POLITICAL ECONOMY
IN THE
MODERN STATE

Political Economy in the Modern State is Harold Innis's transitional and, in some respects, his most transformative book. Completed in 1946, it is a collection of fifteen chapters plus a remarkable preface selected and crafted to address four main themes: the problem of power and peace in the post-war era; the ascent of specialized and mechanized forms of knowledge involving, most particularly, the media, the state, and the academy; the crisis facing civilization and, more generally, the modern penchant for unreflexive short-term thinking in the face of mounting contradictions; and Innis's growing focus on what would be called media bias.

In this new edition, editors Robert E. Babe and Edward A. Comor provide not only a general introduction to Innis's largely forgotten book but also dedicated introductions to each of its fifteen chapters along with a comprehensive index. Together, Babe and Comor demonstrate how Innis's volume reflects a shift in Innis's focus, away from analytical relativism towards, instead, a reflexive search for objective truths.

HAROLD A. INNIS (1894-1952) was a Canadian professor of political economy at the University of Toronto and the author of seminal works on media, communication theory, and Canadian economic hist

ROBERT E. BABE is a professor in the Faculty of Information and Media Studies at Western University.

EDWARD A. COMOR is a professor and faculty scholar in the Faculty of Information and Media Studies at Western University.

Harold A. Innis

POLITICAL ECONOMY
in the
MODERN STATE

HAROLD A. INNIS

Edited and introduced by Robert E. Babe
and Edward A. Comor

University of Toronto Press
Toronto Buffalo London

First Published in Toronto by Ryerson Press 1946

Toronto Buffalo London
utorontopress.com

ISBN 978-1-4875-03840 (cloth) ISBN 978-1-4875-22926 (paper)

Library and Archives Canada Cataloguing in Publication

Innis, Harold A., 1894–1952, author
Political economy in the modern state / Harold A. Innis ; edited and introduced by Robert E. Babe and Edward A. Comor.

Includes bibliographical references and index.
ISBN 978-1-4875-0384-0 (cloth) ISBN 978-1-4875-2292-6 (paper)

1. Economics. 2. Canada – Economic conditions. I. Babe, Robert E., 1943–, editor II. Comor, Edward, 1962–, editor III. Title.

HB171.5.I56 2018 330 C2018-904353-9

This book has been published with the help of a grant from the Federation for the Humanities and Social Sciences, through the Awards to Scholarly Publications Program, using funds provided by the Social Sciences and Humanities Research Council of Canada.

University of Toronto Press acknowledges the financial assistance to its publishing program of the Canada Council for the Arts and the Ontario Arts Council, an agency of the Government of Ontario.

Funded by the Government of Canada
Financé par le gouvernement du Canada

CONTENTS

ACKNOWLEDGMENTS

Both editors thank Siobhan McMenemy for shepherding this project in its earliest and most vulnerable stages, and University of Toronto Press's Mark Thompson for guiding it to fruition. Thanks also to Frances Mundy and copy editor Dilia Narduzzi.

Edward Comor owes a great debt to his wife and son for their love and good-humoured support. He is also grateful to co-editor Robert Babe for his years of inspirational writings, deep understanding of Innis, and, most importantly, his ongoing friendship. Finally, he dedicates the republication of *Political Economy in the Modern State* to Professor Ian Parker. Ian introduced Innis and this book to Edward thirty years ago. His generosity, patience, and sheer brilliance will not be forgotten.

In keeping with Innis's counsel to consider the future as well as the past and present, Robert Babe dedicates this republication to the next generation, and in particular to Keegan, Masen, Patrick, Owen, and all yet-to-be-born grandchildren; may they be suffused with Innis's sense of truth and integrity.

INTRODUCTION TO *POLITICAL ECONOMY IN THE MODERN STATE*

ROBERT E. BABE AND EDWARD A. COMOR

Political Economy in the Modern State is Harold Innis's transitional and, in some respects, transformational book. It is the bridge between his economics and communications studies. Arguably, in terms of his ontology and epistemology, it is his most insightful text. Ironically, it has also been his least understood and appreciated.

Among other things, *Political Economy in the Modern State* (*PEMS*) sheds light on Innis's complex political and cultural concerns – concerns that occupied him in his later years. Indeed, in *PEMS*, Innis provides the intellectual scaffolding for his final six years of scholarship.[1]

Innis lived from 1894 to 1952. He remains, in the eyes of many, Canada's pre-eminent scholar. That was not always the case. Friend, colleague, and biographer Donald Creighton noted that his first decade as a faculty member at the University of Toronto (1920–30) was filled with frustration and loneliness.[2] During that time, Innis was the only one on staff researching Canadian economic history, and what was to become his monumental book – *The Fur Trade in Canada* (1930) – had been rejected by several publishers.[3] By the early 1930s, however, this had changed. The praise Innis then received rested primarily on his staples thesis of Canadian economic history. Recognized internationally not only as a leading figure in economic history but also in the social sciences and humanities,[4] Innis nonetheless began to forsake his staples research (we believe in the mid-1930s). Instead, he set out to develop a new and underappreciated area of inquiry: the political economy of communication, media, culture, and civilization.[5] One might well ask: "Why would Innis do this?"[6] And further: "What distinguishes this later work from his earlier research?"

In this introduction, we maintain that neither Innis's staples thesis nor his communications writings can be understood adequately in isolation from one another. Nor can they be fully understood without a working knowledge of *PEMS*. We will argue that, through this book, Innis sought not only to address contemporary policies and debates in economics but also to transcend them by adopting an ambitiously historical, holistic, and reflexive approach. In fact, the focus of his work shifted from developing a theory of economic history as a guide for emerging economies (especially Canada's) to political and ontological concerns regarding the very survival of Western civilization.

Regarding this latter concern, in his preface to *PEMS*, Innis states that, "the first essential task is to see and break through the chains of modern civilization that have been created by modern science" (vii). In an ensuing chapter he declares also that the "collapse of Western civilization [began] with the [twentieth] century" (94). In another essay republished in *PEMS* we read that "the impression that universities can be bought and sold, held by business men and fostered by university administrators trained in playing for the highest bid, is a reflection of the deterioration of western civilization; to buy universities is to destroy them and with them the civilization for which they stand" (75).[7]

In *PEMS* Innis manifested his inauguration of an extraordinarily grand project. He perceived, at the conclusion of the Great Depression, the onset of the Second World War, and later the dawn of the Cold War, an imminent collapse: "We are faced with the prospect of a new Dark Ages" (138). This expectation required him to respond in a way that would facilitate, at the very least, a deepened understanding of the social and institutional conditions besetting this civilization. Innis related the crisis, in part, to contemporary mass media. More foundationally, however, the book reflects Innis's overwhelming concern with power, which, in his contemporary context, was a dangerously centralized, contradictory, and unreflexive configuration[8] of political, economic, and cultural dynamics.

The very title of the book requires examination. For a century and a half before Innis, "political economy" had been an academic discipline, often accredited to Adam Smith's *The Wealth of Nations* (1776). Through the eighteenth and nineteenth centuries there were many other classical political economists, perhaps most notably David Ricardo, Thomas Malthus, James Mill, John Stuart Mill, and Karl Marx. By choosing "political economy" as part of his title, then, Innis was indicating a treatise that would investigate what political economy had become in the modern era – the era of "the modern state."

In particular, Innis maintained that, in the context of the modern state, a complex of relations, structures, and mediations was undermining the conditions under which political economy as previously understood could proceed (126). This resulted, sadly, in a weakening of political economy as an instrument in the search for truth. The search for truth, he stressed, is inconsistent with the overly specialized and mechanistic forms of thinking characterizing mainstream scholarship of the contemporary period. Moreover, he attributed this new mode of scholarship, in part, to the rise of the modern state. Quoting E. J. Urwick, Innis stated that "specialization runs mad, and when it does so, *never* leads to understanding. Its natural result, is strife and violent dogmatism" (144).

Justifiably, the title also can be interpreted as Innis signalling a treatise on the importance of re-establishing, or pursuing once again, the classical approach to political economic analyses in order to more fully comprehend the nature and impact of contemporary power. In this sense, the book addresses the character and practice of political economic power within and through the modern state. It draws attention, for example, to the underpinnings of conflicts among nation states in the dangerous atomic world of 1946 (as opposed to the marginal, rather apolitical, static equilibrium orientation of much contemporary economics).

Given such an ambitious framework, much analytical territory needed to be traversed. *Political Economy in the Modern State* contains something of a map from which, in retrospect, we can trace and better understand Innis's intellectual journey; why he decided to embark on it; and the foundations for the concerns, concepts, and research he went on to pursue.

~

Ryerson Press published *Political Economy in the Modern State* in 1946, affording it a print run of one thousand copies. From that time to the present, it has been rarely mentioned and, until now, was never republished; commentators have been much more prone to cite *Empire and Communication* (first edition 1950, with many reprints and editions) and *The Bias of Communications* (first published 1951, also with several reprints and editions). Innis's final volume, *Changing Concepts of Time* (1952), recently also benefited from a reprint.

Lack of appreciation of *PEMS* among Innis's commentators is likely related, at least in part, to its chronological position between his staples studies and communications work, to confusion regarding the book's purpose, to dismay that Innis was broaching a new area, and even to a failure to recognize the book as an integral work. *PEMS* was published seven months before Innis delivered what, retrospectively, many recognize to be the piece signalling his transition to media and communications studies; namely "Minerva's Owl," his inaugural presidential address to the Royal Society of Canada, presented in May 1947.[9] One year later, Innis delivered the Beit Lectures at Oxford University (lectures later featured in *Empire and Communications*). Both events were badly received.[10]

Among his colleagues, Innis's shift in research was puzzling.[11] His son, Donald Innis, later revealed that his father was depressed by the fact that this new work was ignored even by those he knew personally to have similar interests. John Nef, Chester Wright, and Frank Knight all acknowledged receiving mailed copies of what Innis sent them, but none responded.[12]

A cursory overview of the contents of *PEMS* makes obvious how it links the author's two main research areas. The first seven chapters concern themes that Innis developed or returned to in his final three books. These directly involve media, communications, culture, public opinion, education, advertising, propaganda, present-mindedness, time/space, and misunderstanding/understanding (arguably, the theme most overlooked by Innis's commentators). Chapters 9 through 14, at first glance, differ markedly from the first seven insofar as they are devoted to economic history or political economic concerns (as commonly understood). These concerns include trade imbalances, staples, overhead costs, unused capacity, liquidity preference, the dynamics of centralization and decentralization, geography/topography, militarization, debt, taxation, transportation, navigation, and tariffs and preferences. As we suggest later in this introduction, these essays invite readers to reflect on Innis's political and cultural concerns (and related communications themes) from the perspective of what then constituted his better-known work. Furthermore, we argue that they reveal the bases of Innis's then emergent conceptual apparatus. Their inclusion in *PEMS* grounds his communications concepts in the soil of his overarching political economy.

Situated between the first seven "media/communication/culture" chapters and the later six "economic" chapters are the titular chapter (chapter 7), and chapter 8, "The Penetrative Powers of the Price System." The latter is the one that most clearly reconciles and integrates Innis's past and future research. As Tom Easterbrook explains, Innis came to recognize that the "key to economic change and much of its dynamic must be sought in changes in communications, for the penetrative power of the pricing system is but one aspect of the penetrative power of systems of communication."[13] By this account, then, Innis had good reason for placing "Penetrative Powers" at the centre of his book, situated immediately after the title chapter.

Although it is important to recognize the continuity in Innis's thought between his early and later periods, and in particular *PEMS* as mediating and to an extent reconciling these two periods, it is equally vital to understand *PEMS* as constituting a fundamental rupture. In important respects, Innis changed his mind. As most clearly set out in *PEMS*, he radically revised (even repudiated) what previously had been a strongly held ontological position. This reversal, which has long gone unnoticed by commentators, arguably did not suit the contemporary zeitgeist and hence likely constitutes yet another reason for the inattention scholars have accorded *PEMS*.

Chapter 15, "Reflections on Russia," closes the volume. Upon first reading, it marks a seemingly abrupt departure, especially when compared to the preceding six chapters. Although there is no direct reference to Russia or East-West relations in the preface, we argue that "Reflections" is a fitting conclusion to *PEMS*. Among other things, it reiterates the book's key themes, squarely directs attention to Innis's political concerns, and clearly anticipates the author's ontological and methodological departure from previous positions going forward.[14]

Seven essays in *Political Economy in the Modern State* were newly published. They include the preface, which of course opens the book, and "Reflections on Russia," which closes it.[15] Normally, scholars make clear their intentions or goals in the opening materials and, in this regard, *PEMS* is no exception. In conclusions, similarly, scholars ordinarily review or summarize their findings and look ahead. In the case of *PEMS*, Innis did not write a "conclusion" per se. However, for reasons we will explain shortly, "Reflections on Russia" fulfils some of the normal expectations of a conclusion.

In addition to the new material, Innis republished eight essays selected from an array of possibilities. In doing this he needed not only to decide which pieces would reappear but also determine their order of appearance (he eschewed chronological ordering). Therefore, part of the our task as the new edition's editors is to speculate on his reasoning in these regards. We believe that *PEMS* is a carefully crafted work – a collection of published and unpublished papers that constitutes more than the sum of its parts.

The chapters that, arguably, go furthest in justifying our understanding of *PEMS* as an integrated work are the preface, "Reflections on Russia," and "The Penetrative Powers of the Price System." These markedly, but by no means exclusively, lay out the book's overarching themes regarding the imminent collapse of Western civilization and the dialectic of understanding/misunderstanding that is directly related to it. More than this, though, particularly through these chapters Innis developed his insistence that there be constructed (or, rather, rediscovered) a reflexive, holistic form of knowledge as a vital antidote to contemporary world crises.[16]

Economics and Staples

Before addressing in more detail the themes and importance of *PEMS*, a selective review of the two major research areas that the book demarcates and mediates will be helpful, beginning with Innis's studies into Canadian economic history.

In formulating his version of the staples thesis, Innis deviated radically from the position initiated in 1923 by W. A. Mackintosh. The latter had proposed that international trade in staples enabled "pioneer communities ... to leave behind the disabilities of a pioneer existence."[17] According to Innis, in contrast, rigidities arising from an undue reliance on staples prevented balanced development in the resource-exporting country and, indeed, perpetuated the exploitation of pioneer economies by older, industrialized ones. Whereas Mackintosh's work resonated with liberal, mainstream economic thought (as exemplified notably by Ricardo's widely accepted "law of comparative advantage"), Innis largely rejected that position, even dismissing claims regarding the universal applicability of social science as it was then practiced.[18]

Two remarkable essays published in 1929 presaged this dissent and foreshadowed his major writings on staples.[19] One was his tribute to the rogue American economist Thorstein Veblen,[20] whose work, Innis claimed, was as significant as Adam Smith's.[21] After commending Veblen's ability to resist the influence of dominant institutions, Innis praised his individualist "revolt against mass education and standardization."[22] Veblen's work, said Innis, constitutes a "monument" in struggles between "static theory and dynamic history, between Frankenstein's monster and Frankenstein."[23]

The other paper, "The Teaching of Economic History in Canada," is even more revealing. There, Innis argued that

> the textbooks of the United States and England pay little attention to the problems of conservation and of government ownership which are of foremost importance in a new country such as Canada. Canadians are obliged to teach the economic theory of old countries and to attempt to fit their analysis of new economic facts into an old background. The handicaps of this process are obvious, and there is evidence to show that the application of the economic theories of old countries to the problems of new countries results in a new form of exploitation with dangerous consequences.

> The only escape can come from an intensive study of Canadian economic problems and from the development of a philosophy of economic history suited to Canadian needs.[24]

Whether Innis was proposing that a universalist economics is impossible or merely that one did not then exist is debatable. What *is* clear is that he did not himself set about developing one. Nor, for that matter, did he tinker with existing mainstream theory. Rather, he set out to develop a more particularist or situationist economics – one based on regional economic history and that was suited to emerging economies (and to Canada's in particular).[25]

These two 1929 essays reveal a primary motivation for Innis undertaking his staples studies. In *The Fur Trade in Canada* (1930) and *The Cod Fisheries* (1940) Innis proposed how the predominance of a given staple for export, combined with geography/topography,[26] institutional conditions, and technological change (particularly systems of transportation), stamped a certain identity on the political economy and culture (involving, to use Mel Watkins's term, "spread effects"[27]). What's more, usually due to irreconcilable contradictions, when a primary staple changed (in Canadian economic history, fur replaced fish, followed by lumber, wheat, and minerals), crises arose and transformations ensued as people (frequently referred to as "vested interests") adapted or failed to adapt to new conditions.

Innis found that during periods of disturbance, new or modified institutions, organizations, and technologies emerge in response. Their development was generally aimed to provide powerful interests with increased or renewed stability or flexibility – namely, greater control over space and/or time.[28] In the case of Canadian political economic development, Innis assessed these in terms of a *longue durée* analysis spanning over four hundred years.

One of the most influential outcomes of this work stemmed from Innis's demonstration that a continuing reliance on staples of all kinds yields a "staples trap"[29] – a perpetual state of incomplete development – and concomitantly an ongoing draining of wealth. In the 1930s, Innis saw past dependencies on Europe being eclipsed by a North American continentalism in which minerals, wheat, forestry products, and hydroelectric power were most at issue.[30]

A related departure from economics orthodoxy was Innis's insistence that, normally, relative prices are inadequate to allocate resources optimally or benignly. Smaller countries, for example, are inherently disadvantaged by an unfettered price system because *their* prices indicate the values and priorities of larger, more powerful trading partners. "The success of *laissez-faire*," he said, "has been paid for by the exploited areas of which we are one."[31] Even for larger economies the price system fails, as it does not reflect collective needs or desires.

From its foundation as a resource-exporting economy – and thereby from its dependence on international trade, demand, and investment – Canada, in Innis's view, had been set on a restricted path. Beginning with the fur trade, but more so in the nineteenth century, the exploitation of staples entailed centralization, massive public expenditures (for example, to build the Canadian Pacific Railway), and debt (most of it foreign-owned). To service those debt obligations, expanding staples activities became even more structurally embedded and existing ways of generating revenues were perpetuated, regardless of the long-term contradictions these entailed. And because of fixed capital's characteristics (see fn. 28 above), the decline of one staple and the emergence of another required a newly formed integration of capital while concurrently utilizing the existing political economic and infrastructural base. Furthermore, Canada's domestic shortage of financial capital (with the exception of the state) perpetuated the tendency to reproduce past relations and conditions, particularly through monopolistic enterprises, centralization, and government planning. As Robin Neill has summarized, "The Canadian problem was the problem of planned growth."[32] The prototypical market system, as Innis's historical studies demonstrated, was a myth.[33]

The Price System

Innis deemed the price system to be a significant medium of communication and of political economic power.[34] His treatment of the price system in *PEMS* is not merely an important dissent from the prevailing mainstream economics discourse (which regarded prices as the not-to-be-questioned indicators of value), but it also directly links Innis's analyses of staples and problems with prices to his subsequent communications work. Rather than assessing prices as neutral or powerful things in and of themselves, Innis treated the price system as a constructed institution, influenced by (and influencing) vested interests, including those administering the state. Prices, to Innis, then, were not the outcomes of seemingly autonomous forces of supply and demand.

As a medium, the price system does not merely link buyers and sellers; its use conveys a sense of relative value to entire populations. Moreover, it reflects and furthers the perceived (but problematic) objectivity of statistics, thereby limiting introspection and discouraging critical questioning. The predominance of the price system, both in theory and in the practice of exchange, also impels, as he wrote elsewhere in *PEMS*, a "neglect of the technological conditions under which prices operate" – namely, the structured circumstances (often involving rigidities, monopolies, and state interventions) that profoundly influence production, exchange, and consumption. The price system also "emphasizes short-run points of view ... rather than long-run points of view which necessitate perspective." "In the social sciences," Innis remarked, there is "a liquidity preference for theories concerned with the present" (85–6).[35]

In chapter 8, and in the other essays Innis selected for *PEMS*, there is an analytical primacy placed on the complexity of historical structures. Moreover, Innis treats these complex structures as the bases of or general superstructural conditions for – *and media through which* – knowledge, culture, beliefs, values, and prices emerge and develop. This process of emergence is for the most part driven by the (biased) efforts of "vested interests" to control (through institutional, organizational, and technological innovation) their activities and power capacities over space and through time in given topographical and technological contexts. We see this history, including its dynamics and implications, reiterated in *PEMS*, especially in chapters 10 through 14.

One profound consequence of Innis's analysis of the price system, particularly regarding its reification and mediation of knowledge capacities, was his turn to even grander topics regarding the historical underpinnings of objectivity and understanding/misunderstanding per se. While his earlier writings assessed Canadian developments in terms of their implications for modern civilization (specifically the rivalry between its European and American forms and, of course, European and indigenous relations),[36] his later work – more abstract, holistic, philosophical, and often explicitly political (especially in *PEMS*) – demonstrated a growing urgency to critique contemporary thinking.

The Origins of Innis's Media and Communications Research

Innis unfolded his mature thinking on media and communications in his final four books, the first being *Political Economy in the Modern State*.

However, his interest in the subject predated *PEMS* and was manifested in three essays published in 1934 and 1935 (although, clearly, his staples research had addressed transportation and communications technology and media in broad terms). As none of these mid-1930s pieces reappear in *PEMS*, some commentary on them is called for.

The first is "The Canadian Economy and the Depression."[37] A key concept in this paper – overhead costs – also plays a significant role in *PEMS*. An overhead is the fixed cost that must be paid irrespective of the level of production. Burdensome or heavy overhead costs (in the fur trade, for example, large scale infrastructural investments in outposts and transportation projects) increase tendencies toward centralization (monopoly) in order to spread those costs over more output. Overhead costs thereby frame business strategies, for example practices intended to influence pricing and demand, and indeed government policy (tariffs, subsidies, regulations, and so on). Innis traced business strategies to the overheads related to railways, canals, newsprint mills, mining operations, and hydroelectric plants, and he found that the drive to meet ensuing debt obligations played a significant role in their histories. "Heavy investment in specialized, long-lasting capital assets," Irene Spry explained years later at a conference celebrating Innis's work, "brought about a profound transformation in the mechanisms of economic organization."[38]

It might already be apparent that Innis's interest in overhead costs and fixed capital structures implied a number of dynamics that constitute templates for concepts such as *bias* and *monopoly of knowledge*. Because most of the costs and investments addressed by Innis entailed the establishment of structures and concerted efforts to redress unused capacities, Innis detected a significant reason for the failure of contemporary economists and policymakers to adequately understand social-economic phenomena.[39] Beyond his critique of the price system, then, Innis also pointed to broader efforts to deal with the problem of overhead costs that generated mechanization, noting in particular that these costs not only occluded precision but also inhibited an ability to engage in the complexities of holistic, historical thinking.

Also in "The Canadian Economy and the Depression," Innis tied the production of pulp and paper (derived from the lumber staple) not only to hydroelectric power, industrialism, and the rise of metropolitan centres (cities) but also to "intensive advertising and revolutions in marketing" through the press and radio. The latter coincided, he wrote, with "the decline of editorials and of freedom of speech, and the emergence of headlines and the modern newspaper." Innis also argued, specifically in the related context of a rising nationalism, that "the coincidence with the advent of radio of dictatorship in Russia, Germany, Italy, the United States, or Canada is not accidental."[40]

This attribution, in 1934, to radio contributing to dictatorship is remarkable. But his claim that Canada and the United States had fallen into dictatorship is even more so. Innis's meaning of and justifications for these claims are clarified in *PEMS* as well as in his later writings (in, for instance, "A Plea for Time" in *The Bias of Communication*). In "The Canadian Economy and the Depression," however, he supported such contentions by arguing that "improved communication such as the press and the radio" enabled "centralized control." Advertising, slogans, the decline of editorials, and the emergence of headlines, according to Innis, had debased public discussion and thereby eroded democracy.[41]

The essential point to emphasize is that this article goes well beyond merely an assessment of the economy and the Depression. In it, Innis's concerns coincided with his analysis of overhead costs and their implications not only for economic development but also for intellectual capacities, persuasion, and modes of governance.

Innis pursued these areas in "Discussion in the Social Sciences," the second of the mid-1930s articles cited above.[42] There, he linked the rise of the newspaper in the nineteenth century to the onset of democracy through the development of printing, the growth of literacy, and the profits possible for press owners who were "concerned with an attack on abuses which concerned those capable of reading or those capable of subscribing to the papers." He explained that "it paid in the newspaper business to attack abuses, or to conjure up abuses and attack them." Thereby, as the press developed into a mass medium in the twentieth century, discussion and debate over issues of public importance were debased: "Circulation has become even more important with the increase in size and efficiency of the newspaper plant," he wrote. "The spread of literacy has provided a market … [and has] accentuated the necessity for wider circulation; advertising has become a basic source of revenues."[43]

Here, notably, Innis distinguished between, and set in contrast, mass literacy and intelligence. He claimed, as well, that the ascent of the former "implies a shift of emphasis from an attack on abuses to *devices* which will attract the interest of the largest possible number of readers."[44] Such features of the modern press included, for Innis, sports, comics, and human interest stories, with their characteristic superficiality and sensationalism.

Like the institutions and infrastructures involved in transportation, communications systems, too, (in particular the newspaper publishing business) entail overhead costs, rigidities, and consequently they are also impelled or biased towards particular methods and innovations. Of course these developments take place within existing conditions and cultural orientations – pre-existing fixed capital structures, for example, which are usually refitted and drawn upon. (Later, Innis would observe that civilizational biases tend to perpetuate themselves through the very institutions, organizations, and technologies that developed in response to the civilization's contradictions.)

Finally, in 1935 – replying to a paper by senior University of Toronto colleague, E.J. Urwick[45] – Innis published "The Role of Intelligence: Some Further Notes."[46] Urwick had argued that the social science paradigm of objectivity is faulty because, unlike the natural world, the social world is inherently unpredictable. The social scientist, like everyone else, is infused with subjectivity. Innis was disturbed by Urwick's dismissal of even the possibility of objectivity (and perhaps ironically so, given Innis's own questioning of objectivity in contemporary economics and the price system).

Innis opened his response by referring to the "major depression after a world war," indicating that, for him, confusion, misunderstanding, and failures of intelligence had taken hold over wide swathes of the population for an extended period of time. He proceeded to itemize obstacles impeding understanding. One such factor, which was consistent with his position on main-line economics set forth in 1929, was scholarship; more specifically, a growing disbelief on the part of scholars (such as Urwick) in the potential for objectivity in the social sciences.[47] Innis also criticized what he deemed to be an uncritical belief on the part of many in the inevitability of progress, reflecting and developing their fixation with change as opposed to continuity. Furthermore, Innis complained, social scientists were increasingly called upon to devise short-term remedies for immediate problems, contributing thereby to an increasingly pervasive present-mindedness.

By urging, in the mid-1930s, that social scientists become familiar with their own biases or limitations and take those into account when undertaking research, Innis, in his own work, began to transition from staples scholar to media and communications theorist.[48] While media, broadly understood, had been a core component of his analysis of economic history, the irrationalities in domestic and international affairs brought to the fore through the First World War and Great Depression induced him to begin directly examining media and communications in conjunction with methodological and philosophical questions concerning knowledge and capacities involving thought.

Significantly, it was also in 1935 that Innis conceived a volume that in just over a decade would become *Political Economy in the Modern State*. Probably the first reference to that prospective work is in a letter to Irene Biss (undated but likely 1935). There, Innis mentions a book in which he would discuss the Depression, approaches to Canadian economic history, the social sciences, and the role of intelligence – topics congruent with *PEMS* as it later appeared.[49]

Ontological Transformation

Commentators generally suggest that in transitioning from staples to media and communications, Innis straightforwardly extended his staples investigations from economic analyses of timber / pulp and paper industries to news, public opinion, advertising, culture, and so forth – seemingly a logical progression.[50] A related proposition has been that the later Innis, in his communications work, simply redeployed tools originally developed for analysing staples, in large part to test the limitations of these tools[51] (indeed, Innis said as much himself).[52]

Whether a logical progression or a conscious extension of conceptual boundaries, we understand this shift to have been more complex than commentators have hitherto recognized; indeed, it was in some important respects transformational. *PEMS*, we believe, not only demonstrates an evolution or development of Innis's economics (e.g., the elaboration and nuancing of concepts such as "capacity"), it also embodies a complex and important ontological shift.

Beginning with the Depression years, Innis became concerned less about Canadian history and more about the interrelated problems of policymaking and developments in the academy. These, he came to realize, were connected to a mounting inability to engage in thoughtful discussion and, in relation to this, the capacity to understand. Yes, the First World War was over, but by the early 1930s an unprecedented economic collapse was gripping the Western world and perceptive observers could see, as well, the violent implications of the rearmaments taking place in Europe. A First World War veteran himself, Innis drew on his analyses of structures and dynamics shaping economic history to associate such crises with problems concerning intellectual and cultural (in)capacities. In this context, his response to Urwick's article and the objectivity-subjectivity debate can be understood as having its roots in larger, more foundational concerns.[53]

By the mid-1930s Innis was worried about what might be called a paradigm shift in Western thinking. The aforementioned "chains of modern civilization" that troubled him (involving industrialization and science) had emerged from the tumultuousness of the past half-century – a period of unprecedented technological innovation and previously unimaginable violence, economic crises, and political fanaticism. These conditions, accompanied by foundational transformations ranging from Einstein's relativity theory to the Russian Revolution, shook previously held Enlightenment presuppositions regarding the potentialities and beneficence of scientific reasoning. In these circumstances a rejection of even the possibility of objectivity resonated widely in the academy and, therefore, research and analyses based on normative and subjective political and social concerns, as Urwick implied, appeared to be justifiable.[54] Innis, in response, turned directly to assess what was structuring and mediating this extraordinary change,[55] and he began to prioritize the role played by modern mass media and other forms of communication.

Whereas in his earlier writings Innis defended Canadian nationhood by opposing the universalist pretensions of mainstream economics, in his media and communications writings he sought after and insisted on the vital importance of reflexively conceived universals. The preface of *Political Economy in the Modern State* demonstrates this through references to "natural law" and "natural order" (xiii, xiv, xvi), likely intended to indicate his interest in counterbalancing subjectivity and normative analyses. Natural law for Innis implied the opposite of the present-mindedness he was to critique in his subsequent work, although, already in *PEMS*, he referenced present-mindedness, stating that it "pulverizes" economics and "other subjects and makes a broad approach almost impossible" (101).

The closing essay of the book, "Reflections on Russia," is likewise revealing. There Innis asserted that "the decision to celebrate the 220th anniversary of the [Soviet] Academy of Sciences is an indication of a broad statesmanlike approach to a world problem of understanding, and recognition of the possibilities of using science as a common approach – almost the only universal common basis left" (262). He continued, arguing that "a common world view has become indispensable" (263) and that "the universities must attack the problem of understanding" (270).

In his communications work, Innis repeatedly endorsed the philosophical approach originated by the ancient Greeks.[56] There are likely several reasons for this. One is their penchant for dialectical thinking and their insistence on seeking balance between and among extremes. Surely, however, another important factor explaining Innis's affinity for the Greeks was their quest for absolutes. In his seminal essay, "A Plea for Time,"[57] for instance, Innis wrote: "The form of mind from Plato to

Kant ... hallowed existence beyond change"; that "form of mind," moreover, was concerned with life beyond "the moment," longing instead for an "absolute or universal value ... a state of permanence beyond time." This quest for absolutes may seem to be at odds with Innis's focus on dialectical materialist reasoning, but that seeming contradiction is muted when we recognize that one of Innis's enduring truths or "absolutes" was precisely the necessity to maintain a dynamic balance between extremes.

We believe that these statements complement what Innis meant when using the terms natural law and natural order in the preface. Also significant are remarks that Innis intended to give as his final address – as president of the American Economics Association – in December 1952 (sadly, he died one month earlier). Although incomplete, those remarks were published posthumously. In those reflections, Innis stressed the need for a universal economics: "Having learned my lesson I must begin by pleading for a general emphasis on a universal approach and by insisting as an economist that economic history is primarily concerned with the task of extending the universal applicability of economic theory and of strengthening a central core of interest."[58] The phrase "having learned my lesson" indicates Innis had, at some point, changed his mind.[59] We believe *PEMS*, and in particular the concluding chapter, "Reflections on Russia," was Innis's primary inflection point.

In *PEMS*, objectivity does not constitute a clear and absolute reality. Instead, Innis begins to treat it as a stance the researcher can attempt to assume in order to develop his/her reflexive capacities. At several points (e.g., viii), Innis bemoans that truth has "superseded the search for truth" (126). Although his historicism could not (yet) accept the possibility of actually attaining some kind of objectivity (as for him the quantitative and qualitative dimensions of knowledge were irrevocably interrelated with the conditions of, and the mediations in, a given political economy), this denial did not preclude the possibility and importance of some kind of ontological objectivity for which humans can and should strive.

In *PEMS*, then, we find the beginnings of Innis's aspiration to develop a standard of truth that could stand alongside the dynamism of his historicism. We also detect an effort to promote an ontology based on the capacity to reflect and understand the historically produced biases and values of one's own culture and, through this method, the biases and values of others. As he wrote in the preface, "States are destroyed by ignorance of the most important things in human life, by a profound lack of culture – which, following Plato, is the inability to secure a proper agreement between desire and intellect" (x).

Preface

The preface is self-contained in two ways. First, it appears before the table of contents, setting it apart from (and arguably giving it a transcendence over) the rest of the book. Second, it makes no specific reference to any of the chapters that follow. Innis was, in effect, asking his readers to themselves detect in the ensuing chapters the themes announced in the preface. That task, evidently, has proved difficult. Consequently, we suggest some connections.

The preface begins by formally stating Innis's main purpose for the book: "This volume has been designed to bring together widely scattered and relatively inaccessible articles published since 1933, for the convenience of students, particularly the large number ... from the armed forces. War veterans have been trained to do difficult things and it is hoped that their training, enthusiasm and self-confidence may be conserved and directed to the tasks of peace more difficult and more complex than those of war. The volume is intended as a guide and as a warning" (vii). Here and elsewhere, Innis gave more than just a passing nod to returning veterans, many of whom were then flocking to university classrooms. One can surmise, therefore, that he completed the preface after May 1945, the month that the war in Europe ended.[60] In declaring that the "tasks of peace [are] more difficult and more complex than those of war" and that the book constituted both "a guide" and "a warning," Innis signalled that he hoped *PEMS* would make a contribution to peace, and that returning soldiers, given their first-hand exposure to the horrors of war, could dedicate themselves to that goal.[61]

Innis's assertion that peace is more difficult than war is explained in part in the next paragraph, after his mention of war veterans, where he provides a concise formulation of his communications thesis (later called "medium theory"): "The difficulty and complexity of the tasks of peace arise from their apparent and deceptive simplicity; the most dangerous illusions accompany the most obvious facts including the printed and the mechanical word." In the same paragraph, he references the apprehensions expressed by Socrates (as represented by Plato) concerning writing and its implications for memory: through their use of "written characters," learners "will be hearers of many things and have learned nothing; they will appear to be omniscient and will generally know nothing; they will be tiresome company, having the show of wisdom without the reality." Innis follows this by immediately incorporating the printing press and radio into his field of concerns, claiming that they also "have enormously increased the difficulties of thought." Finally it is worth repeating Innis's summation of his project which also appears in this remarkable section: "The first essential task is to see and to break through the chains of modern civilization which have been created by modern science" (vii).[62] Near the close of the preface, this guidance is rephrased to again emphasize his new agenda: "The following essays constitute an attempt to interrelate patterns of Canadian development with those of the Western World in the full realization that much remains to be done before the outlines and the details of the pattern can be clearly discerned ... It is perhaps unnecessary to say that it presents no panaceas or answers to questions but rather hopes to raise new questions or at least to draw attention to the necessity of a carefully balanced approach to complex problems" (xvi–xvii).

Through the course of his preface, Innis identified institutions, technologies, and conceptual norms that inhibit or block thoughtfulness and understanding. These include advertising, print, specialization, individualism, mathematics, fanatical nationalisms and regionalisms, religion, lack of tolerance, the "commercialization of language" (xiii), business hierarchies, and a paucity of critical literature and "cultural growth" (xvi).

One response, perhaps the major one to the crises he observed in 1946, is the combination of a reinvigorated political economy with a reaffirmed interest in natural law. "The distortion of the price system," Innis argued, "has weakened the role of political economy in western civilization and destroyed its position as developed by Adam Smith in relation to natural law" (xiii). That statement, of course, raises questions as to what Innis meant by political economy and by natural law.

Regarding the meaning of political economy, in the preface Innis is obscure. He did say that social scientists slanting their work to make "the flames of nationalism burn more brightly," or devising schemes in conjunction with governments to "thwart the human spirit and to fasten the chains more tightly," are antagonistic to political economy (xii). To do political economy, then, scholars must be free of economic and political pressures; they must be located in ivory towers, so to speak. Otherwise, limitations and biases stemming from alliances with or dependencies on vested interests will intrude. Apart from this, however, Innis does little or nothing to unpack what he means by *political economy,* even though the phrase constitutes 50 per cent of his title.[63]

The book's titular chapter (chapter 7), however, helps us better understand his concerns in relation to political economy. While the reader of this book is invited to refer to the introduction we have prepared for it, here we note that chapter 7 addresses issues that were of growing concern to Innis by the early to mid-1940s; for example, the dynamic and contradictory relationships between political, economic, and civilizational centres of power, on the one hand, and their margins, on the other. These tensions, conflicts, and contradictions gave rise, among other things, to opposing pressures for centralization and decentralization. Other issues Innis addressed stemming from these tensions relate to cultural and intellectual capacities or, put another way, historical materialist conditions impacting upon different forms of knowledge. Chapter 7 illustrates Innis's emerging interest in universal tendencies and dynamics involving power and knowledge and, more specifically, bidirectional interactions involving the political/economic/cultural environment of a given place and time (i.e., the "modern state") *and* variations in the intellectual/scholarly practice broadly known as "political economy" (hence, the word "in" of the title).[64]

Regarding natural law, in the preface Innis contrasts and proposes conflicts between written constitutions and natural law (xiv), stating that "the divine right of nations has replaced the divine right of kings" (xv). Given Innis's general antipathy to unchecked or unreflexive authority, including monarchies and religious authorities,[65] it is incorrect to infer that he favoured absolutism over democratic forms of governance. His statement regarding the "divine right of nations" seems to turn, rather, on a distinction in his mind between positive (or legislated) law and natural law. He maintained that in enacting the former legislators routinely ignored the latter. Certainly Innis associated natural law with the rise of science – at least the physical sciences since the Renaissance – and he wrote that "an attempt is made [in *PEMS*] to raise the fundamental question as to the role of science in the Western world" (xvi). But for Innis, natural law also pertained to social, political, and cultural affairs. He claimed, for example, that enacting positive law without regard to natural law leads to the use of force due to a concomitant decline in sustained thought (xiv). Whereas natural law appeals to the intellect, positive law (and rhetoric, involving persuasion, often by irrational means) entails "appeals to force" (xvi).

Here we arrive at the heart of the matter. Recognizing, adhering to, and being compliant with natural law – in Innis's view a requisite counterbalance to raw political-economic power – means that the use of force and rhetoric would likely decline. Conversely, ignoring natural law by according an undue emphasis on positive law and rhetoric increases the use of coercion and, by implication, war. Innis therefore was asserting that the search for ontological universals and for common understandings (but not ones imposed or derived from intellectual limitations or cultural incapacities) are – especially in the context of 1946 – civilizational necessities.

Later writings by Innis confirm our claim that for him natural law pertained more to philosophy (ontology, epistemology, axiology) than to the mathematics of Newton (xvi). Certainly by 1943, Innis recognized that the Newtonian and Euclidean systems of scientific knowledge involving absolutes had limitations and that, in practice, they mediated cultural and analytical simplifications – simplifications involving the mechanized and linear thinking he had already associated with contemporary applications of the price system and statistics.[66] Despite the revelatory implications of Einstein's relativity theory,[67] Innis was concerned by the tendency in modern science to evade "the problems of philosophy," thus severing it from "the problems of human society": "The neglect of these problems and the naivete of separating physics and philosophy as two voices constitute the chief danger of the efforts to popularize science. Energy is drained from the most difficult problems of civilization into a general glorification of the advances in science."[68]

"Reflections on Russia"

It is unlikely that Innis would have anticipated in 1935 (or even as late as 1944) writing a chapter on Russia for *PEMS*. Four months after Germany surrendered, however, Innis visited Moscow and Leningrad upon an invitation from the Soviet Academy of Sciences. In a personal correspondence at the time he wrote: "The whole venture was a tremendous shock to me ... [As a result] I have felt the necessity for a much broader approach in economic history and the very great danger of a very narrow approach such as we seem to get nothing else but. Somehow we must work out approaches in the social sciences which will include the Russian situation ... I think I learned a little about the necessity of being tolerant and to be a little humiliated that I knew almost nothing about the situation."[69] Deteriorating relations between the West and the Soviet Union added urgency to Innis's more general concerns regarding misunderstanding. In "Reflections" he recognized that "two worlds which do not understand each other are suddenly faced with the necessity of working out compromises." This, he added, compels the "search for possible contacts in the broader approach of its history" (257). Innis summarized his position as follows: "The necessity of cutting away the underbrush and of enabling us to see each other has become imperative" (268).

Both in the preface and in "Reflections" Innis identified barriers to understanding: for example, the specialization of knowledge in the West and the partisan character of writings about Russia; the security strategies in the West (oriented towards attack) in relation to those of Russia (focusing on defence); economies based on consumers' goods and the accompanying need for advertising (in the West) contrasted with the Soviet economy's emphasis on producers' goods; and, of course, differences in law, religion, and language. Public discussion in both the West and Russia, Innis lamented, was often confined to inaccurate and pernicious assertions of the superiority of one "system" over the other: "System is a fighting word and the emotional excitement surrounding it obscures even a realization of the necessity of intelligence" (260).

So what, in Innis's view, could be done? Here he is more explicit than he had been in the preface and, we maintain, he anticipated the position he later would articulate in "A Plea for Time" and in his final, posthumously published presentation (mentioned above). In "Reflections" he straightforwardly asserted that, "A common world view has become indispensable" (263).[70]

Innis concluded the chapter with three proposals to redress international misunderstanding. First, he suggested that "cultural achievement may be a device to evade censorship and to provide weapons for the human spirit" (269). But, he added immediately, by itself cultural achievement is insufficient. "Even with repression," he explained, "it produces aberrations in specialization." Specialization for Innis, to repeat, seldom countervails misunderstanding and usually adds to it.

The second concerns science. Innis argued that science constitutes "almost the only universal common basis left ... as a common approach" (269). Again, however, his optimism was qualified, for in the contemporary world "science has become intensely concerned with military secrets" (270). Therefore, he insisted that "the universities must attack the problem of understanding," presumably by discouraging secrecy while, in relation to Innis's critique of scientists (mentioned above), ensuring that philosophical reflection accompany all forms of research.[71]

Third, and perhaps the most important for his work going forward, Innis recommended renewed recognition of the common civilizational roots of East and West and, more abstractly, the potential for understanding that derives from awareness of why diverse institutions and ways of thinking emerged from these shared beginnings. "The significance of Greek civilization to East and West," Innis wrote, "provides an approach to modern problems. Both groups in the word of [Werner] Jaeger are Hellenocentric" (263).[72] "Russia," he observed, "has shared in the heritage of the Mediterranean civilization but she has been dominated by the Greek or the Eastern rather than the Latin or the Western branch" (263).[73]

Thus, by 1946, Innis's interest in cultural capacity – including the capacity to understand – and its interrelationships with political economic structures and mediations was well established. True, he had emphasized capacities throughout his staples writings, but, with *PEMS*, he began using the concept more holistically, involving three principles:

Innis recognized, first, that all activities are bound by physical limitations entailing, among other factors, demographics, the availability of natural resources, and a society's technical and artistic abilities. Second, the determinants of capacity are dialectically interrelated. For example, the recognition that a natural resource is, in fact, a "resource" that can be exploited is in part determined by the knowledge available in a given place and time, while the availability of the resource (such as a staple product) will itself influence the development of this knowledge. And third (and explicitly addressed in *PEMS*), Innis proposed that political economies often operate at less than full capacity – what he termed "unused capacity" (as in chapters 10 and 11). This, in conjunction with his recognition of overhead costs and their implications, led him to view historical developments as being biased through the institutions, organizations, and technologies crafted and used to redress them.[74]

Confusion, Criticism, and Strategy

Political Economy in the Modern State puzzled several initial reviewers. Economist B. S. Keirstead, in 1947, queried Innis's lack of determinism or strict causation: "Human purpose may enter into the totality of social causation more definitely, and in a more precisely discernible fashion, than Dr Innis indicates. If that is so, it would follow that an understanding of the causal processes of the economy would permit more complete control of them, and thus give greater freedom to man than he at present enjoys or than Dr. Innis believes him capable of enjoying."[75] An anonymous review published in *The Economist* judged the book as being almost a total failure: "Incoherence , indeed, is Professor Innes' [*sic*] besetting sin ... Facts and quotations are less marshalled than hurled pell-mell at the reader, who is never certain whether the juxtaposition of two statements is meant to imply a casual connection ... Coupled with a style even more atrocious than is normally to be expected of North American academics, this characteristic goes far to make his essays totally unreadable."[76] By and large, after several negative reviews such as these, the book gathered dust; occasionally it was referenced more for a specific paper contained in it rather than as a significant and coherent work itself.

One likely reason for *PEMS*'s dismissal is related to what Innis called "the disease of specialization" (vii). From his earlier research, Innis had gained the reputation of being a "dedicated generalist" or "macrohistorian."[77] As his junior colleague, J. B. Brebner, wrote in 1953, his research – particularly *The Fur Trade in Canada* – "wove geography, economic history, changing technology, political adaptation, and far more theory than is evident, into such a vivid, variegated, and tough fabric of explanatory exposition that its rough spots and irregularities could be ignored."[78] According to Brebner, by the time *The Cod Fisheries* was published (ten years later, in 1940), Innis faced a "unique problem in exposition" in that he recognized that writing itself (or at least the norms of its contemporary form) tended to mechanize and thus oversimplify his analyses.[79]

Most of Innis's contemporaries, we suggest, dismissed *PEMS* in part because they did not understand his initial assessment of civilizational misunderstanding – nor, and perhaps more fundamentally, did they grasp the unorthodox approach he was pursuing to explain it. "Specialization," Innis wrote in 1945, "has contributed to the rigidity of the social sciences ... We are constantly reminded of the wonders of science and are always forgetting the *eternal* problems of society."[80]

These and similar observations by Innis anticipated how his contemporaries would assess *PEMS*. From a letter written by social geographer Griffith Taylor, dated 7 November (not more than a week or two after the book's publication), it becomes apparent that Innis had confided in his friend and colleague at least one of his goals for the volume. In his brief appreciation, Taylor related *PEMS* to "our modern brand of geography," which he described as "the happy link of science to philosophy – and yet it does help to promote tolerance & world harmony."[81] Cryptic as this correspondence is, its reference to "our modern brand of geography" reflects the newness (if not strangeness) of what Innis was trying to do and the confusion that followed.

There is another probable reason for the book's negative reception, one more directly political in nature. It pertains to what Innis wrote – specifically, his attack on contemporary institutions including the university, commercial interests, state policies, and even democracy itself

– as well as his dismissive comments regarding centralized planning, progress, Keynesianism, academic specialists, and other matters.

PEMS after McLuhan

In the mid-1960s, Innis's communications writings emerged out of the shadows – ironically, a change that occurred simultaneously with a waning of interest in the staples thesis. Arguably, this resuscitation was most attributable to the efforts of Marshall McLuhan (who wrote prefaces and introductions to reissues of *The Bias of Communication* and *Empire and Communications*, published in 1971 and 1972)[82] and to James Carey (who wrote an introduction to *Changing Concepts of Time* in 2004, among other things).[83] Both McLuhan and Carey, however, largely ignored *Political Economy in the Modern State.* We suggest that Innis's other communications books were revived by McLuhan and Carey while *PEMS* was not because the former ones supported the interests of those authors. Carey, for example, appears to have been drawn to Innis because the latter's work did not comply with mainstream communications theory (especially media "effects," which Carey derisively referred to as the "transmission model"). Carey's and McLuhan's inattention to *PEMS* also probably reflected their rejection of the political economic dynamics constitutive in Innis's cultural concerns.

The selective approach to Innis's work – revealing what has been called "a kind of retroactive intellectual schizophrenia"[84] – reflects both the difficulty most have in reading his work holistically and, as Innis anticipated, the effects of specialization in academia. McLuhan publicly proclaimed an immense indebtedness to Innis.[85] However, the extraordinary popularity of his own writings in the 1960s enabled McLuhan to leave behind the more materialist underpinnings of Innis's work – of what would later be called "medium theory." A conceptual move that made McLuhan's treatment of and selective borrowing from Innis effective was the former's claim that media constitute a form of staple.[86] McLuhan's promotion of his (seemingly) deterministic phrase "the medium is the message" further muddied an interest in re-engaging Innis on his own terms, including efforts to comprehend the relationship between his earlier and later work. For McLuhan, the form and content of a medium are interrelated but, in contrast to Innis's historicism, McLuhan unveiled no discernible political economic dynamics shaping the processes at play.[87] Indeed, when building the groundwork for his own interests using what then were Innis's neglected books addressing media and communications, McLuhan excluded *PEMS*. Given his limited interest in a materialist historicism (one directly shaped by political-economic dynamics), there was little reason to revisit *Political Economy in the Modern State* – either as Innis's transitional text or as an important book in and of itself.[88]

Since McLuhan, few have treated *PEMS* in more than superficial ways (beyond, for example, citing specific essays in it). For instance, Alexander John Watson (whose intellectual biography on Innis is unparalleled) gives *PEMS* little more than passing references. Paul Heyer's introduction to Innis, published in 2003, rightly calls it "a pivotal book" that "serves to highlight the direction his future work will take and establishes the critical stance it will employ."[89] Unfortunately, this assessment is not fully developed. John Bonnett's book on Innis devotes a full chapter to *PEMS*, maintaining that it is "an important work, one that deserves the same prominence as *Empire* and *Bias*."[90] However, Bonnett's analysis is selective, locating *PEMS* in the context of his own interest in information studies and systems theory.[91]

For those contemplating a dedicated reading of *Political Economy in the Modern State*, we urge keeping in mind four of the book's interrelated, unifying themes:

i. *Power and International Peace*

One recurring theme is Innis's concerns about power generally and, in his contemporary context, the rising dominance of the United States. Although he treats imperialism as a contradiction-laden fact of international relations (as in his treatment of centre-margin relations), several chapters emphasize his concerns about the monological and unreflexive characteristics of its modern forms.

International understanding and peace, for Innis, require structural counterweights and an engagement with oppositional views. In contrast to efforts to develop more control and precision, Innis recommended a shared and reflexive search for truth as was pursued in the common roots of both East and West: the Greek tradition.

ii. *The Underpinnings of Bias*

PEMS relates patterns and problems in political economic history to structural conditions and mediations. In chapter 10, for example,

Innis argued that the problem of unbalanced cargo involved contradictions that compelled institutional and technological developments. In response to unused capacities, new but similarly oriented ways of organizing and conceptualizing emerged. These, in turn, generated more complex and costly problems. One core outcome, in the case of Canada, was that "the state became capital equipment" (154); it became a dominant (and of course biased) medium in the modern political economy.

In much of the book, the development of staples, their related infrastructures, and the international relations influencing and influenced by their exploitation shape or bias how growth is understood and pursued. From the price system to the press, the university to advertising, economics to science, vested interests are shown to consciously use institutions, organizations, and technologies in ways that often lead to contradictory outcomes for both themselves and society.

iii. *Specialization and Mechanized Knowledge*

Innis states that the book's vague title is in part a response to the ascent of specializations in the academy. Mainstream economics and its obsession with the price system and statistics are examples of social relations being treated in unreflexive ways, more analogous to Euclidean mathematics than the complexities of biology or philosophy. An outcome and a perpetuating precondition of this organization of thought is what Innis later referred to as a monopoly of knowledge. It also reflects and entails a culture dominated by ahistorical illusions and, especially in relation to science and technology, a simplistic pursuit of progress.

In most of his chapters, Innis related these orientations to the forces, processes, and broadly conceived mediations that enabled or facilitated them. Innis pushed the boundaries of his staples research and proceeded to adapt and develop the economic concepts used in this earlier work. As Easterbrook observed, Innis "moved from description of the state of economics to diagnosis of its condition."[92] Through much of *PEMS*, however, Innis went even further and addressed the relationship between how knowledge is produced and a culture's capacity to even ask questions regarding its complexities.

iv. *Civilizational Crisis*

In the opening paragraph of the preface, Innis, to repeat, stated that the book was meant to underline the fact that "the tasks of peace [are] more difficult and more complex than those of war" (vii). Particularly in chapters written during the Second World War, Innis related contemporary developments to past civilizations.

In his critique of the price system, he argued that, when everything is levelled through price, the value of all things, *even life itself,* is lost ("Left to themselves all find their level price / Potatoes, verses, turnips, Greek, and rice" [84]). Mechanized or dead knowledge, stemming from a range of dynamics – from the implications of overhead costs to the institutionalization of vested interests – drowns out cultural vibrancy and living thought.

Arguably, it was the violence of his time, and the inability or unwillingness of scholars to recognize their contributions to that violence, that constituted the conditions under which Innis dedicated himself to researching communications, media, and civilizational history. From these conditions he began to recognize the need to apply a reflexive approach in the context of discerning a universal ontology.

Prescience

More than seventy years after its publication, the themes and concerns conveyed in *PEMS* remain profoundly important. The quest for control and certainty, mechanistic methodologies, short-term conceptualizations, fanaticism and extremism, antiecological ways of living and thinking, and much else continue to undermine the potential development of vibrant and humanistic cultural capacities. Instead of enabling these, contemporary technologies – particularly those used unreflexively to annihilate space and time – are playing constitutive roles in the widening and deepening of international conflicts and other contradictory developments.

Among other forces, the global reach of an oligopolistic market system and the predominance of its requisite price system (facilitated and accompanied by transnational corporations and institutional complexes such as the international financial system) have generated an acceleration of centre-margin contradictions, violent responses, and all kinds of reactionary politics. "The stupidity of nationalism," Innis wrote, "is tempered by the chaos of internationalism" (166). New and reformed institutions and organizations emerge in response, of course, but generally they serve to relocate or postpone crises rather than change their root causes. And, certainly, these foundations – not only in 1946 but also since and continuing into the foreseeable future – remain in place through the largely unrecognized biases of thinking and acting by people who, for Innis, are the agents of history.

Thirty years after *Political Economy in the Modern State*, previously unavailable lecture notes, prepared by Innis for an unspecified presentation during the Second World War, were published. They are significant for a number of reasons, not least of which is that they contain several points that Innis reiterated in *PEMS*; furthermore, some of the political and cultural concerns Innis developed in his book are summarized in these notes. Quite probably, the notes were crafted as Innis was preparing *Political Economy in the Modern State* for publication. In them we find three typically provocative sentences that, to conclude this introduction, may be of interest to the reader: "It is to be expected that you will ask for cures and for some improvement from the state of chaos and strife in which we find ourselves ... There is no cure except the appeal to reason and an emphasis on long-run considerations – on the future and the past. By a determined effort to widen our perspective we may be able to stem the currents of the moment."[93]

Notes

1. Leslie A. Pal uses this analogy in his treatment of Innis's writing on education and the university. See "Scholarship and the Later Innis" in *Journal of Canadian Studies* 12, no. 5 (Winter 1977): 42.
2. Donald Creighton, *Harold Adams Innis: Portrait of a Scholar* (Toronto: University of Toronto Press, 1978), 75.
3. In a private correspondence written in 1929, Innis confided that "a new field has the advantage of being interesting and the disadvantage of being disheartening and at times lonesome." Quoted in Alexander John Watson, *Marginal Man* (Toronto: University of Toronto Press, 2006), 144.
4. For an overview of his status and activities in the early and mid-1940s, see Watson, *Marginal Man*, 223–4.
5. Watson reports that "in terms of print runs and sales, Innis's communications works were not even modest successes ... Only one thousand copies of *The Bias of Communication* were printed, of which 180 remained in stock in September 1959." Moreover, "Clarendon Press declined to reissue *Empire and Communications*, as its original sales had been so meager." *Marginal Man*, 252.
6. For possible answers, see Eric Havelock, *Harold A. Innis: A Memoir* (Toronto: Innis Foundation, 1982), 17; Watson, *Marginal Man*, 223; and Robert E. Babe, *Wilbur Schramm and Noam Chomsky Meet Harold Innis* (Lanham, MD: Lexington Books, 2015), 19–20.

7. This concern remained with Innis for the rest of his life. For instance, in *The Bias of Communication* he wrote that "the conditions of freedom of thought are in danger of being destroyed by science, technology, and the mechanization of knowledge, and with them, Western civilization," 190.
8. "Reflexivity" as used here entails a self-conscious, critical awareness by researchers or policymakers of their predilections, limitations, prejudices, ideological presuppositions, and so on – their "biases" – so as to reduce subjectivity in their scholarship, policy recommendations, and ontology.
9. That paper became the first chapter of *The Bias of Communication.*
10. One of Innis's colleagues in attendance at his presidential address, A. R. M. Lower, recalled that "'Minerva's Owl' took flight in the gathering darkness and flew off into the woods, apparently, and disappeared. Well so did his audience!" A. R. M. Lower, interview for CBC Radio Ideas program on Innis, Fall 2008, Innis Papers, University of Toronto Archives. Graham Spry, who attended the Oxford lectures, said the audience thought that Innis's rendition of classical history "should best be left to the Europeans" (quoted in Watson, *Marginal Man*, 251).
11. This confusion helps to explain the efforts of friend and colleague Tom Easterbrook, shortly after Innis's death, to underline the continuities in Innis's work. "His studies of pre-industrial communications," wrote Easterbrook, "parallel in purpose and method his studies of early staples in Canadian economic history." W. T. Easterbrook, "Innis and Economics," *The Canadian Journal of Economics and Political Science* 19, no. 3 (August 1953): 291–301, here p. 301.
12. Watson, *Marginal Man*, 251. Nef's silence might have been especially hurtful given that, in May 1945, he had written to Innis (speaking both for himself and representing the University of Chicago's Committee on Social Thought) encouraging him to "work out ... some of the implications of what you say" in "Geography and Nationalism." Released in the spring of 1945, "Geography and Nationalism" was a discussion piece that addressed several of the core themes in *PEMS*. In it Innis wrote, for example, that "democracies can survive only on the assumption that there is no single final answer" (303). Arguably, Innis's subsequent writings – *PEMS* and "Minerva's Owl" – constituted the process of working out the very implications Nef was interested in. Harold A. Innis and Jan O. M. Broek, "Geography and Nationalism," *Geographical Review* 35, no. 2 (April 1945): 301–11; Nef to Innis, 5 May 1945, file 06, box 004, Accession B1972-0025, University of Toronto Archives.
13. Easterbrook, "Innis and Economics," 296.
14. As discussed below, the origin of this final chapter was a trip Innis made to Russia in June 1945. In August, he published three articles on Russia for the

Financial Post, and early the next year he published an article called "Comments on Russia" for the *International Journal* 1, no. 1 (January 1946): 31–6.

15. Components of this final chapter were previously released, however (see fn. 14). The other essays newly published in *PEMS* are "Transportation and the Tariff," "An Economic Approach to English Literature in the Nineteenth Century," "The Problems of Rehabilitation," "The University in the Modern Crisis," and "The Political Implications of Unused Capacity."
16. For modern readers the abundance of titles and persons cited in much of *PEMS* might lessen their comprehension of it. This is especially the case in chapter 2. In an effort to help those who find this chapter to be distinctly challenging, we have included a glossary at the end of the introduction to it. It also should be noted that, in this edition, we have endeavoured to correct typographical and other errors found in the book's original publication.
17. W. A. Mackintosh, "Economic Factors in Canadian History" (1923), repr. in *Canadian Economic History: Classic and Contemporary Approaches*, ed. M. H. Watkins and H. M. Grant (Ottawa: Carleton University Press, 1999), 4.
18. Innis critiqued economics for being static and non-evolutionary; for deploying "comparative statics"; for being "mechanistic" (linear in its conception of causality among variables); for being ahistorical; for proposing an eternal tendency of economies to approach equilibrium and optimality; and for favouring abstract, mathematical models; among other things. Innis's dismissal of the economics mainstream is summarized in his quip, "But let me warn you that any exposition by an economist which explains the problems and their solutions with perfect clarity is certainly wrong." Innis, "Government Ownership and the Canadian Scene" (1933), repr. in Innis, *Essays in Canadian Economic History*, ed. Mary Q. Innis (Toronto: University of Toronto Press, 1956), 79.
19. See "The Teaching of Economic History in Canada" (1929), 3–16, and "The Work of Thorstein Veblen" (1929), 17–26, reprinted in *Essays in Canadian Economic History*.
20. As noted by Horace Gray, at the time Innis published his essay on Veblen, an "anti-Veblen campaign [had been plaguing] American universities for a quarter of a century. Some faculty men lost their posts for suspected Veblenism, others were denied appointments and promotions." "Reflections on Innis and Institutional Economics" in *Culture, Communication and Dependency: The Tradition of H. A. Innis*, ed. William H. Melody, Liora R. Salter, and Paul Heyer (Norwood, NJ: Ablex, 1981), 102.
21. "The Work of Thorstein Veblen," 25.
22. Ibid.
23. Ibid, 26.

24. Innis, "The Teaching of Economic History in Canada," 3.
25. According to Innis, "Perhaps the most serious obstacle to effective work in Canadian economics and economic history is the lack of economic history applicable to new countries. The great bulk of the work has been defective through the attempt to fit the phenomena of new countries to the economic theories of old countries; or to give it a slant or bias toward this or that school of political science or history." Innis, "The Teaching of Economic History in Canada," 10.
26. As Innis put it in *PEMS*, "Geography provides the grooves which determine the course and to a large extent the character of economic life" (87).
27. Mel Watkins, "A Staples Theory of Economic Growth" (1963) in *Staples and Beyond: Selected Writings of Mel Watkins*, ed. Hugh Grant and David Wolfe (Montreal and Kingston: McGill-Queen's University Press, 2006), 8.
28. Innis also recognized that political, economic, and, indeed, cultural relations reflect the same tendencies of what have been called fixed capital formations. In the process of change, it is rare that such formations are completely destroyed (even in revolutionary circumstances). Instead, existing capabilities – including institutions, organizations, and technologies – usually are recast or refitted into succeeding organizations. See, for example, Ludwig M. Lachmann, *Capital and Its Structure* (London: Bell and Sons, 1956).
29. Watkins, "A Staples Theory of Economic Growth," 13, 16.
30. One significant and, for Innis, contemporary crisis emerging from this change was Canadian regionalism (reflecting a growing north-south orientation) involving a breakdown in federal governance, the ascent of new and modified political parties, and an elaboration of ideological conflicts. As he wrote in chapter 13 of *PEMS*, to resist ahistorical and unreflexive policy responses, there is a need to modify Canada's "political machinery" and to escape the "hocus-pocus of the economist" (250).
31. Cited in Robin Neill, *A New Theory of Value: The Canadian Economics of H. A. Innis* (Toronto: University of Toronto Press, 1972), 61.
32. Neill, 65. As Innis asked, "What are the results of a situation in which the profit index ceases to operate or operates too efficiently, and the engineer is allowed to run loose, so that the swiftness of development and its unpredictable character are beyond the scope of normal economic theory? … The usual economic practice breaks down … we become involved in a study of economic pathology … We are forced to turn to other devices in this pathological study." Innis, "Snarkov Island," printed in Neill, 148.
33. Daniel Drache, introduction to *Staples, Markets, and Cultural Change*, by Harold A. Innis, ed. Daniel Drache (Montreal and Kingston: McGill-Queen's University Press, 1995), xxxix.

34. In chapter 8, "The Penetrative Powers of the Price System," Innis writes, "The effectiveness of the price system has been shown in the decline of feudalism, the decline of mercantilism, the rise of palaeotechnic capitalism, and the shift to neotechnic capitalism. It has stimulated the growth of inventions and the trend in the movement of goods ... It has hastened the rise of new sources of power and of new industries and accelerated the decline of obsolete regions" (165). (Palaeotechnic capitalism refers to the early stage of industrial and technological development featuring the use of heavy machinery, mineral resources, and fossil fuels. Neotechnic references developments since the late nineteenth century, particularly those dependent on electricity.)
35. Innis also understood that modern mass media (primarily the press and radio) affect relative prices and thereby help to shape and possibly transform the economy and culture.
36. For example, Innis, *The Fur Trade in Canada: An Introduction to Canadian Economic History* (Yale University Press: New Haven, 1930), 383.
37. Innis, "The Canadian Economy and the Depression" (1934), reprint in *Essays in Canadian Economic History.*
38. Irene Spry, "Overhead Costs, Rigidities of Productive Capacity, and the Price System" in *Culture, Communication and Dependency*, ed. Melody, et al., 164.
39. As he put it in "Penetrative Powers" (chapter 8), "Overhead costs have contributed to lack of precision in accounting, and the allocation of costs between the purchaser of goods from department stores and the purchaser of the [news]paper or between the purchaser of the [news]paper and the purchaser of hydro-electric power from plants owned by paper companies, is extremely difficult to determine. In paying for electric light or for groceries one cannot be certain how much is paid for newspapers" (161).
40. Innis, "The Canadian Economy and the Depression," 127.
41. Innis, "The Canadian Economy and the Depression," 127. He added darkly, "Political duplicity has become an asset of first importance in democratic countries" (134). This 1934 article also foreshadows Innis's later treatment of the price system as a space-binding and present-mindedly biased medium of communication. Therein he attributed the failure of the price system to secure well-being to the rigidities (inflexibilities) that stem from overhead costs associated with the production of staples.
42. It was originally presented in 1935 and published in the *Dalhousie Review* in 1936. It is reprinted under the title, "The Intellectual in History," in Drache, *Staples, Markets and Cultural Change*, 446–58.
43. Drache, *Staples, Markets and Cultural Change*, 448.

44. Drache, *Staples, Markets and Cultural Change*, 449; emphasis added.
45. E.J. Urwick, "The Role of Intelligence in the Social Process," *The Canadian Journal of Economics and Political Science* 1, no. 1 (February 1935): 64–76.
46. Innis, "The Role of Intelligence: Some Further Notes," *The Canadian Journal of Economics and Political Science* 1, no. 2 (May 1935): 280. Republished as "The Role of the Social Scientist" in Drache, 429–37.
47. This decline stemmed in part from political economic factors, such as sponsorship of research by vested interests and the political affiliations of scholars.
48. In other words, this shift did not begin with the fall of France in 1940, as has been claimed by several commentators. See Carl Berger, *The Writing of Canadian History: Aspects of English Canadian Historical Writing 1900–1970* (Toronto: Oxford University Press, 1976), 187; Donald Creighton, *The Passionate Observer: Selected Writings* (Toronto: McClelland and Stewart, 1957), 156; and Easterbrook, "Innis and Economics," 292.
49. Likely, the proposed volume also dates substantively to the initiation of Innis's detailed research into the history of paper and printing. See Creighton, "Harold Innis: A Special and Unique Brilliance" in *The Passionate Observer*, 157; see also Creighton, *Harold Adams Innis* (1957), 111–12. Innis's study of the pulp and paper industry was to be part of The Relations of Canada and the United States series sponsored by the Carnegie Endowment in the 1930s, which Innis first addressed in his essay "The Canadian Economy and the Depression" (1934). In that regard Eric Havelock speculated that Innis "became fascinated and perhaps repelled by what the Canadian forests were being turned into – a new means of mass communication by language, conspicuously lending itself to monopoly control." Eric A. Havelock, *Harold A. Innis, A Memoir* (Toronto: The Harold Innis Foundation, 1982), 37.
50. Berger, *The Writing of Canadian History*, 1976; James Bickerton, Stephen Brooks, and Alain-G. Gagnon, *Freedom, Equality, Community: The Political Philosophy of Six Influential Canadians* (Montreal and Kingston: McGill-Queen's University Press, 2006); Paul Heyer, *Harold Innis* (Lanham, MD: Rowman and Littlefield, 2003); Marshall McLuhan, introduction to *The Bias of Communication*, by Harold Innis (Toronto: University of Toronto Press, 1971), vii–xvi.
51. Easterbrook, "Innis and Economics," 292: "Although it is possible to mark out some [phases] in Innis's work," Easterbrook writes, "there is at no point any suggestion of a break or a radical shift in his mode of approach to national or general economic history." Also see Daniel J. Czitrom, *Media and the American Mind: From More to McLuhan* (Chapel Hill: University of North Carolina Press, 1982); Graeme Patterson, *History and Communications:*

Harold Innis, Marshall McLuhan, The Interpretation of History (Toronto: University of Toronto Press, 1990); Rita Watson and Menahem Blondheim, eds., *The Toronto School of Communication Theory: Interpretations, Extensions, Applications* (Toronto: University of Toronto Press, 2007).

52. He wrote in *Bias of Communication* that "it is part of the task of the social scientist to test the limits of his tools and to indicate their possibilities" (xvii). Regarding his communication writings, Innis was more direct: "Certain tools ... have proved effective in the interpretation of the economic history of Canada ... I have felt it wise to proceed with instruments with which I am familiar and which have proved useful." *Empire and Communications*, 6.
53. Robin Neill, "Heyer's Harold Innis: Postmodernism, H. A. Innis, and the Media of Communication," *Research in the History of Economic Thought and Methodology* 24A (2006): 153–66.
54. As Innis wrote in *PEMS*, "The growth of nationalism and the enormous extension of power in the modern state which has overwhelmed the social sciences have meant that power is regarded as an end rather than a means, and that the checks to centralization of power which strengthened the position of the individual have declined in importance" (136). In other words, political goals, as pragmatic justifications, marginalized Enlightenment ideals and, with these, the concerns and interests of those who do not line up with such priorities.
55. Frank Knight, for one, addressed similar concerns. See, for example, his paper titled "Social Science and Social Action" in *International Journal of Ethics* 46 (October 1935): 1–33.
56. From the 1930s, Innis developed relationships with several classicists at the University of Toronto, notably Charles Cochrane. For an insightful analysis of their influence on Innis's work, see chapter 8 in Watson's *Marginal Man*.
57. Innis, "A Plea for Time," *The Bias of Communication*, 90, 89.
58. Innis, "The Decline in the Efficiency of Instruments Essential in Equilibrium," *The American Economic Review* 43, no. 1 (1953): 19.
59. This presentation had two alternate titles: "The Bias of Economics" and "The Menace of Absolutism in Time." Donald Innis, who prepared it for publication, states that, "As the subject of his address he wanted to consider the idea that America's strongest tradition is that she has no tradition." Furthermore, he explains, "The results of this desire for freedom from the past are in some ways unfortunate" as his father "regarded the media of communication of modern America as a sort of trap from which he could see no escape." (In addition to these media, Innis cited the United States educational system.) "For the body of culture which is common to all citizens there are no authorities and all opinions are of equal value. No matter how carefully and objectively a

study of society may be done, anyone is free to dismiss it as just another idea. The freedom of thought which is so dearly loved in America can become freedom from thought … My father," says Donald, "felt that this attitude was very dangerous because … it deprives Americans of any criteria by which they can judge the state of their country or compare it with other countries. When definitions of progress also progress there are no standards by which progress can be measured." Innis, "The Decline in the Efficiency," 23–5.

60. On 7 May 1945, the very day Germany surrendered, Innis asked Lorne Pierce, the book's editor at Ryerson Press, to return the manuscript "as one can always think of changes and improvements." An initial manuscript appears to have been submitted in March of 1945 and the final version submitted one year later. At last the book was published in the fall of 1946. Innis to Lorne Pierce, 7 May 1945, item 0003, file 0106, Lorne Pierce Papers, Queen's University Archives.
61. There is no mention in the preface of strained relations with Russia (as there is in the book's concluding essay). Given that Igor Gouzenko fled the Soviet Embassy in Ottawa with secret documents in September 1945 (arguably inaugurating the Cold War) and that Winston Churchill first referenced "the descent of an iron curtain" in August of the same year, the "Preface" was likely completed in the summer of 1945.
62. And not only "modern science" – but social science, too (viii, xii).
63. "Perhaps no words have been subject to greater strain than those pertaining to the social sciences. The term 'political economy' has been preferred as it has escaped partly because of its cumbersomeness. The most important thing to be said about this term is that it is not important, and by implication the same comment may be made about other subjects. It is useful to turn to the dialogue between Protagoras and Socrates in which the pretensions of the social sciences are effectively exposed. Universities are menaced by specialization and the belief on the part of specialists that no other interest than their own is important … The dangers must be met by an appreciation of the limits of specialization and a recognition of the necessity of perspective" (viii). For further explication, the reader is directed to our introduction to chapter 7.
64. This chapter was derived from a paper Innis read on 20 November 1943 to a symposium of the American Philosophical Society. A slightly shorter version of what appears in *PEMS* was published in the society's *Proceedings* 87, no. 4 (January 1944): 323–41. A few months later Innis sent it to Lorne Pierce (at Ryerson Press) and by October he asked Pierce if Ryerson would be interested in publishing "a volume of essays" related to it. By November – after tinkering with the idea of calling the book *Trends in Political Economy*

– Innis told Pierce that Political Economy in the Modern State would, indeed, be the title. As this essay triggered Innis's meeting with Pierce and bears the same title as the book, Innis likely intended themes in the essay to encapsulate or reflect those in other parts of *PEMS*. We again invite readers to consult our introduction to this chapter for further explication. Innis to Lorne Pierce, 22 October 1944, item 0040, file 0093 and Innis to Pierce, 14 November 1944, item 0041, file 0093, Lorne Pierce Papers, Queen's University Archives.

65. Innis cited James Joyce: "Nationalism, religion, and language are nets set for [a nation's] children" (x). Again: "A friend in power is a friend lost. A decline in morality has followed war and the growth of hierarchies in church, state and private enterprise. Power is poison" (xiii).
66. In 1943, Innis reviewed a book called *Physics and Philosophy* by Sir James Jeans (Cambridge: The University Press, 1943) in which he both praised Jeans for explaining modern (post-Newtonian) physics and criticized him for conceptually segmenting physics from philosophy, particularly as the latter was placed in a subordinate position. Innis expressed concern that by dividing the two subjects, Kant's elaboration of "space and time, of perception and understanding in the structure of the mind" was neglected. *Canadian Geographical Journal* 27 (December 1943): xv.
67. Perhaps playing off Einstein's many remarks concerning mathematics (e.g. "as far as the laws of mathematics refer to reality, they are not certain; and as far as they are certain, they do not refer to reality," 1921), Innis stated in *PEMS* that "God is not a mathematician" (87).
68. See citation in fn. 66.
69. Innis correspondence with Anne Bezanson, n.d., quoted in Creighton, *The Passionate Observer*, 122.
70. In this chapter, Innis also wrote that "political economy as developed in the Western world will be compelled to broaden its range and to discuss the implications of competition between languages and cultural phenomena largely neglected by it" (262).
71. During the Second World War, Innis opposed state-sponsored research in the university, at least for projects involving secrecy and a neglect of peer assessment. Watson, *Marginal Man*, 227.
72. Innis cited classicist Werner Jaeger extensively in both *Empire and Communications* and *The Bias of Communication*. See Watson, *Marginal Man*, 271–4 and 472–3 n. 34. In "Reflections," Innis quoted Jaeger at length, stressing that "the world-wide historical importance of the Greeks … derived from their new awareness of the position of the individual in the community. And in fact there could be no sharper contrast than that between the

modern man's keen sense of his own individuality and the self-abnegation of the pre-Hellenistic Orient ... The beginning of Greek history appears to be the beginning of a new conception of the value of the individual" (263).

73. Innis implicitly raised this point about a common heritage in chapter 5. In "Reflections," moreover, he argued that separate branches developed with Rome, Byzantine, the fall of Constantinople, and then the Renaissance. In the East "political power was monarchical and spiritual power democratic" while in the West "political power was democratic and spiritual power monarchical." (264). As with other chapters, for more insight we invite readers to consult our introduction to chapter 15.
74. Ian Parker, "Staples, Communications, and the Economics of Capacity, Overhead Costs, Rigidity, and Bias" in *Explorations in Canadian Economic History, Essays in Honour of Irene M. Spry*, ed. Duncan Cameron (Ottawa: University of Ottawa Press, 1985), 73–93.
75. B. S. Keirstead in *The Canadian Journal of Economics and Political Science* 13, no. 4 (November 1947): 602.
76. As with other reviews, however, even this author admitted to a degree of fascination with Innis's approach: "[The author's] wealth of knowledge," the commentator writes, "the boldness of interpretation, and the far-ranging alertness and curiosity which these papers display make one feel that to be one of Professor Innes' [sic] students must be an exhilarating, even if exhausting, experience." "Rambles Among the Social Sciences," *The Economist*, 8 February 1947, 239. Also see J. R. Mallory's assessment of *PEMS* in *The American Economic Review* 39, no. 5 (September 1949): 1002–5.
77. Patterson, *History and Communications*, 42.
78. J. B. Brebner, "Harold Adams Innis as Historian," *Canadian Historical Association*, report (1953): 18.
79. J. B. Brebner, "Harold Adams Innis as Historian," 14–15. "The most dangerous illusions," as Innis pointed out in the preface, "accompany the most obvious facts including the printed and the mechanical word. Plato refused to be bound by the written words of his own books" (vii). Marshall McLuhan, in his review of *Changing Concepts of Time*, recognized that Innis's "ability to communicate with his readers seemed to desert him" when he addressed the subject of "communication." Rather than "a collapse into the inarticulate," McLuhan attributed this irony to the complexity of the subject, requiring a "multi-faceted vision of the social process." Marshall McLuhan, review of *Changing Concepts of Time, Northern Review* 6, no. 3 (August 1953): 44–5.
80. Innis, "Geography and Nationalism," 304 (emphasis added). In an undated letter, Innis referred to the emergence of a "social science of totalitarianism"

– the growing tendency for more social scientists to work within paradigms that serve to entrench rather than problematize dominant perspectives. Watson, *Marginal Man*, 476–7 n. 6.

81. Taylor to Innis, 7 November 1946, file 10, box 005, Accession B1972-0003, University of Toronto Archives.
82. According to Watson, "it was McLuhan who is largely responsible for passing Innis's communications works down to us. This is because between the time of Innis's death in 1952 and McLuhan's rise to intellectual stardom in the 1960s, there was virtually no interest in [Innis's later research]." Alexander John Watson, introduction to Innis, *The Bias of Communication*, 2nd ed. (Toronto: University of Toronto Press, 2006), xvii.
83. See, for example, Carey's "Harold Adams Innis and Marshall McLuhan," *Antioch Review* 27, no. 1 (1967): 5–39.
84. Watson, *Marginal Man*, 10.
85. McLuhan wrote that "I am pleased to think of my own book *The Gutenberg Galaxy* ... as a footnote to the observations of Innis on the subject of the psychic and social consequences, first of writing then of printing." introduction to *The Bias of Communication*, ix.
86. McLuhan, introduction to *The Bias of Communication*, xv.
87. McLuhan, in effect, abstracts components of Innis and applies these in terms of absolutes, whereas Innis always framed and tested his approach in the context of material conditions and relations. For an assessment of McLuhan's direct influence in shaping interpretations of Innis, see William Buxton, "The Rise of McLuhan, The Loss of Innis-Sense," *Canadian Journal of Communication* 37 (2012): 577–93. Watson provides an insightful and succinct comparison of McLuhan and Innis (*Marginal Man*, 404–13). For him, McLuhan's interpretation of Innis fundamentally simplified and depoliticized the latter's work. See Watson, introduction, xviii.
88. By the late 1970s, however, essays in *PEMS* were being cited by authors such as Daniel Drache, Robin Neill, Ian Parker, and Mel Watkins, variously assessing Innis's potentials and contributions in relation to critical political economy. In this regard, how *PEMS* has been used is comparable to the posthumously published anthology titled *Essays in Canadian Economic History* (1956). Underlining our argument that *PEMS* is much more than the sum of its parts is the fact that, in contrast to this collection, Innis directly planned, crafted, and, following his trip to Russia, reorganized his book just prior to its publication.
89. Heyer, *Harold Innis*, 34. Robin Neill, in reviewing Heyer's book – "Heyer's Harold Innis: Postmodernism, H. A. Innis, and the Media of

Communication," in *Research in the History of Economic Thought and Methodology*, 24-A (2006): 153–66 – admits that he also neglected *PEMS* in his text, *A New Theory of Value: The Canadian Economics of H. A. Innis* (Toronto: University of Toronto Press). However, Neill's book does draw from *PEMS* quite extensively and it is extremely insightful for those interested in the economic concepts that Innis uses and elaborates.

90. John Bonnett, *Emergence and Empire: Innis, Complexity and the Trajectory of History* (Montreal and Kingston: McGill-Queen's University Press, 2013), 129.
91. To recognize the theme of misunderstanding/understanding in *PEMS* and, more generally, to make extensive use of it in an analysis of Innis, see Robert E. Babe, *Wilbur Schramm and Noam Chomsky Meet Harold Innis* (Lanham, MD: Lexington Books, 2015). Underlining the neglect of *PEMS*, arguably (and remarkably), its most dedicated analysis is an unpublished blog posting titled "Commentary on Political Economy in the Modern State" by an anonymous author called "DCWM." The posting appears to be a graduate student research paper (dated 19 July 2008, http://dcwm-worksanddays.blogspot.ca/2008/07/commentary-on-political-economy-in.html). In it, the author concludes that "we have attempted to show that *PEMS* is more than just a collection of essays; that its parts cohere around the problematic of the role of political economy in the modern state; and that this ethical question, and not the study of pulp and paper, led Innis to study the effect of communications media on the rise and decline of cultures and civilizations through millennia. We have insisted that the heart of Innis's later work is ethical reflection, and this, we suggest, solidifies his later work as work in political economy."
92. Easterbrook, "Innis and Economics," 299.
93. Harold Innis, "This Has Killed That," *Journal of Canadian Studies* 12, no. 5 (Winter 1977): 5.

CHAPTER INTRODUCTIONS TO *POLITICAL ECONOMY IN THE MODERN STATE*

ROBERT E. BABE AND EDWARD A. COMOR

Introduction to Chapter 1

In this opening chapter of *PEMS*, originally published in 1942,[1] Innis addresses misunderstanding through a critical review of newspaper history. Herein, he foreshadows his work on media bias (and what later would be called "medium theory") by relating changes in media to civilizational change.

Innis begins the chapter by observing that previous studies on the newspaper had neglected the impact of advertising on journalism, thereby themselves constituting, in effect, advertisements for newspapers. Building on that insight, he introduces a main theme of the chapter: the press helped forge an intellectual/social/cultural environment supporting its own legitimacy and empowerment. Innis outlines how this and other still broader outcomes involving political, economic, technological, and cultural capacities developed over the course of more than three centuries through the press's relationship with commercial interests, governments, and publics.

He begins by addressing the fundamentally economic character of printing (on page 2), and thereby of journalism and publishing. In this regard, he deals with costs, revenues, scale, demand, product differentiation, advertising, customers, inputs and outputs, industry concentration, competition, applicable legislation, ownership and control, vertical integration, monopoly, and oligopoly – all topics central to any thorough industry study (from an institutionalist economics perspective).

Innis's analysis here is both holistic and dynamic (unlike the comparative statics approach typifying the mainstream or neoclassical economics of his day). When wood pulp replaced rags as the primary input for newsprint, for instance, Innis remarks that a growth in advertising ensued. That growth, in turn, augmented the demand for news as an instrument to attract readers to advertisements. In the process, political control over the press waned and the priorities of advertisers predominated. Indeed, the very nature of "news" changed. Flowing from transformations in journalism, economic, political, and other cultural institutions changed apace, which recursively impacted on journalism and further altered its very nature.

To illustrate: In their quest for circulation, newspapers helped spread literacy – not only by simplifying the language used, but also by advocating for compulsory education (17). These actions enlarged readership and thereby (along with the later advent of radio) brought "lower levels of intelligence" (30) into the political arena – concomitantly debasing political discussion and by extension decision-making. By the early twentieth century, Innis wrote, the "new journalism" had "devastating effects" in the lead-up to the war and in its subsequent culmination through the Treaty of Versailles (20).

As in his staples research, Innis's awareness of centre-margin relations influences much of the chapter. Spaces or opportunities are opened up and capacities developed in political, economic, and geographic peripheries largely in response to efforts to attain or maintain control. For example, early nineteenth century tax burdens on newspapers and the dominance of the Church of England in education enabled competition to emerge from publishers and writers in Scotland (7). Lower taxes in the United States partly contributed to the development of the penny press, stimulating more sensationalist news (9–10). American developments thus influenced those in England, especially after taxation policy in the latter country changed. By the end of the century *The Times* was facing the problem of relevancy, given its entrenched emphasis on political influence as opposed to catering to the demands of advertisers (15). In other words, "the new journalism," facilitated by and itself influencing technological and broader economic and social developments, constituted "frontier points" from which alternatives emerged and monopolies were challenged (20).

The dialectical complexity of Innis's approach warrants further commentary. The arrival of the telegraph increased the capacity to distribute over space information with immediacy including sensationalist news (especially on wars) to the emerging penny presses. "In a literal sense," he writes, "wars are created, as crime waves are created, by the newspaper. Effective news organization makes catastrophes and catastrophes necessitate improvement of the news organization" (22). Moreover, advertising induced technological developments in communications pertaining to electricity, newsprint, printing, type, transportation, photography, cinema, and so forth, which were all designed to accommodate mass audiences. After the First World War, tabloids transformed "the character of news" (29) by emphasizing photography and headlines – visual dimensions appealing to still lower levels of literacy and intelligence (e.g., Sunday comics). The advent of radio redoubled that effect.

On the other hand, the telegraph also augmented the capacity for, and encouraged, the rise of a "more respectable journalism" (11). Its use helped overcome limitations concerning depth of news coverage that had beset early twentieth century papers and, in conjunction with developments in photography, constituted an opportunity for establishing *Time*, *Life*, and other such news weeklies. "Respectable" journalism redressed the hitherto underused intellectual capacities of the literate population and, coupled with a growing demand by advertisers to reach them, facilitated the conditions for both high- and lowbrow journalism.

Although often debasing journalistic standards in the quest for mass audiences, advertising also impelled many news organizations to embrace "accuracy and truth" over "spuriousness" (27–8). Mere sensationalism, Innis explained, was not in keeping with the newspaper as a medium reflecting the "truthfulness" of its advertisements and the corporations they represented.

Nonetheless, although he acknowledged (even emphasized) these contradictory developments, the main trend, in Innis's view, was the former; that is, a trajectory toward superficiality and debasement of knowledge. Quoting the early nineteenth century observations of Sir Walter Scott, Innis referenced the unparalleled impermanency of journalism, its advertising-influenced neglect of political stability, and its antipathy for, as Scott put it, "the deep intensity of thought" (30). "Graham Wallas," Innis added, "pointed to the decline of discussion with the spread of machine industry and to the emphasis on information and facts as destructive of the environment for thought" (30).

Again, however, the unused or underused capacities that emerged were redressed, Innis suggests, by the activities of another institution – the academy. According to Innis, social scientists attempted to "assume the mantle" (31). But, as he develops elsewhere in *PEMS*, the results were far from satisfactory. Indeed, he laments, the rise of the mass-market, advertising-based newspaper and its concerns with current events, accessible explanations, and facts and figures deleteriously impacted on the social sciences. Particularly adverse was the excessive development of specializations (31, n. 48). Universities even found a means of justifying their public funding, as Innis put it, by appointing "press agents to persuade the public of their contributions" (31).

The history outlined in this chapter also touches upon the newspaper's role in pioneering "the development of speed in communication and transportation" (32). With timeliness increasingly defining the value of news and, by extension, the value of scholarly work, Innis argued that a general cultural focus on the speed of information collection, production, and dissemination resulted. Even the natural sciences increasingly came to embrace speed.

For Innis, then, in its institutional development and through the functions it performed, the newspaper mediated much more than mere "news." Rather, the newspaper helped shape the social, cultural, and intellectual environment. Innis repeatedly emphasized that responses to newspaper developments (often involving unused capacities) frequently gave rise to competitive or countervailing activities at the margins. Despite that, a general historical pattern was clear: the perpetuation of cultural norms that demanded yet further stimulants (involving speed-up and present-mindedness) to the neglect of time-consuming thoughts and activities.

Innis's penultimate paragraph draws direct attention to one of his major economic categories of the 1930s – namely, liquidity preference. Here he also provides some suggestive remarks as to how that seemingly staunch economic concept relates to communications and media studies: "Monetary theorists might learn much by extending their attention from the velocity of circulation of money to the velocity of circulation of newspapers. We need to know more about the preference for various commodities before we can discuss effectively the liquidity preference of money" (34).[2] Newspapers, Innis argued in later publications, heighten "present-mindedness," meaning that we become increasingly concerned with the present and less so with either the past or the future. The implication is that with present-mindedness, the desire for liquidity increases.

Finally, we must draw attention to Innis's closing paragraph that, while abstract, is tantamount to a precis of his more famous conceptualization of time-space dialectics (found in later writings). In very few well-chosen words, Innis implicitly invites readers to reconsider what they have just read in a new and much broader context.

Introduction to Chapter 2

Chapter 2 was published in *PEMS* at approximately the same time that it was released in an academic journal.[3] It seamlessly links with the previous chapter by recounting developments in newspaper publishing and relating those to changes in culture, which involve, for one thing, a declining capacity to understand. Unlike chapter 1, however, it addresses recursive impacts between newspapers and other forms of publishing, giving particular emphasis to "technological developments affecting communication" (35).

Regrettably, through an abundance of detail (regarding titles of periodicals, their dates of founding, their owners and contributors, as well as relevant legislation), Innis seems to presume knowledge beyond what most readers are likely to possess. It is tempting, in these circumstances, to quickly skim through his recitations of names in search of nuggets of insight. Those nuggets, however, are often hidden by the plethora of detail. A full appreciation of the depth and breadth of Innis's thought requires careful reading. To encourage and facilitate that, we provide a glossary at the close of this chapter introduction.

According to Innis, the nineteenth century was transitional: it bridged rationalism and irrationalism. The chapter opens by relating developments in literature to irrationalism, psychology, advertising, propaganda, and war. Ironically, the period was one of democratic disengagement as the extension of democratic rights, according to Innis, caused a decline in political capabilities.

To begin with, publishing in the nineteenth century was influenced by changes in technology and resources. Paper production from wood pulp in place of rags, for example, dramatically lowered costs of printed materials (inducing increased printing and publication activity) as did innovations in typesetting and higher speed presses. Also germane were technological developments in news collection (telegraphs, cables, telephones) and in distribution (railroads, steam ships).

Despite lowered production costs, the newspaper industry in London retained a virtual monopoly through the first half of the nineteenth century. The primary factors that enabled this were restrictions by the state (especially through taxes) and its enthusiastic enforcement of libel and sedition laws. As a consequence, journalists and others shifted from news production to other forms of literary activity. The rise of non-news periodicals had repercussions on newspapers, of course, transforming them and, in the process, helping redefine what was deemed to be "news." Newspapers also lowered their prices, relying more on advertising than on subscriptions for revenues. In appealing to mass readers (as consumers) they debased their own standards of literacy. Political debate, opinion, and factual news were often shunted aside in favour of sensationalism (through, for example, war coverage and crime reporting), puffery, human interest, and other entertainments.

Citing the founder of the *Weekly Budget*, a penny press, Innis conveys in graphic terms the cynicism with which the new journalism regarded its readership: "What they want is the lightest and frothiest of chit-chatty information – bits of stories, bits of description, bits of scandal, bits of jokes, bits of statistics, bits of foolery ... Everything must be very short, two inches at the utmost; their attention can't sustain itself beyond two inches. Even chat is too solid for them: they want chit-chat" (46, n. 21). Quoting the *Saturday Review*, as another example, Innis explained that the writings of novelist Charles Dickens (who began his career in journalism) constituted "the apotheosis of what has been called newspaper English" – the popularization of a freedom (or haphazardness) of form, a penchant for lavish description, and, according to Dickens, the habit of making a "pert, actual point at the end of a sentence" (42).

Extensions in the right to vote (1867) and the establishment of mass education through the Education Act of 1870 also affected publication practices in Britain. From this time forward, politicians needed to consider working-class opinions more closely. Proprietors of publications were compelled to cater to "lower levels of literacy," predominantly by accommodating the working class's taste for human interest stories and sensationalism. Advertisers, too, displayed a heightening interest in workers as consumers. With the eventual lifting of taxes and other restrictions (in part as a result of the abusiveness and salaciousness of anonymous authors), direct competition among newspapers increased.

According to Innis, more than just a decline in the quality of news was at issue. Regarding fiction, for example, he quotes George Gissing: "The evil of the time is the multiplication of ephemerides. Hence a demand for essays, descriptive articles, fragments of criticisms, out of all proportion to the supply of even tolerable work" (47, n. 24). In brief, Innis documents a cultural shift: "crude sentimentalism" proliferated, accompanied by a "dislike of all fiction disturbing [the reader's] basic ideas" (52).

It was through the political and cultural changes epitomized by English literature over the course of the nineteenth century, Innis concludes, that "we entered the open seas of democracy in the twentieth century with nothing to worship but the totalitarianism of the modern state" (55). In Innis's view, increased democracy presaged its own demise. And since the general public craved excitement and sensation, publications focused on the same. Thereby, he concludes, "a century of peace gave way to a century of war" (55).

Chapter 2 Glossary

Aberdeen administration. George Hamilton-Gordon, 4th Earl of Aberdeen, was British prime minister from 1852 to 1855. Aberdeen led England into war with Russia, siding with France (Louis Bonaparte), which led to his loss of popular support and the collapse of his government. In this regard, Innis maintained that the press played an important role.

Age. Leading Sunday paper in the 1830s. Edited by Charles Molloy Westmacott (ca. 1788–1868), who infamously accepted money to refrain from publishing certain stories. Edward Bulwer's *England and the English* portrayed Westmacott (there called "Sneak") as an unprincipled gossipmonger.

Ainsworth, Harrison (1805–82). Editor of *Bentley's Miscellany* (1839–41), of which he was proprietor from 1854 to 1868. Also editor of *New Monthly Magazine* from 1845–70 and of *Ainsworth's Magazine*, which he owned, from 1842–54. Also a very popular novelist.

Arnold, Matthew (1822–1888). English poet and cultural critic. Arnold was the first professor of poetry at Oxford to deliver lectures in English instead of Latin. Author of *inter alia*, *Culture and Anarchy* (1869). Credited with coining the phrase "the new journalism" (frequently employed in chapter 2 of *PEMS*), of which he was highly critical, mainly as manifested in the *Pall Mall Gazette* under the editorship of W. T. Stead.

Bagehot, Walter (1826–1877). English economist and journalist, long-time editor of *The Economist*. In *The English Constitution* (1867) he pierced the facade of British "democracy," becoming one of the first to observe that the parliamentary form of government vests virtually absolute power between elections with the cabinet.

Bentley, Richard (1794–1871). As a book publisher in partnership with Henry Colburn, Bentley successfully specialized in "silver fork" novels. Inaugurated *Bentley's Miscellany* in 1837 with Charles Dickens as editor, which began by serializing *Oliver Twist*. Ainsworth succeeded Dickens as editor in 1839, meeting with much less success. Bentley used his *Miscellany* to publicize the books he published.

Blackie, John Stuart (1809–1895). Scottish translator of Goethe's *Faust* and of *Aeschylus*, Blackie was a lawyer by training but a man of letters and classicist by profession and taste. A professor at Edinburgh University, he was a political radical and a Scottish nationalist.

blackmail sheets. See Westmacott and Gregory.

Blackwood's Magazine. English publication between 1817 and 1980. Founded by William Blackwood as *Edinburgh Monthly Magazine*. Conceived as a Tory alternative to the Whig-supporting *Edinburgh Review*.

Bulwer, Edward (1803–1873). British Liberal politician, novelist, diplomat, and playwright. Bulwer coined such expressions as "the pen is mightier than the sword," "the almighty dollar," and "the great unwashed." Subject of much notoriety on the campaign trail due to renunciation by his wife on account of marital infidelity.

Carlile, Richard (1790–1843). Advocate in England for universal suffrage and freedom of the press. As a publisher and bookseller he disassembled political tracts, such as *The Rights of Man*, selling them as a series of pamphlets and thereby making them affordable for a wider audience. For such publishing activities he was charged with sedition, libel, and blasphemy. He also brought out his own journal, *Sherwin's Political Register*, featuring writers such as Byron and Shelley. Upon closure by the government, he changed the title to *The Republican*, to which he was a contributor while serving time in prison.

Carlyle, Thomas (1795–1881). Scottish philosopher, historian, and satirical writer. In *On Heroes, Hero-Worship, and the Heroic in History* (London, 1841) he propounded the "Great Man" theory of history ("history is nothing but the biography of the Great Man"). He maintained, for instance, that "great men should rule and that others should revere them." Wrote a three-volume history of *The French Revolution* (1837).

Chambers, William and Robert. William started *Chambers's Edinburgh Journal* in 1832, later known as *Chambers's Journal of Literature, Science and Arts*; Robert soon became joint editor. The brothers later formed the book publishing firm, W. & R. Chambers.

Chartist movement. Working-class movement for political reform in England, 1838–58.

Cobbett, William (1763–1835). English reformer, pamphleteer, and journalist. Founded the *Political Register* in 1802, which he published until his death. Fled to the United States for fear of being arrested on sedition, where he continued to publish the *Political Register*. Returned to England with Tom Paine's remains, planning to give him a proper reburial. Charged at various times with libel and seditious libel. Elected Member of Parliament in 1832.

Colburn, Henry (1794–1855). Successful author of light fiction. In 1814 he started the *New Monthly Magazine* and later *The Literary Gazette*, the first weekly devoted to the arts and sciences.

Constable, Archibald (1774–1827). Scottish publisher who re-established the *Edinburgh Review* in 1802 (the Tories thought it was an instrument of the Whig Party). Sir Walter Scott, a major writer for the *Review*, split with Constable in 1808 to help found the *Quarterly Review*, a rather staid Tory journal.

Darwin. See Spencer.

Dilke, Charles (1789–1864). An associate of Leigh Hunt. Editor of *The Examiner* and subsequently of the *Daily News*. Also co-proprietor of *Athenaeum Magazine*.

Dominie Samson. A character in Sir Walter Scott's immensely popular novel, *Guy Mannering* (published 1815).

Donaldson, Alexander and John Donaldson v. Beckett (1774). In this case, the English House of Lords (then the final court of appeal) rejected perpetual copyright.

Edinburgh Review. See Constable, Archibald.

Education Act of 1870. Provided that all children between five and eleven in England and Wales would receive education.

Family Herald. Published between 1843 and 1940, this was a weekly magazine of stories, amusement, and useful information. Interestingly, it was one of the few sources of reading material in the Innis farmhouse in Otterville, Ontario, when Harold was growing up. Some commentators speculate that Harold, baptized "Herald," was named after the publication.

Fortnightly Review. Founded in 1865 by Anthony Trollope and others, the *Review* initially aimed to counter the partisan journalism common at the time, but within a few years it was perceived by many to be liberal and partisan. John Morley was editor from 1867 through 1882. Pioneered identifying its authors, as opposed to the practice of anonymity common at the time. Ceased publication in 1954.

Froude, James Anthony (1818–1894). Renowned, albeit controversial, British historian, novelist, and professor. Friend and disciple of the staunchly conservative Thomas Carlyle. An anti–Roman Catholic. Author of the *History of England* (1870) and of *The Life of Carlyle* (1884), among other works. Rabid supporter of the British Empire and colonial rule. Arguably a white supremacist. Editor of *Fraser's Magazine*. Polemical in his historical writings, Froude emphasized the drama of events, making his works popular but not necessarily critically successful.

"Froudacity." A derogatory term (and book title) coined by John Jacob Thomas, in opposition to Froude's views and methods of writing history.

Fraser's Magazine. A general and literary periodical published in London (1830–82). Founded by Hugh Fraser and William Maginn. Edited by Froude between 1860 and 1874. Contributors included Carlyle, Thackeray, and J. S. Mill.

Gifford, William. See *Quarterly Review*.

Gordon, Major General Charles (1833–1885). Sent in 1885 by the British government to the Sudan – in response, according to Innis, to press agitation, principally that of *The Pall Mall Gazette* – Gordon disobeyed orders by refusing to evacuate Khartoum, which soon came under siege. Gordon and other defenders of the city were killed as a result of an attack by Mahdist forces.

Gregory, Barnard. See *Satirist*.

Grub Street. Refers to London's marginal literary scene in the nineteenth century, where there was a concentration of impoverished writers and publishers.

Harmsworth, Alfred. See Northcliffe.

Hearst, William Randolph (1863–1951). Newspaper baron and the American counterpart to Northcliffe in instigating the new ("yellow") journalism.

Hook, Theodore (1788–1841). English playboy and practical joker, often living in penury, in 1820 Hook founded the newspaper, *John Bull*, which ardently supported Conservatism and was antagonistic to Queen Caroline. While domiciled in a "sponging house" from 1823–5, he wrote nine volumes of stories, published 1824–8 under the title *Sayings and Doings*.

Hunt, Leigh (1784–1859). British critic, essayist, and poet, and friend of Keats and Shelley. In 1808 he became editor of the *Examiner*, founded by his brother John. Both brothers became incarcerated for their publications on grounds of libel. Leigh also edited other periodicals, namely *The Reflector* and *The Indicator*, and in the 1840s wrote for the *Edinburgh Review*. In *Bleak House*, Dickens based his character Harold Skimpole on Hunt.

Jerdan, William. See *Literary Gazette*.

John Bull. Sunday newspaper first published in 1892 in London. Founded by Theodore Hook.

Jones, Kennedy (1865–1921). British journalist, editor, and business manager for Northcliffe's press holdings. In 1894 Jones transferred control of the *Evening News* to Northcliffe – the Viscount's first London daily – at which time Jones was named editor. He immediately turned the paper into a more popular (and profitable) vehicle of sports, entertainment, fiction, and sensation (the "new journalism"). Member of Parliament after 1916.

Knight, Charles (1791–1873). Founded *Knight's Quarterly Magazine* in 1823, which published only six issues. In 1827 he was named superintendent of the publications of the Society for the Diffusion of Useful Knowledge.

Literary Gazette. Influential and popular weekly literary review magazine, established 1817 in London by Henry Colburn. As editor, Willian Jerdan wrote much of its material and eventually obtained ownership. Publication ceased in 1863.

Lockhart, John Gibson (1794–1854). Son-in-law of Sir Walter Scott and author of a Scott biography. A writer for the Tory-inclined *Blackwood's*.

London Journal. Popular British penny weekly of fiction, literature, science, and arts, established by George Stiff in 1845. Ceased publishing in 1928.

Mackay, Charles (1814–1889). Scottish poet, journalist, and author of *Extraordinary Delusions and the Madness of Crowds* (1841). From 1835–44 he was assistant subeditor of the *Morning Chronicle*. Appointed editor of the *Illustrated London News* in 1852. As correspondent for *The Times* he discovered and reported on the Fenian conspiracy.

Macaulay, Thomas Babington (1800–1859). Controversial historian. Proponent of a progressive (or "Whig") interpretation of history, particularly with regard to England's history, as manifested in pieces written for the *Edinburgh Review* and his four-volume *The History of England* (1848–55). Winston Churchill and Karl Marx alike deemed Macaulay a "liar," although of his literary prowess there is little disputation. As Secretary of War (1839–41) he helped introduce English and Western concepts to education in India.

Marshall, Alfred (1842–1924). Marshall's *Principles of Economics* (first edition 1890) was the most influential economics text of its time. A founder of modern, or neoclassical, economics.

Meg Merrilies. A character in Sir Walter Scott's immensely popular novel, *Guy Mannering* (published 1815). Also the title of a poem by John Keats.

Minerva Press. Publishing house in the late eighteenth century specializing in romantic and gothic novels.

Morley, John (First Viscount Morley of Blackburn) (1838–1923). British Liberal politician, journalist, and editor. Opposed British imperialism, the Boer War, and England's entry into the First World War. Editor of the *Fortnightly Review* and the *Pall Mall Gazette*. Outspoken in opposition to legislating maximum eight-hour workday on grounds of unduly interfering with market forces, earning him the enmity of labour organizations.

Murray, John (1745–1793). English publisher, renowned for burning the memoirs of his major author, Lord Byron, deeming them likely to damage Byron's reputation. See also *Quarterly Review*.

new journalism. See Northcliffe and Arnold.

New Monthly Magazine. See Colburn.

Newman, John Henry (1801–1890). Left the Anglican Church and his post at Oxford in 1845 and was later received into the Catholic Church where he was ordained a priest. In 1879 appointed a cardinal.

Newnes, George (1851–1910). British publisher and editor, founded *Tit-Bits* in 1881, which was comprised of extracts from books and other publications. Paved the way for popular journalism, most notably Northcliffe's newspapers. Northcliffe (Harmsworth) contributed to *Tit-Bits*. He was also publisher of *The Strand Magazine*, in which Arthur Conan Doyle first published Sherlock Holmes stories. Also founded the *Westminster Gazette* to support the Liberal Party. Elected Member of Parliament in 1885.

Northcliffe, Viscount (Alfred Harmsworth) (1865–1922). Pioneer in tabloid ("yellow") journalism. Bought several failing papers and by introducing sensationalism, simplifying vocabulary, and lowering prices, turned them into highly popular and profitable enterprises targeting the working class. Owner of, among other titles, the *Daily Mail* and the *Daily Mirror*. Also founded *Harmsworth Magazine* (renamed *London Magazine*). Exerted significant influence over English public opinion.

Paine, Tom (1737–1809). Antimonarchist and anticlerical author and pamphleteer, Paine is most famously the author of *The Rights of Man* (1791). In America, Paine helped inspire the independence movement. In France in 1790 he was a major force in support of the Revolution. An adversary of arch-Conservative and monarchist, Edmund Burke, Paine prepared *The Rights of Man* as a rebuttal to Burke's *Reflections on the Revolution in France* (1790).

Pigott letters. Richard Pigott (1835–1889) was an Irish journalist who forged letters, ostensibly from a former business associate and Member of Parliament, with the intention of destroying his foe's career. *The Times* purchased the forged letters and published one of them (18 April 1887). A commission of inquiry concluded the letters were indeed forged, and Pigott admitted the same, soon thereafter killing himself. The reputation of *The Times* was, of course, tarnished.

Political Register. Published by William Cobbett between 1802 and 1835. Initially expounding Tory views, it became increasingly radicalized, particularly as illustrated by its stance on extending the suffrage. To keep the paper out of the hands of the general public, the government enacted the Stamp Act, which endeavoured to confine readership to the wealthy. In 1802 Cobbett began publishing parliamentary debates – at the time an illegal act – as supplements to the *Register*.

Pope's *Dunciad*. A multivolume satirical poem by Alexander Pope (1688–1744), which was published between 1728 and 1743. It "celebrated" the increasing decay and imbecility of Great Britain.

Quarterly Review. A literary and political periodical founded in 1809 by John Murray in association with Sir Walter Scott, primarily to counter the *Edinburgh Review*. Its first editor was William Gifford (1756–1826), who was closely associated with prominent and wealthy Tory families. Opposed to major political reforms, the *Journal* nonetheless supported gradual abolition of slavery and more humane treatments of criminals and those declared insane. Published until 1967.

Queen Caroline (1683–1737). Wife of King George II. She was "unfortunate," in Innis's view, likely on account of severe medical problems in her later years.

Reform Bill (1832). Three Reform Bills in the 1800s were designed to increase electoral participation. The first was the Reform Bill of 1832, permitting about 20 per cent of the adult male population to cast a vote.

Satirist. Sunday paper and scandal sheet (1831–9) published in London by Barnard Gregory, who was jailed on numerous occasions for publishing libellous articles. Gregory frequently demanded bribes from affected parties in exchange for refraining from publishing articles.

Saturday Review. London weekly started by Beresford Hope in 1855. Continued publication until 1938. Benefiting from the repeal of the Stamp Act, the *Saturday Review* initially aimed to counter the influence of *The Times*.

Scott, Sir Walter (1771–1832). Scottish poet, novelist, and playwright; also judge, legal administrator, and major presence in the Tory establishment in Scotland. Served as president of the Royal Society of Edinburgh. His novels include *Ivanhoe* and *Lady of the Lake*. Innis's reference to the "tragedy" of Scott's life (40) likely refers to the bankruptcy of Ballantyne printing, in which Scott held a large investment. Scott devoted his declining years attempting to write himself out of debt.

silver fork school of fiction. A subgenre of the Victorian novel (ca. 1820–40). Deferential to high society. Term coined by William Hazlitt in “The Dandy School” (1827). Often authored by upper-class wannabes, such as Theodore Hook.

Society for the Diffusion of Useful Knowledge. Existed from 1826 to 1848, centred in London. Publisher of inexpensive texts intended to help extend the reading public into the working and middle classes. Associated with University College, London.

Spencer, Herbert (1820–1903). Prolific English philosopher and sociologist. Author of the nine-volume *Synthetic Philosophy* (1862–93) and renowned for applying Darwinian evolutionary theory to society.

Stead, W. T. (1849–1912). Sensationalist editor of *The Pall Mall Gazette*, he was responsible for several of the paper's influential campaigns, including one against child prostitution and, according to Innis, one demanding England's intervention in the Sudan leading to General Gordon's ill-fated expedition to Khartoum. Stead demonstrated how the press (the “new journalism”) could influence public policy, though not always positively, according to Innis. He died aboard *The Titanic.*

three-decker novel. Three-volume novel. Standard form of British fiction in the nineteenth century.

Trollope, Anthony (1815–1882). Popular and prolific English novelist, though not necessarily critically acclaimed.

Westmacott, Charles Molloy. See *Age.*

Westminster Review. Founded in London by Jeremy Bentham in 1823 as rival in opposition to the *Edinburgh Review*, this liberal/progressive/free-thought publication was the official voice of the Philosophical Radicals. Notable contributors included James Mill and John Stuart Mill. Others instrumental in the journal's founding were George Eliot (Mary Ann Evans), Francis Newman, Harriet Martineau, and Herbert Spencer.

Introduction to Chapter 3

“The Problems of Rehabilitation” appeared for the first time in *PEMS.* Given its content, it was almost certainly written during the latter stages of the Second World War.[4] Its subject bridges the book's preceding chapters on the press, intellectual capacities, and contradictory developments in democracy with the one to follow, which addresses what Innis called the university tradition and its role in Western civilization.

More than this, chapter 3 reflects the very heart of the volume. Note, strikingly, the opening and closing sentences: “The *interest* in post-war problems is the post-war problem,” (56, emphasis in original) and “The essential training of returned men is a basic post-war problem" (63). With the end of the war in sight, Innis here was concerned about how this "interest" itself is conceptualized – its character and the dynamics underlying it (and, implicitly, the pedagogical infrastructure available to veterans and other young people). As in 1918, post-war society, he warned, was facing "a fresh depletion of vigorous effective leadership and in a democracy leadership is vital" (57).

More specifically, the interest in post-war problems was itself an issue due to the pervasive triumphalism that was emergent around 1945: "We are promised much in order that our minds be taken off the horror of what is going on around us" (56). People, therefore, were ill-prepared for the complications they would face once the conflict concluded; for example, journalists ("scribblers") who "have learned" (in sync with state propaganda during the war) "how to lie" (56). Innis also recognized this state of affairs to have implications for trust and cooperation as the public "developed a certain resistance to propaganda or a sense of smell. Otherwise," he continued, "it would be difficult to explain the renewed efforts made by governments in setting up various branches for the purpose of informing us" (56).

As in chapter 2, Innis asked why a century of relative peace had given way to a century of war. In chapter 3 he pointed yet again to the press and its symbiotic relationships with government and commerce, and the implications of that for both democracy and for peaceful international relations. Indeed, according to Innis, due to the spread of mass literacy, both the press and state thrived on instability: the press because instability enlarges readership (and in the case of radio attracts listeners), and the state because "bureaucracies must exploit instability to capitalize on fears to show how essential they are" (61). Foreign affairs, for example, "are never interesting unless they are exciting" (59).[5]

In his remarks on the relative peace of the nineteenth century, Innis revealed an arguably uncharacteristic idealism by affirming noblesse oblige. He quotes Bismarck (approvingly): "In England, up to the present, there have been two great parties, whose principals have latterly not differed very widely, and both desired the welfare of the country and nothing for themselves. They were the representatives of a few hundred families who were well enough off not to want more, and who would therefore study exclusively the welfare of the whole community" (62). Those remarks seem quite contradictory to those of the preface where Innis repeatedly claimed that power corrupts and that it usually becomes an end in itself. We speculate that here, in light of the grave challenges facing a cynical and exhausted population (entailing "feelings of instability and bitterness"), Innis was grasping for some "reasoned stability" without resorting to "the sword" (61).

Regardless of how we may judge these uncharacteristically soothing remarks, surely there will be some agreement with his clarion call for increased rationality, a heightened awareness of and resistance to ongoing propaganda, and "some emphasis on the rule of law" in order to resist the extremes "which characterize public opinion" (61).

Introduction to Chapter 4

Chapter 4 was Innis's convocation address at the University of New Brunswick (May 1944).[6] In this chapter he continues to unearth the causes and conditions underlying irrationality. His focus here, however, is on the role of universities.

Innis reminds us that the modern university originated as a creature of the state and church. He employed an analogy: universities as rebellious children. Although science and mathematics, by Innis's account, helped liberate universities from "parental" control during the Enlightenment, these "children" squandered their freedom, losing their way through wanton neglect of the humanities. "Emancipation after such a long period under … supervision," he wrote, "and the discovery of her new freedom, perhaps made this daughter flighty. She began to follow … one fad and then another, to the neglect of her tradition in the humanities and learning. Her influence was sought by business, by political parties, and by ecclesiastical organizations. She came to be known by the company she kept" (64–5).

This long decline – born from the classic dialectics between organization and creativity, force and knowledge, order and freedom – was perpetuated by divisions in scholarship and prompted by the rise of national vernaculars. Moreover, the accompanying ascent of science and mathematics provided little incentive to explore historical questions concerning societal organization and governance – how to keep the peace, for example.

Consequently, in the twentieth century, the humanities, at least their holistic, non-specialized expressions, were all but eclipsed. In the face of pressures from business, political parties, and religious organizations, universities focused on producing "useful" knowledge as *that* leads to reputation and augmented resources (65). While all institutions are committed to self-perpetuation, according to Innis, the university pursued that goal in ways that are antithetical to the scholar's vital role in the perpetuation of civilization. Instead of defending scholarship, he asserted, university presidents and boards of governors became fully complicit in its debasement. Innis called this "the systematic rape of scholarship" (69).

Innis should not be interpreted as calling for a simple reversion to the past. Rather, he recognized that the scholar and what constitutes scholarship are part of a much larger, ongoing dynamic. He also understood that the university, as the institution enabling scholarship, continued to play (or should play) a crucial role in defending society's capacity to produce and preserve living (as opposed to mechanized) forms of knowledge. The "parent" (i.e., the state) provides security; the "child" (the university) provides vitality.

Quoting at length Burckhardt's laudatory summation of Athenian culture at the time of Plato, Innis implied that in that place and time, unlike in his own day, "a general understanding" was possible. In Greece, "people had time and taste for the highest and best, because mind was not drowned in money-making, social distinctions and false decencies. There was comprehension for the sublime, sensitiveness for the subtlest allusions and appreciation of the crassest wit" (67).

Innis concluded chapter 4 with a clarion call "to resist the tendencies to bureaucracy and dictatorship of the modern State" (66), and he offers these parting words to the graduating class the speech was originally written for: "As recent graduates, we dedicate ourselves afresh to the maintenance of a tradition without which western culture disappears" (71). The university alone, according to Innis, has the capacity to defend and promote the reflexive knowledge and practices needed to counter the developments he had just outlined. The young graduates (including returning veterans) were prospectively most capable of appreciating and defending these principles *if* they received educations that were in keeping with the Greek tradition.

One must admire Innis's courage. Convocation is the highest and most formal of university celebrations. In being awarded an honorary degree, Innis was being acknowledged as a pre-eminent scholar. Yet, he used the occasion to castigate virtually every university president in the country for being weak, university boards of governors for being unprincipled and for suppressing scholarship, and many fellow professors for chasing after status and individual security instead of pursuing truth.

Innis's depiction of the plight of universities in this chapter parallels his treatment of press systems in the previous ones. Prior to developing into a mass medium, according to Innis, the press had focused on an objective presentation of factual information for a small, literate class; as it transitioned into an advertising-focused medium, however, it instead presented sensation, propaganda, and amusement. Likewise, universities in the democratic age had acquiesced to pressures from business, political, and religious organizations to provide concrete answers and demonstrable results. Scholars, consequently, had lost sight of their callings.

All of this, for Innis, contributed to the decline in rationality and the crisis of civilization (as he conceptualized it) in the first half of the twentieth century.

Introduction to Chapter 5

Like the previous chapter, chapter 5 originated as a convocation address (this time at McMaster University in May 1945)[7] and focuses on the role of the university in Western civilization. If anything, however, Innis's remarks here are even more damning than those before. For example, he stated bluntly: "Western society has collapsed" (73). It should be underlined how remarkable Innis's cautionary and reproving pronouncements in this chapter are, given that they were delivered six days after V-E Day, 8 May 1945, an event that surely prompted celebration and collective optimism.

Critical public declarations (such as those delivered in this address), Innis advised, are possible only because the university, despite adversity and having largely lost its way, remained a forum where free speech and free discussion were still at least possible. Sadly, neglect of the university, which he viewed as the embodiment of civilization, "reflects the lie in the soul of modern society" (76). Given the then sorry states of democracy, contemporary international affairs, and of course the ivory tower, Innis was adamant in rejecting the popular views of the day concerning the inevitability of progress. These he called "delusions of a better world" (72).

Highly significant to Innis's broader position was W. E. H. Lecky's "double action" thesis, namely that "a healthy civilization implies … the action of great bodies of men … *eventually* governing their leaders; and the action of men of genius or heroism upon the masses, raising them to a higher level" (80, emphasis added). Tragically, in the contemporary period, according to Innis, this "double action" had grown frail and, as a consequence, civilization was imperiled. On the one hand, he proposed, democracy had spread too quickly and the "lowest intellectual levels" (74) had thereby come to participate fully in the polity before "men of genius" had time to elevate them. On the other hand, in the absence of the restraining power of independent judgment (as would be exercised by conscientious scholars protected by independent universities), elites seemingly had lost their enthusiasm to contribute to the development of a discerning public. Instead, evidently, they had become intent to deploy mass propaganda to augment their own power. Even more regrettably, says Innis, intellectuals/scholars with expertise on complicated subjects ("such as money") were now placing their knowledge into the hands "of those who care to exploit them" (73–4) – scholarship-for-hire, in other words.

Note that Innis did not oppose democracy as an ideal. Nor did he support unaccountable power. His main problematic, rather, was the inability or unwillingness of contemporary universities to support and extend the intellectual conditions needed for democracy in the face of co-opting pressures from political-economic power (primarily governments and corporations) *and* from the general public. Regarding government and business pressures, he admonished the university for becoming "one of the kept institutions of capitalism" (75). Demanding practical capabilities and forms of knowledge, businesses increasingly sponsored university institutes, thereby directly encroaching on curriculum design. In effect, universities were asked "to betray their traditions" (75). But "to buy universities," he insisted, "is to destroy them and with them the civilization for which they stand" (75).

Regarding the general public, he lamented that the social sciences were being increasingly scrutinized as to their capacity to deliver demonstrable results. And, regrettably, universities responded to this public pressure by popularizing classes, establishing adult education programs, and by providing "cheap if wholesome entertainment" (74). Like his critique in chapters 1 and 2 of the press in nineteenth century England, in his examination of universities Innis traced the decline in content to the broadening of market forces. He even berated "the professor" for becoming a "sandwich man" instead of a scholar (74) (that is, an advertisement in aid of the university whose primary goal as an institution is self-perpetuation as opposed to defending scholarship in pursuit of truth).

Innis thus identified market forces (involving the price system, the profit motive, marketing concerns, and so forth) as major dynamics debasing universities and degrading intellectual capabilities. A key concept he would later call "the mechanization of knowledge," he referred to here as "the mechanization of modern society" (74). Innis clarified its meaning through a direct citation of Mark Pattison, who explained that there had been a "necessary tendency" with the development of modern society "to divide and subdivide the applications" not only of labour but also of thought.[8]

In this chapter Innis deftly, albeit implicitly, redeployed concepts in his staples studies, such as overhead costs, rigidities, and unused capacities, to address contemporary culture, his epistemological concerns, and his anxieties regarding a potentially apocalyptic future. (More on this in our introductions to chapters 9 through 11.) However, Innis was not without hope. He acknowledged, for instance, that he was speaking "under the protection of an outstanding university [McMaster] free of state support and state dictation." More generally, he recognized that the university remained a place, albeit a "dwindling" one, where people can "discuss the problems of civilization" (73).

Looking ahead, Innis charged new graduates with the duty to take up two challenges: First, in the face of opposition from public opinion and contrary to contemporary propaganda, he asked them to recognize that civilization has indeed collapsed. Second, he urged them to initiate discussions on how civilization might be revivified.

Introduction to Chapter 6

Chapter 6 was Innis's presidential address to the Economic History Association, of which he was then its second president (1942–4). His lecture was initially published in the *Journal of Economic History*.[9] As indicated more clearly by the revised title used for republication in *PEMS*, Innis challenged the common belief that economic considerations alone directly affect or determine cultural relations as, he argued, culture likewise impacts economic affairs.

Another challenge to orthodoxy in this chapter stemmed from Innis's very definition of economics. Usually conceived as the study of how people *choose* to allocate scarce resources among alternative uses (Samuelson), for Innis, in contrast, "economics implies the application of scarce means to *given* ends" (83, emphasis added). Innis, then, was revealing that the mainstream economics discipline normally presumed goals or wants to be given – or as being beyond the discipline's terms of reference[10] – thereby precluding questions or critical appraisals concerning societal aims (e.g., the formation or composition of "consumer demand").[11] In Innis's view, this lapse is more than just a disciplinary failing; when more generally applied, for example in the realm of policy, it is fatal.

Herein, Innis also criticized the penchant of economists to deploy mathematics and other formal mechanisms (such as abstract price theory with its rigorous logic premised on a myriad of unrealistic assumptions) to falsely imply that their analyses and conclusions are "objective" or value-free and, again erroneously, that markets function spontaneously or non-deliberatively.[12] The practice, furthermore, obscures the operation of deep-seated power relations and institutions that help structure market demand.

Innis's excerpt from Lewis Carroll's "The Walrus and the Carpenter," which appears on the opening page of the chapter, provided a further clue as to the unorthodox position he was about to present. Carroll was an Oxford University mathematician (his real name was Charles Dodgson), who intended his poem to be an amusing (albeit thought-provoking) critique of his profession's growing and – for both Dodgson and Innis – absurd propensity to apply quantitative methods as a way of achieving conceptual certainty (as opposed to the Greeks, for instance, for whom the more modest function of mathematics was to aid precision and logical reasoning). Here Innis stressed the need to "overcome" the seeming "omniscience" conveyed by statistics, price theory, and other quantitative tools. The best way of overcoming, he proposed, is to "understand the background of economic thought or of the organization of economic thought or of thought in the social sciences" (83).

Although the chapter's title (in both the original and revised versions) suggests that the subject will be the economic significance of "culture" (or of "cultural factors"), nowhere in the chapter did Innis actually define culture. For that, the reader must return to the preface. There, referring to Plato, Innis proposed that culture is the capacity "to secure a proper agreement between *desire* and *intellect*," remarking also that states "are destroyed by ignorance of the most important things in human life, by a profound lack of culture" (x, emphases added). Clearly, Innis considered culture to be extremely important.

Here Innis deployed (we think for the first time) the concept of "present-mindedness" (101) – an observation or assessment that was to become prominent in *The Bias of Communication.* Present-mindedness, arguably, relates closely to desire, whereas its opposite, namely time-as-duration, relates closely to intellect. If one is consumed by desire, one often quests for immediate gratification, meaning that intellect or dispassionate, objective reasoning (including a reflexive consideration of causes, trends, and possible long-term consequences) fades to insignificance. Another closely related way of reading this chapter, then, is to highlight the connections Innis made between conceptions and practices regarding time (present-mindedness vs. time-as-duration), on the one hand, and economic dynamics and institutions stimulating or responding to desire (including advertising and the price system), on the other.

Innis devoted considerable attention to the importance of a nuanced and, indeed, dialectical-historical understanding in order to counter the aforementioned concerns. Regarding the preoccupation with prices, for example, he acknowledged that, in the past, this interest *increased* rationality and thereby helped countervail the influence of myth, ideology, and religion (98); thus, he spoke of "the rationalizing potentialities of the price system and its importance in developing powers of calculation in the individual" (100). However, in his view, this was far from the whole story, or even the most important one. Countering the rationalizing capacities of the price system is its contemporaneously more powerful thrust – namely, to increase *irrationality*. In that regard he offered several explanations, including the tendencies of the price system to promote present-mindedness (i.e., to foreground desire instead of intellect) and consequently to mask the very "conditions under which prices operate" (85).[13]

Why then, in his view, is ahistorical thinking, or present-mindedness, so dangerous? "When the climate of opinion makes impossible any concern with the past or the future," he declared, "the student finds it exceedingly difficult to discover an anchorage or a point of view from which to approach the problem of European civilization." Conversely, he continued, "a recognition of factors affecting irrationality *is* a beginning" to the task of overcoming these problems (96, emphasis added).[14] From page 87 onwards, Innis demonstrates the "broader perspective" (86) needed to redress these untoward "habits of thought" (85), which is a perspective so dynamic and dialectical that it is seemingly unending (as with a Socratic dialogue) and makes firm or absolute conclusions almost impossible to verbalize.

In our view, the history and analysis presented in this chapter are monumental in the Innis corpus, not only in their own right but also for how they directly link the two main strands of his writing: his economics/economic history and his media/communications/cultural studies. In just one example Innis attributed the sudden decline of architecture from the fifteenth century (to that point, quoting Victor Hugo, "the great handwriting of the human race" [91]) to the inception of the printing press: the publication of words concerning and images of the great buildings became itself a kind of academic art, undermining the prestige and propagandistic power of the buildings themselves. Through this example Innis illustrated an even larger point – namely, that the cultural capacities needed for the Renaissance comprised contradictory and only briefly sustainable conditions. A certain vitality is possible, he maintained, only in times and places supported by economic wealth and by a state of tension/transition involving significantly different but intersecting media (such as parchment/hand copying and paper/typography).

In the final pages of the chapter, Innis addressed directly the tensions between cultural vibrancy and stability, and between revolution and organization, reiterating that in his own contemporary culture the "[r]ationality which accompanies the price system brings its own handicaps in the formation of monopolies" (97). Monopolies, he said, reduce or discourage rational thought: "The price system weakens the profit motive by its emphasis on management [i.e. specialization, centralization, bureaucratization, and control]. Cartels and formalism in commerce paralleled ecclesiasticism in religion and in both cases initiative in thought was weakened" (97). Thus, the reproduction of existing relations and, indeed, biases entail what those in power are wont to resist: openness or competition.

For Innis, centralization and monopolization, however, ineluctably give rise to responses at the margins (Innis's own work being an eminent example of this). Economic history, he proposed to his audience of economic historians, should respond to the ahistorical analyses of mainline economists mesmerized as they are by the price system and mechanistic thinking. What's more, it should be developed to "compel the study of interrelationships between the social sciences and between nations" (100).

"Economic history," Innis concluded, "may provide grappling irons with which to lay hold of areas on the fringe of economics, whether in religion or in art, and with which, in turn, to enrich other subjects, as well as to rescue economics from the present-mindedness which pulverizes other subjects and makes a broad approach almost impossible" (101).

Introduction to Chapter 7

As mentioned in our general introduction, this chapter originated as a paper prepared for the American Philosophical Society (1943) and became the basis of Innis's conversations with Ryerson Press to publish the first edition of *PEMS*. In this context and given the chapter's obvious importance, we address Innis's focus on "Political Economy," "the

Modern State," and his choice of the preposition "in" rather than, say, "of" or "and."

To define "political economy," Innis initially referred to the academic discipline inaugurated by Adam Smith at the University of Edinburgh in the mid to late 1700s. He opened the chapter by delineating conditions of freedom then present in Scotland, deeming them prerequisites to Smith's engagement with political economy. Although Scotland at that time was not a "democracy" (government then was administered by representatives elected by a small minority, males with property and an education), state and church were no longer merged into a single (or "absolute") power (Lord Acton). Instead, the state's power was "circumscribed" by the moral code formulated by John Calvin and promulgated by the Church of Scotland; a code emphasizing "two cardinal laws of human society, self-control as the foundation of virtue [and] self-sacrifice as the condition of the common weal" (105). According to Innis, rivalry between church and state prevented either institution from abusing its powers. That felicitous condition yielded unparalleled freedom for the universities and enabled Scottish intellectuals "to strengthen the extension of civil liberties in the direction of economic freedom" (113). A major thrust of Smith's ("classical") political economy, of course, was his attack on mercantilism to favour freer trade.

So, what was this "authentic" political economy inaugurated by Smith and pursued by classicists like Ricardo, Malthus, and Bentham?[15] Citing Jacob Viner, Innis note d that Smith applied Calvin's two aforementioned ethical principles to both the spiritual and the material realms. On the one hand, Smith's *Theory of Moral Sentiments* (1759) "gave a 'system of ethics on the basis of a harmonious order in nature guided by God;'" on the other, *The Wealth of Nations* (1776) applied Smith's "general doctrine with strict consistency to the economic order" (113). Smith's classical political economy, then, was premised on the dual beliefs that "economic phenomena [are] manifestations of an underlying order in nature governed by natural forces" (114) *and* economic activity should be governed by an inherent or universal system of ethics, elsewhere termed by Innis as "natural law."

In Innis's view, classical political economy was born in and reflected not only the material and intellectual conditions of its time and place but also a universalist moral law. In turn, it affected or mediated the development of those time/space conditions (helping reduce trade restrictions, for instance).

Moreover, Innis insisted, intellectual vibrancy is contingent upon contestation among or between power structures. Competition among vested interests and political beliefs, he maintained, usually gives rise to some kind of enabling spatial-temporal dimension. Peripheral societies (such as the Netherlands, the American colonies, and of course Scotland), in Innis's opinion, were less encumbered regarding intellectual freedom than were centres of political-economic power, and therefore these ancillary societies had relatively more potential for creativity.

In Innis's view, the publication in 1890 of English economist Alfred Marshall's *Principles of Economics* signalled the decline of "authentic" political economy and the ascendance of mere "economics." Innis especially objected to Marshall's major maxim, "*Natura non facit saltum*" (nature never proceeds by leaps), the dictum that grounded Marshall's comparative statics and incrementalist methodology.[16] Perhaps even more fundamentally, Innis maintained that Marshall's methodological individualism ignored Calvin's second ethical principle (self-restraint in the name of the common good), a principle Innis regarded as the very cornerstone of "authentic" political economy. "In the attempt to discover a natural order," Innis writes, the political economy developed by Marshall, Jevons, Walras, Pareto, and Pigou "emphasized the position of the individual, extended the principles of equilibrium and widened the possibilities of mathematics" (127). All of this was detrimental, in Innis's view, to an "authentic" political economy.

As mentioned, Innis insisted that political freedom is requisite for authenticity in political economy. In the then contemporary milieu, which Innis called *the modern state,* that precondition was no longer present. One characteristic of the modern state interfering with intellectual freedom, he argued, is the levelling of hierarchy (associated with the rise of democracy), which results in the "tyranny of public opinion" (120). Quoting Burckhardt, Innis stated the following: "Whatever other merit the opinion of the majority may have, it is, in the present condition of our population, an unenlightened opinion. It must be founded on passion rather than on reason; on prejudice, not on knowledge; it will prefer the interests of its class to those of the whole, and its own immediate to its remote interest" (121). (That archconservative, Burckhardt, of course, presumed that the *upper* classes were not beset by such deficiencies, a supposition, incidentally, that Innis did not share.)

Notably deleterious to the formation of an informed public opinion in the context of contemporary conditions, according to Innis, was a "free press" supported by advertising, and the press's ensuing compulsion to seek the widest possible circulation through sensationalism (among other strategies). (See especially chapter 2.)

Innis maintained, moreover, that this "tyranny of opinion" had infiltrated not just the press and the state (dire though that was) but also the universities. Universities at that time were preoccupied with enlisting support from the broader public, and to do this they were debasing their curriculums by focusing on "practical" knowledge. In addition, for similar reasons, universities were deteriorating into handmaids of the modern state: "The demands of [political] parties have compelled a liquidation of the prestige of learning in the social sciences, universities have become reserve pools of labour to supply political parties during periods of crisis" (124). Innis lamented that in being called upon to proffer professional advice, social scientists "created an impression of scientific finality," adding that "the intensive cultivation of mathematics has enhanced the impression."

The reflexive type of knowledge characteristic of the political economy of the nineteenth century, and its salutary counterbalancing function, in Innis's view, had all but collapsed. Quoting Mark Pattison, Innis wrote that, "Theory [now] exists for the sake of the facts, and not facts for the sake of the theory" (124). Stated otherwise, theory is now developed to "justify" what is, as opposed to facts or conditions being used to test the validity or applicability of theory. Innis further declared: "We have definitely emerged from the happy state described in the last century" (124).

Paradoxically, it was the very success of classical political economy that contributed to its downfall. The decline of mercantilism had generated great wealth that, in turn, gradually enabled "large-scale organizations to extend their activities and compelled the state to restrain them" (128). As the state increased its authority – initially as a means of regulating commerce – its success implied a vast growth of a bureaucracy that called upon social science and university graduates alike for support. Universities responded with research and courses on administration and this in turn further contributed to "the subordination of political economy." Political economy and other fields of inquiry thereby became increasingly mechanistic in their analyses, helping to routinize management. Innis concluded that "thought has been paralysed" (129).[17]

Citing MacIver, Innis identified other factors giving rise to the modern state. Of these, the "decline of dogmatic religion" (135) was key. Moral and ethical principles were no longer effective in curbing state power. In a section of the chapter entitled "The Problem of Power," he made his misgivings abundantly clear: "The supreme and paramount principle of every corporation that has ever existed, whether spiritual or temporal, is to maintain power. Lord Acton summarized the view in his memorable sentence: 'All power corrupts and absolute power corrupts absolutely'" (135).

To summarize, the scholarly discipline known as political economy, as practised *in* the modern state, for Innis, was no longer "authentic." "The increasing power of the state has involved the subordination of political economy in the classic sense if not its disappearance" (128). For Innis, political economy had lost its philosophical/ethical grounding; it had become unduly narrow in order to serve the needs of vested interests.

In a remarkable passage quoting a mentor, Frank Knight, Innis proposed balance as an essential component of a reinvigorated political economy: "A defensible ethic doubtless condemns over-emphasis on power; but it must include both the right use of power and the quest of power – by right methods – for right uses" (136). By implication, freedom to pursue "authentic" knowledge requires protection from the state, but that state power must itself be counterbalanced by other powers.

Appropriately, Innis concluded his essay by reintroducing the theme, "Limitations of the Social Sciences." While leaving the reader to peruse this important section and its review of the conditions underlying cultural florescence and decline, here we conclude by drawing attention to Innis's opening statement underlining the high stakes involved: "In our concern with the problems of modern scholarship we are faced with the prospect of a new Dark Ages" (138).

As befits a titular essay, "Political Economy in the Modern State" is essential for comprehending the book as a whole. Although Innis intended *PEMS* to help guide returned veterans to pursue the tasks of peace, the essay positioned as chapter 7 and bearing the book's title is complex; one speculates that it might have proved challenging even to its original audience of professional philosophers. One wonders if Innis, who lacked trust in the intellectual capabilities of the general public, was himself aware of the irony.

Introduction to Chapter 8

Innis prepared "The Penetrative Powers of the Price System" in 1938 for his inaugural address as president of the Canadian Political Science Association.[18] "Penetrative Powers" mediated Innis's career transition from staples research to communications studies. It also mediates the same transition within *PEMS*. In these pages he critiqued and assessed the implications of the price system as a core institution of mainstream economics and, concomitantly, as a predominant mode of communication in contemporary society.

Innis's starting point was what he termed the "fatal" (145) incursion of statistics, mathematics, and the price system into economic theory and practice. His opening paragraph made his disapproval abundantly clear: "And so the snake entered the paradise of academic interest in economics. Under the stimulus of treasure from the new world the price system ate its way more rapidly into the economy of Europe and into economic thought" (145). Gold is the "treasure" referred to here, largely valued because of its liquidity – namely, its universal acceptance as a means of exchange. Beginning in the seventeenth century, according to Innis, the accumulation of gold was the impetus for England's statistical, linear mindset.

Innis then proceeded to address implications of this mindset, precisely as propagated through the price system and the mathematization of economics. As institutionalized in theories of the price system, mathematics carries distinct biases: it precludes introspection or reflexivity on the part of the scholar and it discourages critical appraisal of the values instantiated through money prices. Furthermore, it sweeps aside all awareness of the technological and historical conditions under which the price system operates. In addition, it endorses "short-run points of view ... [rather than] long-run points of view which necessitate perspective" (85).[19]

By 1946, many economists were defining their discipline as the scientific study of the price system. Innis's critical analysis of market prices and mainstream economic thought – and of the policies based thereon – was, then, both unsettling and radical. A core question directly and indirectly raised by this pivotal chapter is: Why, given the deficiencies noted by Innis, would the price system and mathematized economics have attained such pre-eminence? There ensues also a closely related question: What do mathematized economics and the price system's predominance reveal about relations between institutionalized forms of knowledge and centres or formations of political-economic power? We now respond to those questions by addressing the place of "Penetrative Powers" within *PEMS* itself.

Certainly, in this chapter, Innis addressed several of the book's central themes: (1) he critiqued contemporary economics as being what he would later call a "monopoly of knowledge" (i.e., a predominant knowledge system supported and applied by powerful interests), (2) he emphasized the need to redress imbalanced and ahistorical ways of thinking and the contradictory (even deadly) consequences of not doing so, and (3) he conceptualized money and its messages (i.e., prices) as a powerful medium of communication. We now expand briefly on these three interrelated positions.

The takeover of classical economics (or rather, of classical political economy) by neoclassicists focusing on the price system illustrates Innis's more general position on the political economy of knowledge. Except during times of transition or transformation, he believed, major, widely diffused, and accepted thought systems support and augment established power: "It would be interesting to speculate on the history of economic thought," he wrote, "if England had been an important producer of precious metals and not an importer and an exporter, and if large joint stock companies had not existed to be defended and to support arguments and publication" (146). Here Innis likely had in mind that collapsing all notions of value into the calculus of commodity exchange empowers interests whose main activity is, in fact, commodity exchange (merchants, industrialists, and others). Marginalized by this development, of course, were groups concerned with intrinsic moral, collective, or ethical values (advocates for international peace, religious communities, workers groups, and so on). Also marginalized were countries focused on staples extraction, in this case gold.

However, Innis's even larger point here was that the price system's seeming objectivity or neutrality obscures its *inherent* partiality. Among the several ways it is intrinsically biased include the following: the capacity of monopolies and concentrated industries to set market prices, the capacity of advertisers and PR specialists to affect market prices by creating and strengthening wants or desires, governmental procurements and subsidies that perforce or directly influence prices, and legal systems that fail to account for environmental consequences of private transactions. Thinking and policymaking based on or appealing to the purported efficiency and neutrality of the price system, therefore, will not only cloak the presence and reproduction of power disparities. They may also give rise to grave harms due to actions based on erroneous presuppositions.

Innis addressed a second contradiction as well. Whereas initially the price system was a counterweight to the inefficiencies and injustices of tradition (status by birth, the predominance of religious doctrine, knowledge by fiat, etc.), its ultimate victory destroyed what he conceptualized as a healthy state of tension or balance. A new monopoly replaced the old. The result had been the emergence of a "highly centralized" and eventually "totalitarian" modern state constructed in part to provide the legal framework for the price system. This modern state persisted largely unconstrained by hitherto enduring moral or ethical precepts (i.e., "natural law") (154, 155).

Innis also related the emergence of the modern state to the drive of elites to protect their large-scale investments, to their quest for new and more capital-intensive opportunities and, expressly in the case of Canada, to efforts to resolve the fiscal imbalances that emerged from a staples-based economy. Capitalism's development entailed the ever-deepening role of "governmental machinery" (154).

Directly related to all this was the emergence of new and dangerous expressions of nationalism and regionalism. As in previous chapters, Innis also addressed the debasement of knowledge that accompanied the rise of "organs of opinion" (160) – news media and advertising – and speculated on the "incipient fascism of Canadian intellectuals" (162).

According to Innis, as well, money (or commodification) itself constitutes a powerful and transformative medium of communication. Citing Adam Smith, he remarked that the price system "swept aside the feudal system, and led to the discovery of the new world" (146), gave rise to international trade including the trade in staples and the slave trade, and eventually led to "the defeat of European control" and of the slave trade itself (149–50). The price system also penetrated virtually all aspects of culture: in North America, for example, "religious practices detrimental to trade were replaced by Christianity" and the canals and railways stimulated by the price system "drastically shortened [distances] in space and time" (152). As the analysis he provided in this and other chapters indicates, the penetrative powers of the price system should never be conceived as the dynamics of an autonomous or objective force.

In this chapter, Innis made broad associations that reflect a growing complexity in his thinking. His agenda, in part, was to counter moribund status quo institutions by drawing critical attention to taken-for-granted knowledge systems and their implications on the trajectories of political economies and cultures.

Introduction to Chapter 9

"Liquidity Preference as a Factor in Industrial Development" initially appeared in 1943.[20] It is a fine illustration of Innis's movement from detailed analyses of Canadian economic history to other economic topics and studies on media and communication. It also constituted, perhaps, his most succinct analysis of centre-margin relations in the world's political economy.

The chapter begins by detailing how newly discovered gold fields in the nineteenth century impacted trade and development. It ends, however, by paralleling the impacts of the quest for gold (i.e., for "liquidity") with the rise of new media: "The significance of liquidity preference in economic history extends far beyond monetary policy. It was not confined to the place of gold in trade and production. Improvements in communication had the same effects. The phenomenal expansion of newspapers following the displacement of rags by wood accentuated the intensification of trade, enormously extended the sensitivity of modern economic society, and enhanced the role of liquidity preference" (199–200). According to Innis, "liquidity preference" encompassed not only a favouring of gold over fixed capital (as gold was an almost universally accepted medium of exchange) but also the incentive to improve modes of transportation (railroads, steamships, canals) in order that goods (often staples) and other inputs to the production process (including labour) could be moved more quickly, for greater distances, and in higher volumes, thereby facilitating faster turnovers. Accompanying the mobility of both material commodities and labour, he said, was greater specialization, larger scales of production, freer trade, the advent of responsible government and freedom of contract, and the inauguration of both mass advertising (to stimulate mass consumption) and of mass media (to carry the advertisements). The speed-up of transactions, the widening and deepening influence of the price system to encompass more aspects of life, and the heightened preference for liquidity all implied a new and pervasive present-mindedness. In connecting liquidity preference to this cultural and intellectual shift, Innis tacitly treated money (gold) as a medium of communication. In so doing, money was recognized to be a nodal point of biased (present-minded) thinking, which is to say a medium of international misunderstanding.

As usual, Innis's analysis is nuanced, complex, and dialectical, replete with observations concerning tensions and contradictions. Here the reader's attention is repeatedly drawn to dynamics between the centres and margins (or cores and peripheries) of political economic structures. For example, although gold-mining "brought a reversal in the trend of a spread of money from the centre to the circumference [through] the sudden emergence of money on the fringes" (172),[21] mining's continuing success necessitated the funding of capital equipment, "including roads which implied governmental machinery for the collection of revenue and the carrying of debt" (173). Whereas placer-mining had "stressed individualism" (173), that easily accessible gold supply quickly depleted and therefore yielded "an immediate and strong popular demand for improved transportation to the difficult regions of the gold-mining areas" (173). Innis added, "All the States [of Australia] had appeared on the London market to secure loans to finance capital improvements" (175) and, in turn, "extension of government accompanied improvement of communications" (178). Thus we see Innis associating the preference for liquidity with the rise of the "modern state." He also associated this preference with new unused capacities (entailing instability) stemming from large investments in fixed capital.

A further contradiction set out in this chapter concerned the tension between democratic or "responsible" government versus colonization or imperial control. The rise of commercialism (mercantilism) encouraged by gold discoveries, he argued, "strengthened and consolidated the trend toward democratic government" (173) as labour mobility and new settlements undermined hierarchical forms of political order. In the case of Canada, as the need for the state to act as a credit instrument increased, "political control from Great Britain declined" – a diminution essential, paradoxically, "to the expansion of economic control" (196).[22]

Chapter 9 leads directly into chapter 10 on "Unused Capacity." In their quest for liquidity, governments and investors supported capital-intensive enterprises (railroads, steamships, roads, and canals, as well as large scale manufacturing plants and equipment) involving large sunk costs that were themselves antithetical to liquidity. Not only did technology facilitate economic development in this contradictory way but also it typically lowered per unit costs and prospectively extended markets. Such opportunities for further profits were thereby also opportunities to increase liquidity. But again, the pattern re-emerged whereby more sophisticated technologies were introduced into an increasingly complex time-consuming production, distribution, and exchange process, which gave rise to the rigidities of higher overheads and the political demands of large-scale, long-term investors and creditors.

Put differently, in this chapter Innis demonstrated spatial-temporal patterns and contradictions that belie other versions of economic history and, in the process, demonstrated that the successful exploitation of a resource often entails mounting costs, lengthening time horizons, and growing uncertainties. Transportation and communications infrastructures, while deployed to extend markets and facilitate control, directly altered spatial-temporal configurations, albeit in unpredictable ways. For instance, shipping developments (such as those Innis associated with iron steamships and railways) opened up new sites for economic opportunity, but they also enabled threatening forms of new competition. Again, the telegraph – and with it advertising and the newspaper – enabled the communication of information about prices that could be exploited by producers, but these price-relaying applications in many cases also undermined the cost structures of the production activity in question. Innis used several examples to demonstrate such dynamics, including the Indian rebellion (or mutiny) against the British East India Company that began in 1857.

Innis recognized that the political capacities and orientations of people are not simplistically the outcomes of their relative positions in a particular political economic context. In both India and Canada, the dynamics of centre-margin (including class) relations are variously configured, not least by the historically structured and mediated spatial-temporal conditions at hand.

Introduction to Chapter 10

This chapter was first published in 1936.[23] The ensuing one, titled "The Political Implications of Unused Capacity," is its companion piece. Evidently, Innis believed that "unused capacity" was of such importance to his book that a single chapter applying it to economic history would not suffice. Recall that themes announced in the preface include understanding/misunderstanding, balance/imbalance, war and peace, mechanization and reflexivity. So, predictably, Innis proceeded to connect unused capacity to those themes. It is worth recalling, too, that Innis chose *not* to include other papers that seemingly would have fit well into *PEMS*.[24] The question for this chapter's introduction thus becomes, Why did Innis attribute such importance to unused capacity?

Innis explained unused (or excess) capacity as a source of disequilibrium and of misunderstanding due to its "unbalancing" of relations and activities. To do this, he reviewed over three hundred years of economic history, emphasizing complexities arising from overcapacity. Although the reader must await the chapter's final sentence to find explicit connection to the grand theme of *PEMS* ("Much remains to be done before the implications of unused capacity are understood" [217]), this chapter, in conjunction with the next, provides new insights into the relations and conditions underlying and giving rise to misunderstanding.

The starting point for Innis's analyses was often the capacities and incapacities of people in a given place and time. While, generally, capacities are the historically dynamic parameters of what is feasible or unfeasible, Innis's staples writings focused almost as much on geographic, climatic, and other environmental factors (as in the beginning of this chapter) as they did on political economic and cultural capabilities. Throughout his writings, however, Innis was aware of the dialectical interrelationships between physical and intellectual (as well as quantitative and qualitative) parameters.

Unused capacity, as explained in this chapter, had long been a major (albeit seldom acknowledged) force of disturbance ("un long balance"), one that had set in motion considerable forces seeking to restore balance, order, and control. Often, however, these restorative forces overshot the mark, becoming sources of further disturbance and therefore gave rise to new imbalances. Such contradictory forces, as Innis outlined, included (among others) migrations and new settlements, tariffs and free trade, debt and other forms of state intervention, the construction of transportation infrastructures, the development of new staples for export, and military mobilizations (including wars).

Through his focus on unused capacity, Innis demonstrated a pattern not only in the history of staples-dependent marginal economies but also (by extension and interconnection) world development. In this chapter we see the pattern in the fisheries, the fur trade, the timber trade, the gold rush, and Canada's wheat economy, all requiring the deployment of costly infrastructures to redress unused capacities, as well as related political, financial, military, and cultural mechanisms and arrangements. In effect, Innis was bringing attention to the complex and often deleterious long-term implications of short-term responses to a compounding pattern of overbuilding and overinvestment. The reader is invited to ponder Innis's selection and use of empirical examples in light of an important point he made in an earlier chapter: "The economics of losses is not less significant than the economics of profits" (166). In this chapter, efforts to redress unused capacities were shown to forge the conditions for and the capacities/incapacities of a broad range of "vested interests."

Written in the midst of the Great Depression, one of the chapter's main points was that the calamitous state of the then contemporary political economy had been exacerbated in part by Canada's long-term dependency on staples and the ensuing problems of unused capacity.

The political implications included the reactionary "movement for social credit" in Alberta and the rise of "protests" in other parts of the country. If unused capacities were not redressed, Innis argued, government relief measures and other attempts at stabilizing economic life would prove fruitless. These actions would "not solve the [engrained and long-term] problems of reducing the violence of the swings incidental to the significance of unused capacity" (216).

The reader is reminded that in the preface Innis wrote that "The following essays constitute an attempt to interrelate patterns of Canadian development with those of the Western World in the full realization that much remains to be done before the outlines and the details of the patterns can be clearly discerned" (xvi). This chapter on unused capacity, especially when read as a prelude to the one that follows, enables the reader to better comprehend what is an otherwise murky connection – one that we will elaborate further in our introduction to chapter 11.

Introduction to Chapter 11

"The Political Implications of Unused Capacity" was first published in *PEMS*. Innis explicitly referenced unused capacity in its opening paragraph and then, surprisingly, did not mention it again. In that paragraph, however, he explicitly linked unused capacity with staples and he proceeded to treat the latter at length throughout. This is the connection Innis made: "Unused capacity involved in exploitation of staples had its effect in prolonging the dominance of one staple or in hastening its decline." He then added that through its connection to staples, unused capacity "contributed powerfully to the disturbance of equilibrium in Canada and in Europe" (218).

Before proceeding further, we should note a possible confusion. In Innis's thought, the notion of "capacity," and hence of "unused capacity," has two related but distinguishable meanings. One relates to the physical *size* of a factory or ship (as examples). This meaning has a close connection to supply, economies of scale, overhead costs, efficiency, and other categories common to mainstream economics. The second meaning denotes skills (such as literacy), intellectual potential, and other talents and capabilities. In either case, *unused* capacity is a source of disequilibrium or instability. In the case of human skills, *used* capacity can also be a source of disequilibrium, as illustrated by the spread of literacy (see especially chapters 1 and 2).

The present chapter focuses on the relations, tensions, and power shifts resulting from efforts to exploit natural resources. These efforts gave rise to complex but discernible processes that entailed a systemic elaboration or deepening of unused capacities that, in turn, sped up or slowed down geopolitical change. For Innis, as we have seen, staples are inextricably linked to centre-margin relations; by extension, therefore, Canada's staples are linked to contemporary problems both within Canada and internationally: "The study of the Canadian economy … [is] of crucial significance to an understanding of cyclical and secular disturbances not only within Canada but without" (228).

The unused capacities that Innis assessed were dynamic; those associated with any given staple changed or resisted change in light of a range of factors and conditions in a given place and time. Although media (institutions, organizations, and technologies) are modified or forged in the context of such capacities, use of media recursively changed the parameters of power, including how relations and realities were conceptualized (i.e., the political economy of knowledge). However, such modifications entailed costs and, in the case of Canada, often led to further rigidities that eventually induced limited mindsets (or cognitive biases). More generally, for Innis, patterns and processes related to unused capacity entailed barriers to creativity – what in his preface he referred to as "the chains of modern civilization" (vii).

To illustrate, Innis demonstrated that the economic viability of the fur trade required the presence of an indigenous population possessing particular skills and cultural capacities, as well as the development of certain political, economic, and military relationships among Europeans and native North Americans.[25] As the fur trade developed, however, crises and contradictions emerged concerning, primarily, unbalanced cargoes (a type of unused capacity). These instabilities, said Innis, were compounded through competitive pressures, extreme (and culturally sensitive) fluctuations in the supply and demand of the commodity, and organizational difficulties associated with increasing distances and changing time frames. Such problems spurred efforts to restrict competition and to make the trade more efficient. Control was asserted through centralizing mechanisms involving costly investments and the exercise of state power. The same general pattern recurred time and again through a sequence of staples over the course of Canadian history.

Consider more closely the nexus among staples, unused capacity, and the advent of the "modern state." Mercantilist interests in Britain that first established an international staples economy, according to Innis, unintentionally structured an increasingly uneconomical system whose collapse facilitated free trade and colonial decentralization. Although responsible government in the colonies lightened England's administrative and military burdens, the "problems of trade in staples [became] more acute for the colonies" (228). British North America was largely occupied by immigrants from pre-revolutionary France and by British Loyalists. The generally anti-revolutionary inclinations of those populations, in combination with fear of and competition from the United States, set in motion the parameters for a confederation organized predominantly to defend regional economic interests (as opposed to being an expression of shared interests or democratic ideals). Canada emerged out of the "problems of finance" that resulted from the construction of a national railway that had been conceived to redress the economic difficulties of the regions and provinces. "The federal government," Innis explained, "was concerned primarily with customs for revenue to support transportation improvements ... to pay subsidies largely ... to avoid controversies over religion, and to pay interest on debts incurred chiefly in building railways and canals." (226).

For Innis, then, the dynamic history of unused capacities set forth the grooves (including the political and economic institutions) through which geographically and socially diverse vested interests sought economic gain and/or security. The establishment of the federal government entailed the "use of lands [reserved] 'for purposes of the Dominion,'" and through the construction of the transcontinental railway "the Dominion realized its 'purposes' ... in the enormous increase in the production of wheat in the period from 1900 to 1929" (226). In effect, the conditions for confederation were forged as a means of responding to unused capacities and, in so doing, centralization ensued with the Canadian state responsible for introducing still greater capacity problems. Further political and economic inflexibilities resulted, deepening regional conflicts. In response, "numerous makeshifts have been arranged by which the Dominion has attempted to relieve the burden and that the political atmosphere has become disturbed and confused" (227).

What then is the reader to make of this chapter? On the one hand, given its title, it is the second one ostensibly focusing on unused capacity; indeed, Innis seems to have prepared it specifically for *PEMS*. On the other hand, unused capacity is barely mentioned. Let us speculate that for Innis unused capacity is a sort of *éminence grise*, exerting influence or constituting a historical dynamic that is, for the most part, unnoticed. Once identifying its importance in the opening paragraph,

Innis structured the remainder of the chapter as an illustration of unused capacity's underlying, yet largely invisible power. Due to inattention, unused capacity constituted a major source of misunderstanding in the contemporary international political economy. In the context of 1946, Innis appears to be suggesting that this relatively veiled dynamic – involving complex centre-margin relations and institutionalized ways of organizing and thinking – must be brought to consciousness to illuminate at least some of the worrying developments occurring in the international political economy of his day.

Introduction to Chapter 12

This chapter was originally published in 1942.[26] It included and tied together several concepts from economics (overhead costs, economies of scale, liquidity preference, trade) and related these to their impact on such political economic factors as governance, migration, settlement, debt, competition, and monopoly. Through its focus on the Atlantic fishery, moreover, the chapter can be construed as constituting a succinct case study to illustrate a major conclusion of the previous one: "The study of the Canadian economy becomes of crucial significance to an understanding of cyclical and secular disturbances not only within Canada but without. In a sense the economies of frontier countries are storm centers to the modern international economy" (228). Chapter 13, we will find, further elaborated the implications of the history presented in chapter 12.

Innis began the chapter by implicitly lauding the early Atlantic fishery as a *balanced* economy, featuring "individual enterprise" engaged with "small units of capital" and pursuing common interests giving rise to "co-operation" (229). In merely six pages, he revealed the industry's radical transformation from a relatively low-cost, flexible practice to a major industry characterized by increasingly capital-intensive activities involving entrenched state mechanisms and changing international relations.

The empirical evidence Innis presented demonstrated at a more general level that the conditions in which development unfolds were far from fixed (his position being quite at odds with most contemporary analyses of international relations). According to Innis, structural conditions (or capacities/incapacities) are dynamic. One might infer that the "static" analysis of the economics mainstream manifests the political economy of scholarship as current power arrangements are implicitly depicted as being "normal" or immutable. In this light, the prospect of much-needed "international adjustment" (235) in the face of rigidity is not promising.

A key part of Innis's analysis was his focus not simply on vested interests, cost factors, government policies, and industry practices but also on how these affect one another and influence history differently from place to place and time to time. The technologies used to undertake the fishery (primarily ships and boats), for example, while similar in New England, Nova Scotia, and Newfoundland, led to some very different political economic developments. Moreover, happenings in marginal areas influenced developments in major centres and vice versa (in some cases even thrusting hitherto margins into the position as centres).

As an "attempt to interrelate patterns of Canadian development with those of the Western World," chapter 12 (in conjunction with chapter 13) contributed to a primary goal of *PEMS* as set out in the preface (xvi).

Introduction to Chapter 13

The patterns of political economic development outlined in previous chapters were elaborated in "Decentralization and Democracy." First published in 1943,[27] the chapter focused on "the changes in types of power in the Atlantic basin following the discovery of America" (236).

Here, Innis demonstrated how factors such as dependence on staples, unused capacity, misunderstanding, imperfect competition, and concentrated political economic power played significant roles in shifting alliances, destabilizing international relations, inducing wars, and even inducing the ascendency and decline of empires. He proposed that "the fur trade involved heavy outbound cargo and a light return cargo with the result that settlement was discouraged and that vigorous efforts by government to encourage immigration were made ... The necessity of concentrating on the St. Lawrence [for the fur trade] precluded the development of the [Hudson Bay] route and Radisson and Groseilliers deserted to the English to assist the formation of the Hudson's Bay Company in 1670" (237). In just two sentences Innis here linked the fur trade, unused capacity, the rise of the modern state, shifting alliances, a monopolistic chartered company, and rival empires.

Next, however, Innis presented an even more ambitious theme: We must leave behind simplistic thinking (the "hocus pocus of the economist") if the peace following the Second World War is to endure. Innis situated the history presented in this chapter in terms of the strategies and changing competitive capabilities of the French and English empires in their early exploitation of North American resources. The collapse of French power "profoundly disturbed" the state of tension or equilibrium between the two, yielding a destabilizing English dominance.[28] According to Innis, this was a precondition for the American Revolution and, with it, the end of the first British Empire. Control over much of the Atlantic basin by the imperial centre (Britain) thus led to the successful revolt of one of its colonies (America).

In response to the emergence of the United States, the British were compelled to make significant organizational changes in, for example, the fur trade (involving longer distances, larger capital investments, and, thus, increasing uncertainties). Innis also argued that the end of the second British Empire in the nineteenth century was hastened by the Reform Act in Britain, the decline of mercantilist control over staples activities, and the rise of free trade. Technological improvements, especially in transportation, not only lowered costs but also stimulated growth and increased debts (again presaging the modern state). In response to the end of free trade (an outcome of the North's victory in the American Civil War), changes in British North America included a "policy of division and defence" which "left a legacy of control by the provinces" (245).

More than sweeping, the reader will find Innis's analysis to be remarkably fluid in its overview of changing domestic, regional, and international relations. And far from being a haphazard chronology of influential factors and relational developments, this fluidity was organized through a conceptual framework that emphasized rigidities and flexibilities, states of equilibrium and disequilibrium, crises, centre-margin and imperial power dynamics, and, of course, contradictions.

Chiefly in the closing pages, Innis demonstrated that institutional, organizational, and technological capacities developed directly in relation to changing political economic conditions, and vice versa. In other words, Innis emphasized a historical pattern that is dynamic and dialectical, one in which the "problem of adjustment" (248) surfaces repeatedly. Canada's economy, for example, structured to promote an east-west trajectory in its development, experienced crisis in the twentieth century with the ascent of north-south relations – a crisis that involved declining European markets; obsolescence of existing transportation systems; and the rising importance of hydroelectric power, petroleum, and roads. The structures of decentralized federalism, he asserted, were unable to cope with the political economic power of the United States and its pull of regional interests. Regarding Canada, Innis saw responses to the crisis in the ascent of new political parties, the centralization of power in cabinet, and a growing dependency on barely accountable bureaucracies. These and other developments were facilitated by the reluctance of the press to engage in "effective discussion" and the related popularity of commercial radio (given its intent to reach "large numbers" [248]).

Importantly, Innis did not dismiss democracy itself. Rather, he stressed the inadequacy of Canada's contemporary "political structure" beset by historically entrenched conditions and capacities: "It is imperative that serious attention should be given to the problem of revising political machinery so that democracy can work out solutions to modern problems" (249). "Responsible government," as configured through Canadian history, according to Innis, is antithetical to democracy, and any hope for the latter entails a fundamental rethinking of the structures and political economic underpinnings of the former. Therefore, responsible government and democracy, as he implies elsewhere in *PEMS*, are not identical.

In the last footnote of the chapter, Innis quoted Henry Sumner Maine who commented that a "revolution of ideas is very rare in the West, and indeed experience shows that innovating legislation is connected not so much with Science as with the scientific air which certain subjects, not capable of exact scientific treatment, from time to time assume" (250, n. 3). Through this quote, Innis in effect reiterated questions regarding the supposed precision of economics and other social sciences and their applications in policymaking, stressing yet again the problem of misunderstanding and in particular the need to comprehend the underpinnings and dynamics of society's intellectual and cultural (in)capacities. Rather than more expertise (as with bureaucracies and specialized studies), or more "democracy" (as simplistically formulated in terms of public opinion, for example), Innis stressed the need for in-depth and nuanced analyses of structural conditions and mediating mechanisms in order to ameliorate current crises.

The history presented in this chapter demonstrates the dangerous implications of short-term, narrowly focused thinking and policymaking. In the case of Canada and, by extension, international relations, specialist manipulations of existing instruments in pursuit of "patchwork solutions" (250) only perpetuated and deepened the problems that such responses sought to resolve.

Introduction to Chapter 14

As we have seen, running through *PEMS* is the theme of governments formulating policies and taking actions in the absence of adequate knowledge or understanding. In Canada, for example, royal commissions have been routinely established during periods of crisis to study problems and propose solutions, but what they normally produce, according to Innis, is "panic literature" as opposed to "exhaustive studies of the field as a whole" (251).

"Transportation and the Tariff" is the penultimate chapter of *PEMS*. Indeed, it was added at the last minute and appears to have been written specifically for the book.[29] One can only conclude that, for Innis, this chapter had great importance. However, we believe that its significance today is easily overlooked as tariffs, canals, railway policy, government debt, and so on are likely not of burning concern to contemporary readers. Therefore, here we speculate on the importance of this chapter to Innis in 1946.

In our view, the chapter well illustrates Innis's insistence that deep, broad, nuanced, and complex knowledge is needed for sound policy, as opposed to superficial knowledge (or, just as dangerously, the force-fitting of data into readily available templates as with, for example, price theory). Through Innis's close analysis of actual developments and policies, this brief chapter contains *PEMS*'s most precise policy prescriptions, regarding what the author called the "scientific application of the tariff" (254). Instead of applying tariffs and other policy tools to facilitate the reproduction of a crisis-laden status quo (i.e., its perpetuation in space and time), Innis suggested that they should be used to promote a more diversified and flexible economy. For example, instead of adjusting transportation projects (or even specific railway lines) in response to particular challenges, he recommended setting rates and adjusting dividends with the longer term in mind and, in more general ways, treating the country's transportation infrastructure "as a unit" (251) – taking into account both Canada's "total capital structure" (255) and its (inadequate) banking and financial system.[30]

There is an additional, albeit largely implicit, way in which chapter 14 related to the rest of *PEMS*, even presaging core themes in *The Bias of Communication*. For Innis, transportation developments and tariff policies were mechanisms (or, as his later work would put it, media), forged as means of defending or extending control over space and time. For example, among other implications, most transportation developments extended spatial reach, whereas tariffs constituted spatial barriers protecting and extending the time frames of domestic activities.

In the preface Innis told his readers that a particular concern of *PEMS* was post-war development. In chapter 14 he approached that subject in broad historical terms, interweaving internal limitations (including biases) and external factors that could increase Canada's political economic vulnerability in the post-1945 world. By the chapter's conclusion, he connected the country's contradictory state of affairs to its intellectual and cultural challenges.

In sum, in this chapter Innis reinforced his position that Canada and, by implication, the world are in need of a new approach – one that assesses the present and future through a more holistic, nuanced, and dialectical comprehension of the past. The history it presents recognized, in conjunction with some of the book's other chapters, the need to respond in ways that are both reflexive and practical, emphasizing "unity, strength and flexibility" (256).

Introduction to Chapter 15

Innis began his career by advocating and practising a position of analytical relativism. According to the early Innis, economic models developed in older, industrialized nations should never be accepted without careful scrutiny by emergent ones, for those thought structures might well be used as a means for exploitation. [31] Through his staples thesis, therefore, Innis duly set about developing "an economic theory suited to Canadian needs."[32]

For the early Innis, then, to generalize slightly, competition among thought structures and the development of theories particular to given times and places were routes to emancipation. By the end of his career, however, he had moved to a much different position. In his final address, delivered posthumously to the American Economics Association by friend and colleague Tom Easterbrook, Innis declared: "I must begin by pleading for a general emphasis on a universal approach and by insisting as an economist that economic history is primarily concerned with the task of extending the universal applicability of economic theory and of strengthening a central core of interest" (17).[33]

The inflection point in Innis's transition – between celebrating relativism and his quest for universal truth – arguably, was his trip to Russia in 1945. His reflections on that trip appear in *PEMS* as chapter 15.

Innis opened this final chapter by quoting Sir John Maynard, to the effect that, for a world then facing grave crises, common understanding had become vital (257). Further along, he advised: "The decision to celebrate the 220th anniversary of the Academy of Sciences is an indication of a broad statesmanlike approach to a world problem of understanding, and recognition of the possibilities of using science as a common approach – almost the only universal common basis left" (262). "A common world view," Innis believed, "has become indispensable" (263).

By the end of March 1945, Innis thought he had finalized his manuscript. However, weeks later, on 7 May, he asked his editor at Ryerson Press, Lorne Pierce, to return it, explaining simply that "one can always think of changes and improvements."[34] The day Innis requested the manuscript's return, incidentally, roughly coincided with his invitation from the Soviet Academy of Sciences. Innis visited Russia from 6 June to 4 July. En route back to Canada on 5 July 1945, he wrote in his diary: "Western civilization [has] much to learn from Russia and Russia much to learn from western civilization … The search for truth offers common ground … and the insistence on 'truth' as dogma is an invitation to disaster."[35] By November 1945, among other changes, Innis had added "Reflections on Russia" as his conclusion to *PEMS*. He continued revising the complete manuscript, including "Reflections," until March 1946.[36]

By 1945 Innis had become very concerned about ignorance on both sides of the emerging Cold War, which, he anticipated, leaders on both sides would try to exploit to gain support for their agendas. Also troublesome to Innis was the fact that Canada's anti-revolutionary history, being at odds with Russia's revolutionary zeitgeist, likewise militated against a shared understanding. Alternatively and more hopefully, he suggested that their economic histories did have similarities: unused economic capacities profoundly shaping Canada's economic development, for instance, bore resemblance to the unused capacities associated with Russia's labour force. However, on both sides, policies attempting to respond to these unused capacities had, to that point, constituted merely stopgap measures, giving rise in both countries to political, economic, and cultural inflexibilities that made domestic (and thus international) stability unlikely. For Innis this also made the search for, to repeat, "a common world view … indispensable" (263).

As in some of his previous chapters, "Reflections" emphasized the importance of propaganda. Through the printing press and the rise of vernaculars "it became [in the West] more and more difficult to maintain a common intellectual life ... [and] each nation developed its own narrow outlook" (266). What's more, he argued: "Dependence on the headline and limitations of the press inevitably made for superficial information and an unstable public opinion" (267). In Russia, meanwhile, the state and Communist Party were intent to defend the revolution through all means possible; propaganda, for example, was applied both "in the press but [also] in the development of new shrines such as Lenin's tomb ... and in literature, the stage and the ballet" (267).

A promising approach, said Innis, to emerging international problems is a heightened awareness of and emphasis on the common intellectual/philosophical heritage of East and West, namely Greek civilization. That common legacy, most fundamentally, was grounded in "an awareness of the position of the individual in the community ... 'Other nations made gods, kings, sprits; the Greeks alone made men'" (263). But the dialectic of individual/community, Innis argued, eventually became a primary point of political tension between East and West.

The Renaissance – mediated by Protestantism (having roots in Platonism and St Augustine, as well as the printing press) – could not blossom in the East because, after the fall of Constantinople, the Greek Orthodox Church became part of an absolutist structure. Given the presence of an illiterate population and the absence of the price system, Innis explained, the counterbalancing mechanisms needed to resist the centralization of power (i.e., the abnegation of the individual) simply did not exist in the East. According to Innis, however, those incapacities eventually became capacities: "The weapons of Marx were sharpened and improved in the hands of Lenin and others, atheism was given a more conspicuous position, and the structure collapsed." He asked, hopefully, if the Russian Revolution might yet yield a "second renaissance," this time in the East (265).

Turning to the West, Innis proposed that "a common intellectual life" (266) had been undermined by the mechanizing and divisive impacts of commerce and the printing industry while the dominant economic and political interests "poisoned remaining channels of intercommunication" (267). In Canada, the task at hand, therefore, is "to make determined efforts to understand the Anglo-Saxon world ... and not to become a menace because of our inability to solve our own problems" (269).

In keeping with Innis's emphasis on reflexive capacities, this marvelous chapter again stresses that understanding requires some comprehension of the factors that impede it. He concludes by returning to the role of the academy in what he realized will be a complex and probably irresolvable political and cultural struggle: "The universities must attack the problem of understanding" (270).

As elsewhere in *PEMS,* in this chapter Innis stressed that "our first duty is to conserve and strengthen our heavily depleted intellectual and spiritual resources. The time has at last arrived when the Platonic problem of the state in contrast with the problem of the individual must be solved or rather the problem which Plato left unsolved must be met" (266).

NOTES

1. "The Newspaper in Economic Development," Supplement, *The Journal of Economic History* 2, no. S1 (December 1942): 1–33.
2. According to the quantity theory of money, MV = PQ, where M is the quantity of money, V is its velocity (rate of turnover), P is the price level, and Q is real output. Innis addresses this broader context in, for example, chapters 10 and 11. His concerns there are with interrelations among staples, gold, unused capacity in transportation, and trade, etc., on the one hand, and geopolitical-economic-cultural factors on the other. Innis argues that unused capacity speeds up or slows down political-economic-cultural change, depending on the staple involved.
3. In *University of Toronto Quarterly* 15, no. 1 (October 1946): 37–53.
4. An undated version is held in the University of Toronto archives, filed as an "Address to the Women's Canadian Club Executive Committee."
5. More generally, quoting Bismarck, Innis observes that the art of diplomacy had deteriorated into "veiled menace or tart lecturing" in "a viewless sea of violence and passion" (57). "It became difficult," Innis concludes, "to secure a stable basis from which to view [or understand] the whole with perspective" (57).
6. It was originally published in the *Dalhousie Review* 24 (1944–5): 298–305.
7. Preparing and delivering this commencement address must have been particularly significant for Innis as McMaster was his alma mater for both his bachelor's and master's degrees.
8. Pattison elaborated as follows: "The professions tend to split up into branches; and skill in one becomes more and more incompatible with skill in another ... Cleverness, talent, skill, fluency, memory, all these are understood and rated in the market. A cultivated mind, just because it is above all price, is apt to be overlooked altogether" (77). Contemporary observers will

recognize the parallels between this mechanization of society and the rise of what has been termed Fordism or the Fordist regime of accumulation.

9. Supplement, 4, no. S1 (December 1944): 80–97. For republication in *PEMS,* Innis slightly altered the title (it was originally called "On the Economic Significance of Culture"), dropped the opening paragraph, and rephrased the first couple of sentences of the second paragraph.
10. Gary Becker and George Stigler, both Nobel Laureates, applied a Latin maxim to emphasize the point. See Stigler and Becker, "De Gustibus Non Est Disputandum," *American Economic Review* 67, no. 2 (1977): 76–90.
11. Underlying power relations are further obscured by phrases such as "consumer sovereignty," again indicating that market outcomes are non-deliberative, decentred, and spontaneous.
12. The starkest defence of this neoclassicists' position was published in the year following Innis's death. See Milton Friedman, "The Methodology of Positive Economics," in *Essays in Positive Economics* (Chicago: University of Chicago Press, 1953), 3–34.
13. As prelude to fuller treatments in chapters 7 and 8, Innis invokes "liquidity preference" as a major analytical category, stating that "the use of liquidity preference as a concept in the study of economic history emphasizes short-run points of view acceptable to the price system rather than long-run points of view which necessitate perspective" (85). This point is of such importance to Innis that, employing his characteristically ironic sense of humour, he broadens his target to include all social science: "There is in the social sciences a liquidity preference for theories concerned with the present which is more dangerous in its implications than liquidity preference is to monetary stability" (85–6).
14. Anticipating this assertion and reflecting on Dodgson's cryptic critique on the first page (and, again, foreshadowing his later writings on bias), Innis quotes Ernst Troeltsch: "The apparently objective value of money, and the universal possibility of exchange which this involves, [entails] a strong psychological impulse to become a fixed *habit of thought,* whereas the purely logical process itself, when it only follows its own course, is not subject to these influences, and it then turns these accepted ideas into mere probabilities" (85, emphasis added). "Habit of thought" is a phrase commonly associated with Veblen, and Innis used it with some frequency.
15. Innis writes of "political economy in the classical sense" (128), which for him, we might say, was the "authentic" political economy. We use "authentic" to summarize what Innis valued in terms of solid scholarship. We acknowledge that this is a word distrusted in some quarters of contemporary scholarship, but we deem it very apt in this context. Innis tended to define his

ideal of good, honest ("authentic") scholarship in part by what it was not: It was not unduly influenced by vested interests (religious, political, economic); it was not "present-minded"; it was not specialized; it was not unduly deterministic. It was, however, dialectical and reflexive, and it accounted for the big complex picture of human relations and thinking regarding questions concerning both time and space.

16. "Toynbee and students of civilization," Innis pronounced, "insist that while 'nature never proceeds by leaps,' civilization [in fact] proceeds in precisely that fashion. 'All spiritual growth takes place by leaps and bounds, both in the individual and … in the community' (Burckhardt)" (127).
17. In the twentieth century, Innis says, the economist has become a "political economist," not in the sense of classic political economy but, instead, in that they are now at the service of the party, a pressure group, or the state (130).
18. It was presented in a joint meeting with the Canadian Historical Association and was first published in the *Canadian Journal of Economics and Political Science* 4, no. 3 (August 1938): 299–319. Innis appears to have borrowed the title's metaphor from Matsuyo Takizawa's 1927 book, *The Penetration of Money Economy in Japan and Its Effects upon Social and Political Institutions.*
19. Innis quips that in the social sciences there is "a liquidity preference for theories concerned with the present" (85–6).
20. In *Transactions of the Royal Society of Canada* 3rd series, 37, no. 2 (1943): 1–31.
21. In other words, a reversal of "normal" developments in which liquidity flows initially stem from economic or imperial centres.
22. The liquidity provided through gold, Innis explains, contributed to the lowering of trade barriers and to what we today term "globalization." Innis summarized, "It is significant that Marshall suggested that after 1873 the economic history of one country could not be written" (199).
23. *Canadian Journal of Economics and Political Science* 2, no. 1 (1936): 1–15.
24. These include "The Teaching of Economic History in Canada" (1929), "The Canadian Economy and the Depression" (1934), and "The Role of Intelligence: Some Further Notes" (1935).
25. In contrast Innis explains that the circumstances of Spain's extraction of precious metals in Central and South America and Britain's interest in certain agricultural products produced in the West Indies implied significantly different relationships.
26. In the *Commerce Journal* (April 1942): 21–6.
27. Before *PEMS*, it was published in the *Canadian Journal of Economics and Political Science* 9, no. 3 (August 1943): 236–50.

28. Innis generalizes that "the fall of ... the French Empire" was the "result of the inadequacies of control by France with a continental background; and the dependence on military participation and consequent rigidities. The fall of the British Empire," he adds, "was a result of the inadequacies of control by England with a maritime background and her dependence on naval strength and consequent elasticities" (241).
29. Innis added this chapter to *PEMS* – along with "Reflections on Russia" and "The University in the Modern Crisis" – late in the book's development. The table of contents sent by Lorne Pierce (the book's editor at Ryerson Press) to Innis on 5 March 1945 does not include this chapter. On 7 May (the day of Germany's surrender) Innis told Pierce that he might consider "changes and improvements" to the manuscript. By March 1946, Innis appears to have made his final revisions (*PEMS* was published in October or early November of that year). Pierce to Innis, 22 March 1945, file 02, box 004, Accession B1972-0025, University of Toronto Archives; Innis to Lorne Pierce, May 1945, item 0003, file 0106, Lorne Pierce Papers, Queen's University Archives; Pierce to Innis, 4 March 1946, item 0003, file 0117, Lorne Pierce Papers, Queen's University Archives.
30. Elsewhere, Innis recommends that during periods of prosperity tariffs on equipment used in staples activities should be raised to pay down debts. In depressed periods, these tariffs could be lowered. See Innis, "Snarkov Island" and "A Defence of the Tariff," both in Neill, *A New Value of Theory*.
31. Innis, "Snarkov Island," 149.
32. Innis, "The Teaching of Economic History in Canada," 3.
33. Innis, "The Decline in Efficiency of Instruments Essential in Equilibrium," *American Economic Review* 43, no. 1 (1953): 16–22.
34. Innis to Lorne Pierce, 7 May 1945, item 0003, file 0106, Lorne Pierce Papers, Queen's University Archives.
35. Harold A. Innis, *Innis on Russia: The Russian Diary and Other Writings by Harold A. Innis*, ed. William Christian (Toronto: The Harold Innis Foundation, 1981), 47.
36. This chronology is drawn primarily from correspondence between Innis and Pierce held at the University of Toronto and Queen's University archives.

POLITICAL ECONOMY
IN THE
MODERN STATE

To

DONALD

MARY

HUGH

ANNE

PREFACE

This volume has been designed to bring together widely scattered and relatively inaccessible articles published since 1933, for the convenient use of students, particularly the large number of students from the armed forces. War veterans have been trained to do difficult things and it is hoped that their training, enthusiasm and self confidence may be conserved and directed to the tasks of peace more difficult and more complex than those of war. The volume is intended as a guide and as a warning.

The difficulty and complexity of the tasks of peace arise from their apparent and deceptive simplicity. The most dangerous illusions accompany the most obvious facts including the printed and the mechanical word. Plato refused to be bound by the written words of his own books. He makes Socrates say in *Phaedrus* regarding the invention of writing, "this discovery of yours will create forgetfulness in the learners' souls, because they will not use their memories; they will trust to the external written characters and not remember of themselves. The specific which you have discovered is an aid not to memory, but to reminiscence and you give your disciples not truth, but only the semblance of truth; they will be hearers of many things and have learned nothing; they will appear to be omniscient and will generally know nothing; they will be tiresome company, having the show of wisdom without the reality." Since this was written the printing press and the radio have enormously increased the difficulties of thought. The first essential task is to see and to break through the chains of modern civilization which have been created by modern science. Freedom of the press and freedom of speech have been possible largely because they have permitted the production of words on an unprecedented scale and have made them powerless. Oral and printed words have been harnessed to the enormous demands of modern industrialism and in advertising have been made to find new markets for goods. Each new invention which enhances their power in that direction weakens their power in other directions. It is worth noting that large majorities in political elections accompanied the spread of the newspaper on a large scale in England after the sixties in the last century, and the spread of the radio on this continent. Swings in public opinion are more violent with new inventions in communication, and independent thought is more difficult to sustain. It is scarcely necessary to add, that words have carried a heavy additional load in the prosecution of the war and have been subjected to unusual strains.

Perhaps no words have been subject to greater strain than those pertaining to the social sciences. The term "political economy" has been preferred as it has escaped partly because of its cumbersomeness. The most important thing to be said about this term is that it is not important, and by implication the same comment may be made about other subjects. It is useful to turn to the dialogue between Protagoras and Socrates in which the pretensions of the social sciences are effectively exposed. Universities are menaced by specialization and the belief on the part of specialists that no other interest than their own is important. Special subjects extend their pretensions by posing as co-ordinating subjects. The dangers must be met by an appreciation of the limits of specialization and a recognition of the necessity of perspective. The social sciences have been particularly exposed to the dangers of specialization, and the accompanying curse of individualism at the expense of personality. The problem of the humanities, particularly the classics, is a reflection of the difficulties. The classical tradition precludes the possibility of selling the classics, and is overshadowed by subjects with little other concern than that of selling themselves and even threatening to improve the classics by selling them. We must beware of those who have found the truth. The excesses of individualism rather than the integration of personality have characterized the schizophrenia of Western Civilization. It is the essence of the philosophy of the social sciences that concern should be given primarily to their limitations. "Above all—no zeal."

The influence of specialization in the social sciences has been evident in concentration on the problems of the price system, partly as a result of its deceptive appearance of finality which follows the possibility of extensive use of mathematics, a decisive instrument in the natural sciences. Its advantages have been so important that little question has been raised as to its limitations except in the enormous number of preposterous proposals of monetary reform. These proposals are merely a reflection of the effects of the disease of specialization. Nevertheless the relatively impersonal character of the price system has enormously enhanced the efficiency of industrialism. Its ruthlessness has been the object of voluble complaint but this must be balanced against alternative possibilities. It appears to be the most effective system for introducing freedom and efficiency into hierarchical systems. It has largely avoided the hierarchical limitations of Chinese civilization with its dependence on written examinations, the costs of the ecclesiastical system shown, for example, in celibacy in the Roman Catholic Church, and the dangers of autocracy based on the divine right of kings.

But effectiveness of the price system will depend on a realization of its limitations. It has been dependent on a widespread diffusion of mathematics, i.e., in the ability to make change, and on an intensive study of its mathematical character. The compilation and dissemination of information as to prices has been dependent on the effectiveness of communication in the newspapers, the radio and other media. It operates more intensively in areas where information can be quickly disseminated—in urban rather than rural areas. It is more effective in allocating resources at some times than others. It requires constant attention on the part of accountants, lawyers and other professional groups. The intensity of the belief in the price system will vary in part with the teaching of economics and with the character of the teaching. Its susceptibility to mathematical research facilitates reinforcement of the belief in the price system and contributes to the intensity of the obsession. Its dangers follow obsession and intolerance to a philosophical interest and scepticism.

Perhaps in no country is it more difficult to attain perspective as to the place of the price system than in Canada, precisely because one of our basic industries has been built up on its distortion. The peculiar geographic setting of Canada has made its economy a source of disturbance to the economies of other countries. The enormous importance of water navigation and the vastness of the Precambrian formation have necessitated concentration on large scale production of basic commodities and intense pressure on the markets of other countries. The markets of Europe were bombarded in turn with such staple products as fur, timber and wheat and of the United States with minerals and newsprints. Wheat production, supported by energetic governmental assistance, brought a revolution in British agriculture and led European countries to impose barriers or to undergo revolutions. Pulp and paper production supported by provincial governments facilitated the rapid growth of advertising in the United States, and contributed to the problems of industrialism and the destruction of a stable public opinion. Moreover, the development of a federal structure in Canada, concerned with the occupation of the prairie regions and pressure on Europe, has been twisted by the assistance of provincial governments concerned with the exploitation of the Precambrian formation and pressure on the United States. Our problems have become difficult as a result of our geographic background, and because of our immediate concern with the success of an industry which, in its success, makes for greater instability of public opinion in the United States and in Canada. The pressure of the production of newsprint from the Precambrian formation, and the more intense development of advertising, implies an exaggerated emphasis on the price system and a more unstable public opinion precluding a clear appreciation of our problems and in turn sustained consideration of them.

The results have been evident in our cultural growth. States are destroyed by ignorance of the most important things in human life, by a profound lack of culture—which, following Plato, is the inability to secure a proper agreement between desire and intellect. The state of the arts in Canada is threatened by a fanatical interest in nationalism reflecting our inability to grapple with the problems of Western Civilization. The drain of nationalism on our energies all but exhausts efforts to appreciate our position in the West. Perhaps we are fortunate in our difficulties of establishing a nation or, to paraphrase Oscar Wilde, in having youth as our oldest tradition. In the words of James Joyce, "nationalism, religion, and language are nets set for her children" in Canada as in Ireland. Where Ireland has been called a sow which devoured her young, Canada, it will be said, has produced no young. The traditions of the Church in Southern Ireland have been paralleled in Quebec, and they have combined with nationalism to weaken her rich cultural growth. In Northern Ireland, as in Ontario, the loyalist tradition has meant constant struggle and exhaustion. In Canada the struggle in which the traditions of the Church and language have been intensified by the attacks of the loyalist tradition, and in which the loyalist tradition has been intensified by resistance of the Church, has restrained nationalism. But its restraint has produced a twisted and distorted cultural growth as an appeal to Canadian literature, art or any phase of cultural activity will show. Such resistance, as has been built up in England by the intense interest in regional development, shown for example in Thomas Hardy, has been largely impossible particularly in English-speaking Canada. The hatreds between regions in Canada have become important vested interests. Montreal exploits the hatred of Toronto and Regina that of Winnipeg and so one might go through the list. A native of Ontario may appear restive at being charged with exploitation by those who systematically exploit him through their charges of exploitation, but even the right to complain is denied to him. But it may be a sign of maturity that we no longer talk about the great Canadian novel.

Whether Canada cannot have a literature because she is a nation is an interesting question. Except in French Canada nationalism prevents the growth of a large scale publishing industry. British and American publishing houses are compelled to appoint agents in Canada, and Canadian publishers in competition are reluctant to accept Canadian manuscripts without a reasonable prospect of sales in British and American markets. Canadian writers consequently compete at an unfair disadvantage with American and British publications. In a sense Canada becomes a headless nation with its brains scattered over other countries. Interest in the Canadian scene is restricted by Puritanical traditions and the power of ecclesiastical and business hierarchies. Canadian criticism is handicapped and literature tends to centre around animal stories, United Empire Loyalists, French Canadians and the fly-blown romances of large business organizations and the Royal Canadian Mounted Police. French Canada like France has escaped the necessity of catering to the Anglo-Saxon market.

But both French and English Canada have been influenced by the possibilities of the tourist trade. Self assertiveness, the great Anglo-Saxon characteristic, is exaggerated through the necessity of appearing different from the countries from which we hope to attract tourists. It is imperative that we assume an attitude of superiority toward the United States. Publicity departments have capitalized this attitude with great skill during the war. American media intent on criticizing American practices were used to secure high praise of Canadian practices and this in turn was copied in Canada as the considered impartial view of a detached observer. We must beware of what is said about us in other countries. In her tourist trade Canada offers interesting parallels to Switzerland.

Multi-regional, bilingual and bireligious countries exhaust their energies in compromise. On the one hand the Loyalist tradition assumes that the French Canadians are a conquered race and on the other the French Canadian tradition demands an appeal to history and reliance on spiritual rather than material power. The Protestant churches become Erastian in opposition to the power of the Roman Catholic Church in Quebec. Ultimate power rests in the hands of the army as the outcome of the conscription issue has shown. Cultural development is restricted by the inevitable colonialism which follows. Division makes for intolerance on the part of both French Canadians and Loyalists softened only by trade and debts. The political party is apparently no longer able to provide necessary compromise without the sacrifice of principles. The absence of consistency in the attitude of any English Canadian party or public leader points to the fundamental corruption of Canadian political life. Even the French Canadian has been exposed to the same influence though consistency has been more evident and moral fibre more conspicuous. On all sides the social scientist can be seen carrying fuel to Ottawa to make the flames of nationalism burn more brightly. Or he is constantly devising schemes throughout the Provinces to thwart the human spirit and to fasten the chains more tightly. Fortunately we are sufficiently divided in regions, races and religion to resist his demands for centralization.

Political economy can scarcely be expected to thrive under these conditions. A study of the conditions under which it can flourish would point to Adam Smith, who could write *The Wealth of Nations* in the eighteenth century while supported by a pension secured in return for tutoring the Duke of Buccleuch. The continuity of British public life, with its traditions of leisure and learning, not only created conditions suited to Adam Smith and Gibbon, but also provided the visibility to statesmen and the classical economists and scientists of the nineteenth century which gave significance to the work of Adam Smith, as the names of Pitt, Huskisson, Peel and Gladstone and of Malthus, Ricardo, Mill, Jevons, Marshall, Darwin and Spencer attest. The support of continuous thought in Britain was not evident in France because of the abruptness of the break in the French Revolution. In Germany the dominance of the Prussian state checked revolutionary movements and weakened political economy with Karl Marx and the class struggle as a result. In the United States the continuous change of personalities in government lessened the impact of political economy. The President changed frequently and the life of politicians in Congress was not long. Political life reflected economic pressures and gave little opportunity for sustained philosophical interest. In Canada political interests were concerned with economic expansion of a unified continental character. The Senate became the refuge of party organization. The Canadian Pacific Railway became entrenched in the tariff to the point that it led to the construction of additional competitive transcontinental lines. It is difficult to estimate the burdens of the tariff but they are indicated in part in enormous railway deficits. The inability of economists to make any impression on them has supported the obsession with studies of national income and monetary policy and of politicians with social credit. We have long since ceased to regard the comment of Bagehot to Gladstone in 1863. "Indirect taxation so cramps trade and heavy direct taxation so impairs morality that a large expenditure becomes a great evil."[1] Extensive government expenditure and intervention and large scale undertakings have raised the fundamental problems of morality. A friend in power is a friend lost. A decline in morality has followed war and the growth of hierarchies in church, state and private enterprise. Power is poison.

In turn the problems of world government have become not less difficult. Lord Ripon stated that "parliamentary centralization is an instrument which no power in the world has ever yet successfully applied to the pacification and good government of alien nationalities" and it is hardly probable that Anglo-Saxon countries will succeed where others have failed. The alternative is reliance on benevolent force such as Gibbon described in the Roman empire "with its martial triumphs, legal enactments and social improvements" and such as he implicitly indicated as a model for the British empire, such as Adam Smith suggested for Anglo-Saxon peoples, and Henry Adams for the United States. Armed force based on the effective linkage between economic power and political power becomes supreme.

The distortion of the price system has weakened the rôle of political economy in western civilization and destroyed its position as developed by Adam Smith in relation to natural law. The crystallization and commercialization of language strengthened by the

[1]John Morley, *The Life of William Ewart Gladstone* (London, 1903) II, 63.

development of the communication industries have brought rigidity and division. Obsession with administrative details in areas determined by national boundaries imposes serious handicaps on the work of world organization. Printed constitutions have been stamped on western civilization and the worship of respective fathers of confederation has made impossible the continuation of a system built on natural law. The divine right of nations has replaced the divine right of kings. Constitutions as reflections of types of demand, notably demands for capital, have imposed handicaps to the effective discussion of world problems. Improvements in communication have weakened the possibility of sustained thought when it has become most necessary. Civilization has been compelled to resort to reliance on force as a result of the impact of technology on communication. The limitations of the price system have meant resort to political arrangements in international adjustment and constant emphasis on appeals to force.

The end of the long struggle for re-organization which began with the breakdown of the control of the Church, notably among Anglo-Saxons with Henry VIII, appears on the horizon. The civil war in England with the migration of cavaliers to the South and puritans to the North was reproduced in the Civil War in the United States. The Loyalists who migrated to regions which later became Canada removed the leaven and sharpened the contrast between the society of the south and of the north which broke out in the Civil War. In turn they emphasized the martial atmosphere of Canada and the conflict with the old order reflected in Quebec. Restoration of control by the aristocratic elements in the United States under F. D. Roosevelt coincided with the success of the Loyalists in Canada in enforcing conscription. The imperial concept of Rome as a civil power has been restored with armed force supported by science and technology. "The principal point of greatness in any state is to have a race of military men" (Bacon). Public opinion follows force.

Parliament pushed forward from the absolutism of Henry VIII and his control over the Church to the Civil War, and after a brief retreat under Charles II and James II to 1688. The supremacy of parliament was pushed to the point that the colonies were compelled to withdraw and George III was able to capitalize the reaction. The United States later compelled the readjustments leading to free trade. The growth of independence in the colonies, characterized by the increasing power of the assemblies and the weakening of the governor and council, meant difficulties of co-operation which were temporarily overcome by the military demands of the revolution and the constitution. With the declaration of independence and the energy of Jefferson, opposition to the centralizing tendencies of the federalist emerged. The power of Jefferson and his followers on the left was paralleled by that of the second offshoot of the revolution on the right the loyalists who migrated to the Maritimes and the Upper St. Lawrence. With their emphasis on imperialism and the state they came into conflict with the French dominated by the church. The centralizing trend of the Loyalists was supported by militarism and the Anglican Church, and contributed, particularly in the struggle for control over land, to the outbreak in 1837.

The emphasis of the Constitution of the United States on checks and balances meant that the swing toward Jefferson and Jackson was offset in part by the Supreme Court under Marshall. But the absence of the centralizing power of the army and the Church favoured the growth of centralization in commercial and industrial organizations. In the outbreak of the war between the states centralization of military control in the North was achieved with great difficulty and with great loss of life. With ultimate victory centralization in the North was checked only temporarily by Cleveland. The revolt of the West under Bryan and the work of La Follette in the Republican party enabled Wilson to restore the position of the South. Centralization of the Republican party under Taft brought withdrawal of Theodore Roosevelt supported by Munsey and eastern business interests. The South resumed effective control as seen in the influence of Colonel House and the crucial position of Texas. In the post-war period the swing to supremacy of the Republican party was followed by Roosevelt and the depression. Centralization was carried to new levels. In the United States credit had been given by individual states to support private enterprise and in competition it was necessary for Canada to rely on the federal government to secure credit. Restrictions on the federal government in the United States favoured expansion under the federal government in Canada. Centralization and force have come to dominate the Anglo-Saxon world.

Perhaps the most significant development in the social sciences in the past quarter century has been the interest in the study of civilization following Spengler, Toynbee, Kroeber and others. The importance of cultural growth as a reflection of the tenacity of civilizations compels an intense interest in the subject. It has been observed that cultural florescence has been greatest in Greece, Italy and Germany during periods of political disorganization. While religion may provide a nursery to cultural beginnings, cultural maturity assumes the growth of autonomy and freedom from religious restraint. It would be instructive for the social scientist to attempt a study of his place in cultural growth.

An attempt has been made to raise the fundamental question as to the role of science in the Western World. Greece saw the emergence of science and philosophy and Rome utilized the contribution in an appeal to the natural law of the Stoics. But law and rhetoric implied appeals to force. It was not until the return to Greece in the renaissance and the modern world that science again imposed its will. Mathematics as developed by Newton strengthened the appeal to a natural order evident in the political and economic writings of the eighteenth century. The implications were seen in the rapid spread of machine industry in the nineteenth century and in the collapse of the obsession with money shown in mercantilist systems. But the impact of industrialism on knowledge particularly with the development of electrical transmission has weakened the possibility of a sustained philosophical approach such as characterized the world after Newton. In turn industry has suffered from the renewed obsession with finance in neo-mercantilism. The revolution in communication has favoured a return to rhetoric and force. Industrialism has brought fresh realization of the significant role of language as a divisive force in the modern world. Within linguistic and national boundaries the pressure on savings which has accompanied the rise of insurance and government debt has apparently not been paralleled by the pressure of advertising on the distribution of consumers goods. A falling interest rate and the rise of the neo-mercantilist economics reflect the trend. Machine industry has made impacts on knowledge which have not been realized because it has influenced ways of thinking and left little energy to appraise them.

The following essays constitute an attempt to interrelate patterns of Canadian development with those of the Western World in the full realization that much remains to be done before the outlines and the details of the pattern can be clearly discerned. Duplication has been inevitable as interpretation has relied on the same basic facts. It is perhaps unnecessary to say that it presents no panaceas or answers to questions but rather hopes to raise new questions or at least to draw attention to the necessity of a carefully balanced approach to complex problems. The writer ventures to quote a paragraph from a preface by Goldwin Smith.

> The opinions of the present writer are those of a Liberal of the old school as yet unconverted to State Socialism, who looks for further improvement not to an increase of the authority of government, but to the same agencies, moral, intellectual, and economical, which have brought us thus far, and one of which, science, is now operating with immensely increased power. A writer of this school can have no panacea, or nostrum to offer; and when a nostrum or panacea is offered, he will necessarily be found rather on the critical side. He will look for improvement, not for regeneration; expect improvement still to be, as it has been, gradual; and hope much from steady, calm, and harmonious effort, little from violence or revolution. In his estimation the clearest gain reaped by the world from all the struggles through which it has been going, amidst much that is equivocal or still on trial, will be liberty of opinion.[2]

No reply is necessary to the charge that the essays are the results of dwelling in an ivory tower, since the author is only too aware of the element of national bias which runs through them. The answer to those insisting that sides must be taken is not to take sides. With imperfect competition between concepts the university is essentially an ivory tower in which courage can be mustered to attack any concept which threatens to become a monopoly.

The papers include convocation addresses delivered at the University of New Brunswick and McMaster University and articles from the *Journal of Economic History*, the *Canadian Journal of Economics and Political Science*, the *University of Toronto Quarterly*, the *Dalhousie Review*, the *Queen's Quarterly*, the *Commerce Journal*, *International Affairs*, and the *Transactions of the Royal Society of Canada*. The student should consult M. G. Lawson, *Fur, A Study in English Mercantilism, 1700-1775* (Toronto, 1943), pp. VII-XX, as it is intended as part of a trilogy with chapters 12 and 13.

H. A. I.

[2]Goldwin Smith, *Essays on questions of the day* (Toronto, 1893) V.

CONTENTS

Political Economy in the Modern State

1. THE NEWSPAPER IN ECONOMIC DEVELOPMENT

I

The bibliography of this subject is the subject, and the enormous files of newspapers turned out in the course of over three centuries are formidability itself. To reduce the element of formidability it is necessary to turn to studies of the newspaper in terms of countries, regions, owners, editors and journalists. But again the bibliography reflects the character of the press. Newspapermen have contributed notably, but unfortunately the training in newspaper work is not ideal for an economic interpretation of the subject. The increasing participation of university graduates in journalism provides a basis for more objective studies, but even here the training exercises a subtle influence and weakens the possibility of a sustained and effective interpretation. Throughout the history of the newspaper industry, studies reflect the dominant influence of the moment, or perhaps it is safer to say, represent the dominant influence of the tradition of the industry; hence they show a perceptible lag between the newspaper as it is and the newspaper as it was. In the main they are obsessed with the role of the press in relation to political opinion, the importance of freedom of the press, the fourth estate and so on; they are suffused with innumerable clichés[1] constantly bubbling up from the effervescence of writing.

The dominant role of advertising which followed the penny press and which necessitated active participation in advertising by the press itself has been largely neglected. Studies of advertising are exposed even more than studies of the press to the bias of the subject and they tend to advertise advertising: to show that it is very good or very bad. Publications on the press are an indication of the importance of advertising the press, in showing what a powerful influence such a paper or such an editor or such a publisher has had on the community. Histories of newspapers and biographies of journalists are all too frequently obvious forms of advertising. The modern newspaper dominated by advertising creates an atmo-

[1]See Frederick Hudson, *Journalism in the United States from 1690 to 1872* (New York, 1873), XV-XIX.

sphere which makes a study extremely difficult and hazardous. The claims of the "World's Greatest Newspaper" and of the newspaper with the slogan "all the news that's fit to print" as well as the excellent subtle advertising technique shown in the writings of Oswald Garrison Villard and Upton Sinclair and their opponents illustrate the difficulties. Freedom of the press has made freedom of speech impossible but I can assume that this paper will not be noticed or if noticed will not be read by those concerned immediately with the press. I can perhaps run the risk of violating Mark Twain's dictum that we have freedom of the press and freedom of speech and the good sense not to use either of them. I cannot pretend to have walked unscathed in the crossfire of overdrawn, exaggerated claims regarding the press, and of overdrawn and exaggerated attacks on suppression, brutality, over-statement and misrepresentation. I suspect a bias of my own toward the intellectual revolt voiced by Mark Pattison against the vaunted power of the press when he wrote, "Writers with a professional tendency to magnify their office have always been given to exaggerate the effect of printed words."

II

It has been said that "the fundamental economic character of printing is seen at its fullest in the history of newspapers."[2] At its beginning the printer used the offpeak capacity of a plant concerned with books and pamphlets. The manufacture of paper gave employment to the collectors of rags and may have contributed to the cleanliness of the population and to the gradual decline of epidemics. The sale of papers assisted in maintaining patronage for coffee houses and provided employment to street hawkers. Like books, newspapers were restricted in England and the colonies by the church and by the Crown. In its origins the newspaper was published at short and infrequent intervals, and down to 1641 was restricted to foreign news. During the Civil War the printer was subsidized by the demands of separate factions, and great numbers of newsbooks appeared. After the Restoration, restrictions were more effective and it was not until 1695, after the revolution of 1688, that licensing was abolished. Printers responded with the production of books, pamphlets and newspapers. The party disputes of the reign of Queen Anne were waged by writers in newspapers as well as by the

[2]Stanley Morrison, *The English Newspaper* (Cambridge, 1932), p. 5.

use of taxes and restrictions. The great age of political journalism flourished in the writings of Addison, Steele, Defoe and Swift. Enduring products of the age are found not only in the *Spectator* and the *Tatler* but also in Defoe's *Robinson Crusoe* and Swift's *Gulliver's Travels*. The most effective journalism was that of Swift's *Drapier's Letters,* written under almost insuperable obstacles, and directed against the distribution of coins in Ireland by William Wood. Swift wrote that the "Printer's trade, particularly in this Kingdom, is of all others, the most unfortunately circumstantiated, for as you deal in the most worthless kind of trash, the penny productions of pennyless scribblers; so you often venture your liberty, and sometimes your lives, for the purchase of half a crown; and, by your own ignorance, are punished for other men's actions." Walpole carried political control to its logical conclusion in his domination of the press. The age of authors who wrote for the party press was followed by the dark ages of Walpole corruption, although the light of political freedom continued to burn in such papers as the *Craftsman.* In the colonies, the post office and the demands of the government for printing supported early newspapers. In both England and the colonies an increase in the possibilities of change of those in control of government was fostered by the printer. The prospect of change accentuated the bitterness of journalism between those in control of government subsidies and those who hoped to control them.

The decline of political journalism under Walpole was largely responsible for the decreasing importance of the printer and the increasing importance of the publisher, and of advertising. Commercial expansion after the union of Scotland and England in 1707 and the treaty of Utrecht in 1713 brought increasing specialization in markets, and the demand for information brought buyers and sellers together. On February 3, 1730, there "occurred an event of the highest importance in the history of English journalism,"[3] the publication of the *Daily Advertiser*. Although its first issues contained nothing but advertisements, in three weeks news was added. Commercial intelligence which formed "the entire contents of the early issues, speedily took its important place as the normal constituent of a morning paper." By 1740 all morning papers "gave commercial intelligence and advertising relative and regular space."[4]

[3]*Ibid.,* p. 125.
[4]*Ibid.,* p. 127.

After the fall of Walpole the interest in political news was revived with the outbreak of wars, the dominance of the cabinet and the necessity of expanding the market for advertising. Parliamentary debates were reported surreptitiously. The attempt of George III to dominate the House of Commons with the assistance of Scottish influence represented by Bute, precipitated an acute struggle to secure access to debates. John Wilkes, supported by Junius and London interests, succeeded in 1771, in securing the right of the press to publish the debates. David Hume, a Scotsman familiar with England, doubtless had Great Britain in mind when he wrote that "nothing is more favourable to the rise of politeness and learning than a number of neighbouring and independent states, connected together by commerce and policy." The struggle against Scottish influence was a factor in securing freedom of the newspapers to publish debates. Scottish influence brought relief from the dominance of the book publishing trade, a dominance which was destroyed by a decision in 1774 in favour of Alexander Donaldson, a Scottish publisher in the London market.[5] The sale of cheap books which followed the substantial reduction of royalty privileges opened the way to competition in publishing books and newspapers. The Stuart family, Daniel, Peter, and their brother-in-law, James Mackintosh, and James Perry exercised an important influence on journalism. James Perry gave the *Morning Chronicle* a prominent place by the efficiency with which he organized the reporting of debates. Daniel Stuart was conspicuously successful with the *Morning Post* and later the *Courier.*

Daniel Stuart and John Walter, the founder of *The London Times,* made important contributions to the development of the press by combining features, news, and opinion to support advertising. Booksellers established the *Morning Post* in 1772 but their efforts to control it were defeated by the policy of Stuart. He wrote, "I encouraged the small miscellaneous advertisement in the front page, preferring them to any other upon the rule that the more numerous the customers, the more independent and permanent the custom. . . . Advertisements act and react. They attract readers, promote circulation and circulation attracts advertisements."[6] The booksellers

[5]See A. S. Collins, *The Profession of Letters* (London, 1928).

[6]Frank Presbrey, *The History and Development of Advertising* (New York, 1929), p. 80.

started the *British Press* and the *Globe* to compete with Stuart but without success. John Walter emphasized the importance of advertising in general rather than advertising for particular groups. On January 1, 1785, in the first number of the *Daily Universal Register,* which became *The Times,* he wrote, "It would seem that every newspaper published in London is calculated for a particular set of readers only; so that, if each set were to change its favourite publication for another, the commutation would produce disgust and dissatisfaction to all."[7] "A newspaper . . . ought not to be engrossed by any particular object, but, like a well covered table; it should contain something for every palate." "The great objects . . . will be to facilitate the *Commercial* intercourse between the different parts of the community, through the channel of advertisements; to record the principal occurrences of the times and to abridge the account of the debates during the sitting of parliament."[8] Advertisements were not to be "sacrificed to the rage for parliamentary debates." The extreme length of these debates "so greatly retards the publication of the News-Papers which are noted for detailed accounts of them, that the advantages arising . . . are frequently overbalanced by the inconveniences occasioned to people in business by the delay. . . . Parties interested in *sales* are essentially injured as the advertisements inviting the public to attend them at *ten* or *twelve o'clock;* do not appear, on account of a late publication till some hours after." The *Universal Register* was promised for six o'clock.

John Walter and his son, printers and booksellers, developed the technique of printing to take full advantage of the contributions of the industrial revolution—the application of steam to the press. In 1814 *The Times* used steam for the first time. "The fundamental economic character of printing became most explicit with the invention of the power press, constructed by a newspaper for a newspaper."[9] The application of power to the press was accompanied by its application to the manufacture of paper in the introduction of the Fourdrinier machine which enormously increased production. The price of fine paper in England declined from 49s. 7d. per ream in 1814 to 35s. in 1824; and of printing paper from 24s. in 1831 to 15s.

[7]W. O. Bowman, *The Story of "The Times"* (London, 1931), pp. 1-2.
[8]Morison, p. 182.
[9]*Ibid.,* p. 4.

6d. in 1843. These improvements facilitated the extension of news service to meet the demands for news of the Napoleonic wars. Walter sent Henry Crabb Robinson as one of the first war correspondents to Europe and organized a schooner service to receive early access to war news. Improvements in the transmission of news were accompanied by improvements in the distribution of papers. The mail coach was introduced in the 1790's and rapidly widened the range of circulation.

The French Revolution and the Napoleonic wars brought demands for news, but they also brought demands for the regulation and suppression of newspapers through taxes and restrictions. In spite of the relaxation of the libel law in 1792, prosecutions were severe and numerous, and restrictive legislation was passed in 1798. The press sank to levels of vituperation comparable to those of the early eighteenth century and the civil war. Lockhart refused to accept the editorship of the *Representative* supported by John Murray because of the "loss of caste in society."[10] He wrote that "Ministers . . . consider literary allies as worse than useless unless they be prepared to shift at every breach like the *Courier,* which, by the bye, such shifting has utterly ruined."[11] William Wright supported him in a letter October 3, 1825: "Your accepting the editorship of a newspaper would be infra dig and a losing of caste; but not so I think accepting of the editorship of the *Quarterly Review.* . . . An editor of a Review like the *Quarterly* is the office of a scholar and a gentleman; but that of a newspaper is *not,* for a newspaper is merely stock-in-trade to be used as it can be turned to most profit."[12] On February 24, 1826, Sir Walter Scott wrote of the "touch-and-go, blackguard-genteel which distinguishes the real writer for the press,"[13] and on April 3, 1829, he wrote to Lockhart, "Your connection with any newspaper would be disgrace and degradation. I would rather sell gin to the poor people and poison them by the way."[14] In his journal of April 3, 1824, he wrote, "Nothing but a thorough-going blackguard ought to attempt the daily press, unless

[10]Andrew Lang, *The Life and Letters of John Gibson Lockhart* (London, 1897), Volume 1, p. 365.

[11]*Ibid.,* Vol. II, p 59.

[12]*Ibid.,* Vol. I, p. 367.

[13]*Ibid.,* Chap. I, p. 397.

[14]*Ibid.,* Vol. II, pp. 51-2.

it is some quiet country journal."[15] The breaking out of innumerable sheets preceded the Reform Act of 1832. Agitation in favour of Reform was carried on vigorously by William Cobbett and others, and by the Sunday press, radical in part if only because it was sold on Sundays.

The deterioration of English journalism and restrictions on newspapers were in part responsible for the appearance of the *Edinburgh Review* in 1802. Scottish influence was again in evidence as a competitive corrective. The system of education in England which had been dominated by the clergy, supported monopolies in control of knowledge while the system of national education in Scotland provided a background for healthy competition. In Scotland, according to Adam Smith, "the establishment of parish schools has taught almost the whole common people to read and a very great proportion of them to write and account." The use of English in Scottish universities gave a striking advantage over English universities wedded to the classical system. Frances Hutcheson, David Hume, and Adam Smith had the advantage of the Scottish education, and an open road to England, and indeed to France, which enabled them to escape the tyranny of the Presbyterian Church. Lower printing costs favoured publishing activity in Edinburgh. The first edition of the *Encyclopedia Britannica* was printed in 1771 and later editions in the 1780's. The absence of a Grub Street in Scotland brought an outburst of publishing activity associated with the names of Constable, the Ballantynes, and Scott. The *Edinburgh Review* broke upon a stagnant political and literary world. In Scotland, according to the editor of the *Edinburgh Review,* Frances Jeffrey, the autocratic con-

[15]*The Journal of Sir Walter Scott* (Edinburgh, 1890), Vol. II, p. 262. Frances Jeffrey, editor of the *Edinburgh Review,* wrote to Charles Wilkes on 13 April, 1822, "The most disgusting peculiarity of the present times is the brutal scurrility and personality of the party press, originally encouraged by ministers, though I believe they would now gladly get rid of it; but from their patronage and general appetite for scandal it has become too lucrative a thing to be sacrificed to their hints, and goes on, and will go on, for the benefit and at the pleasure of the venal wretches who supply it." Lord Cockburn, *Life of Lord Jeffrey with a Selection from His Correspondence* (Edinburgh, 1852), Vol. II, p. 200. Jeffrey even had qualms about the *Edinburgh Review.* He wrote to Frances Horner on May 11, 1803, "The risk of sinking in the general estimation and being considered as fairly articled to a trade that is not perhaps the most respectable has staggered me more, I will acknowledge than any other consideration." *Ibid.,* I, p. 145. "From the very first I have been anxious to keep clear of any tradesman like concern in the *Review* and to confine myself pretty strictly to intercourse with gentlemen only as contributors." Nov. 1, 1827. *Ibid.,* p. 280.

trol of Dundas left "no popular representation, no emancipated burghs, no effective rival of the Established Church, no independent press, no free public meetings."[16] The activity of Constable in publishing the poetry of Scott and the *Edinburgh Review* led to the establishment by John Murray of the *Quarterly Review* in 1809 and the sponsorship of Lord Byron's poetry. Scott turned from poetry to novels as a result of the competition.

The effects of restrictions and taxes on newspapers were evident not only in attempts at evasion and scurrility. The technical character of the papers was changed. The important contributions of John Bell to the improvement of typography in the latter part of the eighteenth century disappeared because the burden of stamp taxes compelled the use of small print to increase the contents of the page, which in turn ruined the eyesight of generations of Englishmen in the nineteenth century. The position of *The Times* was enormously strengthened. The inability of John Murray, the publisher, to start a new paper, *The Representative,* to supplement the *Quarterly* was an indication of the strength of papers established firmly on the technical revolutions of the printing industry, and protected by the tax system. After the death of Perry in 1820, the difficulties of the *Morning Chronicle,* with its interest in parliamentary debates, were in part a result of the ability of *The Times* to develop this side of its activities together with its news and advertising. With efficient printing *The Times* could delay publication longer to obtain later news and publish earlier than its competitors. Concentration on the development of printing technique facilitated division of labour and favoured the emergence of the editor. Barnes and his successor, Delane, raised the status of journalism and became intimate with ministers of the government. They had an indirect incentive for the development of close relations with the government because of the importance of legislation favouring their position, and a direct incentive because it gave them access to important political news in an era of important political news and raised the prestige of the paper. Its power became of political importance and *The Times* became the "Thunderer." In 1850 the annual circulation of all London dailies excluding *The Times* was 8,719,840 and of *The Times,* 11,900,000.

[16]Lord Cockburn, *Life of Lord Jeffrey with a Selection from His Correspondence* (Edinburgh, 1852), Vol. I, p. 74.

III

Interrelations between the British and American press varied but by the end of the nineteenth century American influence on the British press was conspicuous. Suppression of the freedom of the press in England had its repercussions in the colonies and in the United States. Benjamin Harris fled to New England and started the first newspaper, *Publick Occurrences,* in Boston before he returned to England after the lapse of the licensing act in 1695. William Cobbett was a journalist in the United States who reversed the trend by sponsoring Great Britain. Compelled to leave, he supported the Tory administration in England until he turned against it in his *Political Register* and was forced to find refuge in the United States. He contributed to the vituperative vocabulary of American journalism. Revenue from job printing and government contracts and party subsidies directly and through subscriptions characterized the acrid political controversies of the period before and after the independence of the United States but was supplemented by advertising. Obsession with political disputes, often resulting in duels, as the one which brought the death of Alexander Hamilton, declined with the end of the War of 1812, the administration of President Monroe, and the decline of the federalist party. Shortage of paper and expensive type which followed restrictions on imports during the wars of the eighteenth and early nineteenth centuries necessitated close printing. Newspapers concerned with commercial development increased in size to the proportions of a blanket, and were supported by advertisements and high subscription prices. Division between papers concentrating on commercial intelligence and those concentrating on political influence left the increasingly literate population without a press. The intense partisanship and scurrility of the English press provided an example which was drawn upon in the sudden outburst of the penny press in the United States.[17] Without the restrictions of the British tax system, the penny press of the United States spread rapidly in the large port centres. In 1829 one newspaper per week was published for every 36 inhabitants in the British Isles; one for every fourth inhabitant in Pennsylvania. The cost in the British Isles was 7d, in Pennsylvania 1½ d. For one year a daily advertisement of twenty

[17]See W. G. Bleyer, *Main Currents in the History of American Journalism* (Boston, 1927), Ch. VI.

lines in a London paper cost £202 16s. and in a New York paper £6 18s. 8. Twelve newspapers in New York had 1,456,410 advertisements and 400 newspapers in the United Kingdom only 1,020,000.[18]

The growth of the penny press led to the adoption of the London system of sale in the streets through newsboys. Cash receipts from circulation were limited and unstable and necessarily supplemented by receipts from advertising. Credit to subscribers and advertisers was replaced by the cash system. The low fixed price compelled concentration on sales to secure volume and receipts, and the increase in circulation attracted advertising revenues. With a rigid small price, the size of the paper in page and in number of pages became the elastic elements. Competition for circulation and advertising compelled a policy of vigorous advertising of the paper which was reflected in the displacement of advertising by news on the front page and finally in the elaboration of the head lines.[19] In the interest of sales to a wide range of literacy, news stories were sensational and local. Domestic news displaced foreign news, and crime news and human interest stories were used to fill pages and attract readers.

Expansion of the press was supported by advances in the technique used in printing, and in the manufacture of paper. The steam press and the Fourdrinier machine were introduced in the United States. The supply of rags was increased both by the use of the chlorine process, which made possible the use of coloured supplies, and by imports from Europe on a large scale. Restrictions on the British press favoured lower costs of rags for the United States. The price of newsprint declined from about $5.00 per ream in 1821 to $3.00 in 1830. The Columbian press, invented by George Clymer of Philadelphia about 1813, substituted the use of a series of levers for the screw. In the early thirties, Richard Hoe enlarged the Napier press and invented a double cylinder press with a capacity of 4,000 papers per hour. Printing inks were manufactured on a large scale. A type casting machine was invented in 1822.

The American press was unhampered in its typography and format by the traditions of book printing of Great Britain and the Continent. The advertiser was more effective in breaking down the

[18]C. D. Collett, *History of the Taxes on Knowledge, Their Origin and Repeal* (London, 1933), pp. 28-9.

[19]See H. M. Hughes, *News and the Human Interest Story* (Chicago, 1940).

conservatism of journalism, and the printer's control was less conspicuous than that of the journalists. Newspapers were unable to secure a dominant political position in the more flexible political machinery of the United States without a clearly marked class structure. A federal system meant that Washington was deliberately chosen as a capital to avoid the jealousies of large commercial and industrial systems and that there was no capital such as London, to support the political dominance of a large paper such as *The Times*. Competition between large urban centres, absence of a tax system, and a guaranteed privileged position under the Bill of Rights ensured the existence of a large number of papers appealing to various groups.

The introduction of the telegraph in the forties brought a marked increase in the supply of news. The Associated Press was formed to provide news to a large number of papers at low cost. The Mexican War, the agitation preceding the Civil War, and the Civil War itself brought a rapid extension of the news service and the organization of war correspondents. The sensationalism of the penny press provided a background for the establishment of the more respectable journalism of Bryant in the *Post*, Greeley in the *Tribune* and Raymond in the New York *Times*. Organization of news which followed the telegraph increased the efficiency of the newspaper as an advertising medium. The pressure of advertising was gradually evident in changes in typography. In the fifties and sixties Bonner of the New York *Ledger*, and the flamboyant advertising of P. T. Barnum brought a change in the use of the single column of agate type. Bennett of the *Herald* refused to make concessions to large advertisers on the ground that no favouritism should be shown and that an appeal should be made to large numbers of small advertisers. Stereotyping was introduced in 1861 and plates of whole pages gave the necessary freedom to advertisers to break the restraints of the single column. The web-perfecting press was installed in 1868 by *The Times* in London and spread rapidly with improvements made by R. Hoe and Company to American newspapers. Paper was fed from a roll, printed on both sides and then cut into flat sheets. Folding machines were invented to complete the operation. A double supplement perfecting press was installed by the New York *Herald* in 1882 and published 24,000 twelve-page papers per hour. The same paper installed a sextuple press in 1889 with a capacity of 24,000 twenty-four-page papers per hour. In

1895, the Hoe octuple press turned out 48,000 sixteen-page papers per hour and further improvements increased the output to 144,000. The four-colour press was used by the *Inter-Ocean* in 1892 and a five-colour press by the New York *World* in 1893. Improvements in the transmission of news by telegraph, cable and later telephone, and increases in printing accentuated the demand for paper. Rags were no longer an adequate source, and after a period of using esparto, wood became increasingly important. Newsprint declined from the high prices of the Civil War to 12c per pound in 1872, 8c in 1877, 4c in 1887, 3c in 1892 and 1 and 4/5c in 1897. In the eighties and nineties, sulphite, in combination with mechanical pulp, gradually replaced paper made from rags. With increased supplies of paper the setting up of type became the bottleneck of the industry. The Mergenthaler linotype was finally invented and installed by the New York *Tribune,* the Chicago *Daily News* and the Louisville *Courier-Journal* by 1890. Typewriters came into general use and supported the linotype in increasing the rate of composition. With these changes, size, circulation, and numbers of newspapers increased.

Advances of the American press had immediate significance for the British press released from the burden of taxes. New papers emerged in the late fifties to contest the monopoly of *The Times.* Levy, who in 1855 founded the *Daily Telegraph,* the first successful penny paper in England, was a close student of J. G. Bennett of the New York *Herald.* With the laying of the Atlantic Cable, American newspapers were quick to extend the lessons learned in the Civil War and began reporting European wars. Russell, the outstanding war correspondent of *The Times* in the Crimean War, was unable to adapt his graphic style to the demands of the cable as Dana of the New York *Sun* learned to his cost. G. W. Smalley, with experience in the Civil War, represented the New York *Tribune* in co-operation with Archibald Forbes of the London *News,* and established new precedents in the development of war correspondence for transmission by cable. Kingslake wrote that "the extraordinary triumphs of European journalism at the time of the Franco-Prussian war of 1870-71 were due, in no slight degree, to the vigour, the sagacity and the enterprise that were brought to bear on the objects from the other side of the Atlantic. The success of that partnership for the purpose of war news . . . which had been forced between one of the

London newspapers and the New York *Tribune* was an era in the journalism of Europe, though, not in that of the United States, where the advance had an older date, deriving from their great Civil War."[20] The telegraph produced a condensation of style and brought an end to "the elaborate ten-column articles and three-volume books." "The home telegraph was diffuse. It was the cable which first taught us to condense."[21] As a further illustration of American enterprise the New York *Herald* with the *Daily Telegraph* sponsored the search by Stanley which ended with the words "Dr. Livingstone I presume."

The impact of American journalism was evident finally in format and typography. The inherent conservatism of the press was shown in the retention of small uniform type in the United States and in Great Britain, especially the latter because of the monopolistic power of *The Times* which continued to use the closely printed page, reflecting the effects of the tax system and the persistent influence of the printer. Morrison explains the slowness with which changes in format and typography were made in spite of the increasing demands of advertising: "the papers," he said, "were too exhausted with the struggle to collect and to digest news which came by telegraph, by cable and—huger novelty still—by telephone, to have time for typographical experiments."

Slow changes in typography accompanied the pressure of advertising in the American press. In turn they had an impact in Great Britain through the evening papers which escaped the traditions of the morning papers and increased in importance after the removal of the taxes and with the decline of *The Times*. With a training in the provincial press, W. T. Stead joined the *Pall Mall Gazette*, and in the early eighties combined the influential reputation built up by his predecessor John Morley with the energy typical of the new journalism. He made effective use of the interview, illustrations, cross heads and unconventional headlines. He relieved the press of conventions, respectabilities, anonymity and party ties, and opened the way to independence from party and wealth. His energetic support of the disastrous expedition of Gordon to Khartoum was an indication of the dangers of transition in the press and of the menace

[20]Royal Cortissoz, *The Life of Whitelaw Reid* (London, 1921), Vol. I, pp. 178-9.

[21]Bleyer, pp. 206-7.

of government by newspapers. Political journalism combined with new techniques had unfortunate consequences. The new journalism was developed and matured under the steadier hand of T. P. O'Connor in the *Star* in the late eighties. Evening papers flourished with the increasing interest in sport facilitated by reliance on the telegraph throughout Great Britain. The spread of American influence was more direct in the establishment of the Paris edition of the New York *Herald* in 1887 and of the London edition in 1889-90. Chester Ives, formerly of the Paris edition, carried the advances in technique in the evening papers to the morning papers and started the *Morning* with the news on the front page. Alfred Harmsworth and Kennedy Jones followed the lead with the establishment of the *Daily Mail* in 1896 but yielded to the pressure of English tradition in making a morning paper look like a morning paper by carrying advertisements on the front page. The final change was associated with the work of R. D. Blumenfeld, an American journalist on the London edition of the New York *Herald,* who, with Arthur Pearson, built up the *Daily Express* with news on the front page. He extended and developed the use of the headline and was supported in the later history of the paper by a Canadian, Max Aitken, the present Lord Beaverbrook.

Mechanical advances in the United States were borrowed by Europe. The Hoe rotary press first used on the Philadelphia *Public Ledger* in 1846 was introduced by *La Patrie* in 1848 and by Lloyds in London in 1856. Oliver Borthwick made a careful study of American designs and introduced them in the publication of the *Morning Post.* The *Daily Mail* introduced the linotype and the monotype from the United States, and thereby had a capacity of 200,000 papers per hour, an output four times larger than that of any competitor, within a period of five years. The *Daily Mirror* as an illustrated tabloid became a success largely through the use of a press purchased from the Goss Printing Company of Chicago. Machinery, perfected in the United States and introduced into England, had enormous significance in the revolution of English journalism after the nineties.

The Times had seized its opportunities in the beginning by taking advantage of the obsession of the *Morning Chronicle* with parliamentary news, although, with the decline of the latter paper, it, in turn, became obsessed with the importance of political intelligence. In the 1850's and 60's taxes on advertisements, newspapers, and paper were removed and the monopolistic position of *The Times* was undermined. Other papers were quick to seize the advantages of the telegraph, and were able to compete on a basis of equality with *The Times*. The *Daily Telegraph* pursued an effective policy in attracting advertisements away from *The Times*. The *Manchester Guardian* and other provincial papers gained access to the debates in the House of Commons and were able to exert sufficient pressure to bring about government ownership of the telegraph system. The prosperity of the *Daily News* began with extensive use of the telegraph in the Franco-Prussian war.[22] The emphasis on political influence brought instability to *The Times* as other papers gained in circulation and influence. Political changes incidental to the British parliamentary system gave other papers an advantage. Lord Palmerston flirted in turn with the *Morning Chronicle*, the *Morning Post*, and *The Times*. After his death and the death of Delane, it became more difficult to establish relations with the government. The political alliances of *The Times* became more inelastic and led it, in its opposition to Gladstone on the Irish question, to the disaster of the Pigott letters. Circulation declined sharply after the death of Delane, and when Moberly Bell became managing editor in 1890, *The Times* was practically insolvent.

IV

The impact of technological change on the press varied not only with major revolutions in printing, paper making, news collection, and distribution of newspapers, but also with the character of the organization by which the processes were performed. The printer was in control of the press until the first half of the eighteenth century when he was largely superseded by the publisher. The continuing influence of the printer was evident in the control of *The Times* by the Walter family. The journalist became influential in the latter part of the eighteenth century, as in the case of Perry and the Stuarts, and the editor emerged in the nineteenth century. With the increasing importance of large-scale capital equipment, good will assumed a role of major significance. The system of advertising developed by the penny press and reflected in the expansion of news on the front page and the development of the head line implied the

[22]See Sir John R. Robinson, *Fifty Years of Fleet Street* (London, 1904).

building up of good will and policies to maintain it. Continuity of titles and of ownership particularly in the family, the unique architecture of buildings, and the publication of books about individual newspapers, publishers, and journalists, reflected the importance of advertising and good will.

In the United States the monopoly accorded the press by the Bill of Rights has facilitated organization and resistance to control from the paper industry. Journalists fostered the development of the paper industry in its origins. William Bradford was financially interested in a mill at Germantown from 1690 to 1707 and had a mill at Elizabethtown in 1728, while Benjamin Franklin is said to have been instrumental in starting 18 mills.[23] During the Civil War a combination of papermakers in the Eastern States increased the price of paper between April and July, 1864, from 15 to 27c. a pound. The substitution of wood for rags defeated the efforts of combinations, but paper, like other commodities, became the concern of trusts in the late nineties with the formation of the International Paper Company in 1898. Newspapers made a concerted and successful drive toward the reduction of the tariff on Canadian raw material. The power of the press was evident in Theodore Roosevelt's conservation projects, in the lowering of tariffs in 1909, in the reciprocity treaty[24] with Canada in 1911, in putting newsprint on the free list in 1913, and in the expulsion of Senator Lorimer[25] in 1912. Large publishers such as the New York *Times* and the Chicago *Tribune* obtained further protection by acquiring ownership or control of Canadian mills. The International Paper Company acquired large mills in Canada, and in 1928 acquired control of newspapers as a means of guaranteeing a market. Loud protests from the press compelled it to abandon the scheme, and it has followed a policy of increasing reliance on the alternative support of hydro-electric power.

In England the papermaker became influential during the periods

[23]L. T. Stevenson, *The Background and Economics of American Papermaking* (New York, 1840). Small papers were probably carried on long credit by paper mills. Josephus Daniels purchased paper on credit from W. F. Askew's mill. Josephus Daniels, *Tar Heel Editor* (Chapel Hill, 1939), pp. 249-50.

[24]L. E. Ellis, *Reciprocity 1911, a Study in Canadian-American Relations* (New Haven, 1939).

[25]See James Weber Linn, *James Keeley Newspaperman* (Indianapolis, 1937), Chap. VII.

of difficulty and depression. After the collapse of 1825 Sir Walter Scott wrote, on Sept. 5, 1827, "Perhaps my genius was Mr. Dickinson, paper-maker, who has undertaken that the London creditors who hold Constable's bills will be satisfied with 10s. in the pound. This would be turning a genius to purpose for 6s. 8d. is provided, and they can have no difficulty with 3s. 4d."[26] Dickinson was a papermaker of Nash Mill, Herts, "a right plain sensible man. He is so confident in my matters, that a large creditor himself, he appears to come down with the support of all the London creditors to carry through any measure that can be devised for my behoof."[27] The same papermaker was an influential counsellor in 1839 in advising Blackwood's to establish a London branch. T. B. Crompton was an influential Lancashire papermaker who took over the *Morning Post* under a mortgage of October 5, 1849, and it was not until 1876, that Algernon Borthwick became editor and proprietor. The monopolistic position of *The Times* and the high burden of taxes on knowledge destroyed large numbers of small mills, and resistance to the removal of the paper duty in 1861 was headed by Mr. Crompton and the Paper Makers' Association.[28] The marked development of newspapers, following the impact of American technique in the nineties, facilitated a vigorous policy of acquiring control of raw materials. The Northcliffe, Rothermere and Beaverbrook interests acquired limits and mills in Newfoundland and Canada.

Newspapers were concerned not only with the freedom of the press as a support to their monopoly position in resisting higher costs of raw material, but also with the measures designed to increase the number of readers and to widen the market. They have exercised a powerful influence on the state by extending the franchise and compulsory education. In the United States literacy was increased indirectly by the support of compulsory education and directly by the establishment of newspapers with a technique designed to penetrate the illiterate fringe and capable of widening the frontiers of literacy. The demands of the penny press necessitated appeals to lower levels of literacy and an emphasis on domestic news and particularly on sensational crime which did not involve libel suits. In

[26] *The Journal of Sir Walter Scott* (Edinburgh, 1890), Vol. II, p. 31.

[27] *Ibid.*, p. 331.

[28] C. D. Collett, *History of the Taxes on Knowledge* (London, 1933), pp. 162-5.

England the monopolistic position of *The Times* in the press, and of the church in education hampered the adoption of compulsory education. The Education Act of 1870 followed the abolition of taxes on knowledge. The demands of a new reading generation were evident in the success of George Newnes in *Answers* and of Alfred Harmsworth in *Tit-Bits.* The *Daily Mail* and the *Daily Express* followed directly from this development. The *Daily Mail* was advertised as "a newspaper not a soporific," and the "heavies" such as *The Times,* which according to Wells "sounded like God talking under the bed clothes," suffered serious loss.

The impact of technological advance on the press was evident in the adaptation of types of control. Family influence and tradition were important in building up good will but were not a guarantee of efficiency. The McCormick family has been conspicuously successful with the Chicago *Tribune,* the New York *News* and other papers, and the Reid family has remained in effective control of the New York *Tribune.* On the other hand the domineering character of pioneers created difficulties. E. W. Scripps quarrelled with his brother and his son but worked out a scheme of organization for a large newspaper chain which has been successful in the Scripps-Howard papers. Pulitzer experimented with various types of control, but his sons were apparently unable to follow his policies in the *World.* The Bennetts gave direction to the *Herald* for two generations, but the death of the younger Bennett brought the paper on the market. The *Dallas News* has followed a policy of systematically destroying the control of absentee family interest.[20] Pulitzer, Bennett, Scripps, and other publishers exercised remote control from steam yachts or from Paris. This device brought prestige and made for the detachment which was necessary in ruthless reorganizations of the staff. The erratic diversions of publishers had advantages and disadvantages for the newspapers. The defects of family control in the reorganization of the press were offset by the ruthlessness of finance. Frank Munsey played a devastating role in reducing the number of New York papers, but the importance of the family is significant in that the New York *Herald,* which he acquired after the death of Bennett, was purchased by the Reid family and merged with the *Tribune.* Decline in the importance of pioneers has been evident in

[20]Sam Acheson, *35,000 Days in Texas, A History of the Dallas News and its Forbears* (New York, 1938).

mutual agreements among members of the staff in the Kansas City *Star*, the Chicago *Daily News*, and the New York *Sun*. In England family influence was important in the provincial press, notably the *Manchester Guardian*, and in the London press, notably in the case of the Walter family in *The Times*. The new journalism had devastating effects on political journalism, and a large number of papers disappeared between 1900 and the early post-war period.

The influence of the family in retarding or sponsoring technological and journalistic change varies not only with the success with which problems of control are solved, but also with the success with which monopolistic positions can be maintained in the political field. The English newspaper has been a combination of political pamphlets and news letters. Kennedy Jones, a powerful figure in the development of the Northcliffe press, has argued that throughout the history of the press, newspapers increase in power by constant attention to public demands, and as they increase in power, they are courted by politicians. Flattered by the politicians, they attempt to influence public opinion, become distrusted, and lose their influence.[80] Governments tend to dominate because they constitute an important source of news, but such dominance brings a loss of prestige to the newspaper. In France, journalism has been regarded as an accepted approach to politics and has not been anonymous but in England, and the United States, exceptions have been the rule in an anonymous press. John Morley was such an exception, but argued that literature repudiated conventions while political action has as its very first working principle compliance with conventions: "All round responsibility for one thing and fuller knowledge of decisive facts makes all the difference."[81] One can only glance at the tragic defeat of Greeley and the newspaper group in 1872, the political reputation of Raymond of the New York *Times*, and the vigorous but unsuccessful efforts of Mr. Hearst to secure admission to public life, to realize the truth of these statements. President Harding was an exception, but he was concerned with a very small newspaper.

The politician can easily exploit the newspaper, and competitors are quick to arouse suspicions as to the political ambitions of rivals.

[80]See D. H. Stevens, *Party Politics and English Journalism, 1702-1742* (Menasha, 1916), Chap. I, shows the influence of parties, especially after 1710, on Addison, Steele, Defoe and Swift.

[81]John Viscount Morley, *Recollections* (Toronto, 1917), Vol. I, pp. 172-189.

In the United States, concessions have been made in cabinet positions, and ambassador's posts were given to Bigelow, Reid, Page and Harvey. In Great Britain the prestige of journalists improved throughout the nineteenth century particularly with the coming of the new journalism, and compromises were reached in appointments to the House of Lords, as shown by the elevation of Lord Glenesk of the *Morning Post,* Lord Northcliffe, Lord Rothermere, Lord Beaverbrook and others of the press peerage. Decline in the influence of the House of Lords after 1911 made appointments less objectionable and more easily achieved. Control of *The Times* by Northcliffe after 1908 was comparable to the control of the *Pall Mall Gazette* by W. T. Stead in the eighties, and the combination of new methods of journalism with prestige had even more devastating effects. They were evident prior to the outbreak of war, were instrumental during the war in replacing Asquith by Lloyd George, and had their effects in the harsh terms of the Treaty of Versailles. The impact of American technique on the British press was evident in the sudden enormous increase in prestige of those concerned with the new journalism, and lack of familiarity with the political problems of Great Britain, introduced an element of irresponsibility which had much to do with the tragedies of 1914 and after. The power of the press began to decline, and Mr. Baldwin enhanced his political strength by refusing to be intimidated by the Plot Press of Lord Rothermere and Lord Beaverbrook. "These men seek power without responsibility. All through history royal courtesans have sought the same thing."

Major changes in the press by which journalism was rapidly adapted to technological advance were fostered by powerful individuals. The effective political press had depended on control under a single hand and avoidance of divisions bringing compromise and weakness. Training in small town and rural newspapers in the United States and in the provincial press in England gave the journalist a knowledge of the details of the industry and an independence which became important in the major changes of the metropolitan press following technological advance. Experienced aggressive journalists moved from frontier points to metropolitan cities. Pulitzer acquired a wide experience in St. Louis which he used effectively in building up the New York *World.* The effects were evident in the difficulties of the New York *Herald* and the New

York *Times*. Hearst was a close student of Pulitzer's methods and developed new methods on the San Francisco *Examiner* before he purchased the New York *Journal*. He attracted prominent members of Pulitzer's staff by large salaries, and the competitive warfare between Hearst and Pulitzer in the late nineties in the New York field brought circulation to unprecedented levels. Northcliffe also lured members away from Pulitzer's staff. Ochs came from the Chattanooga *Times* and reorganized the New York *Times*. Individuals from frontier points were effective in bringing about reorganizations but were less successful in providing for continuous control.

The achievement of large circulations involved the development of appeals to lower levels of literacy. The reading public of large newspapers will not tolerate prolonged controversies and abhors constantly reiterated claims. The average reader is not disposed to spend more than fifteen minutes reading the newpaper. H. L. Mencken puts the extreme limit of the appetite of the newspaper reader at 6,000 words. Kennedy Jones claims that war is of first importance in stimulating circulation, state funerals second, a first class murder third, and after this any big public pageant or ceremony and decisive sporting events. Organization of news services in the Napoleonic Wars gave *The Times* a lead over other papers. The Mexican War, the California gold rush and the Civil War spurred American newspapers to new outbursts of energy. Wars created a demand for extra editions, and the Civil War as the first to be fought by a democratic country on its own soil introduced the terrifying phenomenon of bitterness which saturated the entire community. The Franco-Prussian War gave the evening paper an established position in England. The Spanish-American War and the South African War came at the beginning of the new journalism and were exploited to the full in efforts to increase circulation in New York particularly and in London; the *Daily Mail*, the *Daily Express*, the *Journal*, and the *World* pushed circulation to new levels. They were ideal newspaper wars. To Mr. Hearst was attributed the telegram to Remington, "You furnish the pictures and I'll furnish the war." Prominent funerals played a role in increasing circulation, one need mention only those of Andrew Jackson, the Duke of Wellington, Lincoln, Queen Victoria and King Edward. The death of Queen Victoria hastened the change in format of English papers.

The prospect of Gladstone's sudden death was a nightmare to a generation of English journalists.

The importance of wars, crimes, and major news varies with the activities of the journalist. In a literal sense, wars are created, as crime waves are created, by the newspaper. Effective news organization makes catastrophes and catastrophes necessitate improvement of the news organization. In the history of the Associated Press catastrophes impose sudden strains on the organization, and lead to the discovery of weaknesses and to their elimination. The aggressive newspaper sponsors events which make news—polar expeditions and oceanic flights. Bennett and others have been notoriously successful.

The long run effects of major news events are impossible to predict. It is claimed that the assassination of Lincoln was a shock to Anglo-Saxon people, and actually stimulated policies of peace. The Bulgarian atrocities brought a permanent shift of interest on the part of the people of Great Britain from domestic to foreign news. The trial of Oscar Wilde is held responsible for a sharp decline of interest in poetry.[32] The moral war against Bennett in the early forties brought a decline in circulation of the *Herald*. The assassination of McKinley brought a reaction against the yellow press. Elimination of the "personals" column in the New York *Herald* marked the beginning of its decline. Competition checks the exaggeration of news. Melville E. Stone began a policy in the Chicago *Daily News* of concentrating on condensed news. His influence was perpetuated in his management of the Associated Press. The New York *Times* capitalized the demand for news but treated news items with verbosity. The policy was profitable particularly because of its appeal to advertisers interested in the market of upper income brackets. The folklore of journalists has its parallel in the folklore of businessmen. I have heard a former prominent Canadian in the packing industry attribute a turn in the price of bacon to a news report of the shipwreck of a livestock vessel and the consequent impression of enormous destruction and scarcity. The social scientist would do well to give such folklore closer attention.

The organization of news services has contributed enormously to the extent and accuracy of news, and the handicap of uniformity has been offset by the enterprise of single newspapers or by the growth

[32]James Milne, *The Memoirs of a Bookman* (London, 1934), p. 230.

of competitive organizations. The routine character of Reuter's news provided the background for the spectacular success of the *Daily News.* Protests against the control exercised by members of the Associated Press led to reorganizations and a shift in influence from New York to Chicago. Concern with a single morning paper in each city implied the emergence of a monopoly which favoured the development by the Scripps-Howard chain of the United Press in order to meet the demands of evening papers. Hearst followed with a third organization. Arrangements of the Associated Press with foreign news agencies under Mr. Stone's management brought charges of government influence and led to the establishment of special correspondents on a large scale. The demands of news distribution services also introduced elements of rigidity in newspaper policy particularly as to prices. Changes in the small margin of prices for distribution were responsible for hostility, creating difficulties for newspapers, and competition between news distribution services reached the level of gang warfare.

V

The lumpy character of technological changes in the newspaper industry, the conservative tendencies incidental to the importance of good will, and the trend toward monopolies involve adjustments in relation to advertising. Lowering of prices of newspapers and the widening of circulation have assumed an increasing literacy or an appeal to lower levels of literacy, and a background of commercial activity favourable to advertising. Taxes on newspapers in England contributed to an outburst of outdoor advertising. This spread to the United States where patent medicine firms and other early users of national advertising developed outdoor advertising on an impressive scale[88] especially after the Civil War.

Daily newspapers were published in widely scattered large cities and the concentration on circulation in restricted areas limited the possibility of advertising on a national scale. The development of advertising by L. F. Schattuck in floating the bond issues of the Civil War hastened the establishment of weeklies and monthlies designed

[88]On reaching farthest north in Greenland, Brainard of the Greeley expedition in 1882 wrote on May 14th, "I have never yet visited anywhere without finding Plantation Bitters advertised conspicuously. This is the highest explored latitude, could be no exception, and on the slab in the face of the cliff I carved the familiar characters St. 1860X."

for national circulation. The phenomenal success of the weekly editions of the New York *Tribune* and of other papers, the intense activity of the religious weeklies in the sixties and seventies, and the growth of periodicals sponsored by book publishers such as Putnam, Harper, and Scribner reflected the demand for media for national advertising. Advertising agents became concerned with magazines, and the firm of J. Walter Thompson, established in 1878, was said more than any other to have "developed the magazine field by the end of the century."[34] Frank Munsey applied the principle of low prices with the support of advertising worked out by newspapers to the magazine field and sold *Munseys* for 10c. Periodicals occupied the national political field in the nineties, and in the early part of the century *McClures* and *Colliers* were engrossed in muckraking. The latter was linked with an extensive book selling organization[35] in which national advertising was particularly effective. Cyrus Curtis and his son-in-law, Edward W. Bok, built up unprecedented circulations for the *Saturday Evening Post* and the *Ladies' Home Journal*.

The spectacular success of periodicals based on the sale of features and national advertising pointed the way to the expansion of newspapers obsessed with local news and neglecting national advertising. The legacy of bitterness which followed the Civil War, and facilitated the dominance of the Republican party and the army, compelled the Democratic party to concentrate on the building up of political machines in important northern urban centres. Newspapers devoted their attention to crusades and attacks on the boss system. Corruption in the Republican sphere in the nation was paralleled by corruption in the Democratic sphere in urban centres. Advertising agents emerged in response to demands for the organization of advertising in the newspaper. George P. Rowell developed the list system in the sixties and published the first American newspaper directory in 1869. N. W. Ayer and Son with experience in advertising in religious papers turned to the newspaper. Lord and Thomas began in the seventies to interest manufacturers in national advertising. The importance of advertising technique was evident not only in the starting of *Printers Ink* in 1888 but in the appearance of numerous books on advertising in the nineties. Mail order houses

[34]Frank Presbrey, *The History and Development of Advertising* (Garden City, 1929), p. 272.

[35]See Mark Sullivan, *The Education of an American* (New York, 1938).

emerged in the West to take advantage of markets created by railroads and an improved postal system. Montgomery Ward and Company started in Chicago in 1872 and Sears Roebuck at a later date; both developed techniques of description, half tone and colour in presentation which had their implications in the improvement of newspaper advertising to serve the needs of metropolitan centres.

The use of electric power in urban transit widened the market and electric lighting reduced the fire hazards, facilitating the growth of department stores. It has been said that department stores were founded on "one price, quick sales on low mark-up, multiplicity of offerings under one roof, bargain counters and lavish advertising."[36] Newspapers had served as pioneers in the field of low prices and rapid turnover, and as they were followed by periodicals, so they were followed by other types of goods. As a direct contribution M. E. Stone imported large numbers of pennies in Chicago, where the five cent coin was the prevailing denomination, in order to encourage the sale of his papers, and he persuaded stores to introduce prices ending in nine cents in order to increase their use. The use of small coins facilitated the sale of low-priced goods to larger numbers of consumers in the small income class. The one-price system made possible large scale advertising and standardized salesmanship. A. T. Stewart and Company in New York, John Wanamaker in Philadelphia, and Field and Leiter in Chicago, built up large stores; and advertising consultants, such as John E. Powers, contributed to their expansion.

The effects of metropolitan advertising were evident in the growth of evening papers designed to attract women readers. Department store advertising became news. While morning papers escaped the dominance of male readers[37] characteristic of papers such as *The Times* concerned with political influence, they had not been successful in meeting the demands of lower income groups. Electric lighting made reading easier, and evening papers published news in which the morning papers were handicapped, particularly about sports. They were sold more largely by street sales and

[36] F. L. Mott, *American Journalism* (New York, 1941), p. 596.

[37] "The London *Times* is emphatically a paper for men . . . American women read newspapers as much as their liege lords. The paper must accommodate itself to this fact; and hence the American sheet involves a variety of topics and diversity of contents." Raymond in The New York *Times*, Oct. 14, 1852. Breyer, p. 242.

developed a style with immediate interest and appeal. The success of the Scripps papers reflected the advantages of evening papers and the possibilities of their development in Western centres. Policies were also developed to appeal directly to lower income groups. Deliberately and aggressively chains of smaller papers were built up which emphasized complete independence of advertisers or financial groups in order to appeal to labour. The policy was advertised effectively in the establishment of the *Day Book* in Chicago, a paper which carried no advertising.

Loss of advertising by the morning papers to the evening papers led the former to build up the Sunday paper with its voracious appetite for features.[38] Sunday, morning, and evening papers began to demand features on a large scale and to become competitors of magazines and periodicals. The use of wood pulp and the lowering of the cost of newsprint coincided with the demand for news and feature material. The use of the stereotype brought an end to the blanket sheets, and the production of patent insides, for printing and distribution for news, and later for advertising. Syndicates appeared shortly after the Civil War to provide material for large numbers of small papers. The use of comics and of colour increased from the nineties, and the continued comics became of first importance in capturing and maintaining circulation. Specialization in syndicated material brought improvements in its general character and increased the demand for features. Rural mail delivery in 1897 brought an end to the weeklies and an increase in the circulation of small dailies with further demands for boiler plate.

Major technological changes brought revolutions in journalism in the trend toward inclusiveness. Interstitial media preceding major technological changes were absorbed, and features, news and advertising brought under the domination of the newspaper. Numerous departments were created to cater to the demands of special groups in a specialized society.[39] The growth of chains, syndicates, and press associations reflects the demand for a combination of regional news items with universal features. Metropolitan papers have become increasingly concerned with local news as they have demanded increasing numbers of features. Even in New York

[38]Will Irwin, *Propaganda and the News* (New York, 1936).

[39]James Weber Linn, *James Keeley Newspaperman* (Indianapolis, 1937).

concentration on local news has increased, even though national advertising has also increased.[40] The size of the continent has necessitated variation and uniformity.

Devices designed to increase circulation in order to capture advertising weakened the position of the editorial or changed it into such writing as that of Arthur Brisbane. Mencken has described the editorial page as "our grandest and gaudiest failure." After the defeat of Landon, Captain Patterson pronounced that "the editorial is dead." A comparison of newspapers in St. Louis in 1875 and 1925 shows a decline of total space devoted to news from 55.3% to 26.7% (including an increase in sports from 1.7% to 25.4%); of opinion from 9.67% to 2.2%; but an increase from 6.3% to 10.4% of the space devoted to features; and from 28.9% to 60.5% of that devoted to advertising.[41] Advertising was estimated to have increased 50% from 1899 to 1942.[42] Editorial influence was exercised through the headlines, developed not only to capture attention but also to save the time of the reader faced with papers of increasing size. Slanting of the headlines and the news opened the door to the press agent or publicity agent, not inaccurately described as the praise agent or the pufflicity agent. The constant reiteration of the supremacy of the editor was an indication in itself of the supremacy of the business manager and the advertiser.

The eventual adjustment of the newspaper to changes in the demands of advertising, and to the dominance of advertising, narrows the relations between the newspaper and the commercial world. Large-scale organizations build up good will through newspaper advertising, and the oligopolistic position of the newspaper becomes a part of business firms' monopolistic or oligopolistic position. Large users of advertising have concentrated on technique and its effectiveness, and advertising agents and newspapers have been compelled to develop research organizations. Newspapers at a late date created an Audit Bureau of Circulation and have sponsored pure food laws and "truth" in advertising. Poisoning of the news had led to demands from advertisers for accuracy and truth. Sensa-

[40]See W. C. Crum, *Advertising Fluctuations Seasonal and Cyclical* (Chicago, 1927).

[41]Susan M. Kingsbury, Hornell Hart and associate, *Newspapers and the News* (New York, 1937), p. 195.

[42]*Ibid.*, p. 199.

tionalism without the newspaper cannot be compared to sensationalism with it, and the newspaper has gradually damped down beliefs in witchcraft, astrology, and rumours. But the advertiser demands further improvements and elimination of spuriousness.

The significance of advertising in the American press had its effects on the English press. In spite of competition of the new journalism, *The Times*, with the support of heroic efforts, continued. The effective organization of the sales of books and periodicals in the United States became the example by which new sources of revenue were developed. Horace Hooper and W. M. Jackson, American book agents, were enlisted by Moberly Bell to sell the *Encyclopædia Brittannica* through *The Times*.[43] Other devices included *The Times* Book Club, which brought determined opposition from the book trade. But the influence of the printer continued in the Walter family to prevent the necessary adjustments to the new journalism and in 1908 *The Times* was acquired by Northcliffe. A drastic reorganization followed, and, with the lowering of price, *The Times* was brought into line with modern journalism. After Northcliffe's death, control was returned to the Walter and Astor families but modernization continued. The conservatism of the press was evident in the domination of the book tradition and the printer. Whereas in England and Europe the newspaper grew from the book trade, in the United States the book trade followed the newspaper. American journalists have played an important role in the development of American literature and their output of books is without end. In England, the front page is still predominantly advertisement; in the United States, news. The impact of American advertising became more direct after the last war. Blumenfeld and Lord Beaverbrook in the *Daily Express*, and Selfridge in the department store, continued to introduce American techniques in journalism and advertising. After the last war the drapers became the largest customers for advertising and in 1924 contracts were given to the *Daily Express* for full pages.[44] The race for circulation between the *Daily Express*, the *Daily Mail*, and the *Daily Herald* reflected the full impact directly and indirectly of advertising in the twenties and early thirties.

[43]See F. Harcourt Kitchen, *Moberly Bell and his Times an Unofficial Narrative* (London, 1925).

[44]Lord Beaverbrook, *Politicians and the Press* (London, n.d.).

VI

The last war hastened the trend of development in news, features, and editorials which have become conspicuous since the turn of the century. The high price of newsprint and increasing costs of production brought numerous consolidations and the growth of chains. Advertisers encouraged amalgamations as a means of avoiding duplication. Editorial policy was tempered by the amalgamation of papers and the necessity of maintaining circulation among groups with divergent points of view. The columnist was encouraged as a means of presenting interpretation to different groups. The attempt to attract women readers increased. Because of the dominance of male readers in the English press, Northcliffe started the *Daily Mirror* as a woman's paper, but he quickly learned that the newspaper wants of women differed little from those of men. The tabloid was converted into a pictorial paper, gained wide circulation, and led to the establishment of rivals. The rapid increase in the importance of the cinema and the development of photography brought an appreciation of pictures which was reflected in the newspaper, and particularly in the tabloid. Chicago *Tribune* interests started the New York *Daily News* in 1919, with the support of funds rescued from the war profits tax. Fears of encroachment on readers of his paper led Hearst to start the *Daily Mirror* in 1924. In the same year Bernard Macfadden, after phenomenal success with physical culture magazines and confession stories, started the *Daily Graphic*. In the circulation war of the tabloids, the *Daily News* was crowded into respectability and increasing attractiveness to advertisers. The *Graphic* was compelled to rely on sensationalism, personal journalism centring about sex, new devices such as cosmography, and upon dubious advertising. Circulation based on these features was unstable and unattractive to higher class advertising. The impact of the tabloid war was evident in the rapid increase in the amount of space in newspapers devoted to pictures and in the tendency to play up single large news stories. The invention of the teletypwriter or automatic printer, the teletypsetter, telephotography or wirephoto, the electric flash lamp, and increased speed and the use of numerous colours on the presses supported the change. The character of news since the last war is a reflection of the change in the newspaper. The national field was profoundly influenced by technological changes. Limitations of the newspaper in providing background and interpretation of the news and the importance of photography contributed to the phenomenal success of *Life* and its imitators; to *Time, Fortune,* and the news weeklies. Technological change also contributed to the development of the radio with its serious effects on the reporting of spot news and advertising. The radio capitalized the development of the headline, reduced the importance of the extra edition, and provided interpretation and background. It could reach lower levels of intelligence and literacy and could capitalize on the advances made by advertising in other media.

The implications of the revolution in journalism have been evident in political activity. The franchise has been widened and woman suffrage has accompanied the increased interest of newspapers in women's interests. On the other hand the dominance of advertising and the conservatism of journalism leave little hope of immediate active concern with political considerations. The dominance of political interest which persisted in spite of the growth of advertising becomes extremely difficult to reinstate with the dominance of advertising. Even in the early eighteenth century Lockhart wrote that "no journalist . . . has the undisturbed leisure which literature demands;"[45] "Nothing is less permanent than journalism." Scott wrote, "if you are interrupted eternally with these petty avocations, the current of the mind is compelled to flow in shallows, and you lose the deep intensity of thought, which alone can float plans of depth and magnitude."[46] Graham Wallas pointed to the decline of discussion with the spread of machine industry and to the emphasis on information and facts as destructive of the environment for thought.[47] Shaw has referred to the incurable habit of journalists "of stating public problems without ever having the time to solve them." Kennedy Jones stated to Morley, "you left journalism a profession, we have made it into a branch of commerce." The decline in importance of politics has enormously strengthened the position of autocratic types of government. Radio has become a powerful political instrument and a reflection of the deterioration of

[45]Andrew Lang, *The Life and Letters of John Gibson Lockhart* (London, 1897).

[46]*Scott's Journal,* Vol. II, p. 134.

[47]See Pierce Butler, *The Origin of Printing in Europe* (Chicago, 1940), Chap. I.

the newspaper as a political factor. The rise of dictators, increased length of life of administrations in democratic countries, and the tendency of elections to turn on overwhelming majorities, have been suggested as results of the radio. Slanting of the news which has followed the growth of advertising and the use of press agents and publicity men has enabled government departments to maintain representatives to inform the press. The complexity of legislation and administrative bodies has favoured the use of press agents to interpret and to guarantee the *right* interpretation to newspapers in search of news. Nationalism has become more intense and the position of language groups within nations has been strengthened. It is perhaps not too much to say that the fourth estate has disappeared. The social scientist[48] has attempted to assume the mantle, but in the main he has become a part of government bureaucracies. He has been quick to work in collusion with them, to pretend an omniscience equal to all occasions, and to become the kept class of autocracies. Universities have appointed press agents to persuade the public of their contributions; their curricula have been adjusted; and a rash of departments of university extension has broken out.

VII

In attempting to appraise the economic role of the newspaper, a study of the press in Great Britain has been used as a control device for a study of the press in the United States. The class structure in England and the imposition of taxes on newspapers throughout the first half of the nineteenth century left its impress on every aspect of the press. The concern of the press with political activity was a conspicuous feature and its persistence reflects the inherent conservatism of the industry. Fluctuations in the obsession with political activity have become less pronounced as the power of the press has declined. As political influence became more important, advertising suffered and the full implications of major technological changes were not realized in the effects of advertising on the expansion of

[48]The significance of the newspaper to the social sciences has been evident in the deterioration, since Adam Smith, shown in the increasing obsession with facts and figures in relation to the short run immediate problems of bureaucracies, in the increasing specialization and departmentalization of the social sciences, and in their consequent divisiveness and sterility. Economic history has suffered either as a handmaiden of bureaucracy or a sink of antiquarianism. See B. S. Kierstead, *Essentials of Price Theory* (Toronto, 1942), Vols. V-VIII.

trade. Abolition of taxes on knowledge and the effects of advertising in the American press on the British press have gradually worn down the importance of political influence and made advertising more effective. In the United States political influence long retained its importance; but it became a vested interest, not in a tax structure but in freedom of the press.

The long term trends in the economic role of the newspaper are more conspicuous in the United States where there has been greater flexibility, a more protected position in libel laws which favour the defendant rather than the plaintiff, freedom from taxation, and technological traditions free from the rigidities of the book trade. Technological advance gave the press enormous digestive capacity. Its lumpy type of development, its construction, and the vast area of the United States fostered the growth of national media for advertising and features. Succeeding major advances promoted their absorption in the newspaper. Major technological changes were supported by bombardments from minor developments. Magazines became successful with features, but these were taken over by newspapers and the general illustrated monthly suffered disastrously after the last war.

The newspaper has been a pioneer in the development of speed in communication and transportation. Extension of railroads and telegraphs brought more rapid transmission of news and wider and faster circulation of newspapers; and newspapers, in turn, demanded further extension of railroads and telegraph lines. Cables, postal systems, express systems, aviation lines and radio have been fostered and utilized by newspapers. The concentration of the natural sciences on the problems of physics and chemistry concerned with speed reflects the influence of the newspapers. Educational systems and literacy have been subject to their influence directly and indirectly. Speed in the collection, production and dissemination of information has been the essence of newspaper development. Widening of markets, the effectiveness of competition, lowering of costs of production, the spread of the price system, the evolution of a sensitive monetary structure and the development of equilibrium economics have followed the development of the newspaper. By its drive for the use of small coins it has acted as a spearhead in penetrating to lower incomes. In its effective use of advertising in the selection and exploitation of news, it developed a medium for the advertising of goods. The lifting power of advertising increased from patent medicines to automobiles. The influence of newspapers on communication and transportation has varied with waves of technological advance. Increase in sensitivity in the price system has varied with the efficiency of adaptation of technological improvements. Economic analysis has become more complex and confused. The conservatism of knowledge which resists the impact of improvements in communication breaks down in a conservatism of confusion.

As a pioneer in advertising the newspaper has not been as effective in the advertising of goods as in the advertising of newspapers. Advertising and good will have prompted the growth of oligopolies. The advertising of goods developed more slowly in Great Britain than in the United States. The rapid growth of metropolitan areas supported by newspapers provided room for the establishment of new papers on the basis of technological advance. Established papers were able to resist the full immediate impact of technology. The class structure favoured the conservatism and entrenchment of newspapers in oligopolistic positions among readers of the more literate classes. The New York *Times* and the *Evening Post* of an earlier period with smaller circulations attracted advertising appealing to upper income groups. Advertising rates respond to the principle of charging what the traffic will bear. Technological advance tends to be turned to marginal literate groups in lower income brackets. Members of these groups move up to higher class newspapers or the newspaper, by becoming respectable, retains its control. A marginal group unattractive to advertisers or too attractive to advertising of a dubious sort apparently cannot be reached by a successful newspaper if one may judge from the failure of the *Graphic*. The literate fringe and the low income brackets widen and contract with the business cycle, with the effectiveness of newspaper penetration, and with the lumpy character of modern large-scale newspaper undertakings. Penetration to the larger low income groups becomes almost impossible unless preceded by minor developments such as ballad literature in England and the dime novel and the confession magazines in the United States, the command of enormous capital resources to supply the essential equipment for large scale circulation, or extensive newspaper experience. The large marginal areas of literacy occupied with rapidity and success by the *World* and the *Journal* in the nineties no longer exist.

Under the existing conditions of oligopoly the contributions of the newspaper to the flexibility of the economic structure are restricted. Decline of advertising and of newspaper size and circulation reduces sensitivity of the price system and accentuates inflexibility and rigidity in depression; increase in advertising, size and circulation accentuates flexibility and elasticity. It may be suggested that studies of secular trends and the business cycle would gain from a more adequate appreciation of such technological changes as the manufacture of paper from wood and the use of the linotype, that the long period of prosperity from the 1890's to 1929 was not unrelated to them and that the depression may be in part the result of changes introduced by the radio. It is possible that Professor Schumpeter's interpretation might be modified. The contributions of Professor Gras to studies of the metropolitan area might also gain from an appreciation of the role of the press. Monetary theorists might learn much by extending their attention from the velocity of circulation of money to the velocity of circulation of newspapers. We need to know more about the preference for various commodities before we can discuss effectively the liquidity preference of money. Commodities have a changing significance to the economic structure, to each other, and to the regions in which they are produced and consumed. Equilibria tend to develop in separate metropolitan regions. It may be that Veblen's classification between the pecuniary and the industrial becomes less sharp with an appreciation of the economic role of the newspaper.

Finally this paper is designed to emphasize the importance of a change in the concept of the dimension of time, and to argue that it cannot be regarded as a straight line but as a series of curves depending in part on technological advances. Interest theory would gain by an emphasis on the importance of elasticity in the concept of time. With technological advances in communication the field for long term securities tends to be narrowed in relation to the demand for short term securities. The concepts of time and space must be made relative and elastic and the attention given by the social scientists to problems of space should be paralleled by attention to problems of time.

2. AN ECONOMIC APPROACH TO ENGLISH LITERATURE IN THE NINETEENTH CENTURY

The rationalism of the eighteenth century shed its light on the literature of the early part of the nineteenth century. In the second half of the century with the work of Darwin and Spencer that light began to grow dim. In the twentieth century we have seen the growth of irrationalism reflected in the interest in psychology, advertising, mass propaganda, totalitarian states and war. Mass propaganda of the Anglo-Saxon world, directed by such individuals as Hearst and Northcliffe, played an important role in the defeat of Germany in the last war. Its effectiveness was appreciated by totalitarian states who reinforced their instruction with the assistance of such new methods of communication as the radio and the cinema. The results were evident not only in the totalitarian states. Such phrases as "total war," "full employment," "anti-semitism," and the like, bandied about in the democratic states are a tribute to the influence of totalitarian propaganda, as are the innumerable measures which have been required to offset its effects and to bolster our morale. We have passed from the security and optimism which characterized the belief in progress in the nineteenth century to fear and pessimism and demands for security.

The nineteenth century was a period of transition from rationalism to irrationalism, and its literature reflects the character of the change. On the history of that transition it is hoped that this paper will throw some light. For the moment we shall say with Leslie Stephen[1] that philosophical thought and imaginative literature can have no history, being a by-product of social evolution, "the noise that the wheels make as they go round," and concentrate on technological developments affecting communication.

I

The Industrial Revolution had profound implications for printing and literature, in lowering the costs of paper and introducing steam power to the press. In 1799 Louis Robert at Essone in France designed a machine to make a continuous sheet of paper on an end-

[1]F. W. Maitland, *The Life and Letters of Leslie Stephen* (London, 1906), p. 283.

less wire cloth turned on wheels, and a patent was taken out in England in 1804 by the Fourdinier brothers, after whom the machine was named. The length of time for the manufacturing process was reduced from five weeks to five days, and inventory charges were lowered sharply. The enormous expansion of demand for rags[2] in Great Britain and the United States and the export restrictions in continental countries stimulated a search for substitutes. Esparto grass was used in England in 1857. The abolition of the duty in 1861 brought imports of foreign paper and the removal of obstacles incidental to industrial monopolies which had grown up under the tariff. Chemical and mechanical pulp were used in the sixties and seventies, and by 1882 the shortage of paper could be said to be at an end.

The total production of paper in the United Kingdom increased from 11,347 tons in 1800, all of which was hand-made, to 100,000 tons in 1861, of which 96,385 tons were machine-made. After the removal of the duty in that year production increased to 651,650 tons in 1900, of which 647,764 tons were machine-made. Including imports, consumption by the end of the century reached over a million tons. Prices had declined roughly from 1s. 6d. a pound at the beginning of the century to as low as ¾d. a pound in 1900. They had fallen to 10d. a pound in 1836, and 6½d. in 1859.[3] From 1861 they declined about two-thirds. The proportional cost of paper in publications declined during the century from two-thirds to less than one-tenth.

The use of steam power in the manufacture of paper was followed by its application to the press of *The Times* on November 29, 1814. Production per hour increased from 250 to 1,000 copies. By 1853 Applegath's machine produced 200 copies per minute. The problems of the cylinder press were eventually solved by the Hoe firm in New York. The stereotype, and printing from a continuous sheet, or the web press, was introduced in the sixties, and improvements in folding machinery completed the long line of experiments leading to the fast press. The linotype solved the problem of type-

[2]Rags were imported to the extent of 7,061 tons in 1844, 10,140 tons in 1846, 6,953 in 1849, and 8,124 in 1850.

[3]The costs of fine quality paper declined from 17d. a pound in 1814 to 12d. in 1824, or from 49s. 7d. a ream to 35s. Printing paper declined in price from 24s. in 1831 to 15s. 6d. in 1843. (See p. 5.)

setting in the late eighties and nineties. Development of the book press lagged behind the newspaper press, but the rotary press, the stereotype, and the monotype revolutionized production. Monopoly control in the newspaper field increased the supply of paper available for publication of periodicals and books during the first half century, and the substitution of esparto grass and wood for rags in the making of newspapers increased the supply of raw material available for books in the second half of the century.

II

The diffusion of the principles of free trade, which began with the publication of the *Wealth of Nations,* was perhaps, most significant and least noticed in the field of literature. The monopolies, under taxation and the government regulation with which the press and the stage were distorted, were eventually destroyed with the growing interest in freedom of trade. In the main free trade was achieved in the commodities essential to literature after it had been achieved for other commodities. The monopoly position of the principle of free trade during the early part of the nineteenth century on the one hand weakened the position of other principles and on the other checked its rapid diffusion.

The introduction of machinery under conditions of restriction favoured the growth of monopoly among the dailies. Taxes had increased to a stamp of 3⅕d. net on each paper in 1815, and 3s. 6d. on every advertisement. "Four pages of advertisements and London and foreign reports cost sevenpence."[4] Taxes were being lowered but the monopoly of *The Times* was strengthened. The advertising tax was lowered to 18d. in 1833 and the stamp duty to 1d., and paper duties from 3d. to 1½d. per lb. in 1836. The advertising tax was abolished in 1853, and the stamp duty in 1855. By the middle of the century the annual circulation of *The Times* far surpassed the total of all the other London dailies. The taxes and their changes were of far-reaching significance to literature in the first half of the century.

The tendency of the printing industry to develop monopolies in London had from an early date attracted Scottish booksellers and

[4]W. H. Wickwar, *The Struggle for the Freedom of the Press, 1819-1832* (London, 1928), p. 30.

writers intent on securing a share of the profits. Donaldson had secured a favourable court decision destroying perpetual copyright under the common law in 1774. Constable took full advantage of lower costs of printing in Edinburgh, of improved shipping facilities to London, of the restrictions on newspapers, and of the existence of a small energetic group of men in the law and the Church held back by aristocratic domination in Scotland, to support the launching of the *Edinburgh Review.* He paid unprecedented prices for articles and allowed complete freedom to his editors and contributors. The end of the long spell of drudgery by Grub Street writers, pilloried and made more despicable by Pope in the *Dunciad,* was in sight. The effectiveness of attacks on the Tories annoyed Sir Walter Scott and led him to support the *Quarterly Review,* published in London by John Murray. These reviews reflected opinions of the Whigs and Tories and were followed by the *Westminster Review* representing the radicals. But by the end of the first half of the century their influence had declined. The publishers assumed more active direction—Macvey Napier who followed Jeffrey as editor of the *Edinburgh Review* was also editor of the *Encyclopædia Britannica* for Constable and for Blackie. Lockhart, following Gifford as editor of the *Quarterly Review,* was more closely associated with John Murray in the publication and review of books. By 1855 it was possible for Henry Reeve, a leader-writer on *The Times,* to become editor of the *Edinburgh Review.* J. D. Cook and his staff from the *Morning Chronicle* started the *Saturday Review* in 1855. The increasing prestige of the journalist[5] accompanied a decline in the status of the reviews and a rise in the status of *The Times.* Its monopoly position enabled it to dominate opinion, drove it into competition with the reviews, and left a wider field for periodicals and later for papers emphasizing news.

The high price of newspapers after 1815, and the tendency toward monopoly, provoked a large outbreak of illegal sheets, and the introduction of severe repressive legislation in 1819. William Cobbett began his two-penny *Political Register* in 1816, but fled to the United States in 1817. When he returned in 1819, bringing with him the bones of Tom Paine, he stirred up new interest in his doc-

[5]In the twenties Scott was horrified at the idea of Lockhart's being associated with the press.

trines. The repressive measures of 1819 were powerless to control the outburst of polemical writing centring about the unfortunate Queen Caroline. The scurrilous *John Bull*, edited by Theodore Hook, could not be overlooked by the government in its attempts to repress opposition literature. Richard Carlile, who persisted in printing the works of Tom Paine and with his family and workmen exhausted the resources of his persecutors, after six years of imprisonment was released in November, 1825. The cause of freedom of discussion triumphed with the support of John and Leigh Hunt, Shelley, Southey, Byron, Bentham and James Mill. By 1832 the struggle was absorbed in the larger issues of the Reform Bill.

The restricted development of newspapers, and the decline in importance of news after the Napoleonic wars, favoured not only the publication of scurrilous sheets but also the growth of publishing firms interested in circulating libraries[6] and three-decker novels designed to extract revenue from readers. Sydney Smith wrote of the "customary phrases, union of souls, married in the eye of heaven, etc., etc., and such like diction the types of which Mr. Lane of the Minerva Press very prudently keeps ready composed in order to facilitate the printing of the adventures, etc."[7] Scott's novels dealt a serious blow to the productions of the Minerva Press. Scott had relinquished poetry because (in his own well-known words) "Byron

[6]"For as to the devotees of the circulating libraries, I dare not compliment their *pass-time*, or rather *kill-time*, with the name of *reading*. Call it rather a sort of beggarly day-dreaming, during which the mind of the dreamer furnishes for itself nothing but laziness, and a little mawkish sensibility; while the whole *material* and imagery of the dose is supplied *ab extra* by a sort of mental *camera obscura* manufactured at the printing office, which *pro tempore* fixes, reflects, and transmits the moving phantasms of one man's delirium, so as to people the barrenness of a hundred other brains afflicted with the same trance or suspension of all common sense and all definite purpose. We should therefore transfer this species of *amusement* (if indeed those can be said to retire *a musis*, who were never in their company, or relaxation be attributable to those, whose bows are never bent) from the genus, *reading*, to that comprehensive class characterized by the power of reconciling the two contrary yet co-existing propensities of human nature, namely indulgence of sloth, and hatred of vacancy. In addition to novels and tales of chivalry in prose or rhyme (by which last I mean neither rhythm nor metre), this genus comprises as its species, gaming, swinging, or swaying on a chair or gate; spitting over a bridge; smoking; snuff-taking, tête-à-tête quarrels after dinner between husband and wife; conning word by word all the advertisements of a daily newspaper in a public house on a rainy day, etc., etc., etc." S. T. Coleridge, *Biographia Literaria* (Oxford, 1907), Vol. I, p. 34.

[7]*Works of the Rev. Sydney Smith* (3rd ed., London, 1845), Vol. III, pp. 21-2; see also Dorothy Blakey, *The Minerva Press, 1790-1820* (London, 1939).

beat me. . . . He beat me out of the field in the description of the strong passions, and in deep-seated knowledge of the human breast; so I gave up poetry for the time." After the Napoleonic wars the demand for patriotic poetry disappeared, and Wordsworth wrote such verse as to lead Jeffrey to say in the *Edinburgh*, "This will never do." Murray deliberately refused to publish poetry after Byron's successes and took to tourist guides and cook-books.[8] The firm of Edward Moxon specialized in poetry and, in spite of the popularity of Tennyson, eventually went into bankruptcy. Nor was the change confined to poetry. By 1821 Sydney Smith could write of *The Pirate* as "one of the least fortunate of Sir Walter Scott's productions. It seems now that he can write nothing without Meg Merrilies and Dominie Samson! One other such novel and there's an end; but who can last forever? Who ever lasted so long?"[9] The advantages enjoyed by Scottish writers and publishers in attacking the monopoly in London came to an end in the crash of 1826 and the transfer of the *Edinburgh Review* to Longman and the *Encyclopædia Britannica* to Blackie, and in the tragedy of Sir Walter Scott's life. The fashion shifted from Scott to the realism of the novels of Theodore Hook and the silver-fork school of fiction.

The tax on advertising encouraged publishers to establish journals designed to give extremely favourable reviews of their books. The review replaced the advertisement. Henry Colburn started the *Literary Gazette* with William Jerdan as editor in 1817, and in 1821 converted the *New Monthly Magazine* into a literary periodical edited by Thomas Campbell with the active assistance of Cyrus Redding. He transferred his interest in the *Literary Gazette* to Longman and the latter sold to Jerdan, who was charged with developing his periodical in the interests of prospective advertisers. "However meritorious he may be," wrote Cyrus Redding, "the writer has little chance of attracting the attention of modern criticism without some preponderating influence on the part of the trade in paper and print."[10] Colburn not only exercised control over his own periodi-

[8]See *Autobiography of Henry Taylor, 1800-1875* (London, 1885), Vol. I, p. 193.

[9]Smith to Frances Jeffrey, Dec. 30, 1821, in *A Memoir of the Reverend Sydney Smith* by his daughter Lady Holland with a selection from his letters edited by Mrs. Austin (New York, 1855), Vol. II, p. 217.

[10]*Personal Reminiscences of Eminent Men* (London, 1867), Vol. II, p. 293.

cals but also over other publications. Of the *New Times*, the *Examiner*, and *John Bull* he wrote regarding possible reviews of Lady Morgan's *Italy*: "I am intimately acquainted with the editors, and advertising with them a good deal keeps them in check."[11] It was significant that the *London Magazine*, established in 1820 by Baldwin, Cradock, and Joy, and acquired by Taylor and Hessey, publishers of Keats's poetry, was absorbed by the *New Monthly* in 1829. The failure of the latter was "owing to the extraordinary force of the political tide at that period, the proof of which is manifest from the fact of some of their publications commencing with a rapid sale, and stopping abruptly after the appearance of several virulent attacks from periodicals who were opposed to the politics or liberal sentiments of the writers. The other publishers have ruined themselves from adopting an opposite extreme."[12] S. C. Hall followed Campbell[13] as editor in 1830 and was followed by Bulwer from November 1, 1831, to August, 1833. Colburn formed a partnership with Richard Bentley in 1829 but this was dissolved in 1832, and after Bulwer left the editorship, his novels were published by Bentley. Colburn retained control of the *New Monthly*, and Bentley persuaded Dickens to edit *Bentley's Miscellany* in 1837.

Authors were induced by publishers to take an active interest in writing and editing miscellanies. Harrison Ainsworth had raised the art of puffing his own works to new levels and had developed considerable skill in handling reviewers.[14] His *Rockwood*, published by Bentley in 1834, had an instantaneous success. The fashion for

[11]M. F. Brightfield, *John Wilson Croker* (Berkeley, 1940).

[12]R. H. Horne, *Exposition of the False Medium excluding Men of Genius from the Public* (1833), cited in Edmund Blunden, *Keats's Publisher* (London, 1936), p. 203.

[13]"He suggested the idea of Le Bon Dieu coming to London to seek the copyright of the Bible and going the round of the publishers. He hit off Longman wonderfully. Longman observed to his 'Lordship' that the copyright was of late years deteriorated in value, hazardous to publish, but might still do for a school book; he would be very happy to print it at his Lordship's expense on commission.

"Then Le Bon Dieu goes to Colburn. Colburn does not dispute the general merit of the work but doubts whether it will take with the fashionable world. He suggests a few alterations of high life—the manger and the fisherman are decidedly low—and a few piquant anecdotes about the court of King Herod." Michael Sadleir, *Bulwer: A Panorama* (London, 1931), pp. 204-5.

[14]See S. M. Ellis, *William Harrison Ainsworth and his Friends* (London, 1911).

criminal romances had its influence on Dickens, and *Pickwick* was regarded by Lockhart as "damned low." As editor of *Bentley's Miscellany,* Dickens was followed by Ainsworth in 1839. The latter's *Jack Sheppard* was issued periodically from January, 1839, to February, 1840, and published in three volumes. He started *Ainsworth's Magazine* in 1842, and bought the *New Monthly Magazine* in 1844. Thomas Hood resigned as editor of the latter in January, 1844, and started *Hood's Magazine.*

From the forties to the sixties journalists were crowded out by the disappearance of newspapers in the unequal struggle with *The Times,* and were led to concentrate on weekly periodicals and numbers which, without news, were free from stamp taxes. *Old St. Paul's* and *The Lancashire Witches* by Ainsworth were issued serially in the *Sunday Times.* Dickens, after his short editorship of the *Daily News* in 1846, started his *Household Words* in 1850, replaced by *All the year Round* in 1859. Dickens had begun as a reporter on the *Morning Chronicle* and the influence of journalism was evident throughout his work. Bagehot commented on his style as reflecting "the overflow of a copious mind, though not the chastened expression of an harmonious one." His genius was suited to the delineation of city life since London was like a newspaper: "Everything is there and everything is disconnected." According to the *Saturday Review,* the writings of Dickens were "the apotheosis of what has been called newspaper English." He "makes points everywhere, gives unfamiliar names to the commonest objects, and lavishes a marvellous quantity of language on the most ordinary incidents."[15] The haphazard absence of form encouraged by journalism influenced Thackeray as well as Dickens. "Newspaper writing spoils one for every other kind of writing. I am unwilling now more than ever to write letters to my friends, and always find myself attempting to make a pert, actual point at the end of a sentence."[16]

Monopolistic restrictions characterized the stage as well as the newspaper and contributed also to the development of periodical literature. At the beginning of the nineteenth century Covent Garden

[15]M. M. Bevington, *The Saturday Review, 1855-1868* (New York, 1941), p. 162.

[16]Quoted in Malcolm Elwin, *Thackeray, a Personality* (London, 1932), p. 55.

and Drury Lane theatres still occupied a privileged position. The former was enlarged and reopened in 1810 and the latter in 1812. The stage was used to appeal to the eye rather than to the ear: spectacles and melodrama were the fashion. "At present the English instead of finding politics in the stage, find their stage in politics."[17] Writers such as Theodore Hook and Douglas Jerrold turned from plays to periodical publications, and managers turned to translators and adapters of French plays.[18]

The work of authors who might otherwise have written for the stage was supplemented by the development of illustrations. Almanacs had been produced under monopoly privileges. Competition introduced by Ackermann from Germany in 1822 was astonishingly successful, and was followed by numerous imitations which emphasized increasingly elaborate illustrations, Lamb's "ostentatious trumpery." The work of Bewick in revolutionizing the technique of wood-cutting encouraged the development of illustrations in books and periodicals. The support of writers turned from the stage, merged with the increasing interest in illustrations, and political caricatures introduced from France, to produce the forerunners of *Punch* in the thirties and *Punch* and its numerous imitators in the forties and fifties. The *Illustrated London News* was a product of the same conditions and was strengthened by journalists such as Charles MacKay from the *Morning Chronicle.*

Periodical literature was enriched further by the work of Charles Knight in London and of the Chambers brothers in Edinburgh. Since governmental restrictions were particularly concerned with news, periodicals rigidly excluding news grew rapidly. *Chambers' Journal* had an amazing success from the beginnings in the early thirties. Knight was supported by the Society for the Diffusion of Useful Knowledge, sponsored by Brougham and others, and his *Penny Magazine,* started at about the same time, while successful during the early thirties, eventually succumbed as a result of dullness and the burden of the paper duties. Hazlitt's reference to "the diffusion of useless knowledge about useful facts" summarized the general view. It was the claim of both Knight and

[17]Edward Lytton Bulwer, *England and the English* (London, 1833), Vol. II, p. 14.

[18]See Charles Reade, *The Eighth Commandment* (London, 1860).

the owners of *Chambers' Journal* that the dangers arising from the radical journals which flourished during the long period of the fight against the taxes on knowledge, and which supported the Chartist movement, were materially lessened; and this claim was to some extent justified. In any case, numerous radical journals and the scandalous blackmail sheets, such as the *Age* under Westmacott and the *Satirist* under Gregory, disappeared in the forties.

The rank outgrowth of literature which sprang up as a result of monopoly in the newspaper field brought correctives. *Blackwood's* began in 1817, and under its auspices Lockhart and John Wilson (Christopher North) made vigorous attacks on London writers, which involved a duel and the killing of John Scott, editor of the *London Magazine.* It was followed by *Fraser's Magazine* in the early thirties. Under the editorship of Maginn, the writers for Colburn and Bentley were savagely reviewed. The *Atheneaeum* under Charles Dilke, more sober, refused to accept the dictation of publishers. From the beginning Dilke announced his "direct opposition to *trade* criticism and *paid* criticism." Perhaps the most effective attack on the artificialities of the literature of the first half-century was made by Bulwer who as an author of Bentley's suffered much from the personal abuses of anonymous journalism.[19] He not only replied to the attacks in kind but he became influential in the political field. His speeches in parliament against the taxes on knowledge from 1832 to 1855 were masterpieces of analysis in the tradition of Adam Smith, and contributed powerfully to the removal of monopoly privileges for the newspaper and the theatre. Competition was encouraged with the lowering and abolition of taxes on advertising, paper, and stamps.

III

In the second half of the century the decline in taxes was accompanied by a revolution in journalism. *The Times* was at the peak of its influence in the fifties and its competition had resulted in the disappearance of such rivals as the *Morning Chronicle,* the *Morning Herald,* the *Sun* and others. Thereupon a new group of powerful

[19]See Edward Lytton Bulwer, *England and the English* (London, 1833), Vol. II.

newspapers emerged, including the *Daily News* and the *Daily Telegraph*. The advertising tax had been responsible for the rash of bill posters which broke out over London, and its removal led to the retreat of advertising to the newspapers. Following its success in distributing tea at a uniform price throughout England, the firm of Gillespie actively and successfully sponsored uniform penny postage in 1840. Post-office facilities were improved and extended with the construction of railways. The telegraph and the cable brought a vast increase in news for distribution and facilitated the rapid growth of a large number of provincial newspapers. The extension of the franchise in 1867, and the Education Act of 1870, which reflected the necessity of educating "our masters" (in Lowe's famous phrase), created a large number of readers. Competition was restricted by the government in the first half of the century and subsidized by it in the second half.

The marked expansion of a new group of newspapers in London and in the provinces in the second half of the century was accompanied by the decline of *The Times* to the point of bankruptcy by 1890 and its sale to Northcliffe in 1908. Its emphasis on political influence, which enabled it to destroy the Aberdeen administration in the Crimean War, weakened its position with the increasing importance of news. Editorial support of the South in the Civil War made it impossible for W. H. Russell to duplicate the success as a war correspondent which he had achieved in the Crimea. The training of correspondents in the Civil War (especially with the New York *Tribune*) and the use of the cable enabled the London *Daily News* and Archibald Forbes, in the Franco-Prussian War, to displace *The Times* and Russell. Finally, the publication of the forged Pigott letters destroyed even the political influence of *The Times*. The destruction of its political supremacy was the last phase of the struggle against the mercantile system. The success of Gladstone, the beginnings of large majorities in the House of Commons, and the emergence of the caucus as a device for party control reflected the influence of the *Daily News* and other papers and the provincial press. The increasing susceptibility of Parliament to the influence of the press was shown in the unfortunate expedition to Egypt under General Gordon, a result of the demands of W. T. Stead in the *Pall Mall Gazette*.

The new journalism, in which Stead was a pioneer, received strong support from the development of penny weeklies in London, whose "principal characteristic is a senile imbecility on the one hand, or an irrational sensationalism on the other, equally destructive to anything like masculine vigour of thought."[20] By the early eighties these weeklies had a circulation of between five and six million. The *Family Herald* and the *London Journal* started in the middle forties, were particularly popular because of the emphasis on correspondence. The founders of the *Weekly Budget* had discovered that readers in large cities demanded light amusing reading with news.[21] George Newnes and later Alfred Harmsworth exploited this discovery, the one in *Tit-bits* and the other in *Answers*. From these origins there emerged the *Daily Express* under Arthur Pearson and the *Daily Mail* under the Harmsworth brothers and Kennedy Jones. American experience in the handling of news became important in the evening papers and then spread to the morning papers. But in both Great Britain and the United States the Boer War and the Spanish American War enabled sensational journalism to reach new peaks. Wemyss Reid wrote of the Boer War: "It has been said that this has been

[20]The words are Francis Hitchman's in an article on "The Penny Press" printed in the *Eclectic Magazine* for 1881.

[21]"No article in the paper is to measure more than two inches in length, and every inch must be broken into at least two paragraphs. . . .

I would have the paper address itself to the quarter-educated; that is to say, the great new generation that is being turned out by the Board schools, the young men and women who can just read, but are incapable of sustained attention. People of this kind want something to occupy them in trains and on 'buses and trams. As a rule they care for no newspapers except the Sunday ones; what they want is the lightest and frothiest of chit-chatty information—bits of stories, bits of description, bits of scandal, bits of jokes, bits of statistics, bits of foolery. Am I not right? Everything must be very short, two inches at the utmost; their attention can't sustain itself beyond two inches. Even chat is too solid for them: they want chit-chat" (George Gissing, *New Grub Street*, London, 1904, p. 419).

"I know a man who was once engaged at Jolly & Monk's—the chief publishers of that kind of thing, you know; I must look him up—what a mistake it is to neglect *any* acquaintance!—and get some information out of him. But it's obvious what an immense field there is for anyone who can just hit the taste of the new generation of Board-school children. Mustn't be too goody-goody; that kind of thing is falling out of date. But you'd have to cultivate a particular kind of vulgarity. There's an idea, by-the-bye. I'll write a paper on the characteristics of that new generation; it may bring me a few guineas, and it would be a help to you" (*Ibid.*, pp. 28-9).

a war made by newspapers. Evidently the newspapers are capable of carrying it on."[22]

The enormous expansion of newspapers and periodicals made heavy demands on writing. For his periodical, Dickens was said to have read 900 manuscripts of which he accepted eleven and rewrote them. Even the Rev. Whitwell Elwin, editor of the *Quarterly Review,* wrote in 1854 that "the art of writing pure English is almost lost."[23] By 1875, according to Maitland, "there was hardly a newspaper in England that was fit to read."[24] English journalism had suffered in the first half of the century from the effects of the stamp tax in ways already described but also from its emphasis on size and small type and from the necessity of using quantities of miscellaneous material. Anonymity, the low standard of journalism, and the gap between journalism and politics were in part the result. In France journalism without anonymity was recognized as the highway to office, whereas in England the most damaging charge ever brought against Brougham was that he wrote for a newspaper. The penny-a-liner was employed on an extensive scale to fill the columns of the paper. Even Charles Lamb confessed that he often used the statement, "It is not generally known that the three Blue Balls at the Pawnbroker's shop are the ancient arms of the Lombards. The Lombards were the first money brokers in Europe." The art of spinning out information is again illustrated in the sentence, "He was a policeman and his name was Smith." With the demands of competition the necessity of relying on an organized staff of journalists reduced the work of the penny-a-liner but the demands

[22]Wemyss Reid, "The Newspapers" (*Nineteenth Century,* Vol. XLVI, 1899, pp. 848-64).

[23]*Some XVIII Century Men of Letters, Biographical Essays by the Rev. Whitwell Elwin,* edited by his son Warwick Elwin (London, 1902), p. 130.

[24]F. W. Maitland, *The Life and Letters of Leslie Stephen* (London, 1906), p. 258.

"The evil of the time is the multiplication of ephemerides. Hence a demand for essays, descriptive articles, fragments of criticisms, out of all proportion to the supply of even tolerable work. The men who have an aptitude for turning out this kind of thing in vast quantities are enlisted by every new periodical, with the result that their productions are ultimately watered down into worthlessness" (George Gissing, *The New Grub Street,* London, 1904, p. 31).

"But surely before long some Edison would make the true automaton; the problem must be comparatively such a simple one. Only to throw in a given number of old books, and have them reduced, blended, modernized into a single one for today's consumption." *Ibid.,* p. 95.

for verbiage were still paramount.[25] A. B. Reach was a pioneer in presenting journalistic material in readable and attractive form. George Augustus Sala was a conspicuous artist in the *Daily Telegraph,* of whom Matthew Arnold wrote: "he blends the airy epicureanism of the *salons* of Augustus with the full blooded gaiety of our English cider-cellar. . . . This mixture . . . is now the very thing to go down; there arises every day a large public for it."[26] Professional journalists were influenced in style by popular writers, particularly Macaulay, Mill, and Froude, and by Carlyle in the United States:

> When clever pressmen write this way,
> "As Mr. J. A. Froude would say,"
> Is it because they think he would,
> And have they read a line of Froude?
> Or is it only that they fear
> The comment they have made is queer,
> And that they either must erase it,
> Or say it's Mr. Froude who says it?[27]

The demand for writers was met in part by the universities. The monopoly of Oxford and Cambridge in education was weakened by the establishment of the University of London in 1827. The improvement in status of Roman Catholics, after the Quebec Act of 1774, was eventually followed by their emancipation in 1827.[28] The

[25]"You must know, that the first time I met Angus he told me imprudently some foolish story about a stick that bred a disease in the owner's hand, owing to his pressing so heavily on the ball it had by way of a handle. I touched the story up a little, and made half-a-guinea out of it. Since then that note has been turning up in a new dress in the most unlikely places. First the London correspondents swooped down on it, and telegraphed it all over the country as something that had happened to a well-known Cabinet Minister. It appeared in the Paris *Figaro* as a true story about Sir Gladstone, and soon afterwards it was across the channel as a reminiscence of Thiers. Having done another tour of the provinces it was taken to America by a lecturer, who exhibited the stick. Next it travelled the Continent, until it was sent home again by Paterfamilias Abroad, writing to the *Times,* who said that the man who owned the stick was a well-known Alpine guide. Since then we have heard of it fitfully as doing well in Melbourne and Arkansas. It figured in the last volume, or rather two volumes, of autobiography published, and now, you see, it is going the round of the clubs again, preparatory to starting on another tour." J. M. Barrie, *When a Man's Single* (New York, 1896), p. 234. This volume includes numerous amusing accounts of journalism.

[26]*Friendship's Garland* (London, 1903), pp. 108-9.

[27]J. M. Barrie, *op. cit.*, p. 172.

[28]It was claimed that Irish law-students as reporters of debates played an important role in securing the legislation ("On the taxes on knowledge," *Westminster Review,* July 1, 1831, p. 18).

problem of the established church in Ireland contributed to the Anglo-Catholic movement and the departure of Newman from Oxford. The influence of science began with the appearance of Lyell's *Principles of Geology* (1833) and *The Vestiges of Creation* (1844), written by Robert Chambers but published anonymously, followed by Darwin and the controversy over *The Origin of Species* (1859). Oxford was opened to Dissenters in 1858. Young men who had planned to take orders found their faith weakened and turned to writing and journalism. J. A. Froude and Leslie Stephen renounced clerical orders; the latter calling in Thomas Hardy to witness the ceremony, after the act in 1870 permitting renunciation. He wrote, "I became gradually convinced after the most serious reflection I could give that the Christian position was untenable. I therefore gave up my profession and took to literature."[29] Morley entered journalism and politics. W. L. Courtney on the *Daily Telegraph* and Chenery, the successor of Delane on *The Times,* came from Oxford.

These writers contributed to the revolution in periodicals which accompanied the revolution in newspapers. Periodicals, such as *Fraser's Magazine* which after 1840 represented the Broad Church movement, the *Saturday Review* (1855) which reflected High Church opinion, and other periodicals had been supported by journalists released from newspapers such as the *Morning Chronicle* which disappeared under the monopoly of *The Times.* The interest in religion was evident in the vigorous disputes between Freeman and Froude; its decline was evident in the purchase of *Fraser's* by Longman in 1863 and its absorption in *Longmans' Magazine* in 1882 and in the sale of the *Saturday Review* by the Beresford Hope family in 1891. The effects of the interest in science were shown in the rise of Chapman and Hall, publishers of Herbert Spencer's work, and of Macmillan's supported by the interest of Cambridge University. The *Fortnightly Review* from 1867 to 1882 published numerous articles with powerful attacks on theology. The *Revue des deux Mondes* was used as a model and anonymity was abandoned. The *Contemporary Review* was started in 1866 as a religious periodical and the *Nineteenth Century* in 1877.

Railway construction in the forties was followed by a marked improvement in methods of distribution shown in the organization of

[29] F. W. Maitland, *op. cit.* p. 150.

W. H. Smith and Co. and Mudies. The *Cornhill Magazine* (1860) was started by George Smith of Smith, Elder and Co. with Thackeray as editor. It combined the critical review and the serial novel in a magazine sold for a shilling. Its phenomenal success brought imitators, and fiction serials opened the way for the cheap novel. Authors became less concerned with their own magazines and, like Thackeray, Trollope and George Eliot, accepted fabulous sums for serial rights. The demands for cheap editions of novels brought the yellow-back of the early sixties.[80] By the early nineties the three-decker novel, the staple of circulating libraries, was no longer able to compete with the serial and the cheap novel.

Whatever may be said of the three-decker novel at 31s. 6d., it had the advantage of handsome octavos, clear type, and splendid illustrations. There was no huddling of type and matter, and the pages were not a conglomeration of almost invisible lines.[81] It had contributed to the petty piracy of Thomas Tegg of which Carlyle complained and to the second-hand book trade in which John Lackington had a phenomenal success in the early part of the century. In "The temple of the muses" he kept "about half a million of volumes" which he bought and which he sold only for cash. The novel's size involved Procrustean demands on the author,[82] and its patronage by the wealthier classes and the circulating libraries required puritanical standards. Since novels were read aloud by lamplight in family gatherings the contents had to be harmless. George Moore, in 1885, hastened its decline in his pamphlet *Literature at Nurse or Circulating*

[80]Michael Sadleir, *The Evolution of Publishers' Binding Styles, 1770-1900* (London, 1930).

[81]William Tinsley, *Random recollections of an old publisher* (London, 1900), p. 534.

[82]"Messieurs and mesdames the critics are wont to point out the weakness of second volumes; they are generally right, simply because a story which would have made a tolerable book (the common run of stories) refuses to fill three books." George Gissing, *New Grub Street*, p. 117.

"How is it possible to abandon the three volumes? It is a question of payment. An author of moderate repute may live on a yearly three-volume novel—I mean the man who is obliged to sell his book out and out, and who gets from one to two hundred pounds for it. But he would have to produce four one-volume novels to obtain the same income; and I doubt whether he could get so many published within the twelve months. And here comes in the benefit of the libraries; from the commercial point of view the libraries are indispensable. Do you suppose the public would support the present number of novelists if each book had to be purchased? A sudden change to that system would throw three-fourths of the novelists out of work." *Ibid.*, p. 183.

Morals, and opened the way to French influence and the treatment of sex. The climate began to change. As the influence of Italy was displaced by that of Germany after the defeat of Napoleon, the marriage of Queen Victoria, and the attraction of the brief intensive flowering of German culture in the Romantic era to Coleridge, Carlyle and others, so the influence of Germany was replaced by France after the Franco-German War in which Europe had lost a mistress and gained a master.

The collapse of the three-decker novel followed the destruction of the monopoly of *The Times*. The new literature followed the new journalism. Murray had refused to publish Harriet Martineau's *Deerbrook* because it dealt with the middle classes. *The Times* during the monopoly period, and the *Daily Telegraph* and other newspapers which developed with the lowering of taxes, represented the middle classes of whom Matthew Arnold spoke with such contempt. With the gain in literacy after the Education Act of 1870 and the commercialization of literature, the lower classes made enormous demands for the new journalism and the new literature and these demands were met by cheap paper and printing and the new Grub Street described by George Gissing and Anthony Trollope.[33] The popularity of fiction followed the lower prices of novels. Books were sold in enormous quantities and popular writers, particularly women, wrote incredible numbers of novels. Arnold Bennett in a series of articles written at the end of the century described the work of writers of whom many readers will not have heard: M. E. Braddon, Rhoda Broughton, Sarah Grand, E. T. Fowler, Mary Cholmondeley.[34] Among the defects of the average reader's taste he noted an absence of all sense of beauty of form. "Perhaps the utter collapse of archi-

[33]Gissing has been cited earlier; Trollope likewise complains: "All those who are struggling for success have forced upon them the idea that their strongest efforts should be made in touting for praise. Those who are not familiar with the lives of authors will hardly believe how low will be the forms which their struggles will take—How little presents will be sent to men who write little articles; how much flattery may be expended even on the keeper of a circulating library; with what profuse and distant genuflexions approaches are made to the outside railing of the temple which contains within it the great thunderer of some metropolitan periodical publication! The evil here is not only that done to the public when interested counsel is given to them, but extends to the debasement of those who have at any rate considered themselves fit to provide literature for the public." Anthony Trollope, *Autobiography* (London, 1883), Vol. III, pp. 93-4.

[34]E. A. Bennett, *Fame and Fiction* (London, 1901); see also Q. D. Leavis, *Fiction and the Reading Public* (London, 1932).

tecture the most influential of all the arts, has something to do with this condition of things; perhaps it is only an effect."[35] The average reader showed an inability to perceive art-work as a whole, a taste for crude sentimentalism such as that supplied by Rudyard Kipling, and a dislike of all fiction disturbing to his basic ideas. Arnold Bennett, in spite of his concern for form, studied the art of meeting the needs of the average reader with effect. In the magazines "the final word of editorial cunning" was "the connected series of short stories, of five or six thousand words each, in which the same characters, pitted against a succession of criminals or adverse fates, pass again and again through situations thrillingly dangerous, and emerge at length into the calm security of ultimate conquest. . . . Its universal adoption is a striking instance of that obsequious pampering of mental laziness and apathy which marks all the most successful modern journalism."[36] Conan Doyle, Grant Allen, and above all L. T. Meade, used the formula with effect. To quote Bennett once more:

> The public, which hitherto had accepted meekly what the publisher provided, found itself elevated to a throne, with the publisher obsequiously bowing at the foot therof. . . . The modern editor . . . explores the nature of the demand to be met as patiently and thoroughly as a German manufacturer. With a mixture of logic and cynicism he states boldly that what people ought to want is no affair of his; and in ascertaining precisely what they in fact do want he never loses sight of the great philosophic truth that man is a frail creature. He assiduously ministers to human infirmities. The public would like to read, to instruct itself, educate itself, amuse itself, elevate itself, but no effort and no sacrifice must be involved in the process. The way must be made straight, every obstacle shifted, every lion killed in advance. Inducements must be offered and all the yielding must be on one side. Only by such means can a new market, however vast potentially, be set upon a secure and steady basis.[37]

The large-scale circulation of sixpenny magazines at the end of the century was increased further by the more frequent use of illustrations. Improvements in wood-engraving had been followed by the

[35] *Ibid.*, p. 13.

[36] *Ibid.*, p. 135.

[37] *Ibid.*, pp. 125-6. "I have an idea of offering substantial prizes to men and women engaged in sedentary work who take an oath to abstain from all reading, and keep it for a certain number of years. There's a good deal more need for that than for abstinence from strong liquor. If I could have had my way I would have revived prize-fighting." George Gissing, op. cit., p. 19.

half-tone process, and illustrated periodicals weakened the position of serial publications. Improved machinery for the printing of books and periodicals followed improvements in the printing of newspapers, and lower prices destroyed monopolies in publishing. Mechanization in book and periodical production created a revolution comparable to that in journalism. The low prices of periodicals and books and wide circulation favoured the growth of the one-price system. Alfred Marshall allowed Macmillans to publish his *Principles of Economics* at a fixed net price and the experiment was followed by the organization of publishers for the control of prices. Under the leadership of Sir Walter Besant, authors in turn organized for the protection of their interests. American copyright legislation in 1890 created a new series of rights, and the literary agent emerged to interpret them.

The collapse of the three-decker novel and the circulating library cannot be understood without reference to other European countries and particularly to the United States. The high prices of the three-volume novel in the first half of the century stimulated competition from French and Belgian printers who smuggled copies of English books into England.[38] The high cost of paper made the position of the English author, as compared with the French author, an unenviable one. In turn, the English author had a strong incentive to become editor and publisher and to publish in periodicals as well as in the novel-form, as we have seen in the case of Ainsworth and Dickens.

High prices meant not only smuggling from the continent but also, with the absence of copyright, large-scale piracy of English books in the United States and a smaller-scale piracy of American ones in England. English books were rushed to the United States and hurriedly printed in a wild competitive scramble.[39] One of Carlyle's early works was published first in the United States as were De Quincey's collected writings. W. C. Bryant published one of his first books in England, and Henry Adams deliberately published his attack on the Erie financiers there, in order to secure the widest possible circulation in the United States. English authors, such as Dickens, visited the United States to scold American readers for

[38]G. P. R. James, "Some Observations on the Book Trade as connected with Literature in England" (*Journal of the Statistical Society of London*, Vol. VI, p. 1843).

[39]See a reference to the printing of Moore's *Lalla Rookh* in New York in 1816: T. W. Barnes, *Memoir of Thurlow Weed* (Boston, 1884), p. 194.

their refusal to pay royalties, and to secure a wider market. Harriet Martineau was asked by *Harper's* to write of her experiences in the United States by "Trollopizing" a book. Freedom of the newspapers from taxation encouraged rapid expansion in the United States as compared with Great Britain. The penny-newspaper emerged in the early thirties. The American author found himself driven into journalism by English competition and pulled into it by the demand for newspaper writers. Bryant became editor of the New York *Evening Post*. The English book dominated the American market and American journalism gained from American writing. The newspaper monopoly in England drove writers into periodicals and books, and these in turn drove American writers into American journalism.[40] With the introduction of the steamship in the fifties, *Harper's* was built up with English fiction at the expense of a market for the American writer. The removal of the taxes on knowledge in England left English journalism exposed to the full impact of the advances in American journalism. R. Hoe and Company presses were first used by English papers in the fifties. At the end of the century the new journalism was in command in the United States and in England.

In the economic history of literature and journalism in England and the United States the class structure occupies a dominant position. The reviews of the early part of the nineteenth century were crowded out by the monopoly position of *The Times* and ceased to play a crucial role in political strategy. *The Times* dominated the middle classes from the first Reform Bill to the fifties. The removal of the taxes on knowledge, the extension of the franchise, and the

[40] "Nothing was said about the hatred or fear entertained of literature and its professors by the aristocracy of Great Britain; though much was said about the superior chances afforded in the United States, to men of letters who aspired to a political or a diplomatic career.

In the United States a newspaper editor, if a man of talent and sagacity above the average, and endowed with the power of language, either with the tongue or with the pen, can make himself anything that he pleases—not, perhaps President of the Republic, for that is a post which, for the last forty years, has not been within the grasp of any man of ability, or of anybody but some harmless third-rate politician, who has not made too many enemies in his public career; but a Vice-President, a Secretary of State, or an ambassador to London or Paris. No such chances are afforded to the journalist or the mere man of letters in England, although Mr. Disraeli's career may seem an instance to the contrary. But Mr. Disraeli became a statesman, not because of his being, but in spite of his being an author." Charles MacKay, *Forty Years' Recollections* (London, 1877), Vol. II, pp. 281-2.

development of the telegraphy and cable opened the way for the *Daily News* (1846) and the *Daily Telegraph* (1855), and a penetration of journalism to the lower classes at the expense of *The Times*. Finally the Education Act of 1870, cheap newsprint, and low costs of printing brought a third revolution indicated by the coming of the *Daily Mail* and the *Daily Express*. Public opinion as a reflection of the middle classes became less important, and popular clamour made rapid headway.[41] And so we entered the open seas of democracy in the twentieth century with nothing to worship but the totalitarianism of the modern state. A century of peace gave way to a century of war.

[41]See W. A. Mackinnon, *History of Civilization and Public Opinion* (London, 1849).

"The magic of Gutenberg and Füst hath conjured a wide chasm between the past and the future history of mankind: the people of one side the gulf are not the people of the other; the physical force is no longer separated from the moral; mind has by slow degrees crept into the mighty mass—the popular Cymon has received a soul! In the primal and restless consciousness of the new spirit, Luther appealed to the people—the first, since Christ, who so adventured. From that moment all the codes of classic dogmatists were worthless—the expired leases to an estate just let to new tenants, and upon new conditions." Edward Lytton Bulwer, *England and the English* (London, 1833), Vol. II, pp. 257-8.

3. THE PROBLEMS OF REHABILITATION

The *interest* in post-war problems is the post-war problem. The last war and the brave new world which was supposed to have been ushered in after it is a background for scepticism as to the new heaven and the new earth which is predicted after this war. Social security, full employment and the Beveridge and other plans led A. P. Herbert to write:

> Oh, won't it be wonderful after the war
> For there won't be no war and there won't be no pore
> And we'll all have a pension about twenty-four
> And we won't have to work if we think it a bore
> And there won't be no sick and there won't be no sore
> And the beer will be brighter and better and more
> And there's only one question I'd like to explore
> Why didn't we have the old wa'er before?

We are promised much in order that our minds may be taken off the horror of what is going on around us. Much social legislation has been a means of picking our pockets and preventing us from spending in ways which threatened the war effort.

Samuel Johnson who saw something of the effect of wars in the eighteenth century wrote: "In wartime a people only want to hear two things—good of themselves and evil of the enemy. And I know not what is the more to be feared after a war, streets full of soldiers who have learned to rob, or garrets full of scribblers who have learned to lie." In this war we have most to fear from garrets full of scribblers. We have developed a certain resistance to propaganda or a sense of smell. Otherwise it would be difficult to explain the renewed efforts made by governments in setting up various branches for the purpose of informing us. We are being informed apparently with increasing difficulty but we pay in taxes for such resistance as we try to build up.

But neither the last war nor this will blind us to certain elemental facts about the post-war. And the first fact is the loss of life and the loss of the younger, abler and more vigorous part of life. In every sphere of activity, Canadian life since the last war has been impoverished. In politics, law, the church, medicine, business, there is a preponderance of older men or of very young men, with the generation of the last war without representation. That generation has been lost and its scantier numbers have not the strength to maintain their position. By the irony of fate the sons of that generation are being lost. We face the post-war therefore with a fresh depletion of vigorous effective leadership and in a democracy leadership is vital. Nothing counts so much in any community as the energy and training of young men.

The basic post-war problem is that of stopping the loss of blood or the problem of peace. Plans of the new world or of the new international order can be purchased in large quantities at low price. The question remains as to why there are so many plans for the new world. What is the source of the confusion? Why has a century of comparative peace such as prevailed from the end of the Napoleonic Wars to the beginning of the last war been followed by the breakdown of Western Civilization? Why has European civilization turned from persuasion to force or from ballots to bullets? What has brought about a change of such disastrous consequence? In the first place the delicate machinery for maintaining peace in the last century has apparently disappeared. The press thrived on personalities and instability followed. "It was this personal diplomacy, this attempt to base international relations upon personal sentiments and compliments and toasts after dinner, that had seriously disturbed the mind of Bismarck; and it is this attitude that has kept the German Empire in a ferment and all Europe in a state of periodical crises ever since the reign of William II began."[1] "Diplomacy in their hands always meant either veiled menace or tart lecturing, instead of being the great, the difficult, the beneficent art, which it has been in the hands of its worthiest masters, of so reconciling interests, soothing jealous susceptibilities, allaying apprehensions, organizing influences, inventing solutions, that the world may move with something like steadiness along the grooves of deep pacific policy, instead of tossing on a viewless sea of violence and passion."[2] It became difficult to secure a stable basis from which to view the whole with perspective.

In the last century in England, government, especially with regard to external affairs, was relatively stable. About the middle of the century it began to show signs of instability. *The Times* had achieved, by virtue of a substantial monopoly under the taxes on

[1]Extract from D. J. Hill, *Impressions of the Kaiser*, cited C. E. Playne, *The Neuroses of the Nations* (London, 1925), p. 198.

[2]John Morley, *The Life of Richard Cobden* (London, 1881), Vol. II, p. 150.

newspapers, sufficient power to overthrow the Aberdeen government in the Crimea War. Gladstone pointed to the declining efficiency of parliament which followed the disorganized state of parties. "The gift of eloquence has greatly spoilt Parliamentary life. A great deal of time is consumed as every one who thinks he has anything in him wants to speak, even when he has nothing new to say. There are far too many speeches that simply float in the air and pass out through the windows and too few that go straight to the point. The parties have already settled everything beforehand, and the set speeches are merely intended for the public, to show what members can do, and more especially for the newspapers that are expected to praise them. It will come to this in the end, that eloquence will be regarded as dangerous to the public welfare, and that people will be punisfied for making long speeches."[3] Brougham noted that judges had developed a passion for talking and making bad jokes which he attributed to extensive reporting of trials and to the fact that judges spoke for the press. With the arrogance of power *The Times* began to make mistakes. It backed the South against the North in the war between the states. It published documents on the Irish question which were shown to be forgeries. By 1890 it was practically bankrupt and in 1908 it came under the control of Lord Northcliffe. Wickham Steed became foreign editor of *The Times* in January, 1914. In spite of protests from the Foreign Office he wrote a leader on the eve of war stating that Austria and Germany could not count on English neutrality if they made war on Serbia. "In accordance with its best traditions, *The Times* led the country."[4] Charles Lowe, a former *Times* correspondent in Berlin, wrote, "It is my solemn conviction . . . that there were in particular two men—Lord Northcliffe and Leo Maxse—who will have to answer at the bar of history as main contributors . . . to the causes of the world war."[5] In Northcliffe's hand *The Times* became a powerful weapon used to destroy the Asquith Government.

Deterioration of the position of *The Times* was partly a result of the rise of other papers which came with increasing literacy. Politi-

[3]Moritz Busch, *Bismarck: Some secret pages of his history,* Vol. I, pp. 402-3.

[4]H. W. Steed, *Through Thirty Years* (New York, 1924), Vol. I, p. 412.

[5]Charles Lowe, *The Tale of a "Times" correspondent: Berlin 1878-1891* (London, n.d), p. 207.

cians, the courts, the church became aware of a new master—democracy of which the modern newspaper was a reflection. In 1876 the *Daily News* started agitation over the Bulgarian atrocities and this was capitalized by Gladstone. As Wemyss Reid stated, from that time the British public never lost its interest in foreign affairs and domestic matters receded into the background. Foreign affairs are never interesting unless they are exciting and they are far more exciting than questions of domestic legislation.

As early as 1883 Bismarck could say that low water in political affairs, distress in the journalistic world, is the highest testimonial for a minister of foreign affairs. "Happy are the people whose annals are vacant but woe to the wretched journalists that have to compose and write articles therein" (Bagehot). In the small wars which ominously opened this century, the South African War and the Spanish American War, the press for the first time could expand to its fullest extent. Northcliffe in England in the *Daily Mail* and the New York *World* and the *Journal* in New York capitalized the situation to the full. Dilnot wrote of the *Daily Mail*, "Its unconventional procedure in giving prominence to what was of interest instead of merely to what was considered of importance, its rigid rule that every line in the paper should be justified by its interest to a wide circle, its adoption of extremely short articles, its idea of influencing people through its news columns, as well as of recording facts in them—all these things had not only made the *Daily Mail*, but had already brought about something like a revolution in journalism generally."[6] Norman Hapgood described an interview with Arthur Brisbane, "You are at the critical age," Brisbane went on. "In a man's early years enthusiasm and general interest help him, and if he has moderate ability he is likely to do well enough. Around thirty he is in danger of becoming too seriously interested in something and thereby becoming heavy and monotonous."

"He pointed to a row of shelves built into his motor, and filled. "Do you see those books?" he asked. "It is an encyclopedia; there are thirty volumes; I began at the left, have read straight through fifteen volumes, and shall read straight through the rest. There is a little on every subject under the sun. Young man, if you would succeed in journalism never lose your . . . superficiality.

[6]Frank Dilnot, *The Adventures of a Newspaper Man* (London, 1913), pp. 20-21.

"It was a sound warning. In journalism men are likely to worsen as they grow older, and as they lose excitement. There are not many pen-men who, like Voltaire, are most effective in old age."[7]

Since the turn of the century American influence has become increasingly predominant. The success of the German army in the Franco-Prussian war stimulated an interest in Great Britain in educational legislation, extension of the franchise, parliamentary reform and improved living conditions. "The sudden appearance of Germany as the grizzly terror . . . frightened England into America's arms."[8] Germany's payment of bounties on beet sugar destroyed the cane sugar economy of the Caribbean Islands and contributed to the Spanish American War.[9] The difficulties of Great Britain in the South African War encouraged German aggressiveness. France frightened by a falling birth-rate prepared for co-operation with Great Britain in the final settlement of difficulties over the French shore in Newfoundland and in legislation removing the religious question of French education, and with Russia in her Mediterranean policy. Canada was handled through Great Britain by weakening the position of Laurier in relation to the South African War and by the emotional excitement stirred up over the reciprocity treaty[10] and the naval question. The intensity of the reciprocity campaign was expected to offset the ill feeling following the Alaska boundary dispute. She had no alternative but to serve as a football in the international game between great powers.

The ultimate limits of agitation by the press were reached in the last war. They were evident in the Khaki election, Hang the Kaiser, and unfortunately in the Peace. Since the last war the radio has been added and public opinion has become even less stable. "One of the toughest questions is this: When those who formerly were illiterate and negligible rise in importance, as a mass, so that huge and commonplace diversion is manufactured and sold to them, do they constitute an obstacle to a finer civilization, such as was not constituted by the plowing peasant or the skilled personal mechanic,

[7]*The Changing Years—Reminiscences of Norman Hapgood* (New York, 1930), p. 122.

[8]*The education of Henry Adams* (Boston, 1918), p. 363 also pp. 373-4; also Lionel Gelber, *The rise of Anglo-American friendship, a study in world politics, 1898-1906* (Oxford, 1938).

[9]Brooks Adams, *American's economic supremacy* (New York, 1900).

[10]See W. M. Fullerton, *Problems of Power* (New York, 1913), p. 183 ff.

or are they a soil, full of energy, from which will be drawn upwards to the sun, ever more as our knowledge increases, a minority that will increase the light-forming part of humanity? Moving pictures and radio invite the question as much as do the newspapers."[11] Instability of public opinion brings the paradox of long life for administrations because of the fear which obsesses democracy and the ability to capitalize on fears. Bureaucracies must exploit instability in order to show how essential they are. "The man of the new, post-war epoch is, above all, an anguished man, living in the uncertainty of tomorrow, demanding to be relieved from the effort of thinking and of making decisions for himself, in whom physiological misery and profound demoralization have developed a latent instinct of servitude, a need for being regimented and commanded" (Rougier).[12]

The necessity for some reasoned stability; for some courage which will resist extremes, for some emphasis on the rule of law and the avoidance of extremes which characterize public opinion or its alternative, resort to the sword, is evident. It is important to resist propaganda to secure relative stability of government without the fear of change.

The influence of the press has been evident in the saturation of all classes with feelings of instability and bitterness. The Civil War was followed by an intense bitterness over a long period and much the same might be said of all wars since especially if they have involved conscription. The demand for revenge in France which followed the loss of Alsace-Lorraine could be stirred up in all ranks of society. In Canada we have seen the bitterness between language groups stirred up in the last war, and breaking out more violently in this war. National unity except in our right to pay debts and listen to propaganda becomes almost impossible.

Under the circumstances the problem of parties and of governments becomes exceedingly difficult. "The answer is, the Machine; and this must have workers and payment for workers, in other words, entail corruption in some form, and must bring with it a political morality notoriously, almost avowedly, inferior to the morality of ordinary life, so that you will have the lowest principles of

[11]*The Changing Years—Reminiscences of Norman Hapgood* (New York, 1930), pp. 129-30.

[12]N. S. Timasheff, *Introduction in the Sociology of Law* (Cambridge, 1939), p. 228.

action in the highest sphere. But party is now everywhere in a state of disintegration, brought on by the increased restlessness of intelligence, the multiplication of political sects, the clash of special interests, and the enhanced activity of individual ambition, for which there are not enough prizes or bribes. In Germany, in France, in every Parliamentary country, there is now a multiplicity of parties which is making party government impossible."[13] We are in a fair way to having as many parties as we have provinces or regions. The Liberal Party has made an avowed effort to secure regional representation in Ottawa with the result that weak appointments have been made, and that new parties have grown up. And yet we do not have the personnel to man more than two parties. A great difference has arisen in the attitude toward Cabinet Members. In the last century and the early part of this century discussion centred on the capacities of individuals in terms of Cabinet timber but this appears to be no longer the case in any party.

"Parliamentarism only works where there are merely two rival parties that come to power alternately, and where the members of the legislature are well off and unselfish, and do not find it necessary to struggle for their personal advancement. I am no advocate of absolutism. Parliamentarism is good even here [Germany], as a veto upon the resolutions of unwise governments and bad monarchs—for purposes of criticism. In England, up to the present, there have been two great parties, whose principles have latterly not differed very widely, and both desired the welfare of the country and nothing for themselves. They were the representatives of a few hundred families who were well enough off not to want more, and who could therefore study exclusively the welfare of the whole community—a remark which at bottom also applies to Kings, who should be under no necessity to think of their own interests. The Irish are now coming in as a third party, together with the Radicals, who are still more dangerous. It is worse here in Germany. We have eight or ten parties and the leaders are place hunters, who want to improve their own positions and become Ministers, and who also put themselves at the service of the capitalists—not without a consideration" (Jan. 5, 1886).[14]

[13]Goldwin Smith, *Essays on questions of the day* (Toronto, 1893), p. 103.

[14]Moritz Busch, *Bismarck: Some Secret Pages of His History*, Vol. III, p. 152.

The results have been serious in the collapse of conventions of government. The British tradition of anonymity in the Civil Service has been systematically violated. What has been called the new civil service has apparently no sympathy with the traditions of the old service. A civil servant makes public speeches and expounds the policies of the government apparently without any awareness of the principle of anonymity or of responsible government. No one raises a protest and it is assumed as a normal part of government.

The discussion of post-war problems is a symptom of very deeply rooted significance to this country. We can best meet the problem by facing it and not whistling in the dark about the new order. Having faced the problem it becomes clear that we must realize how prodigal we have been with young life, our most cherished possession, and how careful we must be with that which has been left to us. Care in selection and training comes first. The essential training of returned men is a basic post-war problem.

4. A PLEA FOR THE UNIVERSITY TRADITION

Mr. President, your Honour the Lieutenant-Governor, Members of the Senate, fellow graduates, and guests of the University: The President has asked me to say "a few words of wisdom" to my fellow graduates.

I must begin by expressing my appreciation of the high honour which this University has done me in making me a member of its distinguished alumni. This University, like the University of whose staff I have the honour to be a member, has grown from an institution known as King's College, and has been called into existence by a charter from the Crown. The traditional relations of the University to the Crown may be traced from the University of Paris, which the King of France called his eldest daughter. An eldest daughter in any family is an important person. Her imperiousness may lead members of the family to leave the household, and students rebelling against the University of Paris started the University of Oxford. Again students rebelled against the University of Oxford and started Cambridge. Such a daughter will resent encroachments on her rights, and she was not slow to remind even the Papacy, that there were limits to its authority. She had the interests of the family at heart: to her was intrusted the supervision of writing, printing and associated activities connected with manuscripts and books. But the influence of the eldest daughter depends not only on her relation to other members of her family: it depends also on the position of her father. The Crown has always been jealous of the eldest daughter, and in France gradually removed jurisdiction over the press. Under the close paternal supervision of the Crown and the Church, learning migrated in the late sixteenth century and early seventeenth century to Holland. In England, from the quarrel of Henry VIII with the Papacy to the nineteenth century, the Universities were kept under the close supervision of the Crown, with the result that advancement of learning took place to a large extent outside their walls.

In the nineteenth century in England, perhaps in sympathy with the emancipation of women, the Universities were emancipated by science and mathematics at the expense of the humanities. Emancipation after such a long period under the supervision of the Crown, and the discovery of her new freedom, perhaps made this daughter flighty. She began to follow one fashion after another. In the republics where she lost the parental solicitude of the Crown, she became less conservative and even disrespectful as she consorted with one fad and then another, to the neglect of her tradition in the humanities and learning. Her influence was sought by business, by political parties, and by ecclesiastical organizations. She came to be known by the company she kept.

It is in this period that you and I have been introduced to her and made a part of her community. In what fashion can we best contribute to a strengthening of her position? First we must understand her environment. She is besieged on all hands by villains. She no longer represents western civilization as she did in the Middle Ages, when Latin as a common language made it possible for her to serve as a repository of the highest traditions of western culture. The printing press destroyed internationalism, and accentuated the importance of differences in language: these differences were widened by propaganda and by the use of such terms as "race." Growth of science meant an interest in laboratories and buildings: also the neglect of humanities and of an interest in individuals. The social sciences followed science and talked of organization and planning. Professions emerged to narrow her concern in the problems of life. The University lent her ear to those who on all sides told her they had discovered truth, and she forgot that her existence depended on the *search* for truth and not on truth. But with all these distractions throughout her history, since she assumed the mantle for the promotion of learning from the monastic orders, she has preserved an interest in the search for truth. The interest has been *more* or *less* intense as we have seen, but the University as the *studium generale,* the concern with general studies and the problem of knowledge as a whole, has remained.

Her traditions and her interest demand an obsession with balance and perspective—an obsession with the Greek tradition of the humanities. The search for truth assumes a constant avoidance of extremes and extravagance. Virtue is in the middle way. There are no cures. Always we are compelled to be sceptical of the proposal to cure the world's ills. We cannot tolerate the dominance of any individual or of any group. The University of Paris checked in France the virulence which characterized the Inquisition in Spain.

In our time it must resist the tendencies to bureaucracy and dictatorship of the modern State, the intensification of nationalism, the fanaticisms of religion, the evils of monopoly in commerce and industry. "All the triumphs of truth and genius over prejudice and power," said Macaulay, "in every country and in every age have been the triumphs of Athens." "Nor do the artificial concentrations of good minds in more modern capitals approximate even remotely to the intellectual intercourse of Athens. Men of parts move to the capital only when they are already famous, some of them achieve little afterwards, or at any rate not their best, and one might well imagine that it would be better for them to go back to the provinces. There is not much exchange between them; indeed given the present-day notions of intellectual property, exchange would be looked at askance. It is only very vigorous epochs that can give and take without wasting words. Now, a man must be very rich to allow others to take from him without protest, without 'claiming' his ideas as his own, without squabbling about priority. And then comes that intellectual pest of our time—originality. It supplies the need tired men feel for sensation. In the ancient world it was possible, under the beneficent influence of a free intellectual mart, once the truest, simplest and finest expression had been found for anything, to form a consensus. The most striking example is to be seen in visual art, which (even at its zenith) repeated the most excellent types in sculpture, fresco, and we may assume in all forms whose monuments have not come down to us. Originality, must be *possessed,* not striven for. . . . What the free intellectual mart really achieves is the clarity of all expression and the unerring sense of what men want. The arbitrary and the strange are shed, a standard and a style won, while science and art can interact. The productions of any age clearly show whether they came into being under such an influence or not. In their meaner form, they are conventional; in their nobler, classical. The positive and negative sides are always interwoven.

"In Athens, then, intellect comes out free and unashamed, or at any rate can be discerned throughout as if through a light veil, owing to the simplicity of economic life, the voluntary moderation of agriculture, commerce and industry, and the great general sobriety. Citizenship, eloquence, art, poetry and philosophy radiated from the life of the city. We find here no demarcation of classes by rank, no distinction of gentle and simple, no painful struggles to keep up with others in ostentation, no doing the same thing 'for the sake of form,' hence no collapse from overstrain, no Philistia in shirt-sleeves one day and flashy social functions the next. Festivals were a regular feature of life, not a strain. Hence it was possible to develop that social intercourse which is the background of Plato's dialogues. On the other hand, there was no exaggeration of music, for us the cloak which covers a multitude of incongruities, nor was there any false prudery covering a mean and secret malevolence. People had something to say to each other and said it.

"Thus a general understanding was created. Orators and dramatists could reckon with an audience such as had never before existed. People had time and taste for the highest and best, because mind was not drowned in money-making, social distinctions and false decencies. There was comprehension for the sublime, sensitiveness for the subtlest allusions and appreciation of the crassest wit."[1]

In our time, unfortunately, the power of resistance to extremes has been greatly weakened. In Europe the University has largely ceased as a vital force, though we learn of steady persistent refusal in Denmark to grant degrees, and of a determination in Norway to maintain its traditions. It may be that the University has been strengthened by this ordeal of militarism, but the costs are and will be high. Years will be required to repair the damage. In the allied countries energies have been mobilized and the Universities reduced to a skeleton. In Canada staff and student bodies have been depleted. But in the allied countries there has been a recognition of the necessity of preserving the Universities. In Canada the traditions have been cherished. Many of us who suffered from the neglect of these traditions in the last war, and all of us who have felt the loss of the flower of our youth in the years since the last war, have realized that we must not desecrate the memory of those who fell by a similar neglect in this war. Here I must pay tribute to the resolution of representatives of the Maritimes—to the late Norman Rogers who played an important role in the early formation of government policy with relation to the Universities, to President Smith of the Universities Conference, and, if I may be permitted a personal comment, to your own President. It is through their efforts that many of you have been able to take your degree on this day. As a veteran of the last war, as a member of the generations, our comrades and our sons,

[1]Jacob Burckhardt, *Force and Freedom* (New York, 1943), pp. 214, 217.

of this war and the last, it is with the utmost satisfaction that I participate in these ceremonies of a Maritime institution. I must not break faith with the confidence you have shown in me, and I must speak of the problems of scholarship in Canada as you have demanded.

When one has pointed to the efforts to maintain the position of the Universities in Canada, one is still aware, painfully aware, of the low position of scholarship in the Arts faculties, which are the centre of University traditions, in Canadian institutions. In the public mind the scholar is typified as the absent-minded professor, and all too often the professor is thought of as a salesman of patent medicines. Or he is regarded as an agnostic, a free-thinker and a radical whose primary concern is the corruption of youth. The frustration to which Canadian scholars are subjected through lack of facilities in libraries and laboratory equipment in comparison with those of Great Britain and the United States is evident on every hand. We are scarcely within shouting distance of the scholarship of those countries. In spite of our efforts, scholarship in the liberal arts has been interpreted as not even in the national interest. Books written by Canadian scholars are compelled to resort to the presses of other countries or to support from funds from those countries. Scholars in Canada must be forever grateful to their colleagues in Great Britain and the United States for recognition and support. Only by such recognition and support can they maintain an existence, resist the overwhelming pressure to emigrate to take advantage of higher salaries and better facilities, and hope to strengthen their position. Canada makes heavy demands on her scholars. University presidents, with two or three notable exceptions, including your own, have shown little interest in scholarship. The arts tradition has largely disappeared in appointments—the Church, Law and Business are drawn upon instead. If anyone thinks that University presidents are interested in scholarship, in the humanities and the social sciences in the Faculty of Arts, let him read their pronouncements on those subjects. They are willing to do anything for the Arts courses but get off their backs.[2] In the main they are not

[2]The scholar must regard a University President as Diogenes regarded Alexander. All a President can do is to stand out of the light. An administrator is compelled to make up his mind and make decisions whereas a scholar is under obligation not to make up his mind.

themselves appointed because they are scholars, and it is possible that they never will be and possibly never should be. While it has been the rule to appoint scholars to administrative posts in Great Britain and in the United States, the general low opinion of scholars in Canada makes it largely impracticable.

With the weakening of the power of the Crown, the University has been left to the tender mercies of a stepfather in a Board of Governors. A University president in Canada is required to have some of the qualities of the superintendents of lunatic asylums or of ring masters in circuses. But they should be appointed from those concerned with the protection of scholars against colonialism, imperialism, nationalism, ecclesiasticism, academic nepotism, political affiliations and the demands of special groups and classes, and with encouragement of scholars concerned with the search for truth. The presidents of state institutions are exposed to political influence chiefly through boards of governors. The organization of Canadian Universities tends to have the vices of British and American institutions and the virtues of neither; boards of governors have been known deliberately to torture scholars and students in the interests of political demands. They have been known deliberately to interfere with the content of courses in the interests of particular groups or classes, political parties or ecclesiastical organizations. Apparently they have felt compelled to lend themselves to the systematic rape of scholarship. The suppression of scholarship brings the distortion of scholarship and the necessity for more suppression. Austere associations of scholars have been known to devote whole sessions of their meetings to the discussion of political platforms, and the politician has always been on hand to share in the reflected dignity of discussion and to enjoy the appearance of being taken seriously. No wonder the younger parties have been able to exploit the scholar in their own fashion, when older parties exploit and suppress him in theirs. Nothing has been more indicative of the decline in cultural life in Canada since the last war than the infiltration of politics in the Universities, and nothing has done more to hamper the development of intellectual maturity than the institutional framework of Canadian Universities which permits and encourages the exploitation of scholars, and plays the treasonable role of betraying the traditions for which we fought in the last war and for which we fight in this. Men did not suffer and give their lives for this. This is not a pleasant subject, and is not to be explored further on this occasion. Nor is it the fault of any person or group of persons. The deterioration of intellectual life does not admit of scapegoats. It has come about partly as a result of administrative machinery which has failed to check the inroads of politics and to protect the scholar. Such machinery has been of little avail with the marked decline of interest in classical studies, the disappearance of a generation of scholars from Great Britain, and our inability to replace them effectively with native stock; also, I am sorry to say, with the enormous extension of interest in the social sciences. "Constitutional, radical, social claims were being put forward, supported by the general equalization of rights, and, by the way of the press, were reaching the public on a gigantic scale. Political science became common property, statistics and political economy the arsenal from which everybody took the weapons he could best wield. Every movement was oecumenical. The Church, however, seemed to be nothing but an irrational force; religion was desired, but without the Church."[3] But the University tradition to which we have been formally admitted in these ceremonies compels us to be ever alert to the possibility of protesting against distortion, and of fighting for conditions which make it possible for scholarship to survive and flourish. Scholars have no weapons with which to combat organizations of power always insidiously waiting to prey on them. We have most to lose from encroachments of power. "Power is of its nature evil, whoever wields it. . . . Art and Science have the greatest difficulty in preventing themselves from sinking into a mere branch of urban money-making, and from being carried away on the stream of general unrest. The utmost effort and self-denial will be necessary if they are to remain creatively independent in view of the relation in which they stand to the daily press, to cosmopolitan traffic, to world exhibitions. A further menace is the decay of local patriotism, with its advantages and disadvantages, and a great decrease even in national patriotism."[4]

The arrangement by which Boards of Governors in North American institutions and particularly in Canadian institutions are appointed without reference to the academic staff implies a theory which has reference to public opinion. Members are appointed by governments which provide the funds for political reasons. The

[3]*Ibid.*, p. 226.
[4]*Ibid.*, pp. 297-8.

Presidents appointed by such Boards of Governors are compelled to bridge the gap between the scholarly interest of the staff and the political interest of the Boards and of governments. This is almost a superhuman task, and involves extremely heavy demands on Presidents. Universities have grown beyond the high-school stage of development which this arrangement suggests, and maturity involves a study of the political science of University administration with a view to proper recognition of the role of the scholar and of the University in the nation's life.

The efforts to maintain the traditions of the University are in themselves a testimony to these traditions. As recent graduates, we dedicate ourselves afresh to the maintenance of a tradition without which western culture disappears. We pay tribute to the memory of those who fell in the last war, and of those who have fallen in this war, by the ceremonies in which we have participated. These ceremonies peculiar to an institution which has played the leading role in the flowering of western culture remind us of the obligation of maintaining traditions concerned with the search for truth for which men have laid down and have been asked to lay down their lives.

5. THE UNIVERSITY IN THE MODERN CRISIS

It is to the sober thoughts of those of you who are graduating in this war that a graduate of two wars hopes to appeal. Your Chancellor has asked me to speak on our position as fellow graduates at this time. We are graduating because men have laid down their lives in order that the traditions represented by universities should flourish. I cannot do better than quote a part of that moving funeral oration of Pericles.

For we have compelled everyland and every sea to open a path for our valour, and have everywhere planted eternal memorials of our friendship and of our enmity. Such is the city for whose sake these men nobly fought and died; they could not bear the thought that she might be taken from them; and every one of us who survive should gladly toil on her behalf. I would have you day by day fix your eyes upon the greatness of Athens, until you become filled with love of her; and when you are impressed by the spectacle of her glory, reflect that this empire has been acquired by men who know their duty and had the courage to do it, who in the hour of conflict had the fear of dishonour always present to them, and who, if ever they failed in an enterprise would not allow their virtues to be lost to their country, but freely gave their lives to her as the fairest offering which they could present at the feast. The sacrifice which they collectively made was individually repaid to them; for they received again and again each one for himself a praise which grows not old and the noblest of all sepulchres—I speak not of that in which their remains are laid, but of that in which their glory survives and is proclaimed always and on every fitting occasion both in word and deed. For the whole earth is the sepulchre of famous men; not only are they commemorated by columns and inscriptions in their own country, but in foreign lands there dwells also an unwritten memorial of them, graven not on stone but in the hearts of men. Make them your example.[1]

In following their example we will always be aware that they have gone and that we are the weaker for their loss. It is futile to talk of a brave new world when our youngest and best through whose efforts we might have achieved it have been taken from us. Our first duty to the memory of those who have given their lives is to face the facts of our impoverishment and to avoid dishonouring that memory by delusions of a better world. Most of you know the words

[1]*Cited* J. B. Bury, *A History of Greece.*

of John Donne *For Whom the Bell Tolls,* but I would like to read the full paragraph. "No man is an Iland, intire of itselfe; every man is a peece of the continent; a part of the maine; if a clod bee washed away by the sea, Europe is the lesse, as well as if a Promontorie were; any man's death diminishes me, because I am involved in mankinde; and therefore never send to know for whom the bell tolls; it tolls for thee."

The university must play its major role in the rehabilitation of civilization which we have witnessed in this century by recognizing that western civilization has collapsed. It is the duty of those of us who have participated in this ceremony to discuss the strategy of recovery. This University, which represents the great tradition of freedom from state control, offers a platform on which we may be able to discuss the problems of civilization. We stand on a small and dwindling island surrounded by the flood of totalitarianism. Universities supported by the state have seen the disappearance of freedom of speech and freedom of the press, to say nothing of academic freedom. Privately endowed and denominational universities have their own problems of academic freedom, but state-supported institutions not only have the same problems but also those of political influence. Perhaps the lowest level has been reached in institutions dependent on single occupations. Political pressure becomes direct and disastrous and defeats even the interest of the political groups particularly concerned. But this is only an extreme illustration of an almost universal phenomenon. I am grateful for this opportunity to speak under the protection of an outstanding university free of state support and state dictation, an institution which perpetuates the "discovery reserved for the English separatists" who grasped sincerely and vigorously the principle that "it is only by abridging the authority of states that the liberty of churches can be assured" (Acton).

Bertrand Russell has pointed to the decline of respect for intelligence except in the subject of money and international affairs. But the social sciences scarcely expect a continued refuge even in these complex fields. The professions which have a long tradition and emphasize technical knowledge such as law, medicine and the natural sciences become more difficult, with the result that the attention of the public is turned toward the social sciences. The ivory lab destroys the ivory tower. These subjects are simplified and delivered through adult education courses. The more difficult subjects, such as money, have remained mysterious and accordingly have been exploited in the interests of those who care to exploit them.

The mechanization of modern society compels increasing interest in science and the machine, and attracts the best minds from the most difficult problems of western civilization. The machine is devoted to the simplification of these problems. The technological advantages in communication shown in the newspaper, the cinema and the radio demand the thinning out of knowledge to the point where it interests the lowest intellectual levels and brings them under the control of totalitarian propaganda. The disappearance of the newspaper editorial has been offset by the rise of the comic strip. No group interested in problems of communication can escape the demands of mechanization. State radio stations, adult education programmes, university extension courses all point to the pressure on universities. Nor are universities unwilling to participate in these activities, particularly if they are dependent on public opinion to support their budgets. They become directly concerned in popularizing university education, in condensing whole courses into a single lecture, and in providing cheap if wholesome entertainment. I have already referred in this hall to the boundless confidence shown by university presidents in the efficacy of innumerable speeches in attracting favourable attention to the university. Universities have by no means restricted their efforts to the direct selling of their wares to the public—we have to live—but have sanctioned indirect methods. Low salaries may be made up by leasing competent entertainers, who occasionally find their way into academic circles, to business firms which have a need for this particular type of entertainer in their advertising programmes. I should say of course that the commodities sold in this fashion are dependable. The word "professor" has not always been associated on this continent with the sale of dependable goods. We need a study of the professor as sandwich man—perhaps a doctoral thesis.

This is not to question the competency of business firms to judge as to the value of the entertainment. But one must question the judgment of business men as to the limitations of still another development in universities. Various well-meaning business firms have been actively sponsoring institutes and courses of particular interest to themselves or to what they allege is the general interest of business. For example, industrial relations institutes have been put forward with much unction, but even a university can see that these may every easily become devices for buying the prestige of a university in the interests of capital. Labour groups will be certain that they are precisely such devices, and whatever may be the results of such organizations, the universities will be charged as one of the kept institutions of capitalism. The attempt of business men or of labour or of any group to dictate appointments, type of research, conditions under which the results of research shall be made available, and course of instruction, in the case of state universities, is an attempt to twist the use of public funds in particular directions and to destroy the confidence in, and the prestige of universities. For all universities it is a crime against the traditions of western civilization for which men have been asked to lay down, and have laid down their lives.

When universities weakened by the demands of the war and faced with the obligation of teaching men and women returning from active service are asked to support the demands of various groups, they are asked to betray their traditions. Business and political exploitation of universities by bribes reflects a complete inability to understand that universities honour donors and not donors universities. The impression that universities can be bought and sold, held by business men and fostered by university administrators trained in playing for the highest bid, is a reflection of the deterioration of western civilization. To buy universities is to destroy them and with them the civilization for which they stand. As one of the administrators of my university has said, "A university is not a cheese factory," nor is it a billboard on which advertisers can post their wares. It is to yield to the essential bias of a civilization based on commerce and not to realize that the university is older than modern commerce. We can agree with Mill that "The spirit of a commercial people will be, we are persuaded, essentially mean and slavish, whenever public spirit is not cultivated by an extensive participation of the people in the business of government in detail. Where power extends in advance of education, the art of organizing delusion threatens to keep pace with the agencies which aim at diffusing enlightenment."

It has been said not ineptly of the objectives of universities, "Whatever ideas may be brought to us from whatever source, we will hear them; if they are false we will explode them; if partly true we will sift them; if wholly true, we will accept them—but always provisionally, always pressing onward and seeking something better" (Peter Finley Dunne). Following Locke, "To love truth for truth's sake is the principal part of human perfection in this world and the seed plot of all other virtues."

The descent of the university into the market place reflects the lie in the soul of modern society. The effects are evident in the extreme difficulty of securing recognition for Canadian scholars and of university traditions. They are not recognized by boards of governors or administrators. All across Canada there is an emphasis on buildings, courses, research in applied science and money, and a constant neglect of men. The treatment of scholars in Canadian universities is a standing disgrace. A scholar can only survive by securing recognition outside Canada and even then it will be jealously denied and grudgingly conceded. Instead of recognizing scholars, emphasis is placed on teaching and the adding of new courses. The shift to science accentuated by the war has been offset by the addition of courses in the social sciences and the humanities in the professional schools. A move such as Max Beerbohm proposed of holding veiling ceremonies for unsightly statues in London might well be followed in the university curriculum. The dropping of courses would lighten the loads of members of staff and students so that philosophical interest rather than memorized knowledge might become the rule.

The definition of education given by Milton has never been improved upon. "I call a complete and generous education that which gets a man to perform justly, skilfully, and magnanimously, all the offices, both public and private, of peace and war. . . . It requires much observation of young minds to discover that the rapid inculcation of unassimilated information stupefies the faculties instead of training them."[2] To Lord Elgin is attributed the definition that education fits one for nothing and prepares him for everything. Mark Pattison has enlarged on this subject with advantage. "The necessary tendency of advancing civilization is to divide and subdivide the applications, as of labour, so of thought. The professions tend to split up into branches; and skill in one becomes more and more incompatible with skill in another. The more a subject has been explored, the more time does it take each succeeding student to follow the steps of his predecessors. To prevent the disabling effects

[2]Mark Pattison, *Milton* (London, 1932), pp. 48-9.

of this specialty of pursuit, it becomes the more requisite to secure at starting a breadth of cultivation, a scientific formation of mind, a concert of the intellectual faculties. There is an organization of thought as well as of labour. What is wanted is to get this recognized as the proper remedy; and to have it understood that this commanding superiority, this enlargement of mind, this grasp of things as they are, this clear-sightedness, sagacity, philosophical reach of mind, is to a great degree communicable by training. We, indeed, are far from estimating this power by its applicability. Mental enlargement we know to be self-valuable not useful, but if it can be introduced to notice under colour of being useful in life, so be it, so only that it is introduced. The difficulty is to get the thing recognized at all by those who have it not. Cleverness, talent, skill, fluency, memory, all these are understood and rated in the market. A cultivated mind, just because it is above all price, is apt to be overlooked altogether."[3]

The distrust of universities has become a distressing subject. In one of the provinces of this nation the provincial government has decided to set up its own adult education programme on the ground that the university programme is completely inadequate. In some provinces the departments of political economy are actively solicited to support the prestige of the party and in others the departments are consistently avoided as a prospective menace.

The university has inevitably been a contributor to the breakup of national life. The problem of French and English understanding is as nothing compared to the problems of understanding the programmes of numerous Canadian parties. Regional ideologies are built up on adult education and universities. The English language is deliberately built up as a framework for hocus pocus and unintelligibility. The tendency for each province to have its own party and its own university emphasizes the necessity for special platforms with no possibility of a common approach through rationality. Irrationality assumes fresh importance as a means of capitalizing the necessity of unintelligibility and deliberately avoiding rational contacts. A confederation such as Canada becomes a nation of warring provinces. Irrationality introduces fear and the necessity of bureaucracies as at least a protection in continuity against the frequent changes incidental to fashion. Bureaucracies in the provinces necessitate bureaucracy in Ottawa and bureaucracy in Ottawa compels

[3]*Essays by the late Mark Pattison* (Oxford, 1899), p. 460.

bureaucracies in the provinces. The blight of Oriental despotism which has ever threatened the western world becomes evident in bureaucracy and in turn in militarism. The interest in peace of an intelligent commercial and capitalist society is displaced by the control of the state in bureaucracy, militarism and war.

Political regionalism poisons cultural life in Canada. Nationalism is exploited in the interest of innumerable groups in universities and in other institutions. At times it appears as a device for increasing debts, again as a subject of exploitation by publishers. Authors' associations, writers' associations and the like have an unhealthy number of publishers and publicity agents. And there follows the nauseating back-scratching by editors and authors and the deterioration of standards such as will be evident to anyone caring to make an intensive study of medals and awards. Subterfuges become a part of our national heritage. I am told that Toronto publishers have a rule that the word Toronto must be left out of all their publications. In educational circles all of us know that no scholar can be born outside the Maritime Provinces. Political life has become a blazing furnace burning off material which might have been used for the development of a broad cultural base. The over-emphasis on politics and economics and the social sciences has destroyed a sense of perspective and the necessity of a study of perspective. We have failed to realize that the social sciences have been disastrously weakened by the neglect of a study of their limitations.

These problems are an evidence of the fundamental difficulties of western civilization. The division of the western world in the Roman Empire between Rome and Constantinople created problems which at long last we are compelled to face. Græco-Roman civilization persisted particularly in the influence of Roman law. Following Maine, "It is precisely because the influence of jurisprudence begins to be powerful that the foundation of Constantinople and the subsequent separation of the Western Empire from the Eastern are epochs in philosophical history."[4] . . . "I affirm without hesitation that the difference between the two theological systems is accounted for by the fact that, in passing from the East to the West, theological speculation had passed from a climate of Greek metaphysics to a climate of Roman law. For some centuries before these controversies rose into overwhelming importance, all the intellectual activity of

[4]Sir Henry Sumner Maine, *Ancient Law* (London, 1906), p. 352.

the Western Romans had been expended on jurisprudence exclusively. They had been occupied in applying a peculiar set of principles to all the combinations in which the circumstances of life are capable of being arranged. No foreign pursuit or taste called off their attention from this engrossing occupation, and for carrying it on they possessed a vocabulary as accurate as it was copious, a strict method of reasoning, a stock of general propositions on conduct more or less verified by experience, and a rigid moral philosophy."[5] If we agree with Professor Whitehead that "The safest generalization of the European philosophical tradition is that it consists in a series of footnotes to Plato," we are forced to conclude that its power succumbed in the face of the Industrial Revolution and machine industry and the rise of romanticism. We have seen the effects of the disappearance of the Platonic tradition in the necessity of appealing to force as the unifying and dominating factor. In the words of the late Justice Holmes, "Truth is the majority vote of the nation that can lick all the others." With this collapse Western society has been left exposed to the necessity of meeting the demands of the Eastern empire represented by Russia. The totalitarian state based on the union of church and state which persisted in the Eastern empire and in Russia has emerged as the problem of our time in the West.

These fundamental problems must be faced by the universities. We can no longer temporize. Much ground remains to be recovered. "We are trying to do many and various things and are driven to versatility and short cuts at some expense to truth and depth" (Cooley). Sorokin, a Russian refugee, has remarked that "Step by step we become generous toward the whole of mankind and rather cruel to a living man. We love the whole world, not loving particularly any human being. We talk of the welfare of mankind, not taking any particular care of anybody."[6] The Calvinist tradition of the democracies tends to become inadequate. "Down to the present day the peculiar nature of this structure stamps the life of the Calvinistic peoples with a unique emphasis on the cultivation of independent personality, which leads to a power of initiative and a sense of responsibility for action, combined also with a very strong sense of unity for common, positive ends and values, which are invulnerable

[5] *Ibid.*, p. 367.

[6] P. Sorokin, *Social Mobility* (New York, 1927), p. 543.

on account of their religious character. This explains the fact that all the Calvinistic peoples are characterized by individualism and by democracy, combined with a strong bias towards authority and a sense of the unchangeable nature of law. It is this combination which makes a conservative democracy possible, whereas in Lutheran and Catholic countries, as a matter of course, democracy is forced into an aggressive and revolutionary attitude."

Lecky in the last pages of *The History of the Rise and Influence of the Spirit of Rationalism in Europe,* stated the ultimate problem: "The decay of the old spirit of loyalty, the destruction of asceticism, and the restriction of the sphere of charity, which has necessarily resulted from the increased elaboration of material civilization, represent successive encroachments on the field of self-sacrifice which have been very imperfectly compensated and have given our age a mercenary, venal, and unheroic character, that is deeply to be deplored. A healthy civilization implies a double action—the action of great bodies of men moving with the broad stream of their age, and eventually governing their leaders; and the action of men of genius or heroism upon the masses, raising them to a higher level, supplying them with nobler motives or more comprehensive principles, and modifying, though not altogether directing the general current. The first of these forms of action is now exhibited in great perfection. The second has but little influence in practice, and is almost ignored in speculation."

"This is the shadow resting upon the otherwise brilliant picture the history of Rationalism presents. The destruction of the belief in witchcraft and of religious persecution, the decay of those ghastly notions concerning future punishments, which for centuries diseased the imaginations and embittered the characters of men, the emancipation of suffering nationalities, the abolition of the belief in the guilt of error, which paralysed the intellectual, and of the asceticism, which paralysed the material progress of mankind, may be justly regarded as among the greatest triumphs of civilization; but when we look back to the cheerful alacrity with which, in some former ages, men sacrificed all their material and intellectual interests to what they believed to be right, and when we realize the unclouded assurance that was their reward, it is impossible to deny that we have lost something in our progress."

Rashdall has described the rôle of the university: "But the

name has got to be associated with education of the highest type: to degrade the name of a university is therefore to degrade our highest educational ideal. . . . It is natural and desirable again that efforts should be made to diffuse knowledge and intellectual interests among all classes by means of evening lectures. The English universities may well be proud of having taken the initiative in a movement of the most far-reaching social and political significance. But it would be a delusion, and a mischievous delusion, to suppose that evening lectures, however excellent and however much supplemented by self-education, can be the same thing as the student-leisure of many years, duly prepared for by a still longer period of regular school training. Examinations too, and private preparation for them, are an excellent thing in their proper place: but it is a mistake to suppose that an examining board can discharge any but the very lowest of a university's real functions. The two most essential functions which a true university has to perform, and which all universities have more or less discharged amid the widest possible variety of system and method and organization, hardly excepting even the periods of their lowest degradation, are to make possible the life of study, whether for a few years or during a whole career, and to bring together during that period, face to face in living intercourse, teacher and teacher, teacher and student, student and student."

. . . "But it behoves us not to lose or lower the ideal of the university as the place *par excellence* for professed and properly trained students, not for amateurs or dilettantes or even for the most serious of leisure-hour students; for the highest intellectual cultivation, and not merely for elementary instruction or useful knowledge, for the advancement of Science, and not merely for its conservation or diffusion; as the place moreover where different branches of knowledge are brought into contact and harmonious combination with one another, and where education and research advance side by side. . . ."[7]

It remains to say that you and I have become today members of a community which in a very real sense is the life of Western civilization and that we here dedicate ourselves to its maintenance and enrichment. There have been few convocations in the history of that civilization in which the demands for our devotion have been

[7]Hastings Rashdall, *Universities of Europe in the Middle Ages* (Oxford, 1895), pp. 714-5.

greater. There have been few convocations in which our devotion has been so clearly demanded as in the midst of a second world war in a century which has witnessed a major collapse of civilization. There are few institutions in which the traditions of a university have been so firmly held. We are here because men and women have laid down and are asked to lay down their lives. We dare not desert the tradition for which they have made the ultimate sacrifice.

6. ON THE ECONOMIC SIGNIFICANCE OF CULTURAL FACTORS

I

In discussing the limitations of economic history or of the social sciences or more specifically of the framework of the price system, we can improve our perspective regarding the place of the field of economic history and in turn of the social sciences in Western civilization. We need a sociology or a philosophy of the social sciences and particularly of economics, an economic history of knowledge or an economic history of economic history. Economic history may enable us to understand the background of economic thought or of the organization of economic thought or of thought in the social sciences. The influence of the Greeks on philosophy and in turn on universities compels us to raise questions about the limitations of the social sciences.

We must somehow overcome what Leslie Stephen calls the "weakness for omniscience which infects most historical critics."[1]

> The Walrus and the Carpenter
> Were walking close at hand:
> They wept like anything to see
> Such quantities of sand:
> "If this were only cleared away,"
> They said, "it *would* be grand."
>
> "If seven maids with seven mops
> Swept it for half a year,
> Do you suppose," the Walrus said,
> "That they could get it clear?"
> "I doubt it," said the Carpenter,
> And shed a bitter tear.

Economics implies the application of scarce means to given ends, and the vast range of social phenomena compels a similar strategy of approach.

Within the broad subject of the social sciences we can see clearly the use of obvious strategies. The impact of the natural sciences and machine industry has been evident in the emphasis on pecuniary

[1]*History of English Thought in the Eighteenth Century* (London, 1876), Vol 1, p. 438.

phenomena which are particularly suited to mathematics and mechanical devices developed in relation to mathematics. As slot machines have been built up around the sizes and weights of various denominations of coins so there has been a tendency for economics to be built up around the monetary structure. Walter Leaf wrote of three main causes disposing men to madness—love, ambition, and the study of currency problems, with the last named as the worst. Bamberger wrote that people go mad because of love and bimetallism. Sorokin has described the importance of the quantitative approach in modern society, fittingly enough in four large volumes, and has deplored the emphasis on economic questions as peculiar to the approach.

> Left to themselves all find their level price,
> Potatoes, verses, turnips, Greek, and rice, . . .[2]

The pecuniary slant of economics is as evident in Veblen's elaboration of the pecuniary economy of North America as in the discussion by monetary theorists of liquidity preference. I need hardly refer to the work of the committee on price studies and the important contributions of those working under its directions, mentioning only the studies of Bezanson, Cole, and Hamilton.

The widespread interest in prices reflected in economics and in economic history has effectively broadened the approach to history and corrected the bias which emphasized military exploits or political activities. The state and other organizations of centralized power have had a vital interest in records of their activities and have given powerful direction to the study of political, legal, constitutional, and ecclesiastical history. The mechanics of archival organization have given enormous impetus to the writing of history from the standpoint of centralized power. Administrative machinery and preservation of records have impressed on historical writing the imprint of the state and fostered the bias which made history the handmaid of politics. In the eighteenth century rigid censorship fostered evasions in the form of histories written as political weapons. An interest in history is still fostered as a means of strengthening the church or the state, and the demands of particular groups are reflected even in economic history. The honorific position of military, legal, and

[2]Cited in A. S. Collins, *The Profession of Letters: A Study of the Relation of Author to Patron, Publisher, and Public, 1780-1832* (London: G. Routledge and Sons, 1928), p. 120.

ecclesiastical groups is evident in the history text-book, a form of historical writing which is extremely sensitive to political demands and to nationalistic interests. Scholarship is harassed by the demands of pressure groups. Even though price history has a bias of its own, it can check tendencies favourable to power groups. Economic history can point to the dangers of bias and the necessity for a broader perspective.

On the other hand, the pecuniary approach, when all pervasive, tends to obscure the significance of technology and workmanship. It has threatened to make economics a branch of high accountancy.

> The modern tendency to find mental satisfaction in measuring everything by a fixed rational standard, and the way it takes for granted that everything can be related to everything else, certainly receives from the apparently objective value of money, and the universal possibility of exchange which this involves, a strong psychological impulse to become a fixed habit of thought, whereas the purely logical process itself, when it only follows its own course, is not subject to these influences, and it then turns these accepted ideas into mere probabilities.[3]

Concentration on the price system, driven by mathematics, involves neglect of the technological conditions under which prices operate. The use of liquidity preference as a concept in the study of economic history emphasizes short-run points of view acceptable to the price system rather than long-run points of view which necessitate perspective. An equilibrium of approaches to the study of economic phenomena becomes exceedingly difficult to achieve with the insistence on short-run interests and the obsession with the present. There is in the social sciences a liquidity preference for

[3]Ernst Troeltsch, *The Social Teaching of the Christian Churches* (London: George Allen and Unwin, 1931), Vol. I, p. 408. For a suggestive account of the far-reaching implications of objectivity reflected by the mathematics of the price system, see the description of baseball in Victor O. Jones, "Box Score!" *Newsmen's Holiday* (Cambridge: Harvard University Press, 1942), pp. 162-82: "The one thing which distinguishes baseball from all other sports and which has been the main reason for 'organized baseball's' hold upon the public is its development of a statistical side" (pp. 165-66). For a discussion of the importance of statistics in politicial propaganda see F. C. Bartlett, *Political Propaganda* (Cambridge: Cambridge University Press, 1940), pp. 93-4. "When a statement is 'quantified' it seems to convey to the majority of persons a superior certainty, and it passes without question."—*Ibid.*, p. 94. The Gallup Poll has possibly made politics more absorbing. But statistics has been particularly dangerous to modern society by strengthening the cult of economics and weakening other social sciences and the humanities.

theories concerned with the present which is more dangerous in its implications than liquidity preference is to monetary stability. Marx and his followers sharpened awareness of pressure groups and emphasized the importance of the study of technology and the means of production. While Schumpeter has attempted to bridge the pecuniary and the technological approaches and to avoid the danger of concentrating on the price system and the profit motive and on technology, his efforts have meant the sacrifice of too much in both approaches and particularly in the technological. Moreover he deliberately neglects the important work of political historians. The late N. J. Silberling made a more successful attempt to co-ordinate the political, pecuniary, and technological approaches but his work was limited by national boundaries. In part, the weakness of the technological approach has been a result of the restricted knowledge of technical development. The work of Nef on coal, of Usher on mechanical inventions, and of a large number of students in the field must be supplemented extensively. Such work must emphasize not only technical changes but their significance to economic and political institutions. The interest in legislation, court decisions, and legal systems shown by Commons should be integrated with the work of the historian of prices, technology, and government. Sir Henry Sumner Maine made a comment of profound significance when he pointed to the interrelation of legislation, prices, and technology and the mathematical bias.

> Experience shows that innovating legislation is connected not so much with Science as with the scientific air which certain subjects, not capable of exact scientific treatment, from time to time assume. To this class of subjects belonged Bentham's scheme of Law-Reform, and, above all, Political Economy as treated by Ricardo. Both have been extremely fertile sources of legislation during the last fifty years.[4]

The vast range of studies of business cycles and their significance to unemployment would gain perceptibly by the integration of basic approaches. The conflict between technology and the price system described by Veblen in *The Engineer and the Price System,* in which the restrictions on technology have been of primary concern, can be resolved more easily with a broader perspective. A broader synthesis would enable us to counteract the regression in thought shown by

[4] *Popular Government* (London, 1885), p. 146.

Schumpeter and Polanyi who regard monopoly as a means of resisting the effects of obsession with the short run. In technology as in the price system, advance has been supported by mathematics, but the effectiveness of the application of mathematics varies in the two fields and may make for divergence rather than convergence in the study of economic phenomena as a whole. Since there has been a very perceptible lag in the spread of mathematics in relation to the price system, engineers and scientists such as Douglas and Soddy, social-credit theorists, technocrats, and others have taken advantage of the gap. But it is possible that God is not a mathematician as some philosophers would have us believe.

The intensive demands of technology on students in the social sciences have contributed to the narrowness of its approach and such narrowness has been intensified by the emphasis that political and military history put on nationalism. The important contributions of geography have been restricted to studies of localization such as those of Alfred Weber and of Usher. The significance of basic geographic features has been suggested by Mahan from the standpoint of the sea and by Mackinder from the standpoint of continental land masses but they have not been incorporated effectively in economic history. Nor do we have an effective study of air. In a general way we are familiar with the influence of the sea on the development of democratic institutions in Greece and of the land on the centralizing tendencies of Rome. Although we can trace the influence of Roman institutions in the codified law of Europe and in the Roman Catholic Church as adapted to a continent, and can see the growth of parliamentary institutions and Protestantism in the Anglo-Saxon world in relation to the demands of the sea, it may be doubted whether we appreciate their significance to economic history. But the effects of geography may be offset by technology in that the development of defensive tactics led to the growth of feudalism and the use of gunpowder brought a return to efficient offensive tactics and to increasing centralization in the Western world. Geography provides the grooves which determine the course and to a large extent the character of economic life. Population, in terms of numbers and quality, and technology are largely determined by geographic background, and political institutions have been to an important extent shaped through wars in relation to this background.

II

Geography has been effective in determining the grooves of economic life through its effects on transportation and communication. The lower costs of tonnage by sea than by land strengthened the position of Great Britain in the development of trade in more bulky commodities suited to industrial growth and expansion. France, Spain, and Portugal with a continental background developed connections with the continental hinterlands of the New World. As the late Max Handmann suggested, the Anglo-Dutch trading systems expanded in relation to the sea, continental feudalism in relation to the land. The expansion of Great Britain was in terms of the migration of Englishmen and the development of industries, either, as in the northern colonies, by using English labour in the production of bulky commodities or, in the tropical regions, by organizing imported labour on a large scale for the production of sugar and cotton. Spanish feudalism and militarism exploited native labour primarily for precious metals, and French feudalism for furs. British expansion linked trade with naval strength and limited financial burdens, whereas French expansion meant trade and military strength and enormous demands on finance for the construction of forts and the maintenance of garrisons and bureaucracies. But British maritime expansion meant parliamentary institutions and decentralization characteristic of the Anglo-Saxon world. Federalism became an important feature. In Canada feudalism continued in the ownership of natural resources by the provinces and produced the dual mixture of a capitalistic federal government and feudalistic provincial governments.

The advantages to Great Britain of maritime expansion and of access, with low costs of navigation, to cheap supplies of bulky goods were accompanied by the development of coal mining and industry. Coal began to pull raw materials from the fringes of the Atlantic basin and beyond, and to provide the power for conversion of the raw materials into finished products for export. The effectiveness of the pull began to vary with distances, and distances changed with improvements in manufacturing and particularly in transportation. Timber and cotton from the northern and southern parts of North America could be transported to Great Britain, and penetration to the interior with canals and railways brought steadily expanding trade first in wheat and then in the products of animal husbandry. Successive waves of commodities responded to the lowering of costs of navigation across the Atlantic and of transportation to the interior. As wheat production moved to the interior, older areas became concerned with the production of other commodities. England shifted her fields from arable land to pasture. In these broad trends we see the basis of the stages outlined by Gras and his students in the description of the growth of the metropolitan economy. In the general migration and shift in production of raw materials and, in turn, of semifinished and finished products, we can see the problems that the late Frederick Turner described in his work on the frontiers. Disturbances to these more or less regular trends were a result of sudden developments in which costs were lowered, of geographic factors such as access to the great plains and obstruction by mountains, of cyclonic activities such as accompanied the gold rushes around the fringes of the Pacific, and of the development of new sources of power in the opening up of the coal regions of North America.

The emergence of a complex industrial and trading structure centring about the coal areas of the Anglo-Saxon world assumed not only improvements in transportation but also in communication. Correspondence between individuals and firms with slow navigation, on which Heaton has thrown much light, was inadequate to meet the demands of large-scale industry and large-scale consumption. The rapid and extensive dissemination of information was essential to the effective placing of labour, capital, raw materials, and finished products. Oscar Wilde wrote that "private information is practically the source of every large modern fortune."[5] and the demand for private information hastened the development of communications. The application of steam power to the production of paper and, in turn, of the newspaper, followed by the telegraph, and the exploitation of human curiosity and its interest in news by advertisers anxious to dispose of their products created efficient channels for the spread of information. The state, acting through subsidies, the post office, libraries, and compulsory education, widened the areas to which information could be disseminated. Democratic forms of government provided news and subsidies for the transmission of news.

[5]*An Ideal Husband*, Act II.

As Carlyle wrote, "He who first shortened the labour of copyists by device of *movable types* was disbanding hired armies and cashiering most kings and senates, and creating a whole new democratic world: he had invented the art of printing."[6]

With the rise of a vast area of public opinion, which was essential to the rapid dissemination of information, and the growth in turn of marketing organizations, the expansion of credit, and the development of nationalism, the vast structure previously centring about religion declined. Eric Gill wrote, "Where religion is strong, commerce is weak," but religion played an important role in the growth of commerce. The significance of religion to civilization has been described by Max Weber, Tawney, Toynbee, and others. Centralized religious institutions checked fanaticism but their limitations were evident in the emergence of dissent. Leslie Stephen wrote that "the full bitterness which the human heart is capable of feeling, the full ferocity which it is capable of expressing is to be met nowhere but in religious papers." Adam Smith in his comments on religious instruction noted the handicaps of the established church in England. The clergy had

> . . . . many of them become very learned, ingenious, and respectable men; but they have in general ceased to be very popular preachers. The methodists, without half the learning of the dissenters, are much more in vogue. In the church of Rome, the industry and zeal of the inferior clergy are kept more alive by the powerful motive of self-interest, than perhaps in any established protestant church. The parochial clergy derive, many of them, a very considerable part of their subsistence from the voluntary oblations of the people; a source of revenue which confession gives them many opportunities of improving. The mendicant orders derive their whole subsistence from such oblations. It is with them, as with the hussars and light infantry of some armies; no plunder, no pay.[7]

The restraining influence of religious institutions has limitations, and dissenting groups and philosophical systems emerge on their fringes. Centralization is followed by decentralization.

The printing press and commerce implied far-reaching changes in the role of religion. In Victor Hugo's famous chapter in the *Notre Dame de Paris* entitled "This Has Killed That," he writes:

[6]*Sartor Resartus* (London, n.d.), p. 128.

[7]Adam Smith, *An Inquiry into the Nature and Causes of the Wealth of Nations* (New York: The Modern Library, 1937), pp. 791-92.

"During the first six thousand years of the world . . . architecture was the great handwriting of the human race." Geoffrey Scott has described the effects of printing:

Three influences, in combination, turned Renaissance architecture to an academic art. They were the revival of scholarship, the invention of printing, the discovery of Vitruvius. Scholarship set up the ideal of an exact and textual subservience to the antique; Vitruvius provided the code; printing disseminated it. It is difficult to do justice to the force which this implied. The effective influence of literature depends on its prestige and its accessibility. The sparse and jealously guarded manuscripts of earlier days gave literature an almost magical prestige, but afforded no accessibility; the cheap diffusion of the printing press has made it accessible, but stripped it of its prestige. The interval between these two periods was literature's unprecedented and unrepeated opportunity. In this interval Vitruvius came to light, and by this opportunity he, more perhaps than any other writer, has been the gainer. His treatise was discovered in the earlier part of the fifteenth century, at St. Gall; the first presses in Italy were established in 1464; and within a few years (the first edition is undated) the text of Vitruvius was printed in Rome. Twelve separate editions of it were published within a century; seven translations into Italian, and others into French and German. Alberti founded his great work upon it, and its influence reached England by 1563 in the brief essay of John Shute. Through the pages of Serlio, Vitruvius subjugated France, till then abandoned to the trifling classicism of François I.; through those of Palladio he became supreme in England.[8]

The book destroyed the edifice, and in the religious wars and the French Revolution it destroyed social institutions as well. Brooks Adams wrote:

That ancient channel [the church] once closed, Protestants had to open another, and this led to deification of the Bible, . . . Thus for the innumerable costly fetishes of the imaginative age were substituted certain writings which could be consulted without a fee. The expedient was evidently the device of a mercantile community.[9]

Leslie Stephen in a letter to Charles Adams wrote:

I always fancy that if one could get to the truth, the Puritan belief in the supernatural was a good deal feebler than Carlyle represents.

[8]Geoffrey Scott, *The Architecture of Humanism: A Study in the History of Taste* (New York: Charles Scribner's Sons, 1924), pp. 194-95.

[9]*The Law of Civilization and Decay: An Essay on History* (London: S. Sonnenschein and Company, 1895), pp. 150-51.

The man-of-business side of them checked the fanatic, and the ironsides beat the cavaliers as much because they appreciated good business qualities as because they were "God-fearing" people.[10]

"'We that look to Zion,' wrote a gallant Anabaptist admiral of the age, 'should hold Christian communion. We have all the guns aboard.'"[11]

It is scarcely necessary to elaborate on the significance to the economic development of European civilization of the emphasis which Calvinism put on the individual. This significance was reinforced by the adaptability of the alphabet to the printing press, private enterprise, and the machine, and by the consequent spread of literacy, trade, and industrialism. The Chinese were handicapped by a language ill adapted to the printing press except through support of the state, and there was consequently no expansion of commerce adequate to defeat the demands of religion. We are told of the handicaps of a religion with innumerable devils and gods in contrast with the efficiency of Christianity which reduced their numbers and enhanced economic efficiency. On the other hand, Burckhardt has described the tyranny of religions which emphasized otherworldliness, established a hierarchy to guard the entrance to other worlds, and participated in the most bitter warfare. Morley wrote of "the most frightful idea that has ever corroded human nature—the idea of eternal punishment" and of its deadening effects on the interest in social reform. The terrifying threats of a single organization which inspired Lord Acton to write that "all power corrupts and absolute power corrupts absolutely" were evaded by the printing press and commerce.

Religion has been vitally related to the mysteries of life and death and to the family. The decline of the Church in Europe reflected the impact of birth control on the confessional. The importance of the biological background stressed by Knight in his discussion of the sociological significance of the family was evident in feudal societies with or without primogeniture based on land and military power. Religious sects have fostered the accumulation of wealth over long periods by intermarriage of families. Whereas the Church in its fight for sacerdotal celibacy as a means of preventing

[10]F. W. Maitland, *Life and Letters of Leslie Stephen* (London: Duckworth and Company, 1906), pp. 448-49.

[11]John Morley, *Oliver Cromwell* (London: Macmillan and Company, 1919), p. 478.

the dispersion of wealth left itself open to the looting of its monasteries, the Jews and other sects have been persecuted because of the building up of large fortunes. One needs only to point to the studies of the Jews in relation to trade and economic development and to the peculiarities of economic organization in various sects, for example the interest of the Quakers in developing industries around nonintoxicating beverages, to appreciate their significance. We have no clear understanding of the economics of death and bequest (with apologies to Wedgwood) in relation to the redistribution of wealth among groups and sects.

In the United States the importance of religion to the growth of trade is shown in the large numbers of denominational periodicals and their promising returns to advertisers in a national market. Significantly, among the first advertisers who were alert to these possibilities were those large-scale dealers in human credulity, the patent-medicine firms. Sir William Osler wrote that "the desire to take medicine is perhaps the greatest feature which distinguishes man from animals."[12] Patent medicine capitalized an age of faith in miracles by emphasizing cures and led to the growth of advertising, trade, and scientific development. The railroad and the telegraph steadily increased the efficiency of advertising media—chiefly weeklies, monthlies, and quarterlies—which created a national market. In a country of vast extent the dailies expanded in relation to metropolitan markets and flourished by sensational appeals to larger numbers. After the invention of the electric light and the reduction of fire losses, the department store provided the advertising essential to their success.

The newspaper, with the technological advances evident in the telegraph, the press associations, the manufacture of paper from wood, the rotary press, and the linotype, became independent of party support and became concerned with an increase in circulation and with all the devices calculated to bring about such an increase to meet the demands of advertising. The phenomenal increase in the production of goods and the demands for more efficient methods of distribution stimulated the expansion of newspaper production, and newspapers stimulated production by widening and intensifying the market.

[12]Harvey Cushing, *The Life of Sir William Osler* (Oxford: Clarendon Press, 1925), Vol. I, p. 342.

By the beginning of the twentieth century the new journalism directed by Pulitzer, Hearst, and Northcliffe had become entrenched in the Anglo-Saxon world. The Spanish-American War and the South African War were the preludes to its supremacy. Bismarck, even before 1900, spoke of the power of the press. It had done a great deal of harm.

> It was the cause of the last three wars, . . . the Danish press forced the King and the Government to annex Schleswig; the Austrian and South German press agitated against us; and the French press contributed to the prolongation of the campaign in France.[13]

On January 28, 1883, he said:

> You have only to look at the newspapers and see how empty they are, and how they fish out the ancient sea-serpent in order to have something to fill their columns. The feuilleton is spreading more and more, and if anything sensational occurs, they rush at it furiously and write it to death for whole weeks. This low water in political affairs, this distress in the journalistic world, is the highest testimonial for a Minister of Foreign Affairs.[14]

Bagehot wrote, "Happy are the people whose annals are vacant but woe to the wretched journalists that have to compose and write articles therein." Sir Wemyss Reid, editor of the Leeds *Mercury*, claimed that the interest of the English public in foreign affairs began with the *The News's* agitation over the Bulgarian atrocities in 1876 and Gladstone's shrewdness in capitalizing the agitation. From that time public opinion never returned to its interest in domestic problems. As the "ancient Gothic genius, that sun which sets behind the gigantic press of Mayence" was crushed by the book, so the book was crushed by the newspaper. In turn the newspaper was destined to feel the effects of the radio. With Victor Hugo we can say, "It is the second tower of Babel of the human race."

III

In all this we can see at least a part of the background of the collapse of Western civilization which begins with the present century. The comparative peace of the nineteenth century is followed by a

[13]Moritz Busch, *Bismarck: Some Secret Pages of His History* (New York: The Macmillan Company, 1898), Vol. II, p. 175.

[14]*Ibid.*, p. 346.

period in which we have been unable to find a solution to the problem of law and order, and have resorted to force rather than to persuasion, bullets rather than ballots. "I know only two ways in which society can be governed—by public opinion and by the sword," wrote Macaulay. But Croker, representing the Conservative position, claimed that we govern by the law saving us from extremes of government by public opinion or by the sword. The rule of law became less effective. Where Bismarck had been able to use *The Times, The Daily Telegraph,* and *The Pall Mall Gazette* and say, "It was easier, cheaper, more humane to supply the English journals with news than to fight England,"[15] his master hand was gone, and the newspapers had grown beyond control. They had become something more than his description of "just printer's ink printed on paper." Where diplomacy by paragraphs had reached the point that a reference in *The Times* served as a check to French debates, *The Times* was now in other hands. Northcliffe had control of a power which could break the Asquith cabinet during the war. President Theodore Roosevelt and the big stick had been created by the American press. This vast new instrument concerned with reaching large numbers of readers rendered obsolete the machinery for maintaining peace which had characterized the nineteenth century. Guizot wrote of the great evil of democracy, "It readily sacrifices the past and the future to what is supposed to be the interest of the present," and that evil was accentuated by the reign of the newspaper and its obsession with the immediate. But to paraphrase Hilaire Belloc we must say of democracy,

Always keep a hold of nurse
For fear of finding something worse.

Lippmann's desertion of the study of rationalizing processes as developed with Graham Wallas, following the emergence of Freudian concern with the irrational, was a significant step. It would scarcely be decent in this gathering to refer to the implications to the social sciences, but one notes with alarm the changing fashions in economics. The breakup of the classical tradition of economics is an indication of the powerful influence of fashions in our times. At one time we are concerned with tariffs, at another with trusts, and still another with money. As newspapers seldom find it to their interest to pursue

[15]John Russell Young, M. D. R. Young, ed., *Men and Memories: Personal Reminiscences* (New York and London: F. T. Neely, 1901), p. 271.

any subject for more than three or four days, so the economist becomes weary of particular interests or senses that the public is weary of them and changes accordingly. And this paper will be cited as an obsession with the obsession with the immediate. There is need for a study of economics and insanity supporting that of Durkheim on religion and suicide.

The inability of the twentieth century to find a solution to the eternal problem of freedom and power is basically significant to the study of economic history. When the climate of opinion makes impossible any concern with the past or the future, the student finds it exceedingly difficult to discover an anchorage or a point of view from which to approach the problem of European civilization. A recognition of factors affecting irrationality is a beginning. The church, the army and the police, industry, and possibly the drink trade have been powerful forces affecting fanaticism. A study of the drink trade cannot be undertaken here, but the coffee houses in England after the Puritan revolution in the middle of the seventeenth century weakened the position of the tavern and provided centres of discussion which undermined the position of the Stuarts. The encouragement to sugar production in the West Indies which followed the increase in consumption of coffee, tea and chocolate had its unfortunate consequences in the increased production of molasses and rum. Puritanism in England meant decline in the taverns but a rise in the rum trade of the new world. A change of the whole drinking habits of the United States followed the dumping of tea in Boston harbour, and it may be that the devotion to coffee has had important political results. The relation between beverages and intelligent discussion offers an interesting bridge between economic history and political history. The drink trade has been significant for trade and war. The economic history of North America might be written around the struggle of brandy supported by the French against rum supported by the English. It was the considered view of C. C. Buell, who in the 1880's edited the reminiscences of generals of the Civil War for *Century,* that it "was a whiskey war. With few exceptions, like Howard, all the union generals kept themselves going with hard liquor. The men who came through and succeeded were the ones who could stand up to their drink."[16]

[16]Will Irwin, *The Making of a Reporter* (New York: G. P. Putnam's Sons, 1942), p. 146.

The fundamental problem of civilization is that of government or of keeping people quiet, or following Machiavelli "to content the people and to manage the nobles." All politicians will echo the words of Lord Melbourne, "Damn them! Why can't they keep quiet?" We are aware of the devices of oriental empires and of the empires of Central America through the linking of religion to the state. The Jewish and Mohammedan religions persisted by virtue of discipline and the use of force. Greece used the army and navy as sources of resistance to external domination, and Rome used the army and the road as means of domination. Countries with a revolutionary tradition acquired adaptability and a belief in the power to accomplish change by individual efforts, but the right and ability to protest is not paralleled by an ability to accept responsibility. Vitality assumes the ability to reorganize efficiently. But a revolutionary tradition is safer in the state than in religion. In Germany as the home of the printing press a revolutionary tradition in religion was supported by the state. In England the religious revolution followed the revolution of the state and facilitated the outbreak of Puritanism and the growth of trade. In Canada the revolutionary tradition missed the French in the church, and in turn the English in the state, with the migration of Loyalists after the Revolution, and provided the basis for mutual misunderstanding. Weakening of the Church as a device to destroy fanaticism by the invention of printing, the rise of Protestantism, and the emergence of philosophy in the Age of Enlightenment left commerce as the great stabilizer. Its influence was evident in the comparative peace of the nineteenth century. Samuel Johnson said that there were "few ways in which a man can be more innocently employed than in getting money."

Rationality which accompanies the price system brings its own handicaps in the formation of monopolies. Large-scale effective mechanization of distribution necessitated a single price and the search for devices to prevent outbreaks of competitive warfare. The price system weakens the profit motive by its emphasis on management. Cartels and formalism in commerce paralleled ecclesiasticism in religion and in both cases initiative in thought was weakened. Volumes of economic history were written about business firms, epitaphs in two volumes (George Moore), as part of the literature of the new scriptures. Ecclesiasticism and the devastating effects of the depression brought an acute paralysis of thought and the rush to such illusions and catchwords as security and full employment. The price system brought not only rationality in business but also luxury and freedom from work. The intellectual snob who exploits by telling others how they are exploited and luxurious discussions of the class struggle have been evident enough. We need an economic interpretation of the class struggle, but, as Troeltsch has pointed out, the objectivity of the price mechanism supports the plausible finality of the Marxian interpretation. The price system with its sterilizing power has destroyed ideologies, and broken up irreconcilable minorities by compelling them to name their price. Unrestrained, it has destroyed its own ideology since it too has its price. In a sense religion is an effort to organize irrationality and as such appears in all large-scale organizations of knowledge. Commerce follows the general trends of organized religious bodies as does thought in the social sciences. "Most organizations appear as bodies founded for the painless extinction of the ideas of their founders."[17] Alexander Murray wrote to Archibald Constable, the Edinburgh publisher, on July 7, 1807:

> It will be no wonderful occurrence if, in this age of constitution making and universal improvement, the nations which have long been unscientifically free shall become scientifically servile—for it is only when people begin to want water that they think of making reservoirs; and it was observed that the laws of Rome were never reduced into a system till its virtue and taste had perished.[18]

As in organized religion, dissent appears on the fringes bringing the sceptic and philosopher, or bringing into being the Economic History Association which springs up on the fringes of large ecclesiastical academic organizations.[19] The principle that authority is taken, never given, begins to emerge. Or there may be a palace revolution such as that started by Lord Keynes. "Dost thou not know my son, with how little wisdom the world is governed?" (Count Oxenstierna).

The outbreak of irrationality, which in the early part of the

[17]G. P. Gooch, *Life of Lord Courtney* (London: Macmillan and Company, 1920), p. 416.

[18]Thomas Constable, *Archibald Constable and His Literary Correspondents* (Edinburgh, 1873), Vol. I, p. 261.

[19]See Ernst Troeltsch, *The Social Teaching of the Christian Churches;* also S. D. Clark, "Religious Organization and the Rise of the Canadian Nation 1850-85," *Report of the Canadian Historical Association,* 1944, pp. 86-97.

twentieth century became evident in the increasing interest in psychology following the steadying effects of commerce in the nineteenth century, is the tragedy of our time. The rationalizing potentialities of the price system and its importance in developing powers of calculation in the individual have failed to prevent a major collapse. It has been argued that man as a biological phenomenon has been unable to sustain the excessive demands of rationalism evident in the mathematics of the price system and of technology. Charles Dickens wrote to Charles Knight (January 30, 1854):

> My satire is against those who see figures and averages, and nothing else—the representatives of the wickedest and most enormous vice of this time—the men who, through long years to come, will do more to damage the really useful truths of political economy, than I could do (if I tried) in my whole life—the addled heads who would take the average of cold in the Crimea during twelve months, as a reason for clothing a soldier in nankeen on a night when he would be frozen to death in fur—and who would comfort the labourer in travelling twelve miles a-day to and from his work, by telling him that the average distance of one inhabited place from another on the whole area of England, is not more than four miles. Bah! what have you to do with these![20]

How far does the spread of mathematics and the intensity of modern life create demands for irrationalism and fanaticism? Is the emergence of Freud and the psychologists a result of the spread of irrationalism or an effort to meet the problems of irrationalism? Has commercial development been effective in destroying religious centralization as a stabilizing influence to the point that new sources of power such as nationalism and autarchy with subordination to militarism have taken their place? Morley described the stubborn sentiment of race and the bitter antagonism of the church as the two most powerful forces affecting civilized society. In weakening the church, commerce has been unable to check nationalism, although religious institutions can be more effective than industrialism or commercialism in crushing intelligence. The breakdown of the press shown in the sharp decline in influence of the editorial in the twentieth century points in the direction of nationalism.[21] The printing press and new methods of communication have been developed

[20]Charles Knight, *Passages of a Working Life During Half a Century* (London, 1865), Vol. III, p. 188.

[21]Oswald Garrison Villard, *The Disappearing Daily; Chapters in American Newspaper Evolution* (New York: Alfred A. Knopf, 1944).

as methods of division rather than co-operation. National and linguistic differences have been accentuated and internationalism weakened. The mechanization of art intensified nationalism. Where the stage meant an international interest, the movies and the talkies were subject to customs duties. Following its concentration on the problems of the immediate, commerce has lost its control as a stabilizer of power.

IV

The significance of economic history in all this is shown in its concern with long-run trends and its emphasis on training in a search for patterns rather than mathematical formulae. It should compel the study of interrelationships between the social sciences and between nations. It should rescue the social sciences from the charge of producing books "each with a hundred methods of distributing the fruits of productive labour among those whose labour is unproductive."[22] It should weaken the position of the textbook which has become such a powerful instrument for the closing of men's minds with its emphasis on memory and its systematic checking of new ideas. Biases become entrenched in textbooks which represent monopolies of the publishing trade and resist the power of thought. "Learning hath gained most by those books whereby the printers have lost" (Thomas Fuller). Imperfect competition between economic theories hampers the advances of freedom of thought. Machine industry through printing dispenses with thought or compels it to move in certain channels. The dispersion of thought through the printing industry makes attacks on monopoly increasingly difficult. In emphasizing a long-range approach to social phenomena, economic history should contribute to stability. Not only should it supplement political and social history, it should in supplementing them check the tendency in itself and in them to bias and fanaticism. Within the narrower range of the social sciences it should provide a check against the specialization of mathematical systems peculiar to a monetary and a machine age and should indicate the extent and significance of the irrational as contrasted with the rational. It should offset the superficiality in the mathematical approach of which Wesley Mitchell complains. This is to recognize that the subject is

[22]Henry Holt, *Garrulities of an Octogenarian Editor* (Boston: Houghton Mifflin Company, 1923), p. 104.

more difficult than mathematics and to insist that tools must be used, and not described, if interpretation is not to be superseded by antiquarianism. In the words of Cobden, political economy is "the highest exercise of the human mind, and the exact sciences require by no means so hard an effort."[23]

Economics tends to become a branch of political history and it is necessary to suggest alternative approaches and their limitations, to emphasize sociology with its concern with institutions, geography, and technology. By drawing attention to the limitations of the social sciences and of the price system it can show the importance of religion and of factors hampering the efficiency of the price system. Not only does it introduce a balance to constitutional and legal history, it draws attention to the penchant for mathematics and for other scientific tools which have warped the humanities. Economic history may provide grappling irons with which to lay hold of areas on the fringe of economics, whether in religion or in art, and with which, in turn, to enrich other subjects, as well as to rescue economics from the present-mindedness which pulverizes other subjects and makes a broad approach almost impossible.[24] Economic history demands the perspective to reduce jurisdictional disputes to an absurdity. The use of economic theory as a device for economizing knowledge should be extended and not used to destroy other subjects or an interest in them. Goldwin Smith wrote, "Social science if it is to take the place of religion as a conservative force has not yet developed itself or got firm hold of the popular mind."[25]

[23]John Morley, *The Life of Richard Cobden* (London, 1887), Vol. I, p. 323.

[24]Alec Lawrence Macfie, *An Essay on Economy and Value: Being an Enquiry into the Real Nature of Economy* (London: Macmillan and Company, 1936).

[25]*Essays on Questions of the Day, Political and Social* (New York and London: Macmillan and Company, 1893), p. 39. "It was this youthful religion—profound, barbaric, poetical—that the Teutonic races insinuated into Christianity and substituted for that last sigh of two expiring worlds. In the end, with the complete crumbling away of Christian dogma and tradition, Absolute Egotism appeared openly on the surface in the shape of German speculative philosophy. This form, which Protestantism assumed at a moment of high tension and reckless self-sufficiency, it will doubtless shed in turn and take on new expressions; but that declaration of independence on the part of the Teutonic spirit marks emphatically its exit from Christianity and the end of that series of transformations in which it took Bible and patristic dogma for its materials. It now bids fair to apply itself instead to social life and natural science and to attempt to feed its Protean hunger directly from these more homely sources." George Santayana, *Reason in Religion* (London, 1906), Vol. III, pp. 125-6.

Economic history can contribute to the fundamental problem of determining the limits of the social sciences. Without a solution to this problem there can be no future for them. "There is no use in printing in italics when you have no ink."

The circulation of printed matter cheapened thought and destroyed the prestige of the great works of the past which were collected and garnered before the introduction of movable type. Rational thought and art consequently had more influence. European civilization lived off the intellectual capital of Greek civilization, the spiritual capital provided by the Hebrew civilization, the material capital acquired by looting the specie reserves of Central American civilizations, and the natural resources of the New World. Crozier wrote with regard to England:

> It pays her better to buy her intellect, penetration, originality, invention and so on, when she wants them and where she wants them, than to breed them. . . . Germany and France and other continental nations supply her with nearly all the new departures that have to be made in science and philosophy in medicine, in scholarship and the higher criticism, in the art of war; in new chemical and industrial processes; and in enlargements of the scope of music and of art.[26]

He might have extended the argument to Western civilization.

The enormous capacity of Western European civilization to loot has left little opportunity for consideration of the problems which follow the exhaustion of material to be looted. But this civilization has shown continual concern in the common man and in the distribution of loot. Perhaps economic history can begin from this point to make its contribution in the building up of spiritual, intellectual, and material capital, since it is not concerned with the belief in the common man but with the common man himself.

[26]John Beattie Crozier, *History of Intellectual Development on the Lines of Modern Evolution* (London: Longmans, Green and Company, 1901), Vol. III, pp. 166-67.

7. POLITICAL ECONOMY IN THE MODERN STATE[1]

I. Spiritual and Political Implications of Puritanism

Lord Acton[2] has outlined the historical background of modern freedom essential to the social sciences. The lesson of Athenian experience taught that "government by the whole people, being the government of the most numerous and powerful class is an evil of the same nature as unmixed monarchy and requires for nearly the same reasons institutions that shall protect it against arbitrary revolutions of opinion." In Rome "the vice of the classic state was that it was both church and state in one. Morality was undistinguished from religion, and politics from morals and in religion, morality and politics there was only one legislator and one authority."[3] "The ancient writers saw very clearly that each principle of government standing alone is carried to excesses and provokes a reaction. Monarchy hardens into despotism, aristocracy contracts into oligarchy, democracy expands into the supremacy of numbers."[4] While the necessity of checks as essential to liberty was thus recognized, classical civilization never achieved "representative government, the emancipation of the slaves, and liberty of conscience."[5] These achievements became

[1]From *Proceedings of the American Philosophical Society*, Vol. LXXXVII (4), January, 1944.

[2]First Baron Acton, *The History of Freedom and Other Essays* (London, 1922), p. 13. Cf. Shailer Mathews, *The Spiritual Interpretation of History* (Cambridge, 1916). The latter shows no appreciation of the necessity of securing a balance between centralized organizations as a means to freedom.

[3]Acton, *History of Freedom*, p. 17. Sir James Mackintosh described the burning of Hindu widows as a horror generated by "union of law, of morals, and of religion. When they unite they are omnipotent. The course of nature may be stopped and we may recoil from our most exquisite enjoyments. When these forces oppose each other, their power is proportionately diminished" (*Memoirs of the Life of the Right Honourable Sir James Mackintosh*, London, 1936, Vol. I, p. 155). "So far in history, freedom to think, to observe, to judge men and things severely and dispassionately, has been possible—always be it understood, for a few individuals—only in those societies in which numbers of different religious and political currents have been struggling for dominion" (Pendleton Herring, *The Politics of Democracy*, New York, 1940, p. 429).

[4]Acton, *History of Freedom*, pp. 19-20.

[5]*Ibid.*, pp. 25-6. At least five conditions, according to Acton, must be met by a people in order to preserve their freedom. First, they must never surrender their destiny to any power they cannot control, that is, they must, in spite of all temptation to the contrary, keep the government "so constitutionally checked and controlled, that proper provision is made against its being otherwise exercised." Secondly, they must never cease to participate in the general government:

possible with the rigid discipline under the Hebraic scriptures and the contribution of Christianity.

When Christ said "Render unto Cæsar the things that are Cæsar's, and unto God the things that are God's" those words gave . . . to the civil power, under the protection of conscience, a sacredness it had never enjoyed, and bounds it had never acknowledged; and they were the repudiation of absolutism and the inauguration of freedom. For our Lord not only delivered the precept but created the force to execute it. To maintain the necessary immunity in one supreme sphere; to reduce all political authority within defined limits ceased to be an aspiration of patient reasoners and was made the perpetual charge and care of the most energetic institution and the most universal association in the world. The new law, the new spirit, the new authority gave to liberty a meaning and a value it had not possessed in the philosophy or in the constitution of Greece or Rome before the knowledge of the Truth that makes us free.[6]

The state was circumscribed in its authority by a force external to its own.

The downfall of the Roman Empire was followed by the rise of the Roman Church. Hobbes wrote: "If a man consider the original of this great ecclesiastical dominion he will easily perceive that the papacy is none other than the ghost of the deceased Roman Empire

"for the free classes can only hold their own by self-government." Thirdly, in the government under which they live there must always be a division of power; for "Liberty depends on the division of power." Fourthly, their government and themselves must, notwithstanding much evil and injustice, which reforms rather than revolution can best diminish, persist to tolerate the existence of private property; for "a people averse to the institution of private property is without the first element of freedom." Lastly, their government must remain "so exercised that the individual shall not feel the pressure of public authority, and may direct his life by the influences that are within him and not around him" (F. E. Lally, *As Lord Acton Says,* Newport, 1942, pp. 147-8). All history tells us, that the moment liberty invades property, the reign of arbitrary power is at hand—the flock fly to a shepherd to protect them from wolves. Better one despot, than a reign of robbers. (Edward Lytton Bulwer, *England and the English,* London, 1833, Vol. II, p. 264.)

[6]Acton, *History of Freedom,* p. 29. "Looking back over the space we call the Middle Ages to get an estimate of the work they had done, if not towards perfection in their institutions, at least, towards attaining the knowledge of political truth, this is what we find; representative government, which was unknown to the ancients, was almost universal. The methods of election were crude; but the principle that no tax was lawful that was not granted by the class that paid it—that is, that taxation was inseparable from representation—was recognized not as the privilege of certain countries, but as the right of all. Not a prince in the world, said Philip de Commines, can levy a penny without the consent of the people. Slavery was almost everywhere extinct; and absolute power was deemed more intolerable

sitting crowned upon the grave thereof."[7] In the words of Locke, Christianity made "the one invisible true God known to the world; and that with such evidence and energy, that polytheism and idolatry have nowhere been able to withstand it."[8] Its centralizing tendencies were followed after the invention of printing by the protests of Martin Luther, reinforced by the opposition of political states. He was compelled to take up the position that authority was more dependent on divine revelation and less on ecclesiasticism. His position and the translation and printing of the Bible opened the way, on the one hand, to the growth of the Calvinistic state, as in Switzerland and in Scotland, and on the other, to the growth of Puritanism as it flourished among the sects in Holland and in England. "The substitution of the Book for the Church was the essence of Protestant revolt" (Morley). Calvin evaded the dangers of the Reformation in ecclesiasticism and subservience to the state under Luther by enforcing two cardinal laws of human society, self-control as the foundation of virtue, self-sacrifice as the condition of the common weal, and created a new centre of union for Puritanism.[9] The first English Baptist Church published a declaration of faith in 1611 which stated that "no church ought to challenge any prerogative over

than slavery. The right of insurrection was not only admitted but defined as a duty sanctioned by religion. Even the principles of the Habeas Corpus Act, and the method of the Income Tax were already known. The issue of ancient politics was an absolute State planted on slavery. The political produce of the Middle Ages was a system of States in which authority was restricted by the representation of powerful classes, by privileged associations, and by the acknowledgment of duties superior to those which are imposed by man" (*Ibid.*, p. 39).

". . . The one thing that saved England from the fate of other countries was not her insular position nor the independent spirit nor the magnanimity of her people—for we have been proud of the despotism we obeyed under the Tudors—and not ashamed of the tyranny we exercised in our dependencies—but only the consistent, unintentive, stupid fidelity to that political system which originally belonged to all the nations that traversed the ordeal of feudalism" (*Home and Foreign Review*, July, 1863, pp. 713-54; Lally, *As Lord Acton Says* (p. 54). By consolidating the heterogeneous and anarchical elements that succeeded the downfall of the Roman Empire; by infusing into Christendom the conception of a bond of unity that is superior to the divisions of nationhood, and of a moral tie that is superior to force; by softening slavery into serfdom, and preparing the way for the ultimate emancipation of labour, Catholicism laid the very foundations of modern civilization. W. E. H. Lecky, *The rise and influence of rationalism in Europe* (London, 1913), Vol. II, p. 29.

[7]Leslie Stephen, *Hobbes* (London, 1928), p. 230.

[8]Thomas Fowler, *Locke* (London, 1883), p. 158.

[9]*Essays by the Late Mark Pattison,* collected and arranged by Henry Nettleship (Oxford, 1889), Vol. II, Chap. XII.

any other" and that "the magistrate is not to meddle with religion or matters of conscience nor compel men to this or that form of religion," statements constituting "the first known expression of absolute liberty of conscience."[10]

The divorce of Henry VIII brought the emergence of ecclesiastical power in England as distinct from Rome and the concentration of power under the Tudors in the Crown, Parliament, and the Anglican Church which came into conflict with Puritanism under the Stuarts. The opening of the New World and the expansion of trade across the Atlantic and to the Mediterranean and to India brought vigorous complaints against trading monopolies, the Crown, and the established church. Commercialism, Puritanism, and Parliament reinforced each other. Richard Baxter wrote: "Freeholders and tradesmen are the strength of religion and civility in the Land; and gentlemen and beggars and servile tenants are the strength of iniquity."[11] In the late sixteenth and the early seventeenth centuries Parliament began to reflect the influence of Puritanism.

The problem[12] of religious and civil liberty reached a crisis toward the middle of the seventeenth century. Among the Puritans there emerged the "*dogma of the two orders.* Man as man belongs to the order of nature. . . . God is the creator and ruler of both orders; but they have different economies and are ruled by different laws."[13] Roger Williams insisted "on the natural rights of spiritual men." Separation of the two orders enabled the Puritan to adopt "radical and naturalistic ideas, the sovereignty of the people, and government by consent in the natural field, and to remain dogmatic in the spiritual field. The principle of segregation of the spiritual and the natural, the church and the state, became the basis for the doctrine of toleration on the one hand and the secularization of the state on the other." Moreover, "ideas of liberty, of equality, of democratic organization, of government by the consent of the governed, of truth and agreement reached through free and equal discussion" within the order of grace were carried over to politics

[10] N. H. Marshall, "Baptists" (*Encyclopædia Britannica,* ed. 14). "English separatists grasped sincerely and vigorously the principle, that it is only by abridging the authority of states that the liberty of churches can be assured." F. E. Tally, op. cit., p. 146.

[11] "Puritanism" (*Encyclopædia of the Social Sciences*).

[12] A. S. P. Woodhouse, *Puritanism and Liberty* (London, 1938).

[13] A. S. P. Woodhouse, "Puritanism and Democracy" (*Canadian Journal of Economics and Political Science,* Vol. IV, 1938 (1), pp. 9 ff.).

and the secular field.[14] Harrington wrote: "Where civil liberty is entire, it includes liberty of conscience; where liberty of conscience is entire, it includes civil liberty."[15] Puritanism therefore had its impact on politics in its insistence on agreement through discussion,[16] the separation of church and state, a free state composed of equals pareleling a free church with a democratic form of government. In the struggle between Puritanism and Charles I, the issues were sharply drawn and the King lost his head.

The Puritan revolution strengthened the position of Parliament, but Charles I was an unconscionable time a-dying. His spirit lived on in the restoration under Charles II and nearly a century after the glorious revolution of 1688 was reflected in George III. His influence in the army was weakened partly because England's future was on the sea but it persisted in an established church. But the free press of the Netherlands and the writings of Milton and Baxter and of Locke gradually prevailed in limiting the authority of the state and in extending religious liberty. To quote Lord Acton again: "By arresting the preponderance of France, the Revolution of 1688 struck the first real blow at continental despotism. At home it relieved dissent, purified justice, developed the national energies and resources, and ultimately by the Act of Settlement, placed the Crown in the gift of the people."[17]

It made possible the union of England and Scotland. Encroachments on civil liberty under George III led to the outbursts of Junius and Wilkes in the interests of a free press, and with the success of the American Revolution[18] shifted the responsibility of Parliament to the people rather than to the Crown. Parliament in its earlier struggle with the Crown over-reached itself and, becoming adaptable to control by George III, contributed to the breakup of the Empire.

[14]*Ibid.*, p. 11. "The fact to recognize is the tremendous force of the doctrine of Christian liberty itself, and its fundamental position in the struggle for religious toleration."

[15]*Ibid.*, p. 13. Rainborough's statement expresses the fullest implications: "The poorest he that is in England has a life to live, as the greatest he" (*ibid.*, p. 19).

[16]On the significance of discussion, see Walter Bagehot, *Physics and Politics* (*The Works of Walter Bagehot*, Hartford, 1889, Vol. IV, p. 569)—especially the answer to critics of discussion such as Carlyle. For a contrast with France, see J. U. Nef, *Industry and Government in France and England, 1540-1640* (Philadelphia, 1940).

[17]Acton, *History of Freedom*, pp. 54-5.

[18]John Viscount Morley, *Burke* (London, 1921), Chap. IV.

In New England the Puritan element developed a theocracy comparable to that of Switzerland and Scotland. "Theocrats of all kinds must be persecutors" (Leslie Stephen). Its harshness led to the expulsion of Roger Williams and to the settlement of Rhode Island. The struggle between Crown and Parliament in England accentuated the separatist tendencies of the intensely commercialistic colonies of New England.[19] The insistence of Crown and Parliament on supremacy in the reign of George III brought a variety of protests in England and in the colonies. Lord Camden stated that "taxation and representation are inseparably united. God hath joined them. No British parliament can separate them." Otis in the colonies followed Coke and influenced Adams in arguing that "in many cases the Common law will control acts of parliament and adjudge them to be utterly void; for where an act of parliament is against common right and reason or repugnant or impossible to perform, the common law will control it."[20] The common law occupied an important place in the speculations which preceded the Revolution. Coke, with his reverence for the common law, supported Parliament against Charles I and was used to support the colonies against Parliament. The Assembly of Massachusetts expressed a willingness of compromise by recognizing the Crown but not Parliament. It stated on March 2, 1773: "Our ancestors received the lands, by grant from the king; and at the same time compacted with him, and promised him homage and allegiance; not in his public or politic, but natural capacity only." Feudalism and the Crown were based on land and territorial rights. Parliament emerged with the influence of primogeniture and the importance of maritime trade. Settlement on the North American continent brought conflict with the authority of Crown and Parliament.

The revolt of the colonies against the centralizing tendencies of Crown and Parliament brought them face to face with the problem of framing an acceptable central organization in the Constitution. The influence of Milton and Locke, though weakened in England under

[19]See W. P. M. Kennedy, *Essays in Constitutional Law* (London, 1934), pp. 3-23.

[20]See A. C. McLaughlin, *The Foundation of American Constitutionalism* (New York, 1932), pp. 125-6; also R. G. Green, *Political Ideas of the American Revolution* (Durham, 1932), pp. 124 ff.; C. H. McIlwain, *The American Revolution: A Constitutional Interpretation* (New York, 1923), pp. 152 ff.; C. H. Van Tyne, *The Causes of the War of Independence* (Boston, 1922), Vol. I, Chap. IX.

Walpole and later George III, was reflected in the work[21] of Frederick the Great and Voltaire and carried forward in the philosophy of Jefferson. It favoured decentralization. Hamilton and the federalists favoured centralization. The Declaration of Independence stood in sharp contrast to the Constitution. The compromise of balances[22] in the Crown, Courts, Lords, and Commons in Great Britain emphasized by Blackstone and Montesquieu provided the pattern for checks between sources of power in the President, Congress, and the Supreme Court, and the necessity for appeal to the people.

II. PURITANISM AND LEARNING

The position of learning in the struggle for civil and religious liberty was precarious. "Greatly as the Calvinistic churches have served the cause of political liberty they have contributed nothing to the progress of knowledge."[23] This depended on the discovery of the contribution of the Greeks.

Banished from the Roman Empire in the sixth century, or earlier, the classical conception of beauty of form re-entered the circle of ideas again in the fifteenth century, after nearly a thousand years of oblivion and abeyance. Cicero and Vergil, Livius and Ovid, had been there all along, but the idea of composite harmony, on which their works were constructed, was wanting. The restored conception, as if to recoup itself for its long suppression, took entire possession of the mind of educated Europe. The first period of the renaissance passed in adoration of the awakened beauty and in efforts to copy and multiply it.

But in the fifteenth century, "educated Europe" is but a synonym for Italy. What literature there was outside the Alps

[21]The conditions of the order which was established after the confusion of the fall of the Roman power before the inroads of the barbarians; and which constituted the Europe of the early and middle ages, are now tolerably well understood, and the historic continuity or identity of that order is typified in two institutions, which by the middle of the eighteenth century had reached very different stages of decay and possessed very different powers of resisting attack. One was the German Empire, and the other was the Holy Catholic Church. Frederick dealt a definite blow to the first, and Voltaire did the same to the second" (John Viscount Morley, *Voltaire*, London, 1921, p. 134). See *Ethics*, July, 1943.

[22]See Goldwin Smith, *Essays in Questions of the Day* (n.p., 1893), pp. 95-7; also James Bryce, *The American Commonwealth* (New York, 1915), Vol. I, Chaps. I-III; C. A. Beard, *Economic Origins of Jeffersonian Democracy* (New York, 1915); V. L. Parrington, *The Colonial Mind 1620-1800* (New York, 1927).

[23]*Essays by the Late Mark Pattison*, Vol. II, p. 41.

was a derivative from, or dependent of, the Italian movement. The fact that the movement originated in the Latin peninsula, was decisive of the character of the first age of classical learning (1400-1550). It was a revival of Latin, as opposed to Greek, literature. It is now well understood that the fall of Constantinople, though an influential incident of the movement, ranks for nothing among the causes of the Renaissance. What was revived in Italy of the fifteenth century was the taste of the schools of the early empire—of the second and third century. There were, no doubt, differing characteristics, for nothing in history ever exactly repeats itself. But in one decisive feature the literary sentiment of the fifteenth century was a reproduction of that of the empire. It was rhetorical, not scientific. Latin literature as a whole is rhetorical. There are exceptional books, such as the "Natural history" of Plinius, but, on the whole, the idea of science was Greek, and is alien to Latin. To turn phrases, and polish sentences, was the one aim of the litterateur of the empire. . . . This divorce of the literature of knowledge, and the literature of form, which characterized the epoch of decay under the early empire, characterized equally the epoch of revival in the Italy of the popes. The refinements of literary composition in verse and prose, and a tact of emendation founded on this refined sense, this was the ideal of the scholar of the Italian Renaissance.

The decay and extinction of the artistic enthusiasm of the Italians was gradual, but may be said to have been consummated soon after the middle of the sixteenth century.[24]

As the eye, captivated at first by charms of person, learns in time to see the graces of the soul that underly and shape them, so the classics, which had attracted by their beauty, gradually revealed to the modern world the rich wisdom which that beauty enshrined. The first scholars of the Renaissance enjoyed, without labour, the harmonies of language, the perfection of finish, which the great masters of Latin style had known how to give to their work. Just when imitation had degenerated into feebleness, mannerism, and affectation, the discovery was made that these exterior beauties covered a world of valuable knowledge even in the Latin writers. And underlying the Latin literature, it was perceived, was one more valuable still, the Greek. The interest of the educated world was transferred from the form to the matter of ancient literature. Masses of useful knowledge, natural or political, the social experience of many generations, were found to have lain unnoticed in books which had been all the while in everyone's hands. The knowledge and wisdom thus buried in the Greek writers presented a striking contrast to the barren sophistic, which formed the curriculum of the schools.

It became the task of the scholars of the second period of the

[24]Mark Pattison, *Isaac Casaubon 1559-1614* (London, 1875), pp. 507-8.

classical revival to disinter this knowledge. The classics, which had been the object of taste became the object of science.[25]

The first period of humanism in which the words of the ancient authors had been studied, was thus the preparatory school for the humanism of the second period, in which the matter was the object of attention. . . . The *first* period in the history of classical learning may be styled the Italian. The *second* period coincides with the French school. If we ask why Italy did not continue to be the centre of the humanist movement, which she had so brilliantly inaugurated, the answer is that the intelligence was crushed by the reviviscence of ecclesiastical ideas. Learning is research; research must be free, and cannot coexist with the claim of the Catholic clergy to be superior to enquiry. The French school, it will be observed, is wholly in fact, or in intention, Protestant. As soon as it was decided, as it was before 1600, that France was to be a Catholic country, and the university of Paris a Catholic university, learning was extinguished in France. France, "noverca ingeniorum" saw her unrivalled scholars, expatriate themselves without regret, and without repentance. With Scaliger and Saumaise the seat of learning was transferred from France to Holland. The *third* period of classical learning thus coincides with the Dutch school. From 1593, the date of Scaliger's removal to Leyden, the supremacy in the republic of learning was possessed by the Dutch.[26]

With the assassination of Henry IV, Casaubon migrated from France to England.

The struggle in England was disastrous to its universities.

When twenty years of tranquillity and order had restored the possibility of intellectual life, we find two results. First, that taste, poetry, and literature were the first intellectual fruit to revive after the moral pestilence which had desolated the nation. The reign of Elizabeth produced accordingly a rich harvest of poetry and general literature, but it was not till the beginning of the next century that speculative thought and the severer studies again raised their heads. Secondly, that the movement of the national mind is carried on no longer, within the universities, but without them. From that time to the present, the universities have ceased to originate, to rule, even to respond to, or be affected by, such intellectual activity as the nation has possessed. The whole of that sphere of thought in which a liberal training consists, or by which it can be accomplished, has been abandoned by them. So far as it has gone on at all, it has gone on without them. Ever since Henry VIII's first interference with opinion here, the universities have been kept in dependence by the State; under Elizabeth, and under James and Charles, the fetters

[25] *Ibid.*, p. 509.
[26] *Ibid.*, pp. 510-11.

were drawn tighter and tighter, and education, starved by its severance from the living current of thought and opinion, gradually died out.[27]

The measures then taken in the cause of order, security, and permanence, had the effect of drying up the very springs of our life, and cut us off from giving or receiving from the nation at large a healthy intellectual impulse. Then was laid the foundation of that fatal divorce between the universities and the national mind, which has lasted ever since. This alienation reached its acme, politically, about the middle of the last century, when Oxford had become identified with the sullen and anti-national Jacobite faction; morally and intellectually, about the close of the century, when it can scarcely be said that the university gave any education at all. We sustained our very existence by means of our political connection and our landed property, and had altogether lost our hold on the national mind. Speaking only of Oxford, and omitting exceptional instances, such as the prelections of Sanderson on Moral Philosophy in 1643, or those of Blackstone on English Law in 1754, we may say that from the Laudian Statutes of 1636, till the First Examination Statute of 1801, the University *curriculum* became more and more narrow, the efficiency of what remained, less and less.[28]

The results have been described by writers in the late eighteenth century. "In the University of Oxford, the greater part of the public professors have, for these many years, given up altogether even the pretence of teaching." (Adam Smith.) For Gibbon it was the home of port and prejudice. Sydney Smith[29] wrote, "The only consequences of a university education are the growth of vice and the waste of money."[30]

Advances in philosophy came from the Continent and particularly Holland. Advances in astronomy and mathematics after Galileo and the discovery of circulation of the blood by Harvey early in the seventeenth century provided the background for the philosophy of Descartes and Spinoza and the writings of Hobbes. Bacon gave an impetus to the study of science particularly by his attack on the dialectics of the school men. Locke toward the end of the century stimulated an interest in psychology, and Newton made notable advances in mathematics and astronomy. While England made its contributions, Pattison has written:

[27]*Essays by the Late Mark Pattison,* Vol. I, p. 449.

[28]*Ibid.*, p. 452.

[29]See *The Works of the Rev. Sydney Smith* (London, 1848), Vol. I, pp. 383-93.

[30]G. W. E. Russell, *Sydney Smith* (London, 1905), p. 12.

If we take the philosophical and religious literature of England for the earlier half of the eighteenth century, we shall find upon it the stamp of a second-hand and derivative character. The writings of the English Deists—Shaftesbury, Chubb, Toland, and Woolston—have that sort of originality which proceeds from ignorance of what has been thought or written. The speculative impulse came from the Continent: from two or three leading minds—from Descartes, Spinoza, and Bayle. In England it obtained notoriety, publicity, and diffusion.[81]

While the vigorous struggle for civil and religious liberties in England was being prosecuted in the late eighteenth and early nineteenth centuries and their position in the United States was being strengthened and consolidated, the principles of economic liberty were being formulated and advanced in Scotland, "the only kingdom in which the Reformation triumphed over the resistance of the state." Union with England in 1707 provided the background for an escape from the intolerance of religious tyranny in the expansion of trade[82] from Glasgow and in the attractions of law[83] and literature in Edinburgh, "that garret of the earth—that knuckle-end of England—that land of Calvin, oatcakes and sulphur."[84]

The universities of Scotland escaped from the heavy hand of the state, and while the church attempted to excommunicate Hume, it was possible for him and for Hutcheson and Adam Smith to strengthen the extension of civil liberties in the direction of economic freedom. Adam Smith presented a systematic extension of principles first in the spiritual and then in the natural field. His *Theory of Moral Sentiments,* published in 1759, gave a "system of ethics on the basis of a harmonious order in nature guided by God, and in an incidental manner applies his general doctrine with strict consistency to the economic order."[85]

[81] *Essays by the Late Mark Pattison,* Vol. II, pp. 402-03.

[82] W. R. Scott, *Adam Smith as Student and Professor* (Glasgow, 1937).

[83] "Every youth, of every temper and almost every description of character, is sent either to study for the bar, or to a writer's office as an apprentice. . . . Is a lad stupid, the law will sharpen him—is he too mercurial the law will make him sedate—has he an estate, he may get a sheriffdom; is he poor, the richest lawyers have emerged from poverty—is he a Tory, he may become a depute-advocate—is he a Whig, he may with far better hope expect to become" (*The Journal of Sir Walter Scott,* Edinburgh, 1890, p. 36).

[84] G. W. E. Russell, *Sydney Smith* (London, 1905), p. 28.

[85] Jacob Viner in *Adam Smith, 1776-1926* (Chicago, 1928), p. 119. See also G. R. Morrow in *Ibid.,* Chap. VI.

Smith's doctrine that economic phenomena were manifestations of an underlying order in nature governed by natural forces, gave to English economics for the first time a definite trend toward logically consistent synthesis of economic relationships, toward "system building." Smith's further doctrine that this underlying natural order required for its most beneficent operation a system of natural liberty, and that in the main public regulation and private monopoly were corruptions of that natural order, at once gave to economics a bond of union with the prevailing philosophy and theology and to economists and statesmen a programme of practical reform.[86]

While "the doctrine of self-reliance and self-denial, which is the foundation of political economy, was written as legibly in the New Testament as in the *Wealth of Nations,* it was not recognized until our age."[87] Scotland became "the land of porridge and political economy."

Professor Hollander has traced the influence of the master's work in the establishment of the classical school of political economy. The lectures of Dugald Stewart, in which the doctrines of the *Wealth of Nations,* were expounded, were attended by James Mill, the father of John Stuart Mill, Sydney Smith, John Ramsay McCulloch, and Henry Brougham. "The 'gospel of mammon" according to some entered the university curriculum." "The word *corn* sounded strangely in the moral class and *drawbacks* seemed a profanation of Stewart's voice."[88]

The *Edinburgh Review,* which first appeared in October, 1802,

[86]*Ibid.,* pp. 116-17.

[87]Acton, *History of Freedom,* p. 28.

[88]*Adam Smith, 1776-1926,* p. 33. "When an University has been doing useless things for a long time, it appears at first degrading to them to be useful. A set of lectures upon Political Economy would be discouraged in Oxford, possibly despised, probably not permitted. To discuss the Enclosure of Commons, and to dwell upon imports and exports—to come so near to common life, would seem to be undignified and contemptible. In the same manner, the Parr or the Bentley of his day would be scandalized to be put on a level with the discoverer of a neutral salt; and yet what other measure is there of dignity in intellectual labour, but usefulness and difficulty? And what ought the term *University* to mean, but a place where every science is taught which is liberal, and at the same time useful to mankind? Nothing would so much tend to bring classical literature within proper bounds as a steady and invariable appeal to these tests in our appreciation of all human knowledge. The puffed-up pedant would collapse into his proper size, and the maker of verses and the rememberer of words would soon assume that station which is the lot of those who go up unbidden to the upper places of the feast" (G. W. E. Russell, *Sydney Smith,* London, 1905, p. 11).

gave an important place[39] to economic criticism. Malthus, Say,[40] and Ricardo and later John Stuart Mill came under the influence of the *Wealth of Nations* and devoted their energies to its extension, its simplification, and the widening of its influence. Marshall described the period 1770-1820 as the classical epoch in which the author "by the form or the matter of his words or deeds . . . has stated or indicated architectonic ideas in thought or sentiment which are in some degree his own and which once created can never die but are an existing yeast ceaselessly working in the cosmos.[41] But the followers of Adam Smith lost the great concept of society as a whole. Ricardo, and the utilitarians destroyed it in the interests of a market economy with its sale of land and labour (Polanyi).

In his attempt to elaborate the natural order as understood by Adam Smith and immediately to combat the notions of Godwin as to the perfectibility of human nature, Malthus wrote his *Essay on Population* and its extensive later revisions. His thesis that population tended to outrun the food supply was a profound contribution to the subject of political economy, as a branch of biology, and to the subject of biology. Both Wallace and Darwin, who developed the theory of evolution independently, have paid tribute to the crucial

[39]Francis Jeffrey, who became editor, made an abstract of the *Wealth of Nations* in 1792 and in the winter of 1800-1 attended a course of lectures in political economy by Dugald Stewart (Lord Cockburn, *Life of Lord Jeffrey*, Edinburgh, 1852, Vol. I, p. 64). Francis Horner wrongly argued that Turgot's *Reflections on the Formation and Distribution of Wealth* was "a work . . . truly denominated, by Condorcet, the germ of Adam Smith's Inquiry" (*Memoirs and Correspondence of Francis Horner, M.P.*, London, 1853, Vol. I, p. 68). "The perusal of this beautiful chapter of Smith on the corn trade has suggested to me the propriety of studying his work as a model of argumentative composition. I should imagine, that his style of reasoning, so artificial and yet so perspicuous, so ingeniously minute and yet so broad and comprehensive, would be admirably adapted to the subjects of law" (p. 117). Smith's system is "evidently imperfect; and yet it has so much the air of a system, . . . that we are apt to adopt erroneous opinions because they figure in the same fabric with approved and important truths." Smith might have "contributed more powerfully to the progress of political science, had he developed his opinions in detached essays" (pp. 126-7). Later he wrote: "We owe much at present to the superstitious worship of Smith's name; and we must not impair that feeling, till the victory is more complete. There are few practical errors in the '*Wealth of Nations*,' at least of any great consequence" (p. 237). Horner as well as Lauderdale and Dugald Stewart found the fifth chapter extremely difficult if not unintelligible (pp. 164-5, 244-5). Nor did Horner and Lauderdale find Quesnay's Economic Table intelligible (pp. 204-5). Adam Smith's *Moral Sentiments* was "the most scientific and acute description . . . in any branch of . . . the natural history of the mind" (pp. 328-9).

[40]*Adam Smith, 1776-1926*, Chap. VII.

[41]*Ibid.*, p. 28.

position of his work. In a letter to Wallace dated April 6, 1839, Darwin wrote: "I came to the conclusion that selection was the principle of change from the study of domesticated production; and then reading Malthus (October, 1838) I saw at once how to apply the principle."[42] Both Malthus and Darwin were exposed to bitter attacks, but their contributions to the science of biology, including economics, cannot be denied. Herbert Spencer elaborated the significance of Darwin's contributions to the social sciences. His influence ranged from the academic work of Thorstein Veblen in the United States to the important political achievements of John Morley in Great Britain.

The influence of Adam Smith and the political economists was strengthened by the outcome of the struggle for civil and religious liberty. In the last half of the eighteenth century deism declined. Newman has remarked that the Roman Catholic Church suppresses reason and the Anglican Church feeling, and that consequently Anglicans become Methodists and Roman Catholics infidels. The religious influence of Wesley, and the humanitarianism of Wilberforce and the Clapham Sect brought an interest in reform and the end of the slave trade. The American and French Revolutions on the one hand tightened the bonds of the aristocracy[43] and on the other accentuated the demands for release. Burke wrote in favour of the American Revolution and against the French Revolution. Wordsworth was sympathetic to the French Revolution but turned to hostility. Coleridge adapted Kantian philosophy to the demands of the Conservative position. Godwin, Shelley, the Hunts, and Hazlitt sponsored an interest in revolution. The energies of Cobbett and Place and the radicalism of James and John Stuart Mill, Bentham, and writers for the *Westminster Review* stiffened the influence of the Whigs for reform. Sydney Smith and writers in the *Edinburgh Review* and Albany Fonblanque in the *Examiner* were effective in securing Catholic emancipation, the Reform Acts, the reduction of taxes on knowledge and eventually the destruction of the mercantilist system. Robert Burns gave a fatal blow to ecclesiasticism in Scotland.

[42]*More Letters of Charles Darwin* (London, 1903), Vol. I, p. 118. See also Geoffrey West, *Charles Darwin* (New Haven, 1938), p. 167; and H. Ward, *Charles Darwin* (Indianapolis, 1927), p. 288.

[43]Anthony Lincoln, *Some Political and Social Ideas of British Dissent, 1763-1800* (Cambridge, 1938).

The effects of the contributions of Puritanism to political liberty evident in the revolt of the American colonies, and to economic liberty in the publication of the *Wealth of Nations,* have been described at great length. They compelled the shift from centralization to decentralization in the British Empire.[44] The clearing away of the vast accumulations of mercantilism[45] in the introduction of free trade and in the repeal of the Navigation Acts, the escape from vested interests, centring about staple products under mercantilism, the improvement of the conditions of the working classes in England, the contributions of Romilly, Bentham and Brougham in the improvement of legal machinery—all these far-reaching changes were a part of the achievements of the early nineteenth century.

The reform movements had their significance for education not only in the attention of the state to popular education[46] and in voluntary organizations such as the Society for the Diffusion of Knowledge, but also in the universities. The establishment of the University of London brought competition with the old universities, and the intrusion of the state particularly in education in Ireland led to the Anglo-Catholic movement under Newman and the decline of interest in theological controversy.

The railway mania of 1847 and King Hudson was the first material that rushed in to fill up the vacuum. G. V. Cox says, "Instead of High, Low, and Broad Church, they talked of high embankments, the broad gauge, and low dividends. Brunel and Stephenson were in men's mouths instead of Dr. Pusey or Mr. Golightly; and speculative theology gave way to speculation in railway shares" (Recollections, p. 238). The truth is that this movement, which swept the leader of the Tractarians, with most of his followers, out of the place, was an epoch in the history of the university. It was a deliverance from the nightmare which had oppressed Oxford for fifteen years. For so long we had been given over to discussions unprofitable in themselves, and which had entirely diverted our thoughts from the true business of the place. Probably

[44]See *The Cambridge History of the British Empire,* Vol. II, *The Growth of the New Empire, 1783-1870* (Cambridge, 1940), Chap. IV.

[45]"That great juggle of the 'English Constitution'—a thing of monopolies, and Church-craft, and sinecures, armorial hocus-pocus, primogeniture, and pageantry" (John Morley, *The Life of Richard Cobden,* London, 1881, Vol. I, p. 130).

[46]"The schoolmaster is abroad. And I trust more to him, armed with his primer, than I do to the soldier in full military array, for upholding and extending the liberties of his country" (Brougham, in speech, January 29, 1828).

there was no period of our history during which, I do not say science and learning, but the ordinary study of the classics was so profitless or at so low an ebb as during the period of the Tractarian controversy. By the secessions of 1845 this was extinguished in a moment, and from that moment dates the regeneration of the University. Our thoughts reverted to their proper channel, that of the work we had to do. . . . More than this, the abject deference fostered by theological discussion for authority, whether of the Fathers, or the Church, or the Primitive Ages, was incompatible with the free play of intellect which enlarges knowledge, creates science, and makes progress possible. In a word, the period of Tractarianism had been a period of obscurantism, which had cut us off from the general movement; an eclipse which had shut out the light of the sun in heaven. Whereas other reactions accomplished themselves by imperceptible degrees, in 1845 the darkness was dissipated, and the light was let in in an instant, as by the opening of the shutters in the chamber of a sick man who has slept till midday. Hence the flood of reform, which broke over Oxford in the next few years following 1845, which did not spend itself till it had produced two Government commissions, until we had ourselves enlarged and remodelled all our institutions.[47]

Scholarship[48] at last emerged to a foremost place. In Cambridge mathematics had checked the growth of obscurantism and provided the environment in which Marshall wrote his *Principles of Economics*. In Oxford political economy found a place. The historical school was gradually adapted to new demands.

[47]Mark Pattison, *Memoirs* (London, 1885), pp. 235-9.

[48]"Dorat (died 1588) represents that moment in French literature—a moment which has never recurred—when Greek learning was in alliance with public taste and polite letters. In England this phase of accomplishment, which survived till within the present century, monopolized the name of scholarship. The English word 'scholar' has no equivalent in any living language. In Germany the word 'Gelehrte' is characteristic of a country which has learning without a literature. France, which has a literature pauperized by the absence of knowledge, has no word which can represent 'scholar,' as for nearly three centuries it has not known the class" (*Essays by the Late Mark Pattison*, Vol. I, p. 20). "It appears, meanwhile, that the representatives of the historical sciences have no place in this category. They fall under a purely literary valuation because, however superb their knowledge and their power of communicating it, they are only concerned with the knowledge of parts of the world and not with the formulation of laws, for 'historical laws' are indefinite and contested. Whether economics, with its laws of life, has already produced representatives of unquestionable greatness is doubtful.

"In mathematics and science, on the other hand, there have been universally acknowledged great men.

"All thought was first liberated when Copernicus dismissed the earth from the centre of the universe and assigned it to its place in a subordinate orbit of a single solar system" (Jacob Burckhardt, *Force and Freedom*, New York, 1943, pp. 310-11).

Indeed, the desuetude and even direct discouragement of the academical study of the Roman law during the last two centuries has been a concurrent cause with the neglect of philosophy, of that contracted habit of the national mind to which this country owes at once its success and its littleness; its success in the practical employments of commerce, its incapacity for enlarged views either of national welfare, or of foreign policy. The same superstition of Puritanism, which in the seventeenth century proscribed the speculative theology and philosophy as being popish, operated too against the imperial constitutions, which were tainted by their Roman origin.

For the general student in the History School, however, a more valuable scientific element even than the civil code is offered by political economy. Indeed, history, unless combined with a study of the positive laws of human welfare, is little better than a portion of elegant literature. It is void of any instructive power, and sinks into an amusement, into curious research, or at best becomes so much information for conversational purposes. This subject we may hope to see grow upon this School. It should not be treated as a special subject, which, like Roman law, may or may not be known. It should be understood to be *the* theoretical science of history, and should be required of all candidates, except the law students, who have not time for it. Besides the vital connection of this subject with history, this science is especially the home growth of Britain. It is the only science of which it can be said that the principles have been discovered and extended chiefly by Englishmen; the best books on it are written in the English language, and the very facts themselves on which its inductions are based have been supplied by the mercantile and industrial development of Great Britain. The treatise of Ricardo is almost the perfection of a logically reasoned science applied to an adequate collection of carefully examined phenomena.[49]

The economic expansion of England in the nineteenth century gave it a peculiar place.

In one department of progress the English development has indeed been complete, regular, and from within. In commerce and manufactures, England may be said to have conducted on behalf of the world, but at her own risks and perils, the one great commercial experiment that has yet been made. Our practice has been so extended and diversified, that from it alone, with but little reference to that of the other trading nations of antiquity, or of modern times, the laws of economics have been inferred, and a new science constructed on a solid and indisputable basis.[50]

[49]*Ibid.*, p. 486.
[50]*Ibid.*, Vol. II, pp. 400-1.

These far-reaching changes based on economic expansion increased the divergence with the continent.

"It has often been remarked with regret [writes Sir Henry Maine] that while the learned in the exacter sciences abroad and in England have the most perfect sympathy with each other—while the physician or the mathematician in London is completely at home in the writings of the physician or the mathematician in Berlin and Paris, there is a sensible, though invisible, barrier, which separates the jurists, the moral philosophers, the politicians, and the historians of the Continent, from those who follow the same pursuits in England." The divergence—a divergence not of opinion, but in our mode of thinking—is even more manifested in our Theology, than in the moral and political sciences.[51]

Political economy never flourished in competition with law in the universities of France and Germany. The imperial system of Rome was too strongly entrenched. Europe began to specialize, and with specialization came the dangers of division.

In quite modern times it would seem as if the burden and labour of human progress were pretty evenly shared between the three nations of Europe who have any liberty of action at all. The French had hitherto the working out of the political problem. To the share of the English has fallen the social and industrial difficulty. Speculative Germany has claimed for her own the problems of thought, the abstract matters of Philosophy and Theology. To each of these separate tasks is attached its own burden, its own peculiar danger.[52]

III. THE TYRANNY OF OPINION AND LEARNING

Dangers were accentuated in England by the growth of the press and the importance of public opinion.

These causes are to be found in the general levelling tendency exerted by the advancing tide of civilization. In its superficial aspect, this tendency shows itself in that spectre of the Tory party which they call "democracy." Its deeper forces are found in the increasing influence exercised over Government by a certain dead level of "public opinion." Our national Church has happily escaped political revolution which is leavening society. The tyranny of opinion has been making steady advances in Western Europe; nowhere more rapidly

[51]*Ibid.*, p. 212.
[52]*Ibid.*, pp. 216-17.

than in England. At one time it was worth the Church's while to ally itself with the State, i.e., with the Government. But it is now understood that Government has a master, and it is found to be better policy to contract the alliance directly with that master. This master is the public opinion of the majority. He who has a good understanding with this can afford to quarrel with power, even though it be the power of a Napoleon. Whatever other merit the opinion of the majority may have, it is, in the present condition of our population, an unenlightened opinion. It must be founded on passion rather than on reason; on prejudice, not on knowledge; it will prefer the interests of its class to those of the whole, and its own immediate to its remote interest. The numbers of the wise who think are little capable of increase at any time; but the numbers of the public who are influenced by opinion become yearly greater. Knowledge has less and less influence on affairs, and opinion more and more. This is not only the case in secular politics, but in religion also. Theology has absolutely no weight in this country, where there is not even any faculty of canonists. But religious opinion operates over a larger area than any other opinion whatever.[53]

In an essay on "intellectual responsibility and the political spirit" Morley wrote:

Practically and as a matter of history, a society is seldom at the same time successfully energetic both in temporals and spirituals; seldom prosperous alike in seeking abstract truths and nursing the political spirit. There is a decisive preponderance in one direction or the other, and the equal balance between free and active thinking and coherent practical energy in a community seems too hard to sustain.[54]

These conclusions were supported by his observations on English life in the latter part of the last century. Earlier in the same essay he wrote:

The political spirit has grown to be the strongest element in our national life; the dominant force, extending its influence over all our ways of thinking in matters that have least to do with politics, or even nothing at all to do with them. There has thus been engendered among us the real sense of political responsibility. In a corresponding

[53]*Ibid.*, pp. 298-9. "We are not sure that the amount of illiberality pervading public opinion in England is not more powerful for evil, than the amount of repression exerted over public opinion in France" (*Ibid.*, p. 402).

[54]*On Compromise* (London, 1921), p. 61.

degree has been discouraged . . . the sense of intellectual responsibility.[55]

Again:

The undisputed predominance of the political spirit has a plain tendency to limit the subjects in which the men animated by it can take a real interest. All matters fall out of sight, or at least fall into a secondary place, which do not bear more or less directly and patently upon the material and structural welfare of the community. In this way the members of the community miss the most bracing, widening and elevated of the whole range of influences that create great characters. First, they lose sincere concern about the larger questions which the human mind has raised up for itself; second, they lose a fearless desire to reach the true answers to them.[56]

This impoverishment of aims and depravation of principles by the triumph of the political spirit outside its proper sphere cannot unfortunately be restricted to any one set of people in the state. It is something in the very atmosphere which no sanitary cordon can limit.[57]

On the North American continent opinion has occupied an even stronger position. Precisely because of the character of its commercial civilization the Anglo-Saxon community, especially in North America, has linked trade to opinion. Advertising has become an integral part of the activities of the press with vital implications to opinion. Political activity and trade are facets of this civilization. This background implies a distinct and possibly unbridgeable gap between Anglo-Saxon and other European communities.

In England we have been less affected than other nations by the two main sources of interference, viz., the authority of government and the influence of foreigners. . . . In Germany we see an unhealthy tripartite division: (1) the Governments; (2) the Intellectual Class; (3) the People. The governments exclusive, narrow-minded, inquisitorial, meddlesome; the small intellectual class, possessing a compass of knowledge, and a breadth of thought, which make it lead the speculative intellect of the world; the people more superstitious, more really unfit for political power, than the inhabitants of England. This divergence of interests between classes is due to the fact, that the intellectual stimulus of Germany was a stimulus administered from without. They received their impulse from their contact

[55] *Ibid.*, p. 60.
[56] *Ibid.*, p. 62.
[57] *Ibid.*, p. 71.

with French intellect imported wholesale by the Great Frederick. Hence the highest intellects in Germany have so far outstripped the progress of the mass of their fellow-countrymen, that they have absolutely no influence upon them. . . . The stock of American knowledge is small, but it is the common property of the whole nation; the stock of German knowledge is immense, but it is in very few hands. Thus Germany is unfitted for our purpose by a serious failure in the diffusion of knowledge; American by a deficiency in its amount.[58]

In Anglo-Saxon countries the spread of democracy has accompanied the penetration of politics. An American pertinently asked, "Why it is that when Canadians meet they always talk politics?"; but the vice is not peculiar to Canadians. The implications of opinion to institutions of learning in Anglo-Saxon communities have been evident on every hand. The tyranny of opinion can be read in the speeches of university presidents and in the degree lists of most universities. A highly respected university in Canada has the distinction of giving the same honorary degree twice to the same premier of a province. Another university refused a degree to the premier of a province presumably for political reasons. The effects of the tyranny of opinion have been evident in the commercialization of universities. One might cite the neglect of an interest in Russia and the Orient and the unseemly haste to repair the damage and the tenuous position of labour in university curricula.

The university must be the intellectual capital of the country, attracting to itself, not all the talent, but all the speculative intellect. It should be an independent body, fenced round by its own privileges —prescriptive rights too sacred to be easily invaded—with its own annals and code of laws. But political independence is of less consequence to it than social. It should have sufficient social status for its honours and dignities to be in themselves rewards, and that its members should not be under the temptation to secure for themselves other positions, political or ecclesiastical, to which their academical place would then rank as subordinate. If there be not some proportion between the prizes which public life, or the professions, and those which the university itself, offer, the former will always draw off the highest talent, and leave only the second-rate and mediocre for academic labours.[59]

[58]*Essays by the Late Mark Pattison*, Vol. II, pp. 398-9.

[59]*Ibid.*, Vol. I, p. 419. The civil service, notably the judiciary has developed various devices, such as high salaries, to check the influence of political opinion. At least one university president has argued that low salaries were paid in universities to facilitate participation in outside activities.

The significance of political influence has been striking in the social sciences since the depression and the war. The demands of parties have compelled a liquidation of the prestige of learning in the social sciences, universities have become reserve pools of labour to supply political parties during periods of crisis. Government as an art has been largely free of academic traditions in democracies, but the crises of the depression and the war have led to a demand on all sides for men bringing prestige. Unfortunately the social sciences have created an impression of scientific finality and the use of the word sciences suggests the power of the fallacy. Large heavy volumes of a statistical character written by committees in a mechanized style gave the appearance of finality. The intensive cultivation of mathematics has enhanced the impression. We have definitely emerged from the happy state described in the last century.

> This is true of all science, but it is more particularly true of History and Economy. Here, more than in any other field, do we feel that theory exists for the sake of the facts, and not facts for the sake of the theory. In these practical sciences we are less liable to that science-worship which infests the more theoretical, in which the more abstract and general the expression the better. The economists and statisticians have not yet learnt this fanaticism.[80]

We have learned fanaticism. Research, like Mesopotamia, has become a blessed word.

The gap between research and teaching has widened perceptibly with the result that the practicability of the conclusions of research have not been constantly exposed to the tests of teaching experience and of their adaptability to communication to students and even more to a democratic community. The divorce between research and education has been evident in the establishment of specialized insti-

[80] *Ibid.*, Vol. II, p. 424. "The Civil Wars which may be expected, I think (judging from certain fashions which have come in of late) to spread through many countries—together with the malignity of sects which have crept into the place of solid erudition—seem to portend for literature and the sciences a tempest not less fatal. and one against which the Printing office will be no effectual security. And no doubt but that fair-weather learning which is nursed by leisure blossoms under reward and praise, which cannot withstand the shock of opinion, and is liable to be abused by tricks and quackery, will sink under such impediments as these. Far otherwise is it with that knowledge whose dignity is maintained by works of utility and power" (R. W. Church, *Bacon*, London, 1910, p. 72).

tutes[61] attached or not attached to universities, manned by a staff which does no teaching, part-time teaching where they are attached to universities, or full-time teaching when members of the staff are on leave of absence in such institutes. Specialization has meant the emergence of institutes unconnected or loosely connected with teaching and the creation of organizations which may easily be drawn upon by political parties in times of crises. Such organizations may serve as buffers between the universities and political parties, but the advantage is offset by their inefficiency as buffers and by the decline in efficiency of teaching. The conclusions presented by specialized institutions become less assimilable to students[62] and more suitable to the demands of bureaucratic exhibitionism. The prevailing trend toward education of larger numbers of students and the establishment of institutes have made it impossible for university administrators to adapt themselves to new developments in the field of knowledge.[63]

[61]The "present-mindedness" described by Professor Schuyler (*Proceedings of the American Philosophical Society,* Vol. LXXXVII (4), 1944, pp. 342-51) has dominated research in the social sciences in the period between the two wars. The interest in the organization of research on a large scale, beginning in the last war, gained momentum in the upswing of business cycle during the twenties and was given elaborate support by governments during the depression. The handicraft was steadily displaced by the machine. As in other industries, large-scale capital equipment brought, if not monopoly, a substantial oligopoly. Research became concentrated with special reference to its own peculiar regard for location theory, of which the details need not be enumerated here. The adaptability of the monetary system with its mathematical bias to the calculating machine has done much to validate the predictions of Veblen in his emphasis on the pecuniary and industrial bifurcation of Western civilization. See Thorstein Veblen, "Economic Theory in the Calculable Future" (*American Economic Review,* Vol. XV (1), 1925, supplement; pp. 48-55). Large buildings and fixed capital equipment and the production of volumes unintelligible to the majority parallel the large endowments and mystic rites of ecclesiastical institutions. Economic mysticism displaces religious mysticism as may be seen in the interest of the Church in economic movements such as co-operation. On the other hand, organizations have emerged to provide excuses for avoiding intensive research. Scholarship is deliberately directed by purchase to stimulate present-mindedness. Wealth, prestige and academic pretensions have been used as stepping stones for academic and political preferment. "Disinterested activity and the slow opening of long term projects become well-nigh impossible as situational pressures call for quick results" (Logan Wilson, *The Academic Man,* New York, 1942, p. 219).

[62]F. W. Maitland wrote of Leslie Stephen: "He had not the advantage—the inestimable advantage—of constantly endeavouring to explain his theories to beginners and to construct a highway in which fools cannot err" (*The Life and Letters of Leslie Stephen,* London, 1906, p. 327).

[63]See *Essays by the Late Mark Pattison,* Vol. I, p. 460.

The results have been evident in a rapid deterioration of public opinion. A few years ago we had in this country a premier who occasioned much jeering by a political programme which offered $25.00 a month to the electors. With the aid of the social sciences we have far outstripped this proposal in our offers to provide full employment or, more modestly, reasonable employment. "Never surely was so much promised to so many for so little" (C. R. Fay). Research has made us perhaps very learned but not necessarily very wise. One is always impressed by the contrast between the ripe judgments of men with long experience in business and in politics and the parade of intensive research. Learning is overloaded with precocities. The importance of the obvious has been overlooked by research. The rapid growth of bureaucracies recruited from highly specialized social sciences has brought the rapid growth of ecclesiasticism and the rapid decline of scepticism. Democracies are becoming people who cannot understand, run by people buttressed and protected by the ramparts of research. In this country I am told it is customary for members of the bureaucracy to prod members of the opposition in Parliament to follow a line of policy which will compel members of the Government to yield to their wishes. Well might they accept the words of Locke[64] as their motto: "The greater part cannot learn and therefore they must believe." "Truth" has superseded the search for truth, and little respect is paid to Professor Knight's claim:

> Only on . . . the subject matter of price theory economics can it be said that any great headway toward satisfactory treatment has been made and that is but a limited aspect of the total problem of action. Without an adequate ethics and sociology in the broad sense, economics has little to say about policy.[65]
>
> The direct effects of "preaching" about economic relations and obligations are in general bad; and the kind of legislation which results from the clamour of idealistic preachers—and from the public attitude which such preaching at once expresses and tends to venerate or aggravate—is especially bad. All this is the natural consequence of exhortation without knowledge or understanding—of well meaning people attempting to meddle with the workings of extremely com-

[64]Thomas Fowler, *Locke* (London, 1883), p. 158.

[65]F. H. Knight, "Ethics and Economic Reform" (*Economica.* n.s., Vol. VI (24), 1939, p. 422.

plicated and sensitive machinery which they do not understand. . . . Christianity affords no concrete guidance for social action, beyond an urge to do "good and avoid evil."[66]

The rise of political economy reflected the growth of economic liberty. In the attempt to discover a natural order it emphasized the position of the individual. Marshall with Jevons, Walras, and Pareto and Pigou extended the principles of equilibrium and widened the possibilities of mathematics. The phrases, "Natura non facit saltum" (Nature never proceeds by leaps), "the one in the many, the many in the one," of Marshall's *Principles of Economics* and *Industry and Trade* reflect the philosophy. The combination of the mathematical and the biological fallacies has been challenged by the insistence that civilization is an art. "In art, as in life, the chief problem is a right choice in sacrifices. Civilization is the organization of values."[67] Toynbee and students of civilization insist that while "nature never proceeds by leaps," civilization proceeds in precisely that fashion. "All spiritual growth takes place by leaps and bounds, both in the individual and . . . in the community" (Burckhardt).

Economic liberty followed civil and religious liberty and was less firmly rooted in Western civilization. As the most tender plant it has suffered first from the disappearance of civil liberty. Economic liberty as supported by the classical school assumed an economy of resources in the policies of government and was effective in the destruction of the wasteful policies of the mercantile systems. It pointed to policies by which large organizations were allowed to grind each other down and to make way for smaller organizations.[68]

[66]*Ibid.*, pp. 418-19. "Political Economy, as I venture to think, has been especially valuable in what I have called the negative aspect. It has been more efficient in dispersing sophistries than in constructing permanent theories. . . . But the complexity of the problem is so great—and the working of industrial forces so essentially bound up with other more inscrutable forces, that I confess to a certain scepticism as to the truly scientific character of their more positive conclusions" (Leslie Stephen, *Life of Henry Fawcett*, London, 1886, p. 449).

[67]Geoffrey Scott, *The Architecture of Humanism* (London, 1926), p. 163.

[68]George Unwin's favourite quotation was from William James: "I am against bigness and greatness in all their forms. . . . The bigger the unit you deal with, the hollower, the more brutal, the more mendacious is the life displayed " (*Studies in Economic History*, London, 1927, p. 462). See "The Passing of Political Economy" (*Commerce Journal*, March, 1938); W. M. Daniels, "The Passing of the Old Economist" (*Harvard Business Rev.*, Vol. XII, 1933-4, pp. 297-303).

The state intervened as a policeman concerned with more or less fair play[69] between organizations and in the interests of the operation of competition. But the very success of political economy of the classical school evident in the efficiency of industrialism and free trade implied limitations. The advance of Western civilization provided the prosperity which enabled large-scale organizations to extend their activities and compelled the state to restrain them. "Vexatious interference . . . the ordinary treatment of commerce by power" (Pattison) became an obligation. The overpowering demands of administration have been reflected in the decline in emphasis on philosophy in the study of political economy. The curricula of universities are concerned to an increasing extent with the routine and details of administration,[70] and students are taught more and more about less and less. Larger numbers of poorer students can be trained in the details of routine, and routine demands larger numbers of poorer students. We have all the answers and none of the questions.

The increasing power of the state has involved the subordination of political economy in the classical sense if not its disappearance. Art has been displaced by science. "Not poetry, but science, not sentiment but calculation is now the misguiding influence."[71] The

[69]See F. H. Knight, *The Ethics of Competition and Other Essays* (New York, 1935).

[70]One is reminded of the comments on Oxford in the last century. "Young M.A.'s of talent abound, but they are all taken up with the conduct of some wheel in the complex machinery of cram, which grinds down all specific tendencies and tastes into one uniform mediocrity. The men of middle age seem, after they reach thirty-five or forty, to be struck with an intellectual palsy, and betake themselves no longer to port, but to the frippery work of attending boards and negotiating some phantom of legislation, with all the importance of a cabinet council—*belli simulacra cientes.* Then they give each other dinners, where they assemble again with the comfortable assurance that they have earned their evening relaxation by the fatigues of university, and who give the tone to it—a tone as of a lively municipal borough; all the objects of science and learning, for which a university exists, being put out of sight by the consideration of the material means of endowing them" (Mark Pattison, *Memoirs,* p. 90).

[71]See Geoffrey Scott, *Architecture of Humanism,* p. 92. The importance of political economy as a branch of biology and as an art is emphasized by Polanyi who argues for an approach through society and culture as a means of avoiding the dangers of sudden changes incidental to exposure to machine industry and the market economy. "No specifically human motive is economic" (Knight). See Karl Polanyi, *The Great Transformation* (New York, 1944), p. 250.

advances in political economy have been concentrated on mathematical analysis and a narrowing of the subject to a small number of experts and a consequent decline in interest in the philosophical and political background. Lip service is paid to the plea that free trade is better than dominion.[72] "When goods cease to move across boundaries armies will begin" (Cordell Hull). But since 1914 the modern state has drawn more heavily on the social sciences and thought has been paralysed. The extension of government boards and innumerable royal commissions have in one way or another drawn the social scientist into the service of the state. Social scientists in the service of the state necessitate the appointment of social scientists in the service of private enterprise to combat their encroachment. There are few economists who will say, and none who will say so well, as Adam Smith: "People of the same trade seldom meet together, even for merriment or diversion, but the conversation ends in a conspiracy against the public, or in some contrivance to raise prices." In these times an economist[73] will be among them. If the social scientist is drawn into the civil service, royal commissions, or industry, or even if he is not, he is attracted to the

[72]"Warriors and despots are generally bad economists, and . . . instinctively carry their ideas of force and violence into the civil policy of their governments. Free trade is a principle which recognizes the paramount advantage of individual action. Military conquerors, on the contrary, trust only to the organized efforts of bodies of men directed by their own personal will" (John Morley, *The Life of Richard Cobden*, p. 460). "All power is military; but military power requires success to establish it and exercise to preserve it. In such wretched governments therefore peace is a source of anarchy. Military government is beyond all others, subject to personal revolutions, because it requires a degree of vigour and vigilance of character to maintain it, to which no passion less powerful than that of ambition, and no education but that of struggle, can discipline the mind" (*Memoirs of the Life of the Right Honourable Sir James Mackintosh*, Vol. I, p. 472).

[73]The emphasis on large-scale research between the two wars has brought to a sharp focus the problem of status of the social scientist. Without a tradition of professionalism the social scientist has been the prey of governments and of private enterprise. The results have been scandalous. It would be invidious to point to illustrations, but it may be worth noting that in the United States the great seductions have been made by private enterprise and in Canada by political parties and governments, but exceptions are so obvious that it would be unsafe to make generalizations. Until the social sciences can develop effective deodorants and then disinfectants, the subject must continue at a stage comparable to the age before Lister in medicine. See Stephen Leacock, *Canada* (Montreal, 1941); David Lewis and Frank Scott, *Make This Your Canada* (Toronto, 1943); Ernest Gruening, *The Public Pays: A Study of Power Propaganda* (New York, 1931).

problem of politics and power. Within limits an "economist"[74] is something to conjure with and in the hands of the politician he has been used to foster the interests of the party and the state. The economist becomes a political economist. He has enlisted with pressure groups in the struggle against other pressure groups or he has enlisted with the state as centralized power. The decline in communicability in the social sciences has made the social scientist an ally of the modern state as the great pickpocket. Absorption of the social scientist in bureaucracy in the present crisis has left the community exposed to a flood of arrant nonsense.[75]

IV. THE ECONOMIC EFFECTS OF LIBERTY

In North America westward expansion after the War of 1812 made enormous demands on the energies of the people. The importance of agriculture was evident in the strength of Jeffersonianism, the emergence of Jacksonian democracy, and the abolition of the national bank. Penetration to the interior of the continent and increasing distances brought demands for free land and precipitated the clash with the representatives of the cotton kingdom of the South. The desert of the southern great plains brought the expansion of cotton-growing to an end and led to the struggle over slave-holding

[74]"It is no explanation of the universal regret, that he was a considerable political economist: no real English gentleman, in his secret soul, was ever sorry for the death of a political economist: he is much more likely to be sorry for his life. There is an idea that he has something to do with statistics; or, if that be exploded, that he is a person who writes upon 'value': says that rent is—you cannot very well make out what; talks excruciating currency; he may be useful as drying machines are useful; but the notion of crying about him is absurd. The economical loss might be great, but it will not explain the mourning for Francis Horner" (Walter Bagehot, *Literary Studies*, London, 1879, p. 20). This description is no longer accurate.

[75]"Of all things, they love a long and an expensive war, and fear peace; for peace produces order, and gives the Prince leisure to enquire into the abuses of the state; it lets him into a right knowledge of persons in the kingdom, and the dregs which float upwards when the liquor is stirred, must sink to the bottom in quiet times; peace restores liberty of speech, whereas in war all is silenced with the single word necessity; in peace there is no need to court factions, turbulent spirits are not so useful, thrift may be introduced, and such sudden fortunes cannot be raised out of the public. Grievances may be calmly debated, the management of the revenues inspected, the conduct of the ministers may be examined; and good laws may be proposed, without the perpetual objection of, 'Are you for bringing in the French and "Popery"?' But war will better answer their designs, who mean to thrive by the loose administration with which war is generally accompanied, and who propose to prosper by the calamities and misery of their country" (*The Political and Commercial Works of Charles Davenant*, London, 1771, Vol. II, pp. 311-12).

in the territories which ended in Civil War. The highly organized aristocratic society based on cotton and slave-owning effectively resisted over a long period the loosely knit democratic society of the North. With the eventual success of the North and the collapse of the South, northern policies prevailed. Industrialism forged ahead with the production of iron, coal, and oil and the construction of railways. It had the support of financial technique worked out by such pioneers as Jay Cooke during the Civil War. Lack of resistance was apparent in the domination of the Republican party and the limitation of Democratic presidents since the Civil War to Cleveland, Wilson, and F. D. Roosevelt. The Democratic party strengthened its position in the South and in urban centres such as New York. The Supreme Court,[76] built upon foundations laid down by Marshall, survived the critical period of the Civil War and strengthened the position of industrialism. The increasing strength of the Democratic party in the South and the urbanization of population eventually brought a demand for new types of control in economic life. The diversities of a vast region and a constitutional system with its emphasis on appeals to the voting public and on checks on power have enabled a republic to sustain a civil war and to support adjustments over a long period. Absence of a large army, an established church, and a landholding class and the adoption of a constitution emphasizing balance hastened economic development and facilitated strategic control over natural resources by relatively small numbers.

In Canada severance of political relations with France after the fall of Quebec enhanced the power of the Church along the lower St. Lawrence. The American Revolution was followed by the migration of Loyalist elements particularly to regions in the Maritimes and in the region which became Upper Canada. Small colonies were organized on a militaristic basis as a means of resisting the United States. Settlement and land policy reflected the centralizing effects of military demands. Immigrants from Great Britain especially Scotland and from the United States and French Canadians opposed these centralizing tendencies to the point of rebellion in 1837. William Lyon Mackenzie was thoroughly steeped in Scottish life and tradition.[77] In Nova Scotia the traditions of the New

[76]See Brooks Adams, *The Theory of Social Revolutions* (New York, 1913).

[77]R. A. Mackay, "The Political Ideas of William Lyon Mackenzie," *Canadian Journal of Economics and Political Science*, Vol. III (1), 1937, p. 1.

England colonies in the Assembly survived, and responsible government was achieved under the leadership of Joseph Howe without the bloodshed of the St. Lawrence.

The dominance of Scottish influence in the Strachans, the Galts, the Macdonalds, and the Mackenzies provided the solution to religious, political, and constitutional problems in the development of government in the interests of capital expansion through canals and railways. The Act of Union and the British North America Act were instruments designed to secure capital funds, and the skill of Macdonald dominated political and religious groups. Confederation provided no basis for the balancing of powers which characterized the constitutions of Great Britain and the United States. The influence of the Senate was nullified by control of the House of Commons and of the Supreme Court by subordination to the Privy Council. The influence of the Crown was steadily reduced by the House of Commons. Resistance to centralization in the House of Commons was limited to the brief opposition of the administration of Alexander Mackenzie. The complexity of the task of controlling religious groups, evident after the execution of Louis Riel, and conscription, reduced the power of one centralizing group and shifted it to the other. But each was concerned with the major task of capital expansion chiefly in the improvement of transportation—railways and canals—the one favouring private enterprise, the other public ownership. The dominance of the church, neglect of the army, and absence of an aristocratic landholding class facilitated concentration on control over railways and natural resources. Outside the House of Commons, the Privy Council alone served as an effective bulwark in resisting the powers of the federal government and supporting the powers of the provinces. Resistance by the provinces was effective through the influence of language, religion, race, and control over natural resources. The governmental machinery of the provinces has been strengthened in struggles with the federal government by the gradual extinction of legislative councils. Freedom in Canada rests on the tenuous support of the Privy Council and on continued struggle between the provinces and the Dominion. The weakening of Parliament with the dictatorship of the Cabinet or of a small group of the Cabinet or of a small group of civil servants who control the small groups of the Cabinet, and the present unanimity of all parties on expansion of state control weaken the prospect of continued freedom. The lack of unity which has preserved Canadian unity threatens to disappear. The necessity of continuous compromise in the interests of religion, regionalism, and race explains the paucity of political thinking and the importance of pretence in mediocrity to political leaders.

Defeat of the Southern States in the Civil War which brought to an end the compromise arrangements, including the Reciprocity Treaty from 1854 to 1866, was followed by railway construction, occupation of free land, and tariffs. The United Canadas on the St. Lawrence were compelled to improve and extend the system of canals and railways, and to develop a federal structure. After Confederation the federal government built the Intercolonial from Halifax and Saint John to connect with the Grand Trunk Railway and generously supported construction of the Canadian Pacific Railway to the Pacific coast. The government and the railway entered into energetic competition with the railways of the United States for settlers and capital. After the turn of the century two additional transcontinental lines were built to the north of the Canadian Pacific Railway. During the World War these railways and the Grand Trunk and the Intercolonial came into the hands of the federal government. Centralization in Canada was hastened by the defeat of the Southern States and the necessity of competing with an aggressive and successful North. The return in influence of the South in the success of the Democratic party under President F. D. Roosevelt facilitated co-operation with Canada.

The phenomenal economic expansion of Great Britain and North America followed political, religious, and economic liberty. The century of achievement in the Western world has been traced in Professor Clapham's monumental work on the economic history of Great Britain, France, and Germany, and in Professor Wright's *Economic History of the United States.*[78] The enormous increase

[78]See also C. W. Wright, "American Nationalism: An Economic Interpretation" (*Facts and Factors in Economic History*, Cambridge, 1932).

"The pressure and activity of business here [New York] can hardly be conceived. Even London does not give an idea of it; for here all are men of business and all seem to have more to do than they *can* do" New York, November 24, 1836 (*Letters of Anna Jameson to Ottilie von Goethe*, ed. G. H. Needler, New York, 1939, p. 66).

"In England (says Thicknesse), one may trust the honour of a respectable tradesman; in France and Flanders I never experienced a single instance of it. On the continent merchants and tradesmen were looked upon in a degrading point of view, merely for being of that class; nor would the most honourable or

and redistribution of population, the unprecedented extension of capital equipment and production, the phenomenal rise in the standard of living (expenditure as some would call it), and the prosecution of major wars were a result of increasing efficiency of machine industry, especially through inventions affecting communication and transportation and the utilization of vast natural resources, including two new sources of power, petroleum and hydro-electric power, and the increasing effectiveness of the price system.[79] In the production and distribution of goods the assistance of the state has been enlisted on an extensive scale. In the last sentence of his three volumes, Professor Clapham issues a warning that while

> almost the least propertied of their countrymen was already a privileged member of the human race; that the talk of a world of plenty which needed only to be organized, a way of speech then coming into fashion among social experimentalists, was not yet relevant to a world some two-thirds of whose inhabitants had not, by western standards, decent clothing for their backs or plain food enough to eat; and that the privileged position of Britain and indeed of the white races though much less insecure than some pessimists maintained, was not quite certainly a part of the permanent divine order of things.

These achievements were attained with the collapse of mercantilism and the rise of economic liberty. But from the high point at the middle of the last century with the Reciprocity Treaty between

respectable behaviour ever raise them in the ideas or estimates of the nobles or gentry, who are taught to treat them with neglect and even contempt. Thus being deprived of that great motive to noble and liberal actions, the love of honour, rank, the notice of the great, etc., etc., their minds became depressed and degraded" (*Memoirs of the Forty-Five First Years of the Life of James Lackington*, London, 1827, pp. 294-5). Primogeniture in England checked the multiplicity of titles which were evident on the continent (Abraham Hayward, *Selected Essays*, London, 1878, Vol. II, p. 253). Polanyi points out that the English aristocracy assimilated the wealthiest of newcomers of both England and the United States and broadened the upper ranks of the social hierarchy. On the continent the absence of primogeniture hermetically sealed the feudal aristocracy from the *bourgeoisie*. On the other hand, the celibacy of the Catholic clergy saved Europe from a hereditary priesthood, the evils of Brahmanism, and the abominations of the Asiatic system; and made the Church a channel by which ability in governmental administration could be recruited from the people (See *Memoirs of the Life of the Right Honourable Sir James Mackintosh*, Vol. II, p. 14). Michels emphasizes the role of the Socialist party as a channel similar to that of the Catholic Church open to the talents of the people.

[79]See H. A. Innis, "The Penetrative Powers of the Price System" (*Canadian Journal of Economics and Political Science*, Vol. IV (3), 1938).

Canada and the United States from 1854 to 1866 and the Cobden treaty between England and France, free trade has rapidly receded. Rising tariffs reflected the growth of nationalism, the shift from commercialism to capitalism, and the decline of economic liberty. Professor MacIver has listed the fall of the birth-rate, the decline of dogmatic religion, the dominance of finance over industry, the spread of economic consolidations, the growth of urbanization, and the establishment of a mechanical basis for modern society as characteristic of the period.

V. THE PROBLEM OF POWER

Wordsworth in a letter dated June 22, 1817, wrote: "There is, in fact, an unconquerable tendency in all power, save that of knowledge, acting by and through knowledge, to injure the mind of him by whom that power is exercised."[80] The supreme and paramount principle of every corporation that has ever existed, whether spiritual or temporal, is to maintain power.[81] Lord Acton summarized the view in his memorable sentence: "All power corrupts and absolute power corrupts absolutely." "Power tends to expand indefinitely and will transcend all barriers abroad and at home until met by superior forces." This "produces the rhythmic movement of history." "The passion for power over others can never cease to threaten mankind, and is always sure of finding new and unforeseen allies."[82] "It is by the combined efforts of the weak made under compulsion to resist the reign of force and constant wrong that in the rapid change but slow progress of four hundred years, liberty has been preserved and secured and extended and finally understood."[83]

Power is a machine, but it is one of which the moving force is passion, much oftener than knowledge. This is the agent with whose effects and consequences history has to occupy itself. This is the force which moves the world, small and great, from the intrigue that turns out a minister, to the revolution that changes the face of a continent: passion, creating and animating power, degrading knowledge to be the skilled artificer that forges chains for its sub-

[80]Baron Acton, *Lectures on Modern History* (London, 1930), p. 340.

[81]H. T. Buckle, *Introduction to the History of Civilization in England* (London, n.d.), p. 686.

[82]Acton, *History of Freedom*, p. 32. See Ernst Troeltsch, *The Social Teaching of the Christian Churches* (London, 1931).

[83]*Ibid.*, p. 51.

jects. Power, once constituted, has a tendency to perpetuate itself: it is at the discretion of power how much, or how little, intellectual progress its subjects shall be permitted to make. For though knowledge be itself a power yet as it grows up and finds passion already seated on the throne, it cannot raise its head, except so far as the monarch in possession licenses it. Power, however, though excessively jealous is not clear-sighted. It has always entertained suspicions of knowledge, and has usually set its face against it, and kept it under. But it has not done so in all countries with the same thorough-going consistency which it has in some, and which it always could show. Hence, in these countries, as in England, the classes in possession of knowledge were able to wrest a considerable share of power from the classes in possession of the landed property, i.e., capitalized power. And as knowledge, the moment it is at all free, has an irresistible tendency to increase, it has, in England, made those encroachments on property, and shows that disposition to encroach more and more on the prerogatives of property, which theorists mistake for a uniform law of progress, and ascribe to the inherent vitality and expansiveness of knowledge. The history of Europe teaches quite another lesson. In it we see written in characters of blood, the weakness of intellect when separate from force and passion—its utter powerlessness when against them.[84]

Professor F. H. Knight has written that "civilized life under mundane conditions simply cannot be pictured without quite extensive power relations between human beings in addition to power over nature. A defensible ethic doubtless condemns over-emphasis on power; but it must include both the right use of power and the quest of power—by right methods—for right uses."[85] The growth of nationalism and the enormous extension of power in the modern state which has overwhelmed the social sciences have meant that power is regarded as an end rather than a means, and that the checks to centralization of power which strengthened the position of the individual have declined in importance. The effectiveness of the price system and of technological advance which strengthened the position of the individual also provided support through which the state increased its powers. Militarism and the civil service have encroached on liberty. Economic liberty has provided the basis for encroachment on civil liberty.

The problem of power has become more complex with the

[84]*Essays by the Late Mark Pattison,* Vol. II, pp. 427-8.

[85]"Ethics and Economic Reform" (*Economica,* n.s., Vol. VI (24), 1939, p. 421).

marked increase in the size of technological units. Physics and chemistry have dominated biology.[86] The state has increased in strength, by fostering and attempting to control the growth of such concentrations of power with their implications to the problems of war and peace. While the state is, as Professor George Unwin has said, a large number of bald-headed men in offices, the civil service has been greatly extended and has become much more inflexible and powerful. "For every bald-headed man in the office there must be a policeman in somebody else's office" (R. S. Warren). "Great as is my admiration for many of the qualities of our civil service, I am afraid that they are becoming a heavy handicap in our struggle with the totalitarian states, and in making ourselves safe from them. They cramp our energy and spoil or discard our ideas.[87] In Canada the powers of Parliament have been usurped by the Cabinet and the extension of government by orders-in-council. Responsible government perished in Newfoundland with scarcely an audible protest. In the United States there is a fourth term and in Great Britain, national government.

[86]R. E. Parks, "Physics and Society" (*Canadian Journal of Economics and Political Science*, Vol. VI (1), 1940).

[87]J. M. Keynes in the *New Statesman and Nation*, Jan. 28, 1939. In Canada efforts have been made to strengthen the civil service by conspicuous notification to members of Parliament that petty patronage will not be tolerated. On the other hand, the sudden incursion of large numbers of individuals to the civil service unfamiliar with parliamentary tradition has led to public discussion by civil servants on an unprecedented scale—further disquieting evidence of the shallow soil of Parliament in Canada. Nor have members of the Government protested against these violations of convention. Rather than participate in active discussion themselves, they have apparently preferred presentation of policy by civil servants. Announcements of orders-in-council with mysterious numbers and continuous shuffling of departments and of the personnel of departments are unhealthy signs of intense activity and inefficiency. Even such public pronouncements as have been made by members of the Government in and out of Parliament have smacked of the phraseology of the civil servants. The hand is the hand of the Government but the voice is the voice. . . . (See "Notes on Politics since 1918," *Acta Victoriana*, 1941; also R. MacG. Dawson, "Our Bashful Bureaucrats," *Winnipeg Free Press*, Dec. 18, 1942.) Extension of government control increases the difficulties of the police and leads to resort to "the system of common informers" described as "clumsy, upon the principle, that what is left to be every man's business will either become nobody's, or be assumed by those who had better attend to their own affairs, and who will manage their own so much worse for meddling with this; and it frequently has proved very troublesome and impertinent in England, where corrupt people have tried to make a profit, and conceited fanatics to glorify God, by the revival of penal prosecutions, which the necessities of commerce or more rational manners have sunk into disuse" (Francis Horner to J. A. Murray, September 13, 1804, *Memoirs and Correspondence of Francis Horner, M.P.*, Vol. I, pp. 276-7).

VI. LIMITATIONS OF THE SOCIAL SCIENCES

In our concern with the problems of modern scholarship we are faced with the prospect of a new Dark Ages. The recovery of France, Germany, and Italy will be necessarily slow. Nor will Great Britain be able to recapture a position achieved in her universities within the last fifty years without enormous efforts. Nor can we see the possibility of an immediate flowering in North America. It has been said that "of all the practical arts that of education seems most cumbersome in its method, and to be productive of the smallest results with the most lavish expenditure of means."[88] What can be done to foster the growth of the tender plant of scholarship? Hume argued that "it is impossible for the arts and sciences to arise, at first, among any people unless that people enjoy the blessing of a free government."[89] "From law arises security, from security, curiosity, and from curiosity knowledge."[90] "All these causes render free governments the only proper nursery for the arts and sciences. Nothing is more favourable to the rise of politeness and learning, than a number of neighbouring and independent states connected together by commerce and policy. Limited territories give a stop to both power and authority."[91] "The divisions into small states are favourable to learning, by stopping the progress of authority as well as that of power."[92] "A strong genius succeeds best in republics, a refined taste in monarchies. And consequently the sciences are the more natural growth of the one and the polite arts of the other."[93] "When the arts and sciences come to perfection in any state, from that moment, they naturally or rather necessarily decline and seldom or never revive in that nation where they formerly flourished."[94] "Here then is the chief triumph of art and philosophy. It insensibly refines the temper and it points out to us those dispositions we should endeavour to attain by a constant *bent* of mind, and by repeated *habit*."[95] "The same age which produces great philosophers and

[88]Mark Pattison, *Milton* (London, 1932), p. 45.

[89]David Hume, *Essays Moral, Political and Literary*, ed. T. H. Green and T. H. Grose (London, 1875), Vol. I, p. 177.

[90]*Ibid.*, p. 180.

[91]*Ibid.*, p. 181.

[92]*Ibid.*, p. 182.

[93]*Ibid.*, p. 187.

[94]*Ibid.*, p. 195.

[95]*Ibid.*, p. 221.

politicians, renowned generals and poets, usually abounds with skilful weavers and shipcarpenters." "Industry, knowledge and humanity are linked together by an indissoluble chain and are found from experience as well as from reason to be peculiar to the more polished and what are commonly denominated the more luxurious ages."[96]

We have attempted to indicate the circumstances which have been favourable to the growth of freedom and the spread of learning. The collapse of the political power of the Roman Empire was followed by the rise of the spiritual power of the Roman Church. The shift from political power to spiritual power was favourable to the growth of learning, but the organization of spiritual power led to the break of Luther and Calvin, to the Reformation and the counter Reformation, and to the migration of learning to Holland.

Enthusiasm being founded on strong spirits, and a presumptuous boldness of character, it naturally begets the most extreme resolutions, especially after it rises to that height as to inspire the deluded fanatic with the opinion of divine illuminations and with a contempt for the common rules of reason, morality and prudence.[97]

The Church ceased at the Reformation to do that which it had done ever since the first promulgation of Christianity. The education of mankind was from that time forward handed over to the impersonal and irresponsible moralists of the press. That education went on, but outside the Church, under its ban. On the other hand, looking to the temporal and selfish interests of the Church as a corporation, it was the wise choice. It was the wise instinct of the Italian statesmen that led them to choose ignorance and the masses as the solid foundation for the edifice of their ecclesiastical power. An aristocracy of intellect is a very precarious institution. Power always finds its way back to the majority in the long run. The press may be troublesome at times; but the majority can always tie it up when they please to do so.[98]

The Church having once committed itself to the fatal principle, that what it once sanctions becomes irrevocable, there is no retreat for it from the accumulating arrears of blunders—errors of policy or principle, to which all long-lived societies, even the best managed, are liable. Consequently the Catholic Church has never been able to re-enter upon the common line of European progress. All the social ameliorations which European states have made for many centuries

[96] *Ibid.*, pp. 301-2.
[97] *Ibid.*, p. 149.
[98] *Essays by the Late Mark Pattison*, Vol. II, p. 307.

have been made outside the Church, and in spite of its most strenuous opposition. It has been the consistent foe of every attempt on the part of the wise and good to employ past experience for the correction of legislative error, or for softening the harsh pressure of political institutions. Since the sixteenth century its power has declined, its consistency has never yielded. The consequence is, that the sum total of our intellectual and political gains has accumulated itself outside of the pale, if not of Christianity, yet of the historically legitimate and venerable fabric of the Western Church. The Church's position, with feeble pertinacity anathematizing in the name of religion all the triumphs of human reason and genius, has often provoked the sarcasm of the scorner and the satirist. It is beginning now to awaken other thoughts among us. We are now disposed to mourn over the invincible barrier which the attitude of the Church opposes to that reunion of the intelligence of the West to its religious traditions, which must be regarded as a preliminary condition to the final organization of society on a basis which shall preclude crises and revolutions. Instead of sneering at the impotence of the papal pretensions, we stand in dismay before the impregnable strength of the position in which human Unreason has entrenched itself.

The Reformation, so far as it was an intellectual movement, was an attempt to restore the equilibrium of science and religion, which had been disturbed by the gradual growth of human knowledge.[99]

Learning retreated to the fringes of power regions. Religious freedom emerged in Holland and economic freedom in Scotland and the American colonies. The achievements of the nineteenth century included the revival of learning in England and the United States, but the end of the century saw the clouds which became the tyranny of opinion. Political economy flourished with political, economic, and religious freedom. It withered with subordination to mathematical abstractions and science, and became the handmaid of centralized power in the modern state. The problem of the social sciences is the problem of the arts in Western civilization.

It may be sufficient at present to have pointed to the general fact of the sequence—science, speculation, educational impulse—in the history of civilization, which, indeed, is that of education; for education is only the natural result of the instinct to communicate our culture; an instinct active in proportion as the culture is vigorous and enlarged. An accomplishment, or a skill, its possessor desires to monopolize; talent excites admiration, not sympathy. Enlargement of mind, as of character, seeks to propagate itself; the more that share it, the greater our gain. Intellect attracts intellect in proportion

[99] *Ibid.*, pp. 282-3.

to its capacity: there is a freemasonry of intelligence, as such; even while we are young, we are conscious of this before we can comprehend it. . . . Turning to history, we may mark two great periods at which this annihilation of mental activity by itself, and the consequent loss of the higher education, has occurred. One such epoch may be found in contrasting the fifth with the middle and close of the fourth century of the Christian era, though in this instance the case is so complicated with other conditions, that we cannot stay to disentangle our point of illustration. The second is more generally known, the silencing of the Latin philosophy by itself, and the consequent decay of University life which had arisen with it, till it was a second time re-invigorated at the classical revival, or the restoration to the world of a new material for thought and observation.[100]

We may ask whether we are at the beginning of a third period of intellectual torpor.

The place of the social sciences in Western civilization must be seen in relation to the role of universities. The university has played its greatest role in serving as a stabilizing factor. However inadequately it has played this role in various periods in the history of civilization, it has served as a repository of the reasoning of the ablest minds attracted to it. It has preferred reason to emotion, Voltaire to Rousseau, persuasion to power, ballots to bullets. Rashdall has described the influence of the University of Paris, in checking in France the dangerous tendencies of the church shown in the Inquisition in Spain. It must continue its vital function in checking the dangerous extremes to which all institutions with power are subject. The extreme tendencies of modern civilization shown in the rise of the modern state and in the tyranny of opinion compel universities to resist them. The trend of the social sciences in response to the demands of the new bureaucracy has been toward increasing specialization. And in this it has threatened the influence of universities. The university must deny the finality of any of the conclusions of the social sciences. It must steadfastly resist the tendency to acclaim any single solution of the world's problems at the risk of failing to play its role as a balancing factor in the growth of civilization. The Marxist solution, the Keynesian solution, or any solution, cannot be accepted as final if the universities are to continue and civilization is to survive. It is the task of the social sciences in the universities to indicate their limitations in their cultural setting.

[100]*Ibid.*, Vol. I, pp. 441-3.

Their contributions to the universities and to Western civilization will depend on their success in that task. If they fail they will add to confusion. It is possible that an application of demand-and-supply[101] curves may assist in determining their limitations, but the character of civilization suggests that the problem is philosophical and perhaps beyond their power to solve.

Nor does it seem probable that much hope can be expected from the specialization of the humanities and perhaps of philosophy itself. The social sciences and in particular political economy[102] have

[101]Democracy demands simplicity. The complexity of the social sciences leads to an emphasis on the class struggle—an indication of illiteracy and intolerance to complexity. The division in Canada between French Canadians, English Canadians, Colonial Canadians and Imperialistic Canadians increases the difficulties of democracy and leaves the common basis of union one of debts and taxes. Unlike other Anglo-Saxon communities Canada has no revolutionary tradition. The counter-reformation in Quebec is paralleled by the loyalist tradition in the older English provinces. Confederation became a compromise between church and state and not a basis of union.

"These ferments, however, conflict with the money-making current, and ultimately the latter proves the stronger. The masses want their peace and their pay. If they get them from a republic or a monarchy, they will cling to either. If not, without much ado they will support the first constitution to promise them what they want. A decision of the kind, of course, is never taken directly, but is always influenced by passion, personalities and the lingering effects of former situations" (Burckhardt, *Force and Freedom,* p. 209).

[102]"This, or something like this, is the scheme of progress which political economy reveals. It differs essentially from the schemes of most moralists in the fact that its success depends not upon any radical change in the nature of mankind, not upon any of these movements of enthusiasm which are always transient in their duration and restricted in their sphere, but simply upon the diffusion of knowledge. Taking human nature with all its defects, the influence of an enlightened self-interest first of all upon the actions and afterwards upon the character of mankind, is shown to be sufficient to construct the whole edifice of civilization; and if that principle were withdrawn, all would crumble in the dust. The emulations, the jealousies, the conflicting sentiments, the insatiable desires of mankind, have all their place in the economy of life, and each successive development of human progress is evolved from their play and from their collision. When therefore the ascetic, proclaiming the utter depravity of mankind, seeks to extirpate his most natural passions, to crush the expansion of his faculties, to destroy the versatility of his tastes, and to arrest the flow and impulse of his nature, he is striking at the very force and energy of civilization. Hence the dreary, sterile torpor that characterized those ages in which the ascetic principle has been supreme, while the civilizations which have attained the highest perfection have been those of ancient Greece and modern Europe, which were most opposed to it.

"It is curious to observe by what very different processes the antipathy to asceticism was arrived at in these two periods. In the first it is to be ascribed mainly to the sense of the harmony of complete development and above all to the passionate admiration of physical beauty which art contributed largely to sustain." W. E. H. Lecky, *The Rise and Influence of Rationalism in Europe* (London, 1913), Vol. II, pp. 367-8.

emerged from a background of political, religious and economic liberty. The *Wealth of Nations* was written in a Calvinistic community. "Down to the present day the peculiar nature of this structure stamps the life of the Calvinistic peoples with a unique emphasis on the cultivation of independent personality, which leads to a power of initiative and a sense of responsibility for action, combined also with a very strong sense of unity for common, positive ends and values, which are invulnerable on account of their religious character. This explains the fact that all the Calvinistic peoples are characterized by individualism and by democracy, combined with a strong bias towards authority and a sense of the unchangeable nature of law. It is this combination which makes a conservative democracy possible, whereas in Lutheran and Catholic countries, as a matter of course, democracy is forced into an aggressive and revolutionary attitude."[108] But Calvinism was undermined by the growth of science in biology and in physics and chemistry. It can no longer offer effective resistance to the centralizing trends of secularization. The weakening of economic liberty has been a part of the weakening of religious liberty and political liberty. The bureaucracy of the state and private enterprise rule by division into irreconcilable minorities. Large numbers of parties as in Canada become a guarantee of weakness of political leadership and of the strength of bureaucracy. The development of advertising and mass propaganda masquerading as education compel the consent of the governed. Legal institutions like religious institutions tend to be weakened as bulwarks of liberty. The overwhelming amount and complexity of legislation inspired by bureaucracies weaken the influence of the courts by adding to their burdens and stressing the spread of administrative law. The social sciences reflect the demands of industrialism and capitalism. There has been little discussion of the political implications of full employment and this probably assumes that political changes incidental to prosperity and depression disappear and that democratic government atrophies and disappears. The universities like the churches have concentrated their attention on public opinion as the source of power whether in extension courses or in the shaping of curricula and content. "I despair of a return to the sane atmosphere in which Adam Smith quite naturally combined the moral sentiments with his scientific

[108]Troeltsch, Ernst—*The Social Teaching of the Christian Churches* (N.Y., 1931), Vol. II, pp. 619.

thought about economic forces. The whole trend today is to exalt the rationalist scientific approach and to discard the philosophical. I am not thinking only of the worship of the physical and mechanical sciences, but rather of the attempt to make ethics, philosophy, sociology, etc., conform in method and language to the physical sciences—with disastrous results. Specialization runs mad, and when it does so, *never* leads to understanding. Its natural result, is strife and violent dogmatism. I wonder whether we shall get into a saner atmosphere within the next two or three generations" (E. J. Urwick).

8. THE PENETRATIVE POWERS OF THE PRICE SYSTEM

Economics is an older subject than statistics, but this paper is confined to the period since statistics began to leave its impression on economics and reached that stage, fatal to economics, when it came of age. Professor G. N. Clark in *Science and Social Welfare in the Age of Newton* (Oxford, 1937) has traced the background of statistics, in the growing importance of mathematics through astronomy, surveying, and book-keeping which followed the discovery of the new world, prior to its beginnings with the publication of John Graunt's *Observations upon the Bills of Mortality* in 1662, or four years before the census of Talon in Canada. An important statistical department was set up in England under an inspector-general to collect statistics on imports and exports about 1695. The effects of the imports of treasure from North America were becoming increasingly evident and William Fleetwood with a strong vested interest in stability in the value of fellowships published his *Chronicon Preciosum* in 1706. And so the snake entered the paradise of academic interest in economics. Under the stimulus of treasure from the new world the price system ate its way more rapidly into the economy of Europe and into economic thought.

"A project of commerce to the East Indies, therefore, gave occasion to the first discovery of the West."[1] The rise in prices[2] in the late sixteenth and early seventeenth centuries stimulated the flow of trade from Europe to the new world and to the old world, from the West Indies to the East Indies. With the beginning of the seventeenth century, the formation of the East India Company was accompanied by the settlement of Virginia. Dried fish from Newfoundland provided food for the fishing industry and for shipping. It was carried to Spain and exchanged for treasure, and used as food for ships going south of the line for the East Indies to exchange treasure for spices, calicoes, raw silk, and other East Indies goods. Exports of treasure from England evoked the protests of mercantilists and

[1]Adam Smith, *Wealth of Nations* (New York, 1937), p. 531.

[2]See E. J. Hamilton, *American Treasure and the Price Revolution in Spain* (Cambridge, 1934); Adam Smith, *Wealth of Nations*, p. 202. Bodin wrote the *Discours sur les causes de l'extrême cherté qui est aujourdhuy en France* in 1574.

precipitated the discussion which became the basis of the interest shown by English economists in problems of foreign trade. It would be interesting to speculate on the history of economic thought if England had been an important producer of precious metals and not an importer and an exporter, and if large joint stock companies had not existed to be defended and to support arguments and publication. The defence of the East India Company by Thomas Mun in his pamphlet in 1621 was accompanied by the battle between divergent views of Misselden and Malynes. The rise in prices stimulated the trade described by Adam Smith: "The silver of the new continent seems in this manner to be one of the principal commodities by which the commerce between the two extremities of the old one is carried on, and it is by means of it, in a great measure, that those distant parts of the world are connected with one another."[8] Under its drive, the commercial system of England expanded in the new world and in the old. With limited shipping facilities, the production and trade of light valuable commodities from the new world became evident in tobacco from Virginia and sugar from the West Indies. Manufactured products were sent to Africa for slaves and gold to be carried to sugar and tobacco plantations. New England was fostered by Virginia for the production of fish for exchange of specie in Spain rather than of tobacco. She expanded to produce not only fish for Europe but also lumber, fish, and agricultural products, and ships to carry these cheap bulky commodities for short distances to the English plantation colonies of the new world. I hope the historians will concede a claim to the effects of rising prices not only in the expansion of settlement in the new world but also in the Puritan Revolution, the passing of the Navigation Acts, and the establishment of the colonial system, and the defeat of a powerful commercial rival in the Dutch.

While Adam Smith attacked the system which emerged, he was aware of its advantages in defence. He saw it as part of the spread of the price system which had swept aside the feudal system, and led to the discovery of the new world, and with his support, to the wiping out of the inequities of the colonial system itself. "But what

[8]Smith, *Wealth of Nations*, p. 207. "Of all the commodities, therefore, which are bought in one foreign country, for no other purpose but to be sold or exchanged again for some other goods in another, there are none so convenient as gold and silver" (*ibid.*, p. 516).

all the violence of feudal institutions could never have effected, the silent and insensible operation of foreign commerce and manufactures gradually brought about."[4]

A revolution of the greatest importance to public happiness was in this manner brought about by two different orders of people, who had not the least intention to serve the public. To gratify the most childish vanity was the sole motive of the great proprietors. The merchants and artificers, much less ridiculous, acted merely from a view to their own interest, and in pursuit of their own pedlar principles of turning a penny wherever a penny was to be got. Neither of them had either knowledge or foresight of that great revolution which the folly of the one, and the industry of the other, was gradually bringing about. It is thus that through the greater part of Europe the commerce and manufacture of cities, instead of being the effect, have been the cause and occasion of the improvement and cultivation of the country.[5]

His predecessor, Richardson, wrote in 1750 "That the giving trade the utmost freedoms and encouragements is the greatest and most solid improvement of the value of lands."[6]

The character of trade which emerged in relation to the growth of cities in Europe was described by Nicholas Barbon in *A Discourse of Trade* (London, 1690), who wrote: "The chief causes that promote *trade,* (not to mention good government, peace and scituation, with other advantages) are industry in the poor, and liberality in the rich." "Those expences that most promote trade, are in cloaths and lodging: in adorning the body and the house, there are a thousand traders imploy'd in cloathing and decking the body, and building and furnishing of houses, for one that is imploy'd in providing food. . . . Fashion or the alteration of dress is a great promoter of *trade,* because it occasions the expense of cloaths, before the old ones are worn out: It is the spirit and life of *trade.* . . . The next expence that chiefly promotes *trade,* is building . . . it imploys a greater number of trades and people, than feeding or cloathing." "Beside, there is another great advantage to *trade,* by enlarging of cities; the two beneficial expences

[4] *Ibid.,* p. 388. For an excellent account of the decline of the feudal system in Japan as a result of the introduction of money see M. Takizawa, *The Penetration of Money Economy in Japan and its Effects upon Social and Political Institutions* (New York, 1927).

[5] Smith, *Wealth of Nations,* pp. 391-2.

[6] W. Richardson, *An Essay on the Causes of the Decline of Foreign Trade* (London, 1750).

of cloathing and lodging, are increased; Man being naturally ambitious, the living together, occasions emulation, which is seen by outvying one another in apparel, equipage, and furniture of the house; whereas, if a man lived solitary alone, his chiefest expence would be food" (pp. 31-4).

External trade was an extension of internal trade. Commodities carried long distances under primitive conditions of navigation were necessarily light in bulk, high in value, and suited to the demands of the luxury class in metropolitan areas. Consumption goods, especially those involving the introduction of habits, created a steady demand. Tobacco consumption spread rapidly after the seventeenth century. Sugar was imported in increasing quantities to sweeten the tea and chocolate brought from the East especially in the latter half of the seventeenth century. Furs met the demands of fashion in clothing and in the case of durable commodities, such as beaver hats, were passed down through various strata of society. The demands of the upper classes, encouraged by imports of specie and increasing fluidity of resources, stimulated production of luxury goods, expansion of trade, and the penetration of luxuries to lower classes.

The characteristics of production, distribution, and consumption of these commodities imposed strains on any colonial system aiming at comprehensiveness and the interests of the mother country. In the fur trade France sent vessels of goods to be traded with the hunting Indians of the Precambrian formation north of the St. Lawrence, and its development involved continued penetration to the interior. Settlement and agriculture were restricted and exposed to the fluctuations in the price of a commodity determined by fashion and by uncertain supplies from the Indians. The agricultural base in the St. Lawrence was consequently not adequate to the establishment of a sedentary fishery in the Maritimes and neither could be linked to the demands of the French sugar plantations of the West Indies. In the English colonial system the demands of the plantation commodities, such as sugar and tobacco, differed from those produced in the commercial colonies, such as fish and lumber for the West Indies, and those produced in Newfoundland, namely fish chiefly for European consumption. The plantations[7] required slaves, foodstuffs to supply the slaves, lumber for buildings, and live-stock to operate the mills. These cheap bulky secondary commodities supplied by New

[7] C. R. Fay, "Plantation Economy" (*Economic Journal*, Dec., 1936).

England and other colonies were extremely sensitive to regulations which affected prices of luxury goods. The colonial system encouraged the plantations through monopolies of the English market and the fisheries and agriculture as a base of supply for the plantations. "To increase the shipping and naval power of Great Britain, by the extension of the fisheries of our colonies, is an object which the legislature seems to have had almost constantly in view. Those fisheries, upon this account, have had all the encouragement which freedom can give them, and they have flourished accordingly. The New England fishery in particular was, before the late disturbances, one of the most important, perhaps, in the world."[8] With the expansion of the fishery, shipping increased, larger quantities of goods were available, and protests were more vigorous against restrictions imposed at the instigation of the plantations in the interests of cheaper supplies and provisions. The colonial system had inherent contradictions stimulating production by a policy of freedom in colonies producing secondary commodities and restricting the market for those commodities by a policy of preferences for colonies producing staple commodities. New England shipping encroached consequently on the French Empire and capitalized its limitations by profitable smuggling. It supported expansion of trade from secondary bulky commodities into the luxury commodities of the new world, through the manufacture of molasses, a by-product of sugar, into rum and its exchange for furs, slaves, and fish. The difficulties of European commercial systems in North America were evident in the retreat of the French and finally in the withdrawal of the English to the St. Lawrence. The effectiveness of the commercial development of New England with the advantages of freedom of trade supported by the fishery and shipping, broke down the colonial system of France and in turn of England. Shipping implied commercial strength, naval power, and defeat of European control.

The decline of the British commercial system proceeded rapidly after the American Revolution and the publication of the *Wealth of Nations*. After the War of 1812, the colonial trade Acts of the twenties, and admission of the United States to the British West Indies in 1830, became landmarks in the steady trend toward free trade. The attacks of Adam Smith and the group of government

[8]*Wealth of Nations*, pp. 544-5.

interventionists, who were his disciples and followers, on the vested interests of the merchant class bore fruit in clearing away the shackles of the colonial system. Decker had written in 1744, "Restraint is always harmful to trade." "Nothing but freedom can secure trade."[9] Adam Smith declared that "Of the greater part of the regulations concerning the colony trade, the merchants who carry it on, it must be observed, have been the principal advisers. We must not wonder, therefore, if, in the greater part of them, their interest has been more considered than either that of the colonies or that of the mother country."[10] "The sneaking arts of underling tradesmen are thus erected into political maxims for the conduct of a great empire; for it is the most underling tradesmen only who make it a rule to employ chiefly their own customers."[11] The slave trade was finally abolished in the West Indies, the Reform Bills destroyed the power of vested interests in Parliament, the timber preferences were reduced, the Corn Laws repealed, the Navigation Acts abrogated, and responsible government established in the colonies. The free trade system in North America was extended by the Reciprocity Treaty with the United States. The abolition of slavery in the Civil War was an important landmark in the transition from status to contract. The disappearance of the East India Company was followed by the purchase of Rupert's Land from the Hudson's Bay Company. The price system had gradually but persistently eaten out the rotting timbers of European colonial structures and as it destroyed feudalism so it destroyed the defences of commercialism.

Commercialism left a powerful stamp on the history of the East and West. Great Britain emerged as a dominant metropolitan unit. The Americas became politically independent but continued to carry the culture of people from Spain, Portugal, France, and England. In Canada a large French population had grown up on the lower St. Lawrence in response to the demands of the fur trade. Across the northern half of the continent the aborigines had felt the powerful influence of the commercial pull. Sir George Simpson wrote, "Connubial alliances are the best security we can have of the good will of the natives," and half-breeds are evidence of the policy.

[9]Sir Mathew Decker, *An Essay on the Causes of the Decline of Foreign Trade* (Dublin, 1749).

[10]*Wealth of Nations*, p. 550.

[11]*Ibid.*, p. 460.

Religious practices detrimental to the trade were replaced by Christianity. Of one tribe Simpson wrote: "They have made a poor hunt in consequences of the death of a relation and in the agony of grief according to ancient usage rent their garments so that they are now destitute of every necessary." Again he wrote:

> There may be a difference of opinion as to the effect the conversion of the Indians might have on the trade; I cannot however forsee that it could be at all injurious, on the contrary I believe it would be highly beneficial thereto as they would in time imbibe our manners and customs and imitate us in Dress; our Supplies would thus become necessary to them which would increase the consumption of European produce & manufactures and in like measure increase & benefit our trade as they would find it requisite to become more industrious and to turn their attention more seriously to the Chase in order to enable to provide themselves with such supplies; we should moreover be enabled to pass through their Lands in greater safety which would lighten the expence of transport, and supplies of Provisions would be found at every Village, and among every tribe; they might likewise be employed on extraordinary occasions as runners, Boatsmen, etc., and their Services in other respects turned to profitable account.
>
> The Honble Committee I am satisfied will take this view of the subject and there are a few of the most enlightened in this Country who would do so likewise but there are others (and I am almost ashamed to say Members of our Council) who would condemn it as being wild & visionary and ruinous to the Fur Trade without even taking the trouble of thinking seriously thereon or looking at the question in all its bearings and important consequences.[12]

Duncan McGillivray wrote: "For the prairie Indians the love of rum is their first inducement to industry; they undergo every hardship and fatigue to procure a skinful of this delicious beverage, and when a nation becomes addicted to drinking, it affords a strong presumption that they will soon become excellent hunters."[13] With monopoly control Simpson reduced imports of spirits to a minimum. The fur trade left a framework for the later Dominion. The timber trade, based on preferences and the specific gravity of white pine, hastened English settlement in Upper Canada. The fishing industry left a region divided between four national interests, France, Newfound-

[12]Frederick Merk, *Fur Trade and Empire* (Cambridge, Mass., 1931), p. 108.

[13]A. S. Morton, *The Journal of Duncan McGillivray* (Toronto, 1929), p. 47.

land, Canada, and the United States. These divisions in northern North America illustrate the general divergent effects of commercialism.

Into the moulds of the commercial period, set by successive heavier and cheaper commodities, and determined by geographic factors, such as the St. Lawrence River and the Precambrian formation; by cultural considerations, such as the English and French languages; by technology, such as the canoe and the raft; by business organization, such as the North West Company and Liverpool timber firms; and by political institutions peculiar to France and England, were poured the rivers of iron and steel in the form of steamships and railways which hardened into modern capitalism. Improved transportation, increasing specialization in Great Britain, the spread of machine industry in relation to coal and iron, and migration of population to urban centres involved imports, of wheat, live-stock, and dairy products from North America for foodstuffs, cotton from the United States and wool from Australia for clothing, timber from Canada and New Brunswick for housing, and raw materials for manufacturing, and exports of manufactured products. Steamships and railways lowered costs of transportation and hastened the shift to imports of bulky, low value, and perishable commodities from more adjacent regions. The discovery of gold in the Pacific basin, in California and British Columbia, and in Australia and New Zealand, was followed by immediate migration of population, exports of gold, and later, of bulky commodities, and rapid extension of transportation facilities. The Suez Canal and the Union Pacific Railway were opened in 1869, the Canadian Pacific Railway in 1885, and the routes from Great Britain via the East and the West to the Pacific drastically shortened in space and time.

The rise of industrialism in the first half of the nineteenth century was hastened by the demands of the Napoleonic Wars[14] for iron and steel and by the increasing effectiveness of the price system. It was the reverse side of the decline of the commercial system. The emergence of free trade by the middle of the century reflected and enhanced the efficiency of the price system and the growth of industrialism. The ebb of commercialism was the flow of industrialism. The establishment of responsible government in Canada marked the

[14]T. S. Ashton, *Iron and Steel in the Industrial Revolution* (London, 1924).

collapse of the colonial system and the beginnings of capitalistic development. Government was unified in the Act of Union and broadened in Confederation. The divisive trends of the United States disappeared with the success of the North in the Civil War.

Again war was followed by rapid expansion of the iron and steel industry, rapid construction of railways and improvement of steamships. What Geddes has called palæotechnic society,[15] emerged in full bloom with its coal mines, industrialism, and urbanization. Credit facilities were improved with additional supplies of gold, completion of the Atlantic cable, development of financial structures, especially during the Civil War and after the improvement of political structures, and the improvement of the exchanges[16] for handling commodities and securities. Legislation improved the position and effectiveness of corporations, and new developments for the amassing of large quantities of capital and capital equipment, such as the trust and the holding company, were introduced. Institutions for the collection and direction of funds, such as banks, bond houses, and insurance companies, became more effective. Inefficiency was weeded out through ruthless competition, the long depression, and improved bankruptcy legislation. Marked increase in production and lowering of costs of transportation contributed to falling prices.[17] With the advantages of industrial leadership and lowering of the costs of raw material in Great Britain and the influence of mathematics and the natural sciences, the interest in the concern of Marx with the exploitation which accompanied industrial change shifted to that of Jevons, Marshall, Walras, and Pareto in the development of equilibrium analysis. The gold standard operated in the fashion familiar to all students of text-books of economics, and the prices between countries were automatically adjusted. The price system operated at a high state of efficiency in the occupation of the vacant spaces of the earth. In countries producing cheap and more bulky raw materials, improved transportation was dependent on funds from industrial areas. They were repaid in part in areas dominated by government activity, such as Canada, by revenue from tariffs on manufactured

[15]See L. Mumford, *Technics and Civilization* (New York, 1934). Also E. F. Heckscher, "Recent Tendencies in Economic Life," *The World's Economic Future* (London, 1938), pp. 97-110.

[16]H. M. Larson, *Jay Cooke, Private Banker* (Cambridge, 1936).

[17]"Memorandum to Royal Commission on the Depression of Trade and Industry" (*Official Papers of Alfred Marshall*, London, 1926, pp. 4-5).

goods from industrial areas or were avoided in part by bankruptcy in areas dominated by private enterprise, such as the United States. Competition of manufactured goods led to the protective tariff and schools of economics which traced their origins to List in Germany, Carey in the United States, and Buchanan in Canada. Canada attempted to secure revenue and to check competition from industrial countries, and to participate in the development of more extensive projects by facilitating credit expansion.

The outbreak of the Great War has been regarded as the signal for the collapse of capitalism. Sombart has traced the history of capitalism to its final stage of *hoch capitalismus*. Geddes would describe it as the rise and decline of the palæotechnic (or coal and iron) society and the beginnings of the neotechnic (or new sources of power and base metals) society. But with the shift from commercialism to capitalism, so with the shift from capitalism to what may be called later phases or whatever the war and post-war period may be designated, the ebb of one was the rise of the other. Where capitalism followed the more rigid channels of surviving commercialism or where it arrived later in a highly centralized state, it was a part of governmental machinery. In Germany,[18] Italy, and Japan and in the British Dominions the state became capital equipment. The twentieth century was Canada's; and Germany wanted a place in the sun. In Canada the federal government supported, and engaged in railway building on an extensive scale, and the provinces, strengthened in their power by Privy Council decisions, shared in railway construction and engaged in the development of hydroelectric power and in the expansion of mining and the pulp and paper industry. In Great Britain and the United States, on the other hand, regulatory boards were conspicuous for railways and public utilities, and control was developed to combat trusts and monopolies and to meet the problems of monetary disturbance.

The war brought a marked increase in government activities in all nations.[19] The conduct of military and naval activities over a long period brought encroachment of the state on private organization, especially in the fields of banking and transportation. In

[18]See T. Veblen, *Imperial Germany and the Industrial Revolution* (New York, 1915).

[19]See the small library on war history published by the Carnegie Endowment for International Peace.

Canada the federal government became an owner of railways on a large scale. Most significant developments appeared in the field of finance and in its influence on the price system through the fixing of prices of commodities by governmental bodies set up for war purposes and the floating of loans by governments on an unprecedented scale. The end of the war found the participants with debts of astronomical figures. The Treaty of Versailles riveted a debt structure on the German nation. These debts were followed by a long series of revisions and disturbances, including ruinous inflation in Germany and Austria, the Dawes Plan, the Young Plan, the League of Nations Plan, the collapse of Austria, *de facto* cancellation of debts, depreciation of sterling, the franc, and the dollar, and increasing reliance on nationalistic measures ranging through various stages of totalitarianism.

The war and post-war period to 1929 was marked by a continuation of the prosperity which had its rise in the late nineties of the last century. The state was more effectively utilized as a monetary device[20] and political disturbances reflected economic disturbances more directly. Capital equipment begun in the war and the pre-war periods was extended and completed. Railways in Canada, the Panama Canal (opened in 1917), and the release of shipping after the war contributed to marked expansion based on accessibility to the Pacific. These extensions of palæotechnic structure were accompanied by a marked development of the neotechnic structure. Significant inventions and new sources of power were utilized and extended. Oil displaced coal in ships and vastly increased their range, especially in the Pacific. The internal combustion engine played an increasingly important role in transportation, agriculture, and industry in the densely populated areas and in the remote areas. Roads and hotels were built on an extensive scale. Hydro-electric power was developed with and without government support in the non-coal areas and contributed to a marked increase in the supply of non-ferrous metals such as nickel, zinc, lead, aluminum, and gold. Following the stimulus of the war these neotechnic developments contributed to the expansion of Russia, Japan, Italy, France, Germany, the British Dominions, and the United States. The radio

[20]See W. A. Mackintosh, "Gold and the Decline of Prices" (*Proceedings of the Canadian Political Science Association*, 1931, pp. 88-110).

and expanding newsprint production were reinforced by the nationalistic energies released by new inventions and new sources of power.

While the palæotechnic and the neotechnic developments reinforced each other in the war and carried forward the boom of the twenties they began to diverge and to conflict in the depression. The coal areas as the basis of palæotechnic industrialism were the centres of development because of the importance of coal as a weight-losing raw material[21] which attracted other raw materials. Its significance was evident to neotechnic industry in the importation of petroleum in large quantities and in the importance of iron and steel to the automobile industry. But the difficulties of the coal industry in the twenties, evident in Great Britain especially in the depressed areas, in contrast with the emergence of the light industries, such as the automobile, radio, and electrical equipment in new locations, indicate the character of the change. The railway problem in Canada and other countries followed the emphasis on heavy equipment in rails, right-of-way, locomotives, and cars, and extensive financing for handling increasingly bulky, heavier, and cheaper commodities and the consequent effectiveness of motor competition with its stress on light valuable commodities, light equipment, and ease of finance. Wheat production was rapidly extended in the war and during the twenties by intensive and extensive cultivation, with railroad construction and motor transportation, in trucks and tractors, while industrialism centred on the coal areas was in distress and the market was narrowed. Tariffs emerged with increasing nationalism to protect agriculture in the wheat markets of the world.

Hydro-electric power is less mobile and flexible than petroleum. Distance from the power site has been an important factor but the handicap has decreased with inventions and new materials. It has facilitated the exploitation of the resources of non-agricultural areas with resistant formations and broken topography distant from coal formations. The conspicuous resources have been minerals and newsprint and pulp products, but with the depression, production of metallic minerals supported by gold has become an important competitor for power and has strengthened the radio against the newspaper.

[21]C. J. Friedrich, *Alfred Weber's Theory of the Location of Industries* (Chicago, 1929).

The implications of neotechnical industralism have been evident in the growth of cities and metropolitan areas. On the one hand the skyscraper and increasing compactness of population in large apartment houses have been encouraged by developments in electrical equipment and on the other hand population has spread out over wide areas as a result of the automobile and metalled roads. Population has been released by machine industry in agriculture and has migrated to the more densely populated areas. Rising standards of expenditure and congestion have been accompanied by declining birth-rates. Building booms have characterized the sharp depreciation through obsolescence of housing equipment, and governments have attempted to encourage the construction of houses in the face of competition from more efficient apartment houses and at the expense of unfortunate individuals who have been encouraged to own their own homes. The demands of population in congested areas under the direction of scientific work in nutrition have shifted from carbohydrates to vitamins or from wheat to dairy products, live-stock, fruits, and vegetables. Improved transportation facilities, especially in the development of refrigeration, have increased the range of supply of proteins, fats, and vitamins. The wheat-coal economy, which involved hauling bulky commodities to the dominant coal areas, has been broken by the emergence of a large number of metropolitan centres dependent on new types of supplies and new types of transportation characteristic of recent industrialism. The strengthening of the Dominions and of the provinces in the Statute of Westminster and with the benefit of Privy Council decisions since the war reflected the decreasing importance of the metropolitan demand of Great Britain and the expansion of new metropolitan areas on the North American Continent. The city has sharpened the cultural background established under the influence of commercialism.

Neotechnic industrialism superimposed on palæotechnic industrialism involved changes of tremendous implication to modern society and brought strains of great severity. The institutional structure built up on iron and steel and coal has been slow to change. Governmental machinery in those regions in which palæotechnic society developed late has been extended and government intervention in regions in which it developed earlier has been intensified as a result of the rigidities of labour organization and corporate finance.

Regions which continued primarily commercial, as Newfoundland, in the export of dried fish and in which capitalism, represented by the railway and the steamship, involved heavy burdens, failed to survive the effects of the new industrialism and the impact of the depression and lost responsible government. The effects of government intervention have been less severe in regions dominated by neotechnical industrialism and enhanced in regions dominated by palæotechnical industrialism. Wheat areas and coal and iron regions have been penalized. Adjustment by tariffs, railway rates, bounties, bankruptcy legislation and other devices which characterized palæotechnic industrialism has become inadequate and compelled the intervention on a large scale of monetary devices.

The price system has been thwarted by the burden of debt hanging over from the old industrialism and stimulated by the support of government in the growth of the new industrialism as in the Ontario Hydro Electric Power Commission. Private enterprise has been exposed to conflict and defeat in the fields of labour and capital in the old industrialism and has been conspicuously successful in the new industrialism. The search for liquidity favoured the new industrialism. Profits from tobacco were turned into the development of hydro-electric power on the Saguenay and supported substantial profits from the production of aluminum. The Ford Motor Company has been a conspicuous tribute to individual enterprise and the use of petroleum, as has also the development of Radio City. Private enterprise has been handicapped by the inconsistencies of political decisions but it has adapted itself with amazing facility. With monetary policy the state has been compelled to concentrate on vast areas and has been less effective in major undertakings such as the St. Lawrence water-ways with the consequent profits which accompany disturbances on a large scale. In democratic countries with a strong labour organization or a large and vocal agricultural population, monetary policy is an important device but limited by an essentially conservative outlook.

The problem of debt in the war and the post-war period arising from this background of capitalism has had significant repercussions on the effectiveness of the price system. It was enhanced by the rise of continental economies, by the construction of transcontinental railways following the discoveries of gold on the Pacific, and by the dominance of coal and steel. Short term credit which characterized the commercial system dominated by an island was followed by long term credit dominated by continents. The unmanageable character of long term credit in terms of allocation of yields in relation to costs became evident in the enormous reduction in value of railway securities in the United States, in the emergence of large fortunes through reorganizations and the formation of trusts, and in the evolution of the Canadian federal structure as an instrument capable of carrying an expanding debt. The problem of debt is the problem of Canadian federalism as the federal structure is a credit instrument. To confine ourselves to Canada, the so-called railway problem has emerged with the problem of wheat, the competition of roads and motor transport and of new routes such as the Panama Canal, and has been evident in the disappearance of dividends on Canadian Pacific Railway stock and the continuation of deficits on the Canadian National Railways. The intensity of the problem incidental to the enormous amounts of capital involved in transcontinental railways, and the burden of overhead costs incidental to the economic, political, and geographic background has been evident in the first decade in the pronouncements of Sir Henry Thornton, and in the second decade in the pronouncements of Sir Edward Beatty. On the one hand, the Canadian Pacific Railway as the bulwark of private enterprise has shown little evidence of weakening in the struggle, and its plea for arrangements which appear to provide for operation of all Canadian railways at the expense of government is in danger of being regarded as an attempt at participation in the old game of tired business men in Canada. On the other hand, the Canadian National Railways are directly under the sovereign power of Parliament and should not be used to lay conduits under the name of co-operation from the Treasury to the pockets of Canadian Pacific shareholders, or be exposed to the subtle sabotage of maintaining an empty hotel in Vancouver and an empty hole in Montreal for nearly a decade in order not to injure private enterprise. It is the hope of democracy in Canada that both will continue to strive earnestly but that neither will succeed, and that the impossibility of running two competitive railways will continue. Dictatorship for the advantage of the Canadian Pacific Railway and a balanced budget is a prospect to be contemplated with concern. Those who argue for the abolition of the Canadian National deficit must suggest alternative and more effective devices for offsetting the burden of the tariff and the relief of depressed areas. Dictatorship proposed by the Canadian National in the form of a compulsory arbitration tribunal should be resisted as an encroachment on the powers of Parliament and on the rights of the Canadian Pacific. Both railways should be warned against talking nonsense about scientific rate structures and uneconomic costs in their attacks on road transport. Political agitation as to savings rather than earnings gives rise to the suspicion that the problem of efficient administration of transcontinental railways has not been solved or that administration, adapted to expansion, has been inadequate with its cessation. The public would like more indication of attempts to increase earnings rather than to be asked to make more sacrifices in the interest of savings. We may hope that the aggressiveness of the Canadian Pacific Railway will keep politics out of the Canadian National and that the aggressiveness of the Canadian National Railways will keep the Canadian Pacific out of politics and out of the Canadian Treasury, and that the results will permit the continuation of democratic government. The vested interests of the social scientist will suffer less from the attacks of Sir Edward Beatty than from the indifference of an amalgamated railway.

Organs of opinion reflect the increasing significance of regional and metropolitan growth in demands for economies in the interests of finance or for protection against the possibilities of poorer service and discrimination which would accompany the various proposals for economic dictatorship. Montreal and Toronto have chiefly reflected the financial interests of the St. Lawrence in the demands for railway amalgamation, but the exceptions and Western Canada support the outlook of wheat in fears of rigidities of economic dictatorship. Interests representing the new industrialism have been evident in striking fashion in control by the pulp and paper industry of the *Mail and Empire* and then by mining and hydro-electric power in the amalgamation of the *Globe and Mail*. Newspapers tend to reflect to an increasing extent the influence of rapid transportation and efficient distribution characteristic of metropolitan development. The pressure of overhead costs incidental to large scale capital equipment in newspaper plants and newsprint mills has increased the importance of large scale circulation and of good will or the stereotype of Walter Lippmann. Dependence on advertising, particularly from department stores, has become a vital issue[22] in policy as to news, editorials, and features. The cheap newspaper is subordinated to the demands of modern industrialism and modern merchandising. Overhead costs have contributed to lack of precision in accounting, and the allocation of costs between the purchaser of goods from department stores and the purchaser of the paper, or between the purchaser of paper and the purchaser of hydro-electric power from plants owned by paper companies, is extremely difficult to determine. In paying for electric light or for groceries one cannot be certain how much is paid for newspapers. The patterns of public opinion or the stereotypes have become blurred, and amalgamations of newspapers and the fusion of editorial policies lead to demands for general programmes which appeal to the business mind. Broad stereotypes are typical such as the belief in the stability of governments, or as social scientists, who have logically taken the place of millennialists, have been wont to put it, the dangers of civilization crashing, whatever that may mean. The Canadian variant points to the break-up of Confederation.

Periodicals emerge to meet the demands of any group whenever that group becomes sufficiently specialized to demand goods which warrant advertising on a sufficient scale to support the periodical. Specialization of this character is largely restricted to cities and regions. Such periodicals attempt to build up fresh stereotypes but are forced to compete with constantly improving technique designed to reach new and possibly lower levels of intelligence, especially those who prefer to look at photographs rather than to read. Those who prefer to read have hived off as supporters of pocket-book digests. Illustrations have reached a place of dominant importance and writers have been compelled to illustrate the illustrations including the advertisements. The difficulties of new parties unable to build up sharp stereotypes through newspapers or periodicals have been less evident in the publication of large editions of cheap books. New educational

[22]Freedom of the press and freedom of speech have always been relative terms assuming a moderate tolerance. Newspaper space involves a substantial outlay of funds as does an hour's broadcasting. In private conversation where talk is said to be cheap, one is inclined to revise Mark Twain's dictum and to say that we have freedom of speech and freedom of the press and not the good sense not to use either of them. Small talk, bores, and other terms are in constant demand. In so-called conferences freedom of speech is paraded as a special feature, but it usually amounts to common scolding or saying things calculated to get the conference into the newspapers—in other words, advertising space for nothing. See H. A. Innis, "Discussion in the Social Sciences" (*Dalhousie Review,* Jan., 1936).

movements and reform programmes make the world safe for publishers. The support of religious bodies to publishing houses has weakened and been replaced by the state with its demands for educational texts. Education comes under the jurisdiction of the provinces. A substantial publisher of text-books is not in a strong position to publish literature other than that of a strikingly nationalistic or local character. The incipient fascism of Canadian intellectuals, the group which cannot distinguish a bar association from a trade union, in Winnipeg, Toronto, and Montreal, evident in nationalism, isolationism, and the boosting of Canadian literature in the interests of Canadian publishers, has deep roots. School texts handled on a mass production basis in an off-peak period by large organizations such as mail-order houses and providing as a by-product, advertising, reduce the volume of publishing houses and, who knows, may injure the possibility of developing Canadian poetry. Abolition of standard texts in favour of the publication of a wide variety of books increases the cost of education to the publishers, the state, and the purchaser of books, but it tends to break down broad stereotypes.

The decline in value of political stereotypes which accompanies the decline of the party newspaper has been partly a result of the increase in importance of the radio as a political weapon. Competition between newspapers and the radio for advertising, as well as in the handling of news, has been evident in the concerted attack by the press on the Canadian Broadcasting Corporation following contracts with American firms. From the standpoint of the public, it is a choice between Moon Mullins and Charlie McCarthy. The radio capitalizes the disadvantage of the large newspaper in appealing to stereotypes which refuse to be blurred as is evident in the strength of religion in the rural areas. While it has served the dictatorship of Russia, Germany, Italy, and Japan, it has assisted in escape via the provincialism of Mr. Aberhart and the federalism of Mr. Roosevelt. As a new invention the radio threatens to circumvent the walls imposed by tariffs and to reach across boundaries frequently denied to other media of communication, but like the newspaper it is adapted to the demands of metropolitan areas. Saskatchewan elections may provide a rough indication of the range of the Calgary stations.

In a political entity such as Canada in which the forces of

centralization are so strong, the element of size involves powerful counteracting forces of decentralization. The wheat-coal economy and the enormous burden of debt which has accompanied its decline have involved rigid interest and transportation charges supported by broad general stereotypes involving imperialism, nationalism, demands for railway amalgamation, union of the Prairie Provinces and of the Maritime Provinces, the dangers of communism, the dangers of fascism, and the like. Adam Smith might have said of capitalists as he said of merchants: "The government of an exclusive company of merchants is perhaps the worst of all governments for any country whatever."[23] "I have never known much good done by those who affected to trade for the public good."[24] Wide fluctuations in prices of raw materials such as furs, fish, timber, wheat, pulp and paper, and minerals involve a large element of elasticity, in marketing structures as in barter and the truck system, in the standards of living of producers, and in financial structures as reorganizations will attest. Expanding metropolitan areas dependent on the new industries such as pulp and paper, minerals, and hydro-electric power were provided with cushions in relief, in relative financial independence, and in the more direct impact of new inventions. The exposed areas have been of the wheat-coal economy and the favoured areas have gained with the new industrialism. In spite of the hard core of rigidity of the debt structure, the monetary policies of other nations, especially of Great Britain and the United States, compelled a change in monetary structure and monetary policy in Canada. A prominent Canadian banker stated at an annual meeting of a bank largely concerned with the new industrialism in January, 1931: "For the future it is absolutely essential that means should be devised to prevent the drastic changes in the price level which have been characteristic of the period since the close of the war."[25] A representative of the same bank stated in 1938: "Experience will have taught us nothing, if as a result of occurrences of the last seven years we do not conclude that positive action from a monetary point of view is the first essential in controlling excesses of both boom and depression."[26] The effects have been evident in defaults with and

[23]Smith, *Wealth of Nations*, p. 537.

[24]*Ibid.*, p. 423.

[25]*Proceedings of the Canadian Political Science Association*, 1931, p. 122.

[26]S. R. Noble, "The Monetary Experience of Canada during the Depression" (*Canadian Banker*, April, 1938).

without benefit of the political success of Mr. Aberhart. A monetary policy which might have softened the effects of the depression in the wheat-coal areas might have spurred on the activities of the new industrialism in the hydro-electric power, mining, and pulp and paper areas and increased the internal strain already severe as attested by the major disasters of debts necessitating the Royal Commission on Dominion-Provincial Relations. The difficulties of the wheat-coal regions are not less because of the declining sympathetic interest of the regions of the new industrialism.

The limitations of the price system in overcoming the handicaps of rigidities of debt burdens and in accentuating internal strains have been evident in the rise of monetary nationalism and the increasing importance of the state as a monetary instrument. Bankruptcy is no longer accepted as an effective solvent and is no longer possible with the state as a credit instrument and the possibilities of controlling inflation. It is "unthinkable." The increasing strength and influence of institutions concerned with long term credit, such as bond houses and insurance companies, based on the application of mathematics in the calculation of mortality tables and bond yields has left no alternative. Within the state, large scale capital equipment and the drive to operate at capacity have accentuated the importance of alternative production and intensified competition in off-peak periods. Ridges formed by buckling under competitive pressure are conspicuous in basing point systems, intensive advertising, and monopolistic arrangements. The tendency toward fixed prices has been accompanied by more intense competition in other directions as in the case of railway service and train schedules and political agitation. The realm of intangible services assumes increasing importance and the skyscraper has become the modern cathedral. Long term credit is the new basis of modern belief. The difficulty of competition in prices compels a shift in cost items and a realignment of accounting. The rigidity of accounting systems accentuates the importance of fixed prices with the result that the accountant is bribed to present accounts with limited value for interpretation or accuracy.[27] Accounting systems have met the demands of corporations for release from control of debt by facilitating the development of policies by which reserves and surplus have been built up, and

[27]See C. A. Ashley, "Some Aspects of Corporations" (*Essays in Political Economy in Honour of E. J. Urwick*, Toronto, 1938).

control lost to the shareholder. Dependence on the capital market for new supplies of capital has been materially lessened, with the result that it becomes more speculative. Short term credit and the importance of liquidity intensify speculation. Concentration of control in the hands of management, with the possibilities of interlocking directorates and the like, involves possibilities of unwise developments in large organizations, and lack of information regarding their policies. The monetary system with its mathematical implications facilitates the development of mechancial control devices, ranging from improved accounting machinery to the adaptation of automatic services to the nickel and other coins and of the Canadian nickel in size and weight to the American nickel.

The price system has stimulated minor correctives in persuading the consumer to educate himself through consumers' research organizations, societies to stop propaganda (of all things), and other devices, and still permits many of us to live in comparative peace. Its handicaps have been stressed to an increasing extent by economists who have been concerned with monopoly theory and with the decline of competition or with the rise of economic warfare and what someone has called the decline of the idea of competition. The effectiveness of the price system within the state is evident in the attempts to reinforce pecuniary by political values. The successful politician is precluded from policies which indicate class or self-interest but he is successful in so far as he succeeds in enlisting the support of the price system. He should be the orthodontist of the social sciences pursuing his way by gradual but persistent pressure, but he continues with analogies of the machine in "pulling levers" or with violent medical treatments in giving "a shot in the arm."[28]

The effectiveness of the price system has been shown in the decline of feudalism, the decline of mercantilism, the rise of palæotechnic capitalism, and the shift to neotechnic capitalism. It has stimulated the growth of inventions and the trend in the movement of goods from light and valuable raw materials to heavy and cheap raw materials, and to light and valuable finished products. It has hastened the rise of new sources of power and of new industries and accelerated the decline of obsolete regions. The drive of the price system on the economic and social structure within the state has been

[28]V. F Coe, "Monetary Theory and Politics" (*Essays in Political Economy in Honour of E. J. Urwick*).

accompanied by continual disturbance between the states. The role of the state in assuming the burdens of depreciation through obsolescence of the wheat-coal economy and of stimulating the development of new industrialism involves rapid expansion of public debt and necessitates the continual revision of currencies in relation to other countries. The relative lack of rigid structure in the international field has probably reduced the dangers of international disturbance. The stupidity of nationalism is tempered by the chaos of internationalism. Losses through nationalism are offset by realignments of national boundaries, trade agreements, international cartels, foreign balances, world fairs, and subsidized tourists. Monetary nationalism is a reflection of the role of the state in the expansion of industrialism and the means by which the state is compelled to rely increasingly on expanded public debt and to avoid increasingly its effects. Employment and the demands for consumers' goods must be stimulated by state activity. To obtain bread we must build a gun or lay down a stone. Monetary nationalism and the constant necessity for readjustments of exchange have become normal phases of the recent effects of the price system. Responsible government in the vital sense of control over funds has disappeared in favour of secret operation of equalization funds. The automatic system which centred on London has come under divided control with the rise of North America and the opening of the Pacific. We seem destined in economics to follow the meteorologist in modifying equilibrium analysis and turning to what he has called the polar front theory in which the meeting of economic masses becomes important rather than trade between nations. There are serious weaknesses in the analogy of flowing from high to low pressure areas, and great advantages in discussing pressure groups. The economics of losses is not less significant than the economics of profits.

Economists have reflected the confusion introduced by machine industry. The decline of vested interests peculiar to the period after Adam Smith was a tribute to the economic value of the *Wealth of Nations,* but the emergence of vested interests (i.e., the legitimate right to something for nothing) under capitalism has reduced the value of economic theory based on Adam Smith and increased the value of economic theory adapted to nationalism. To extend the thesis of Mr. Keynes as to the influence of rising prices on literature, it may be said that they tend to correspond with free will systems of economic thought. Jevons might have added economic systems to Acts of Parliament and sun spots. Scientific advance and the application of science to industry through inventions are characteristic of periods of prosperity. The philosophic outlook based on scientific achievement leaves its stamp on economics. Periods of prosperity may be characterized by most intensive work in economics but periods of depression have been characterized by attempts at application, particularly in the field in which mathematics provides a convenient channel between science and economics, namely money. Economics becomes a branch of physics and chemistry rather than of biology. Politics have become a method of revolt. The word political has been restored to its place with economy, and equilibrium analysis must be modified and extended throughout the social sciences. A study of the elasticity of demand for autarchies is significant to a study of the elasticity of demand for wheat.[29] Depressions produce deterministic systems and arguments such as have been advanced in this paper.

[29]See *The State and Economic Life* (Paris, 1934), pp. 252-4, 289-90.

9. LIQUIDITY PREFERENCE AS A FACTOR IN INDUSTRIAL DEVELOPMENT

The last half of the nineteenth century was characterized by a series of erratic outbreaks of economic activity along the Pacific coast of North America and in Australia which suddenly transformed vast scantily populated areas into regions producing enormous quantities of raw materials for a highly industrialized Europe. Traffic to the Pacific had been restricted to commodities of high value and light bulk, such as furs, wool, and tea. The encircling movement of world trade which surrounded the globe first in the fur-trade in which traders from Russia met traders from Europe and North America in Alaska was strengthened by the sudden economic cyclones which followed the gold-rushes. The discovery of placer gold in California in 1848 was followed by the rush of 1849, and the opening up of other areas in the Pacific region. Possibilities of enormous wealth, the enhanced value of gold following depression and a secular decline in prices, and the uncertainty of yield, led to the immigration of large numbers, chiefly young men, with at least sufficient funds to pay the expensive passage and to buy large quantities of expensive supplies. The influx of labour and capital into regions chiefly mountainous in character, and with restricted economic development, necessitated importation of goods and supplies on a large scale. High prices as a result of sudden increase in demand and the addition of large supplies of gold provided enormous profits on imports and on shipping. The profit motive in its most intense form was in evidence in the rush of labour and supplies to new gold-fields.

Influx of population was followed by rapid exhaustion of the accessible gold-fields and the necessity of searching for new regions or of developing alternative natural resources. The return of prospectors from California and the intimate knowledge of the peculiarities of the country which accompanied the spread of sheep-raising over wide areas in Australia led to the discovery of gold in New South Wales and in Victoria and to an influx of immigrants in 1852. The hope of the Chief Secretary who wrote, "If this is a gold country it will stop the Home Government from sending us any more convicts and prevent emigration to California" at Sydney in

1851 was fulfilled. Population increased rapidly from 437,665 in 1857 to 1,168,149 in 1871, and gold production in the period totalled £124,000,000. Decline in the yield of the placer fields and the introduction of capitalistic methods of exploitation and displacement of labour were followed by migration, search for gold in other regions, and the rush to New Zealand (Otago in 1861, and Westland in 1865). The arrival of large numbers of young men equipped with supplies and with experience in Australian fields led to rapid exploitation.

On the Pacific coast of North America, miners pushed northward from California in search of new fields and in 1858 "about 10,000 foreign miners" were attracted to the bars of the Fraser River. Large numbers of disillusioned, among them Henry George, turned back, but others pushed up the Fraser to make the important discoveries on its tributaries in the Cariboo in the early sixties. The total yield of gold from 1858 to 1876 was estimated at $40,000,000. The population of British Columbia totalled 36,247 in 1871, when it entered Confederation.

The effects of the discovery of gold in the Pacific regions were evident in the demand of large numbers in relatively densely populated areas for ships to carry them to the gold-fields. The discovery of gold in California quickened the demand for American sailing ships. Clipper ships carried passengers around the Horn for San Francisco and thence proceeded to China for a cargo of tea to be taken to London. The increasing demands for raw materials and for markets for manufactured products from Great Britain were met by the migration of ships and trade. News of the gold strike of 1851 in Australia was followed by a demand for fast, comfortable ships from England and the abandonment of the miserable emigrant ships of the forties. The Blackwallers employed from London to India were diverted to Australia. The fast sailing ships of New England and Nova Scotia were in demand in Liverpool for the Australian route. James Baines, with the Black Ball Line, purchased the famous ships of Donald McKay, a native of Nova Scotia; and his rival, the White Star Line, joined in competition for mail contracts, landing mail in Australia in from sixty-five to sixty-eight days, and for passengers. The *Marco Polo* (1,625 tons), pioneer of the Black Ball Line, built in Saint John, New Brunswick, in 1851, and her Master, Captain James Nicol Forbes, became famous in the

Australian trade with a record passage by the Horn from Melbourne to Liverpool of fifty-six days, and a round trip of five months and twenty-one days. Time was reduced as a result of the theories of M. F. Maury as to wind directions and as to routes. New England and British North American ships were in demand as larger, better sailing vessels and built of softwoods of cheaper construction. As the timber trade of British North America contributed to support industrial change in Great Britain in the first half of the century, the softwood ships of North America supported commercial change in the Pacific. But steamers to Colon, a railway thence to Panama, completed in 1855, and steamers thence to California almost displaced sailing ships by Cape Horn.

The increase in settlement along the coast of Australia, following the gold-rushes, created a demand for more efficient services between the ports and from the ports to the interior. The Australian Steam Navigation Company and other companies established services in 1851 and later dates between Melbourne and Sydney, Sydney and Brisbane and Melbourne and Adelaide, and Melbourne and Newcastle. Railway mileage in Victoria and in New South Wales increased from two miles in 1854 to 171 miles in 1859 and total railway mileage in Australia to 1,042 in 1871. In 1854, a mail service was established between Melbourne and Wellington, New Zealand. Steamers ran from Melbourne to Dunedin, and Sydney to Auckland, and, after the gold-rush in New Zealand, from Melbourne to Otago. New Zealand coastal steamers ran between Wellington and Dunedin, and in the gold-rush to Hokitika. Steamships engaged on short runs were extremely mobile and capable of being shifted according to demands. They were taken as troopships for the Crimean War, and were engaged after 1860 in the Maori Wars in the North Island of New Zealand. Telegraph communication was established between Sydney, Melbourne, and Adelaide in 1858, and a line was opened from Perth to Fremantle in 1869. A submarine cable was laid from Tasmania via Circular Head and King Island to Cape Otway in 1859 and in the Cook Strait in 1866. In New Zealand a wooden tramway was built from the Bluff to Lake Waktipu and a railway was built from Christchurch to Lyttleton early in the sixties, and from Invercargill to Bluff Harbour in 1867. In 1870, 1,887 miles of telegraph line had been laid.

The entrance of the steamship in the Pacific trans-oceanic

trade was infrequent and slow to develop in spite of assistance through mail contracts. In 1853, mail was taken by the P. and O. from Singapore to Sydney, but the Crimean War necessitated withdrawal of steamships and cancellation of the service. After considerable difficulty the P. and O. began a monthly service from England to Australia via Mauritius in 1859 but this was abandoned for connections at Galle in Ceylon. After several unsuccessful efforts, a steamship service was started from Panama to Sydney. The island of Rapa was selected as a coaling station in 1866, but the service disappeared with the completion of the Union Pacific to San Francisco in 1869 and the establishment of a line from San Francisco to Sydney in 1870.

On the American coast, steamers were employed to run from Panama to San Francisco, and to Oregon and British Columbia. Steamboats were brought up from California to be employed on the route from Victoria to Langley, and from Langley up the Fraser River to Emory's Bar. The rapidity of development of British Columbia placer mining was hastened with the plant and technique which had been developed in the California gold-fields. Location of placer gold-fields tended to concentrate in the upper reaches of the swift waters of relatively montainous regions. In British Columbia, discovery of gold on the bars of the Fraser River was followed by discoveries in the Cariboo, with the result that improved land transportation was essential since navigation was not feasible. Goods were handled from Emory's Bar to Yale by smaller craft and eventually the Cariboo Road was extended to Barkerville.

The effects of placer-mining on the movement of population and on transportation facilities were cyclonic in character. Rapid increase in population created demands for shipping and improved transportation, and led in the distant regions of the Pacific to the development of numerous subordinate industries. Funds brought out by immigrants from densely populated industrial areas, supplies of gold obtained from the gold-fields, and a scarcity of manufactured products and provisions, led to a sharp rise in prices. The intensely speculative character of gold-mining with the uncertainty of returns, the disturbances created by new discoveries, and the decline of production in relation to primitive methods, necessitated a high rate of depreciation and reinforced the trend toward high prices. The short life of a placer camp involved fabulous charges.

I

Gold-mining introduced an advanced state of monetary organization which accentuated flexibility in the specialization of production. It brought a reversal in the trend of a spread of money from the centre to the circumference in the sudden emergence of money on the fringes. Mercantile systems which favoured devices increasing imports of specie and accentuated the importance of liquidity were outstripped by the production of large quantities of gold.

The demand of a large population for foodstuffs was followed by agricultural expansion. The total land under crop in Australia increased from 491,000 acres in 1850 to over a million acres in 1858: New South Wales, 223,000; Victoria, 299,000; Tasmania, 229,000; South Australia, 264,000; and Western Australia, 21,000. "All wages rose, all accessible good land was in great demand, the dealers in produce found the advantage of prices rising in the article as it passed through their hands, live stock increased in value, shipping was profitably employed."[1] The dominance of the wool trade in both Australia and New Zealand became less conspicuous. Labour was attracted to the gold-fields, and wages of shepherds increased. A rise in the price of meat led to emphasis on the production of mutton. Cattle became increasingly important.

Labour was released from gold-mining with the exhaustion of shallow diggings, and the displacement of primitive technique by capitalistic devices which could be adopted with the improvement of transportation. In 1861, the Victoria gold-fields employed 711 steam engines (10,782 horse-power). Alternative employment was limited. Shipping in relation to gold-mining implied a heavy outbound cargo and a light, highly valuable, return cargo. Ample space was available on ships returning to England and improved transportation to the gold-fields facilitated a return to wool production and wool exports. Lower freights and higher prices contributed to strengthen the position of wool following the disturbances of the gold-rush. But wool production did not involve a substantial demand for labour. Industries which emerged in relation to the demands of the large population of the gold-fields offered greater possibilities for absorption of labour, provided new markets for manufactured products were available. In 1861, Victoria had 403 factories employing 3,830 persons. Attempts to encourage industry were accom-

[1]Cited, *Cambridge History of the British Empire*, Vol. VII, Part II, p. 151.

panied by attempts to increase revenues and to stimulate agricultural development in addition to wool production.

Placer-mining, with its emphasis on labour and on supplies of funds, stressed individualism, but continued exploitation necessitated capital equipment including roads which implied governmental machinery for the collection of revenue and the carrying of debt. An immediate and strong popular demand arose for improved transportation to the difficult regions of the gold-mining areas. While the outlay for improved transportation was heavy, miners were extremely reluctant, as a result of high prices, to contribute to the support of transportation.

Placer-mining strengthened and consolidated the trend toward democratic government. The Australian Colonies Government Act of 1850 was followed, with the stimulus of a rapid increase in population, by responsible government in New South Wales, Victoria, and Tasmania, in 1855. Self-government implied control over lands and of revenue[2] from land sales.

Following the abolition of the preference on goods from the United Kingdom in 1851, and the demands for revenue, import duties were imposed by Victoria in 1855. Under the determined and energetic leadership of David Syme, a policy of protection was adopted in 1866 and employees increased to 28,000 in 1874. This development involved industrialism, protection, and extension of agriculture. The struggle between the wool producer and the agriculturist which characterized Australian land policy became severe and was followed by the Land Act of 1862 with its emphasis on settlement.

New South Wales had been less seriously influenced by the gold-rush. Population had been drained to Victoria and industrial development was weakened. In 1852 duties[3] were imposed on

[2]Licence fees were introduced in New South Wales and in Victoria, but at rates which were inadequate and which became increasingly unpopular with attempts at rigorous collection and exhaustion of the gold-fields. As a result of determined protests, fees were reduced in Victoria in 1853, and following the Ballarat riots of 1854, miners' rights, conferring the franchise, displaced the licence fee, and an export duty of 2s. 6d. per ounce on gold was imposed in 1855. Local courts were established in the gold-fields to settle disputes.

[3]Miners were forced to pay licence fees but, with the example of Victoria, an export tax was introduced in 1857 and licence fees abolished. Wool production increased in importance, and the number of sheep increased from 5,615,054 in 1861 to 16,278,697 in 1871. The position of the squatter tended to defeat, through "dummying," the efforts of the farmer in the Land Act of 1861. Land under crop increased to 378,592 acres in 1870-1.

selected commodities. The importance of wool exports and dependence on a staple product precluded attempts to develop manufacturing by protection. The free-trade policy of New South Wales was in striking contrast to the protectionism of Victoria. South Australia responded to the demands of the gold-fields with increased production of wheat. With relative decline in local demand, and the introduction of agricultural machinery, particularly the stripper, exports of wheat were sent to Great Britain in 1866. The area under crop increased to 801,571 acres in 1870-1. Robert Torrens contributed to the solution of the land problem of agricultural expansion through the system which was introduced in 1858, and the Strangeways Act (1868) gave further encouragement. Tasmania, Western Australia, and Queensland increased the area under crop during the period, but the total advance was not relatively important.

The diverse economic development of the colonies of Australia involved conflicts in policies. The contrast in tariff policy between New South Wales and Victoria, and their limitations in treaty-making power, caused the failure of numerous conferences. In 1867 an agreement was reached between the two colonies, but it was not until 1873, in the Australian Colonies Duties Act that the imperial authorities conceded the right to make trade agreements.

Agreement was conspicuous, on the other hand, in the exclusion of Chinese. Migration of Oriental labour was a result of the immediate demands for labour in the gold-fields, of the high costs of labour in temperate areas of the Pacific coast with light density of population and at long distances from the Atlantic seaboard,[4] and of the existence of areas of intense population density along the Asiatic fringe.

Expansion of transport facilities and improvement of navigation,

[4]Prospects of profitable occupation induced Chinese brokers to provide capital to pay the costs of transportation (the ticket credit system) to the gold-fields. It was estimated that 2,000 Chinese coolies were employed in the Victoria gold-fields in 1854. The Restriction Act in 1855, prohibiting the arrival of Chinese by vessels, was followed by migration to South Australia and immigration to Victoria by land. In 1857, Chinese in the Victoria gold-fields had increased to 26,370, and South Australia was persuaded to pass a restriction Act. Victoria, in the same year, imposed heavy taxation on the Chinese population. In spite of legislation, population totalled 42,000, with the result that previous Acts were replaced by legislation imposing still heavier taxation. Chinese population declined with exhaustion of the gold-fields, and in 1864 restrictive legislation was repealed. In New South Wales, 12,988 Chinese were engaged in the gold-fields in 1861 and a bill similar to the Victoria Act of 1855 was enacted.

particularly the iron clippers and the beginning of regular steam traffic, supported the rapid economic growth which followed the gold-rush to the distant areas of Australia. Concentration on wool as a commodity adapted to the demands of distant transportation was accentuated. Public borrowings accompanied improved transportation facilities and expansion of production. All the States had appeared on the London market to secure loans to finance capital improvements: Victoria, 1859; New South Wales, 1855; South Australia, 1854; Queensland, 1861; Western Australia, 1845; and Tasmania, 1867. Free trade in Great Britain and development of Australia through staple products in relation to the demands of that area were accompanied by financial support from Great Britain and in turn by responsible government and the institution of suitable financial machinery designed to secure adequate revenue. The geographical characteristics of Australia with its extensive coast-line implied decentralization of governments and competition for labour rather than for capital, whereas in Canada concentration on the St. Lawrence implied centralization and competition for capital for construction of canals and railways. Confederation appeared early in Canada as a result of competition from the United States and later in Australia as a result of difficulties between decentralized states.

The effect of the gold-rush of Australia on New Zealand in the fifties was to provide a base to support the expansion which followed the gold-rush to New Zealand in the early sixties. As in Australia, high prices of agricultural products stimulated production and decline in gold production released labour for the development of other industries. Canterbury and Otago, as the chief centres of sheep-raising, and the South Island generally, increased in importance with demands for provisions, supplies, labour, and shipping. The number of sheep increased from one and a half million in 1858 to nearly ten million in 1871, wool exports from nearly four million pounds to nearly thirty-eight million, and land under cultivation from one hundred thousand acres to one million, two hundred thousand acres. Grain exports declined from 118,740 bushels in 1859 to 3,238 bushels in 1863, but increased to 1,032,092 bushels in 1871. South Island definitely established economic supremacy until the end of the century over North Island which had been harassed in the sixties with the Maori Wars. In 1871 population in South Island totalled 159,918, and in North Island 96,875. The development of railways and public works followed the increase in revenue incidental to the gold-rush. In 1870 the debt of the government totalled £4,543,316, and of the Provinces, £3,298,575.

The effects of the gold-rush in British Columbia were similar to those in Australia and New Zealand. Rapid increase in population created demands for provisions and supplies. The immediate demands and high prices of foodstuffs led not only to a rapid increase in imports, but also to local production. In spite of geographical limitations of soil and climate the colony was self-sufficient in its supply of wheat by 1866. Salmon were caught in large numbers for local consumption. Timber and planks were imported from American mills during the early building boom in Victoria, but local sawmills were rapidly introduced and by 1870 were installed on the Fraser and in the Cariboo to meet the demand of towns, and of miners for construction of flumes and sluice boxes. As placer creeks were exhausted and capitalistic methods of extraction increased in importance, surplus population moved outwards to new creeks or contributed to the more stable development in the support of new industries. Built up to meet the immediate demands of gold-mining, industries served as a basis for expansion in the production of exports. As ever, gold-mining involved a heavy inbound cargo and a light outbound cargo, and the lumber industry provided the raw material for an outbound cargo and for the rapid development of various regions in the Pacific. Operations begun at Alberni and Barclay Sound in 1861 were sufficient to support exports of over eleven million feet in 1862 to New Zealand, Australia, Hawaii, the Orient, South America, and even to England and Italy. Cheap lumber was essential to support the rapid transient changes in the economies of Pacific countries. The importance of industrialism as shown in the coastal steamers led to the development of the coal resources of Vancouver Island. A first shipment of 1,840 tons from Nanaimo to San Francisco in 1852 was followed by an increase of sales to a peak of 44,005 tons in 1868.

The inrush of immigrants in 1857 and 1858 led to the cancellation of the Hudson's Bay Company's licence to trade in British Columbia in 1858. Various forms of taxation were necessary to finance local construction to the interior, and included mining licences, a head tax, a tonnage tax, an import tax, and tolls. Decline of gold-mining and difficulties of taxation led to an increase in the debt of the colony. A free-trade policy abandoned by Vancouver Island involved higher duties, union of the colonies in 1866, and union with Canada in 1871 in which a debt of $1,666,200 was assumed by the Dominion. Like Australia, British Columbia was faced with the Oriental problem, and as early as 1864 about two thousand Chinese were employed in the gold-fields, but it was not until a much later date that restrictive legislation was enacted. The cycle of sudden immigration, exploitation and the use of capital equipment, the emergence of government and debt, and the shift to new natural resources continued in British Columbia as in other placer-mining regions.

The expansion and later contraction of the gold-fields of British Columbia was followed by increasing interest from the Atlantic. The long and difficult route overland began to compete with the long route by the Panama or the Horn. Milton and Cheadle crossed the Rocky Mountains in 1862 in the footsteps of fur-traders and miners. Construction of an overland telegraph to Asia was brought to an abrupt stop with completion of the Atlantic cable in 1866. Alaska was added to American territory in 1867. These developments were the forerunners of the agreement by which British Columbia joined Confederation on condition that a transcontinental railway was built. The gold-rush of British Columbia, expansion of the United States, and the problem of debt in Canada precipitated the demand for political unity across the northern half of the continent and in turn for economic unity. Gold-mining and its consequent economic development was a powerful factor pulling the westward extension of Empire to meet extension eastward.

II

Economic development in the Pacific prior to the completion of the Suez Canal and particularly in Australia emphasized the importance of the Cape of Good Hope and South Africa. The need of regular steam communication from England to Cape Town was increased by the internal difficulties in South Africa and by the requirements of a squadron based on Cape Town for the suppression of the East Africa slave trade. Better harbour accommodation for troop ships and passenger ships proceeding to India, and Australia, and the use of Durban coal supported steamship development and traffic to the Far East. The Union Steamship Company began monthly mail service from Southampton to Cape Town in 1857. It was extended to Durban in 1865 and made semi-monthly in 1868. A telegraph was completed from Cape Town to Simonstown in 1860 and to Grahamstown in 1864. Railways were built from Cape Town to Wellington, fifty-seven miles, in 1863, and to Wynburg in 1864. The Cape Town harbour works were completed in the decade from 1860 to 1870 and the Castle Steamship Company established a line in 1872. Extension of government accompanied improvement of communications. In 1853 representative government was established in Cape Colony, but responsible government was delayed until 1872. Natal continued as a Crown Colony and Basutoland came under a protectorate in 1869. As a result of the rush to the diamond fields of Kimberley in 1867-8, the British government assumed responsibility for maintaining order among the mining population in 1871, and annexed the Transvaal in 1877.

Expansion in the gold regions of the Pacific and improvement of transportation facilities strengthened extension to India and the Far East. Steamships had shortened the route to Suez, and from Suez to India. The Peninsula and Oriental Company signed a contract in January, 1853, for a fortnightly service between England and Alexandria, between Marseilles and Malta, and between Suez, Calcutta, and Hong Kong with a service every two months from Singapore to Sydney. A supplementary contract in 1854 provided for a service from Suez to Bombay, but the outbreak of the Crimean War reduced a fortnightly service from Bombay to China to a monthly service. The Indian Mutiny was followed by an extension of the line between Bombay, Aden, and Suez, and with a fortnightly service from Marseilles to Alexandria and arrivals and departures alternating from Calcutta and Bombay, a weekly service was given to India. Completion of the railway from Alexandria to Cairo in 1857 and its extension to Suez facilitated the change from Marseilles to Alexandria rather than to Malta. In 1864, a telegraph line with cable was completed from London to Karachi and in 1870 a cable was completed under British control. In 1867 a weekly service was provided to Bombay, and a fortnightly service to and from China and Japan. The Suez Canal was completed in 1869 and in the same year Marseilles as the port of arrival and departure was displaced by Brindisi. With this extension of steamship service, coaling stations were established and facilities for handling steamships were developed. Coastal steamship services were extended with the formation of the British East India Navigation Company in 1857, and included the coast from Singapore to Zanzibar in 1862. Interlocking directorates with the Netherlands East India Company formed in 1866 extended a line from Singapore to the Dutch East Indies and to Brisbane, Sydney, and Melbourne by Torres Strait.

As in North America improvement of navigation contributed to the development of railways and canals in the interior, so in India, railroads extended from terminal ports, canals and river steamships reduced costs of transportation, and involved increasing government support. The energy of Lord Dalhousie prepared the way for capital expenditures in numerous directions. Lower Burma was annexed in 1852, Jansi and Nagpur in 1853, and Oudh in 1856. The pressure of industrialism and the Indian Mutiny in 1857 were to be followed by final surrender of governmental control on the part of the East India Company in 1858. The Ganges Canal was completed in 1857, and the Kistna delta canals in 1855, and the Ravi Canal in 1859. The programme of energetic railroad construction outlined by Lord Dalhousie in 1853 was followed, particularly after the Mutiny by rapid progress. In 1853 a road was completed from Bombay to Lhana, in 1854 from Calcutta to Raneegunje (37 miles), and in the following year 120 miles were built in Madras. The depression in North America in 1857 and the importance of development of transportation facilities after the Mutiny led British contractors and capitalists to turn their attention to India. In 1858, Brassey began construction of a railroad from Calcutta to Khoostea on the Ganges (112 miles; completed 1862). In the following year one was built from Nulhattee to Azimgunje (27 miles) and in 1864 from Arkonam to Conjeveram (18 miles). The Delhi railway from Ghazeaabad to Umritsir (304 miles) was completed in 1870. Railway mileage in India increased from 35 in 1853-4 to 4,771 in 1870. In spite of government guarantees and other privileges, development was slow, but the serious famines of 1860 and 1866 led to active participation by the state in railway construction in 1869. The capital invested in railways in India has been estimated as follows:

(in thousands of pounds)

Year	Amount	Year	Amount
1858	£5,500	1864	£3,800
1859	7,150	1865	5,400
1860	7,580	1866	7,700
1861	6,500	1867	7,000
1862	5,800	1868	4,500
1863	4,750	1869	4,400

The telegraph preceded and accompanied the railroad. In the suppression of the Indian Mutiny it was said that "The electric telegraph has saved India." Before the advent of railways troops could be moved only about ten miles a day, whereas by rail they could cover four hundred miles in a day.[5]

The railway provided cheap transportation for raw materials from, and for manufactured products to, the interior. Access to the Raniganj coal fields by railway in 1854 contributed to the spread of industrialism. Wars in Russia and America accentuated the development of trade in tropical products from new sources, such as India, and had effects similar to gold in other regions. Imports of wheat in Great Britain following the abolition of the Corn Laws, and prior to the development of bulk handling, required extensive use of jute bags and the importation and manufacture of jute. The Crimean War cut off supplies of grain from Asia and necessitated increasing reliance on America for grain and on India for jute. The manufacture of jute in India began in 1855, the first power loom was introduced in 1859, and several mills were opened in the sixties. The average annual export from Calcutta from 1858 to 1863 was nearly 1,000,000 hundredweight. The cotton famine in Lancashire precipitated by the American Civil War was accompanied by high prices of textiles and increased exports from Bombay and from Egypt. The value of exports of cotton from Bombay increased from £5,500,000 in 1862 to £35,000,000 in 1866. The first cotton mill was established at Bombay in 1853, but the high price of cotton during the Civil War period, and the collapse of the speculative period of the cotton boom, hampered industrial expansion. Egypt owing to her advantages in nearness and in the production of a long staple cotton could outbid India, and her exports to England increased rapidly.

Cultivation of Indian tea increased rapidly in the sixties in Assam, Bengal, southern India, and Ceylon. According to one account, a plantation of 1,876 acres in 1850 produced 216,000 pounds, and 295 plantations of 31,303 acres produced 6,251,143 pounds in 1870. After the boom of the early sixties and the crash of 1866, cultivation expanded slowly and about 10,000,000 pounds were exported to the United Kingdom in 1869. Coffee exports from the Wynaad in South India totalled nearly 20,000,000 pounds in 1860-1. In 1865, 14,613

[5] L. C. A. Knowles, *Economic Development of the Overseas Empire* (London, 1924), p. 300, note.

acres were under cultivation in this region. The district of Coorg began production in 1854 and had 73,306 acres under cultivation in 1870.

As a result of the increasing consumption of coffee, 176,000 acres were planted in Ceylon from 1853 to 1869 and produced a crop valued at £4,000,000 sterling. Exports reached a maximum of 1,054,030 hundred-weight in 1870. Unfortunately the spread of the coffee blight began in 1862 and eventually ruined the industry, but after a few years of sharp strain it was replaced by tea and cinchona. Cinnamon production increased in the latter part of the period but chiefly at the expense of quality. As a result of active government intervention and substantial expenditures on irrigation canals after 1856, the production of rice increased. Roads were built throughout the island and products were brought to the markets at lower costs. In 1867 a railroad was completed from Colombo to Kandy (75 miles) and in 1871 from Peradanuja to the important coffee district at Nawalapituja. Decline of coffee production in the Far East brought a shift to Brazil as at a later date decline in rubber production in Brazil followed the shift of rubber to the Far East.

Extension of steamship navigation to the Far East produced an expansion of trade. The cession of Hong Kong and the opening of treaty ports in 1842 was followed by persistent efforts to extend trade, and the treaties of Tientsin of 1858 were extended and enforced in 1860. Similarly, treaties with Japan in 1859 were extended and enforced in 1865, and supplemented by a tariff convention of 1866. The way was opened for rapid expansion after 1868. The strategic importance of Singapore and the Malay States on the route to the Far East was evinced by the creation of the Crown Colony in 1867.

The extent of development of trade between the United Kingdom and the Pacific is suggested in an increase in imports of India and Ceylon from £9,094,349 in 1850 to £30,055,138 in 1860, and to £31,856,422 in 1870, and in exports from £7,874,584 in 1850 to £13,811,961 in 1860, and to £30,705,844 in 1870. British shipping entered and cleared to India and Ceylon increased from 1,081,511 tons in 1860 to 4,701,765 tons in 1870. Imports of Australia and New Zealand from the United Kingdom increased from £2,744,671 in 1850 to £16,316,853 in 1860, and amounted to £14,102,897 in 1870, and exports to the United Kingdom increased from £2,622,762 in 1850 to £12,502,378 in 1860, and to £13,343,356 in 1870. British shipping entered and cleared, exclusive of coastal trade, increased from 310,161 tons in 1850 to 2,355,399 tons in 1860 and to 3,912,429 tons in 1870. British shipping entered and cleared to Hong Kong increased from 724,693 tons in 1860 to 1,649,250 tons in 1870. Imports of the Cape of Good Hope from the United Kingdom fluctuated from £1,165,624 in 1850 to £2,187,207 in 1860 and £1,956,305 in 1870, and exports to the United Kingdom from £611,817 in 1850 to £1,547,351 in 1860 and £2,123,061 in 1870. British shipping entered and cleared increased from 300,937 tons in 1850 to 388,217 tons in 1860 and 314,063 tons in 1870.

III

Attraction of the remunerative passenger traffic to the gold-fields of California and Australia hastened the decline of sailing vessels and the development of the steamship in the Atlantic. The clipper ship in the United States accompanied the boom days of ship-building in the fifties in Quebec and New Brunswick, and of ship-building and shipping in Nova Scotia in the sixties. The application of steam to navigation lagged behind its application to land transport, but received a strong impetus from the demand for cheaper and faster service, the influence of invention, and government subsidies. The liberal subsidies granted by the United States to their steamships (1845-7) contributed to the breakdown of the British Navigation Acts. The repeal of these Acts in 1849 and the admission of foreign ships to the coasting trade of Great Britain in 1854 increased the mobility of shipping. Areas with advantages in abundance of ship-building material, and in skill and technique, responded to the demand for wooden sailing vessels. But such advantages were eventually offset by the superiority of iron, coal, and steam, and the industrial development of the United Kingdom. The pressure of industrialism based on railroads and ports was evident in the transformation of shipping. The displacement of American softwood by British hardwood, and of British hardwood by iron, prepared the way for the iron steamship. Wooden and iron steamships were at first concerned primarily with passengers and mail and superseded even the fastest clippers. The reduction in the thickness of the hull with the use of iron actually reduced the weight of ships, provided space for more cargo, involved less danger from fire, permitted the construction of larger ships to carry coal, enabled them to stand heavy driving in head seas and overcame the handicap of spars and masts in limiting the size of ships. The increasing efficiency of marine engines, the introduction of the screw, and the decline in fuel consumption[6] widened the range of steamships. Steamships from Great Britain began to penetrate the non-coal areas of Africa, South America, and the Pacific.

The effect of the Pacific gold-rushes was evident first in the rapid extension of steamship services to the West Indies and the Panama. A contract with the Royal Mail West India Steam Packet Company was extended to include a monthly service to the Brazils in 1852. Later contracts in 1857 imposed a faster schedule and development of the service to Rio de Janeiro and River Plate. In 1866 and 1868 the time from England to the Panama was reduced. The Pacific Steam Navigation Company developed a coastal trade between Panama and Valparaiso. In 1868 a profitable monthly service was established from Liverpool via the Straits of Magellan to Valparaiso. This became a fortnightly service and was extended to Callao in 1870. Additional steamship lines were organized, particularly from Liverpool to the West Indies and the Panama with the energetic activities of Alfred Holt beginning in 1855. With the Limited Liability Act of 1862 amalgamations were formed, the West India and Pacific Steam Navigation Company in 1863, and the Liverpool, Brazil and River Plate Steamship Company in 1865. In that year a steamship of the Holt Line made an 8,500-mile non-stop trip from Liverpool to San Francisco.

Sailing ships were challenged further by completion of the Suez Canal, and of the Union Pacific Railway in 1869, which cut the continents in half and removed support from sheltered routes. The

[6]

	Gross tons	*Coal per day in tons*	*Bunker capacity*	*Cargo capacity*
1855, *Persia*, iron steamship, paddle simples side lever engines...	3,300	150	1,640	1,100
1865, *Java*, iron steamship, screw, simple inverted engines	2,697	85	1,100	1,100
1874, *Bothnia*, iron steamship, screw, compound engines	4,556	63	940	3,000

C. E. Fayle, *A Short History of the World's Shipping Industry* (London, 1933), p. 241.

eighteen-fifties were a most interesting decade in the history of Atlantic shipping for they saw the steamer making real headway against the sailing ship, principally because iron construction and screw propulsion obtained recognition. They were, too, a period of cut-throat competition, which in addition to providing excitement for the lookers-on who did not stand to lose dividends by it, invariably meant technical development.[7] Steamship lines supported by mail subsidies were organized for regular schedules. Following the disappearance of the Collins Line, keen rivalry continued between the Cunard, Inman, Allan, and Dominion lines in the fifties and sixties. Competition for passengers penetrated to the immigrant trade. The percentage of immigrants arriving in Canada by steamships increased from forty-five in 1863 to over ninety-five in 1869. Finally, steamships encroached on bulk cargo traffic and extended development from coastwise to ocean traffic. Improvements in navigation on the Atlantic were significant in strengthening the position of the more highly industrialized areas by lowering the costs of the cheapest form of carriage, that by water. The improvements were hastened by the advantages resulting from the increased size of the unit employed and from rapid depreciation, accentuated by losses, from mobility as to routes, and the severity of competition between large capitalistic organizations. The early improvements were concentrated on speed and were designed to increase the mobility of labour. Improvements in relation to the movement of labour hastened the production and movement of raw materials in new areas and enlarged the demand for the manufactured products of Great Britain.

The increasing importance of iron and coal contributed to the strength of the merchant marine of Great Britain. In the depression of 1857 large numbers of American vessels[8] were sold to Great Britain, and with the outbreak of the Civil War and the ravages of Confederate cruisers half a million tons of shipping were transferred to British registry. Total shipping cleared and entered in ports of

[7]F. C. Bowen, *A Century of Atlantic Travel, 1830-1930* (London, n.d), p. 53.

[8]In the decade from 1850 to 1860 the tonnage of the American merchant marine increased from 3,535,000 to 5,049,000, and in 1861 a maximum of 2,494,984 tons were engaged in foreign trade. As a result, the percentage of British tonnage entering and clearing United Kingdom ports declined from 69 as an average from 1847 to 1849 to 56 in 1860.

the United Kingdom increased from 24,700,000 tons in 1860 to 36,600,000 tons in 1870, and the percentage of British tonnage from 56 to 68. Ship-building activity in the United Kingdom was great in 1863-5, when the Civil War checked American industry, and reached its peak of 275,000 tons in 1864. By the end of the sixties the steamship had surpassed the sailing vessel in Great Britain.

		Total number of vessels	*Total tonnage*
In 1860	Sail	818	168,420
	Steam	198	93,590
In 1870	Sail	541	123,910
	Steam	433	364,860

The iron steamship capitalized the advantages of Great Britain in her possession of iron and coal and of ports accessible all the year round. Her striking competitive advantages in ship-building bound her formal and informal Empire more closely to her. The advantages of areas which produced wooden sailing vessels rapidly depreciated and the expansion of canals and railways to the interior of new lands was encouraged with a consequent increase in the production of raw materials and demand for finished products. The supremacy of Great Britain in ship-building hastened this shift of energies in the outer Empire to internal exploitation. Ship-building and shipping were the basis of her expansion. Thus the increasing importance of British shipping, particularly with the development of the iron steamship on the Atlantic, and the migration[9] of about two and a half million people in each of the decades from 1850 to 1870, coincided with the internal development of North America and other regions.

The Sault Ste. Marie Canal, completed in 1855, gave access to the iron ore resources of Lake Superior, and the Civil War and railways created demands for iron and steel. Ship-building tonnage on the Great Lakes increased from 212,000 in 1851 to 547,267 in 1866, and railways extended inland from Atlantic ports to Chicago in 1852 and the Mississippi in 1854. Mileage in the United States increased from 9,021 in 1850 to 52,922 in 1870. The Homestead Act of 1862 opened up new lands for rapid occupation, and exports of wheat from the United States, particularly with rise in prices

[9]W. A. Carrothers gives a total of 2,844,512 emigrants from the British Isles from 1853 to 1870 of which 61 per cent. went to the United States and 28 per cent. to Australia in eight years 1853-60, and 72 per cent. to the United States and 17 per cent. to Australia in the ten years 1861-70.

to the peak of 1867 and the increasing use of machinery which accompanied scarcity of labour in the Civil War, totalled 188,000,000 bushels in 1870. The Civil War was in part a result and in part a cause of concentration on western expansion. It involved a profound disturbance to trade. Exports of cotton were practically wiped out from 1862 and reached about three-fourths of the total of 1860 in 1870. The financial drain of the war weakened the monetary and credit structures of both North and South and contributed to the sharp upward trend of protection in the post-war period. With the end of the Civil War, restrictions on settlement in the West were removed and settlement was encouraged. Destruction of the influence of the South was favourable to an increase in the tariff in the North. Reciprocity which had served as one of the compromises between the North and South to delay the Civil War, in which Canada was expected to offset for the North the extension of slavery to Texas in the South came to an end. Free land, loss of revenue from land sales, and war debt involved higher tariffs and protection as new sources of revenue. The South was no longer a factor restraining the tendency toward protection.

Internal expansion in the United States created a demand for capital and labour, and increased competition with less fortunate areas. These areas were consequently drawn more closely to the United Kingdom through the production of raw materials, and the demand for finished products, and were forced to adopt a definite policy of encouragement of capital and labour. The Reciprocity Treaty, during its existence from 1854 to 1866 created an immediate relationship between expansion in the United States and Canada. But the Civil War marked the end of the break between the South and the North, between staple production and industrialism, and between free trade and protection, and sharpened the contrast between an economy built up around the St. Lawrence, with its emphasis on water transportation, on staples and on the markets of Great Britain, and an industrialism with its emphasis on railroads, and led to abrogation of the Reciprocity Treaty. The election of Lincoln from the marginal free soil state of Illinois marked the end of compromise and the supremacy of the North.

In Canada the improvement of transportation facilities by canals and railways was stimulated by the possibility of sharing in the rapidly expanding traffic of the Middle West and thereby reducing overhead costs. The Welland Canal and the St. Lawrence Canals, enabling steamships from the Upper Lakes to descend to Montreal, were completed by 1850, and were intended to reduce costs of transportation[10] from Upper Canada and to compete with the Erie Canal which carried traffic from Buffalo to New York.

Handicaps of seasonal navigation on the St. Lawrence necessitated the construction of railways to ports on the Atlantic seaboard open all the year round. Reciprocity and the Civil War brought a marked increase in trade with the United States. A railway was built from Portland to Montreal in 1853, and from Montreal to Toronto in 1856, and to Sarnia (1855). Portage roads to offset the limitations of the St. Lawrence system were built across the Welland Peninsula and to Collingwood (1855). The completion of the Victoria Bridge at Montreal in 1859 provided a through line not only to develop traffic in Canada, but also to tap the traffic of the Middle West.

The Suspension Bridge (1855) provided a shorter route for American lines to New York, and the importance of propellers on the larger vessels of the Upper Lakes in the sixties rendered the Welland Canal increasingly obsolete. In spite of the construction of the Welland Railway in 1858, Montreal failed to increase materially its share of traffic. In 1871, three-fourths of the tonnage could not be taken through to Lake Ontario. Shipments of flour and wheat, reduced to bushels, increased to 11,425,167 in 1869, but the total was slight compared to exports from New York. In spite of a lower rate from Chicago to Montreal, "such has been the commanding influence of that great commercial metropolis New York in drawing trade to itself and in keeping down the price of ocean transport that

[10]Attempts to strengthen the position of the St. Lawrence included a contract in 1852 with the Canadian Steam Navigation Company requiring a fortnightly service to Quebec in summer and a monthly service to Portland in winter. Difficulties led to cancellation in 1855 and a new arrangement with Messrs. Allan of the Montreal Ocean Steamship Company for similar service. Weekly sailings winter and summer to Portland and Quebec respectively were begun in 1859 but it was not until 1864 that a satisfactory postal route was introduced on the St. Lawrence. Lighthouses were installed on the river and on the gulf, and telegraph lines were extended from Quebec to Father Point in 1859. The channel to Montreal was steadily deepened to 22 feet in 1878. In turn, as railways were built to New York construction of railways to Montreal to obtain a larger share of traffic was essential. Insurance charges were gradually reduced on the St. Lawrence and the competitive position strengthened.

those efforts, though not fruitless, have not been so successful as at first anticipated."[11] High rates of ocean freight to Quebec and Montreal, partly as a result of insurance and other costs, but particularly of the inability of Montreal to provide a balanced cargo and of the seasonal character of navigation, were a serious drawback.

Inability to compete with American routes reduced long haul traffic on the canals and railways, and necessitated increased reliance on local traffic. Revenue was reduced and the interest charges on capital invested in canals, and to a less extent in railways, were paid by increasing demands on the government. The importance of water navigation, competition from the United States for capital, labour, and traffic, and importation of skill and capital from Great Britain for construction purposes, involved government assistance on a substantial scale. The completion of the major railway systems in England by the middle decades of the century increased the demands for raw materials, and released railway contractors alert to the possibilities of guarantees from the colonial governments. The achievement of responsible government facilitated credit arrangements but involved difficulties with Great Britain and the United States.

The repeal of the Corn Laws and Navigation Acts involved the loss of preferences on colonial wheat and, coinciding with depression, led to the Annexationist Manifesto of 1849 and the demands for reciprocity with the United States.[12] The Reciprocity Treaty of 1854 was designed to increase trade between Canada and the United States, i.e. to create a free trade area in North America, and to encourage traffic on the St. Lawrence. It hastened the migration of American technique through opening a market for sawn lumber and other products. The position of the square timber trade and of wooden ship-building for the British market was weakened and the advantages of the St. Lawrence in the production and export of white pine as square timber and wooden ships became less conspicuous with the increasing importance of the American market for sawn lumber. Removal of the preference in Great Britain, and competition from Baltic lumber and iron steamships coincided with increasing demands for foodstuffs and especially wheat. The cessation of imports of wheat, which had become important with the

[11] *Canada, Sessional Paper,* No. 3, 1863.

[12] See *Cambridge History of the British Empire,* Vol. VI, pp. 382-4; also H. A. Innis, *Problems of Staple Production* (Toronto, 1933), Chap. II.

abolition of the Corn Laws from the Black and Baltic seas, during the Crimean War, accentuated demands from Canada and the United States, and contributed to the rise in the price of wheat and to increasing emphasis on railroads and the steamship. The proportion of lumber and timber to total exports from lands was below 50 per cent. in the fifties, and the trend, with wide fluctuations, continued downward to below 30 per cent. in 1870.[13] Dependence on wheat and heavy fixed charges incurred with the introduction of railways and steamships precipitated difficulties in finance. The depression of 1857 brought a sharp decline in the price of wheat which was followed by fluctuations in price and yield. In spite of the abolition of seigniorial tenure and of clergy reserves in 1854 the want of good land in Upper Canada in the early sixties was accompanied by difficulties of wheat production incidental to exhaustion of virgin soil, by the introduction of agricultural machinery from the United States, especially after the Civil War, and by increasing diversification of agriculture. The demand for livestock and livestock products during the Civil War, and the migration of dairying technique from the United States contributed to increasing exports of dairy products (particularly cheese) to Great Britain after the abrogation of reciprocity. In the late seventies, the steamship contributed to the development of substantial exports of livestock.

Problems of wheat and lumber exports were reflected in the crisis of 1857 in decline in imports, decline in revenue, and government deficits. The financial structure was profoundly affected by fluctuations in exports and by the shift in economic life shown particularly in the growth of towns which accompanied the railroad and the steamship. Speculation in real estate, difficulties with exports, and expansion of credit affected private as well as public finance. The more important banks of Upper Canada collapsed after 1863 and were followed by legislation restricting banks to commercial credit and to new developments.

An important step in meeting these problems was taken in 1858 with an increase in the tariff of 20 per cent. In 1855, Great Britain opposed negotiations for free trade between Canada and the

[13] A. R. M. Lower, "The Trade in Square Timber" (*Contributions to Canadian Economics*, Vol. VI, 1933).

West Indies, but a rise in the tariff was more serious.[14] Galt argued that the improvements in transportation paid for by revenue received from customs were more than sufficient through lowering of rates to offset the addition of duties, and that in this sense customs duties were designed to stimulate free trade.[15]

The Tariff Act was not disallowed, nor was it adequate to meet the problem. In 1866, with a debt of $77,020,082, the government was "unable to raise more than half of a moderate loan even when offering eight per cent. interest" as a result of "the disastrous effect on Canadian credit of the experience of British investors." The solution of the problem consisted in part in increasing traffic by intensive economic development, and more particularly by extensive economic development. Mr. E. W. Watkin, representing the directorate of the Grand Trunk, advised extension of the railway eastward to the Maritimes and westward to Rupert's Land. With the encouragement of the British government, he succeeded in securing a reorganization of the Hudson's Bay Company in 1863, with a view to

[14]The Duke of Newcastle, with the support of the Sheffield Chamber of Commerce, protested in a letter dated August 13, 1859, and Alexander Galt, the Minister of Finance, replied on October 25, 1859: "Self government would be utterly annihilated if the views of the Imperial Government were to be preferred to those of the people of Canada. It is therefore the duty of the present Government distinctly to affirm the right of the Canadian legislature to adjust the taxation of the people in the way they deem best, even if it should unfortunately happen to meet the disapproval of the Imperial Ministry. . . . The fiscal policy of Canada has invariably been governed by considerations of the amount of revenue required. . . . It is certainly ungenerous to be reproached by England, when the obligations which have caused the bulk of the indebtedness of Canada have been incurred either in compliance with the former policy of Great Britain, or more recently assumed to protect from loss those parties in England who had invested their means in our railway and municipal bonds" (*Canada, Sessional Papers,* No. 38, 1860, cited in E. Porritt, *The Fiscal and Diplomatic Freedom of the British Overseas Dominions,* Oxford, 1922, pp. 455-6). See also *Cambridge History of the British Empire,* Vol. VI, p. 349.

[15]"All these improvements have been undertaken with the twofold object of diminishing the cost to the consumer of what he imports, and of increasing the *net* result of the labour of the country when finally realized in Great Britain."

"If by an increase of five per cent. on the duty, a reduction of ten per cent. on the other charges were produced, the benefit would accrue equally to the British manufacturer and to the consumer, and the indirect but legitimate protection to the home manufacturer would be diminished; the consumer would pay five per cent. more to the Government, but ten per cent. less to the merchant and forwarder. In this illustration lies the whole explanation of the Canadian customs" (*Canada, Sessional Papers,* No. 23, 1862). This argument had been developed by Adam Smith. See H. A. Innis, "Significant Factors in Canadian Economic Development" (*Canadian Historical Review,* Vol. XVIII, 1937, pp. 374-85).

arrangements for construction of the railway, but it was not until 1869 that the Dominion government extinguished the rights of the Hudson's Bay Company and not until 1870 that Manitoba was added to Confederation. British Columbia, seriously injured by decline in gold production, joined Confederation in 1871 on condition that a connecting railway should be built within ten years. The debts of both provinces were taken over by the Dominion, arrangements were made for the payment of subsidies to contribute to the costs of local administration, and the Canadian Pacific Railway was completed in 1885.

In the Maritimes, railways were designed as portage railways to give Halifax short connections to Windsor on the Bay of Fundy and to Pictou on the Gulf of St. Lawrence; and Saint John, a short connection to Shediac on the Gulf of St. Lawrence; and totalled 365 miles in 1866 costing $15,000,000. Confederation between United Canada and the provinces of New Brunswick and Nova Scotia involved arrangements by which the debts incurred, chiefly as a result of transportation, were assumed by the Dominion. Moreover, capital was made available through a guarantee of a loan by the imperial government for extension of the Grand Trunk Railway through British territory to the winter ports of Halifax and Saint John, and the Intercolonial Railway was completed in 1876.[16] The new Dominion served as a credit structure by which capital became available with government support, and transportation facilities were extended. The St. Lawrence route, with its dependence on extensive governmental intervention in the reduction of transportation charges, and its inability to compete with American roads for through traffic, was forced to rely on fresh government support for the development of new sources of traffic. The political structure was adapted to these demands.

The establishment of fiscal autonomy in relation to Great Britain involved similar changes in relation to the United States. The competition of American manufactured products during the depression of 1857 coincided with the demand for revenue and, with the pressure of Canadian industrial interests, reinforced the trend toward higher tariffs. Protests arose from the United States against a violation of the spirit, if not the letter, of the Reciprocity Treaty. The

[16]See *Cambridge History of the British Empire*, Vol. VI, pp. 444 ff., 460 ff.

outbreak of the Civil War brought a marked increase in trade with the United States, but the end of the war and the financial difficulties of the United States and removal of the South as a free-trade influence led to increasing protests against the treaty, and to its abrogation in 1866. The Civil War, and especially the *Trent* affair and the Fenian raids, were accompanied by increasing attention on the part of Great Britain to the North American colonies, and hastened the enactment of the British North America Act.

The trend toward centralization which characterized the economic development of the St. Lawrence was in contrast to the trend toward decentralization in the Maritime Provinces, particularly Nova Scotia. Confederation was in some sense imposed by the needs of the St. Lawrence. The Atlantic steamship on the St. Lawrence, industrialism in Montreal, and the railroad in the Maritimes, created demands for coal from Cape Breton and the Pictou fields, while reciprocity encouraged trade, particularly from the Atlantic coast of Nova Scotia and the Bay of Fundy, to the United States. Confederation and a compromise between a high Canadian tariff and a low Nova Scotian tariff involved additional burdens to the western portion of the Maritimes which were not entirely offset by the advantages of new markets in the St. Lawrence to the eastern portion. Reciprocity permitted American fishermen to fish in inshore waters and to compete with Maritime fishermen, but the advantages to the United States were lost through the dearth of shipping during the Civil War. The fishery and settlement extended from Gaspé and from Newfoundland to the north shore of the St. Lawrence and Labrador with the result that Nova Scotian vesseels were compelled to search new grounds and Lunenberg vessels went for the first time on the Grand Banks in 1873. The Washington Treaty encouraged the Canadian industry.

Reciprocity between the United States and the colonies of British North America included Newfoundland and coincided roughly with the introduction of responsible government in that area in 1855. Competition from the French had effects similar to the effects of competition on Canada from the United States. Introduction of the seine in the cod fishery along the French shore and of the trawl on the banks adjacent to St. Pierre and Miquelon was followed by determined efforts to restrict their operation by Newfoundland. Conservation measures and control over sales of bait to the French were designed to check French competition stimulated by bonuses and large-scale operations. A treaty of 1857 arranged between Great Britain and France as to the disposal of the Newfoundland fishery was not enforced as a result of the hostility of Newfoundland and its insistence on responsible government and the recognition of its implications by Great Britain. Control was extended through the customs to the Labrador, with the result that the position of St. John's was strengthened at the expense of Nova Scotian, American, and British fishing interests. In spite of her proximity to Great Britain the effects of steam navigation were not evident until a late date. As a result of success with a submarine cable between Carleton Head, Prince Edward Island, and Cape Tormentine on the mainland completed November 22, 1852, F. N. Gisborne introduced the telegraph in St. John's in the same year and planned construction of a trans-Atlantic cable. In 1856 a cable was completed and telegraphic communication established with North America but it was not until July 27, 1866, that a permanent trans-Atlantic cable was laid by the *Great Eastern* from Valentia to Heart's Content. In 1869 a French cable was laid from Brest to St. Pierre, and in 1873 extended to Canso, Nova Scotia. Mail was carried under contract from St. John's to Halifax in winter months, and direct steamship lines to Galway began in 1856 and to England under the Allan Line in 1873. Internal development was fostered by responsible government, protection, and the spread of industrialism. The steamship was introduced in the sealing industry in 1863, and improved methods of extracting seal oils were introduced in the fifties. The herring and salmon fisheries became increasingly important. Abrogation of the Reciprocity Treaty was a logical development in Newfoundland as it had been in the other colonies. Commercial credit continued of dominant importance and the Union Bank was established in 1854 and the Commercial Bank in 1857. The demand for roads and capital improvements involved insistence on the part of the Newfoundland government on the right to impose duties and collect revenue. While the Maritime Provinces had joined United Canada in spite of differences in economic and political structure, Newfoundland, less influenced by the railway, had found the differences too great to permit of political union with the continent. Capital demands were not adequate to stamp the economic life of Newfoundland in a mould adapted to the requirements of Confederation, and the dispersion of economic life, characteristic of the fishery extending along the coast, precluded political unity.

IV

The series of gold-rushes hastened the trend toward increasing mobility of labour. The effects of industrialism particularly through the steamship and the railway contributed to expansion of free trade and responsible government in the temperate areas and to the spread of freedom of contract in the tropical regions. Further, the spread of the humanitarian movement led to protracted and finally successful efforts to suppress the trans-Atlantic slave trade. These, however, were complicated by the decline of preferences on sugar with the adoption of free trade. West Indies planters attempted to meet the difficulties by encouraging immigration of Chinese coolies. Capital was supplied by the planters, and labour was brought out under the contract system. "By judiciously promoting emigration from China and at the same time vigorously repressing the infamous traffic in African slaves, the Christian governments of Europe and America may confer benefits upon a large portion of the human race, the effects of which it would be difficult to exaggerate." So wrote Lord Russell to Earl Cowley on July 11, 1860.[17] Chinese officials were not impressed by the advantages, and emigration to tropical countries was restricted. Emigration beginning in 1852 was checked until 1859 and carried on with numerous difficulties after that date. British Guiana brought in about fourteen thousand Chinese in the period 1853 to 1879. For the more tropical West Indies, Indian coolies were more promising. In 1844, the East India Company granted permits to Jamaica, British Guiana, and Trinidad to recruit coolie labour, and in 1847 to Ceylon; also the British government granted similar permits in 1858 to St. Lucia, in 1860 to St. Vincent and St. Kitts, and in 1867 to Grenada. Many liberated slaves were brought to the West Indies, especially from Sierra Leone; also a large immigration came from Madeira.

In 1851 Lagos was captured from a powerful slavery gang with heavy losses and the rightful king restored. His successor, being under the control of slaves, was deposed and in 1861 Lagos was

[17]Cited, P. C. Campbell, *Chinese Coolie Emigration to Countries within the British Empire* (London, 1923), p. 129.

annexed. From this beginning Great Britain checked the slave trade on the Slave Coast. Also mercantile efforts on and near the Niger secured a basis for expansion of control over Southern and Northern Nigeria.

In Cape Colony, representative government in 1853 tended to emphasize equal political rights for blacks and whites. The contrast with the policy of the neighbouring Dutch republics involved difficulties with native tribes, which forced Great Britain to assume an increasingly strong position as a means of assuring order. The shift to free trade coincided with the spread of industrialism in the coal-bearing formations of the temperate regions and with the disturbance of economic life in the tropical regions. Mobility of labour and capital which accompanied the trend toward freedom of trade was of profound significance to the relatively unpopulated areas of the temperate regions, and of serious implication to the densely populated areas of the tropical zones. The abolition of slavery through the Civil War in the United States was a part of the general trend among countries dominated by Anglo-Saxon races. The long struggle of the British Navy off the coasts of West Africa to put down the slave trade, with little or no support for a long time from other powers, ended successfully in 1863-6 owing to the annexation of Lagos, to the efficiency of screw steamers in capturing slavers, to the complete abolition of slavery in 1862 by the United States, and, later, by Brazil and Cuba. The migration of Oriental labour to the gold-fields of the Pacific and of coloured labour to the tropics were indications of the far-reaching changes of the period.

The tremendous impact of the gold discoveries of the Pacific was evident in the enormous demands for capital equipment and manufactured products and also in the contributions of gold imports toward the changes of British capital structure. With increasing industrialism, the ample resources of commercial credit in Great Britain became inadequate to meet the internal and external demands for long-term credit. The crash of Overend Gurney and Company in 1865 was in part a result of the depression and in part of far-reaching changes in the financial structure. More effective organization of long-term credit facilities was evident in the extension of legislation to provide for limited liability companies in 1855 and 1862, and in the emergence of a holding company such as the International Financial Society in 1863. The completion of the Atlantic cable in 1866, the extension of cables, telegraphs, and mail steamships linked the financial structures of North America to Great Britain and to the Far East and facilitated capital movements and more direct control of economic and political development. Improvement of financial machinery hastened the decline of the East India Company and of the Hudson's Bay Company, and the development of industrialism in Great Britain and within and without the Empire beyond. Responsible government and the realignment of political structure in the temperate and in the tropical regions provided efficient credit instruments by which shipping and transport were revolutionized with industrialism. Political control from Great Britain declined in importance, but its decline was essential to the expansion of economic control. Guarantees and bonuses were provided by colonial governments with and without the support of the imperial government for the construction of railways; for example, the Grand Trunk Railway, under private or government construction. The weak position of Empire countries through their dependence on staple products, the timidity of capital which had suffered losses in foreign countries in the forties, and the competition of expanding industrial areas such as the United States, implied dependence on governmental support. The vested interests which characterized an Empire dependent on Navigation Acts, staple products, and commercial credit were weakened with the emergence of the Reform Acts in Great Britain, responsible government, and the progress of industrialism. The shift to navigation and land transport linked to steam was followed by the demand for, and the supply of, new staples more essential to the increasing industrialism of Great Britain, such as wheat and wool. Public finance and private finance, and political and economic institutions alike, reflected the expansion of industrialism in the Empire and the Western World.

The downward trend of duties of the period ending in 1850 continued practically to vanishing point. The British budget of 1853 abolished the duty on cotton yarn, the excise tax on soap, and the advertisement tax, and halved the duties on fruits and dairy products. In 1855 the stamp duty on newspapers was removed, and in 1860 all duties on imported manufactures. The excise duty on paper was abolished in the following year. The Cobden agreement with France was negotiated in 1860. The timber duty followed in 1866, and the sugar duty, after a series of gradual reductions, disappeared in 1874.

These changes completed the movement toward free trade, and the removal of protection from the vested interests which had grown up in the colonies producing the staples, sugar and lumber, and they encouraged internal trade dependent on advertising and newspapers. With the repeal of the Navigation Acts (1849) the advantages of industrial maturity and leadership were practically unhampered by governmental restrictions.

Advantages accruing through removal of duties and taxes, and increasing efficiency of the fiscal mechanism, were supplemented by technical improvements, particularly as applied to shipping. Commodities were imported cheaply, and with improved railways, ports, and ships were carried over longer distances and at lower costs. The stream of goods and commodities moving toward and away from an enlarged metropolitan centre increased in speed and ran with less friction. The completion of a railway and canal system in the United Kingdom by the middle decades of the nineteenth century created an industrialism based on iron and coal, with the growth of an urban population, an increasing demand for raw materials and an expanding market for finished products.

Extension of the influence of Great Britain in the Pacific and Atlantic under the impetus of technological advance, particularly in relation to navigation and transport in the Atlantic regions, and the impetus of the profit motive, particularly in the gold regions of the Pacific, implied an economic balance in which disturbances of one area were offset by advances in the other. The Civil War and the opening up of a continent in the United States involved its retreat from the sea and opened the door more widely to Great Britain. The Crimean War checked Russian exports of wheat and stimulated production and exports from Canada and the United States. The depression of 1857 in North America and the Civil War were followed by a shift of British interest to Central Africa, India, and the Pacific. The Civil War and the Crimean War forced extension outwards of Empire. The shifting of interests strengthened the position of Great Britain. The possibilities of increasing traffic reduced overhead costs on expanding industrial equipment. Improved technique, such as the introduction of steel, hastened the process of expansion. The increasing efficiency of industrial Britain was accompanied by the increasing efficiency of financial and fiscal Britain. The impact on Great Britain of wide fluctuations in the economic activity of regions producing raw material, exposed to shifts from gold to wool and to variations in the yield and price of raw materials, as in the case of wheat, was softened by the balancing of regions. The costs of shifting to the more permanent base of industrialism in terms of iron and steel were borne largely by the obsolescence of areas supplying quantities of raw material, such as timber and wooden ships, and were offset in part by lower costs of transportation and the development of new staples. Agriculture in England felt the impact of competition from new areas and arable land was converted into pasture. Diversity of demands for capital as a result of the economic and political divergences of regions producing raw materials, ranging from New Zealand to the United States, involved competition for labour and capital from the aggressive, rapidly expanding, continental area of the United States, with the weaker areas of the old Empire, and the evolution of types of government and guarantees adequate to secure metropolitan growth. Canada felt more directly the effects of American expansion and of British demands for guarantees, with the result that her experiences with tariffs and political structure were destined to establish precedents for later developments in the other Dominions. The period from 1849 to 1870 was a watershed in imperial history in the spread of industrialism to new regions.

The impact of free trade and industrialism, particularly in relation to steam navigation, accentuated the emphasis on specialization of production of raw materials in new countries and on the production of finished products in more highly industrialized regions. Water transportation and the increasing distances of the Pacific stressed production of specialized raw materials. Gold production emphasized the advantages of a highly industrialized area in its ability to supply promptly and abundantly supplies of finished products. The heavy cost of production, particularly in terms of transportation of raw materials suited to the demands of an increasingly industrialized area such as wheat and wool, and the enormous costs involved in the shift to new staples, implied in the pressure of free trade and industrialism and of gold-rushes, involved extensive government support. Free trade in Great Britain brought increasing emphasis on staple products in new countries and in turn the introduction of capital equipment, steamships, canals, roads, and railroads, and problems of finance and governmental activity along the lines of responsible government, federation, and protection. Dependence on staples involved more sweeping fluctuations of price, yield, and returns, and accentuated reliance on governmental intervention. Limited liability in its relations to the growth of corporate activity in Great Britain was paralleled by government guarantees in the regions producing raw materials. Commercialism began to give way to capitalism.

Expansion of trade brought improvement in transportation, the emergence of public debt, responsible government, and nationalism. Capital became relatively immobile and inflexible in the government securities of the Dominions. Access to bankruptcy which characterized more mature regions was denied. Political institutions were elaborated in relation to the increasing problems of debt. Dominions, provinces, and municipalities resorted to conversions and even to bankruptcies. Monetary policies were widened on an extensive scale, nationalism intensified and capital rendered still less mobile.

The cyclonic effects of the gold-rushes in the Pacific region were evident in the expansion of shipping and trade on the Atlantic and the Pacific and in the development of Great Britain as a metropolitan centre of the world. It is significant that Marshall suggested that after 1873 the economic history of one country could not be written. At a later date the gold-rushes had profound effects on continental development. Transcontinental railways were built to San Francisco and in turn from Montreal to Vancouver to link up the economic areas based on the discovery of gold with the eastern seaboard of North America. Construction under private enterprise in the United States hastened railway construction with substantial government support in Canada. The Klondike gold-rush had its effect in hastening construction of two additional transcontinental railways which became the basis of the Canadian National Railways. The vast resources of a continent were opened up with transcontinental lines. The discovery of placer gold reversed the basic trends of liquidity preference which favoured the growth of metropolitan areas particularly with the support of mercantilistic policies. The discovery and production of gold on a large scale shifted the impact of liquidity preference from trade to production, from established areas to new areas and enormously widened the bounds of production and trade.

The significance of liquidity preference in economic history extends far beyond monetary policy. It was not confined to the place of gold in trade and production. Improvements in communication had the same effects. The phenomenal expansion of newspapers following the displacement of rags by wood accentuated the intensification of trade, enormously extended the sensitivity of modern economic society, and enhanced the role of liquidity preference.

The effect of liquidity preference was evident in the distortion of economic development in relation to staple production. The attractive power of gold hastened the opening of the Pacific and in turn contributed powerfully to the rapid expansion of wheat production following the construction of transcontinental railways on the North American Continent and of animal products, wool, mutton, and dairy products in Australia and New Zealand. The pressure of agricultural products on the markets of Europe hastened industrial development and contributed to the rise of protection in industry and agriculture.

Distortion by the gold-rushes of more normal trends of metropolitan development—in which improved techniques in transportation and communication gradually led to changes in types of product from the hinterlands, more easily handled products being replaced by less easily handled products, fur by timber and timber by grain—by the speeding up of transportation improvement with construction of transcontinental railways was offset in part by their effectiveness in stimulating changes in staple production. Concentration on staples implied a highly specialized economy from which changes were accomplished with great difficulty and with distress. The Napoleonic Wars and high preferential duties brought the shift from fur to timber in the St. Lawrence. The Rebellions of 1837 were in part a result of the difficulty of shifting from timber to grain.

The gold-rushes hastened the shift to new staples and contributed to the difficulties of the long depression, but once the shift was made the basis was provided for the great boom. There were no gold-rushes to soften the depression of the thirties, and the shift from wheat to livestock and dairying in Western Canada was accomplished with intense difficulty.

10. UNUSED CAPACITY AS A FACTOR IN CANADIAN ECONOMIC HISTORY

The significance of navigation in the economic development of a region penetrated by the St. Lawrence to the south and by Hudson Bay to the north has been evident in concentration on production of raw materials for consumption in the highly industrialized[1] area of Europe, and in problems which have arisen with intense specialization, such as unused capacity in terms of vessel space as a result of inability to secure a balanced two-way cargo. The green fishery as conducted from French ports on the banks and along the coast required heavy outbound cargoes of salt to balance return cargoes of fish, but the dry fishery, which became important with the development of Spanish trade at the beginning of the seventeenth century, required smaller quantities of salt and equipment on the outgoing voyage and made necessary the carrying of ballast.[2] The English dry fishery in Newfoundland involved a further lack of balance in that crews necessary to carry on the industry were larger than those necessary to man the vessels, and, because of the seasonal fluctuations and agricultural limitations of that area, men were carried back at the end of the season. Sale of fish in the markets of Spain and the Mediterranean necessitated the dispatch of vessels to England with the men necessary to carry on the fishery, and additional larger vessels (sack ships) with cargoes of fish to market. The addition of sack ships lowered the cost of provisions and facilitated the beginnings of a settlement in which men remained over the winter. Consequently, competition between sack ships and fishing ships for cargoes of fish and for profitable return cargoes of salt, tropical products, and specie from Spain and the Mediterranean to England, contributed to the long severe struggle which dominated the history of Newfoundland and placed severe restrictions on the introduction of political institutions. New England, with a winter fishery and a favourable area for the development of agriculture, lumbering, and shipbuilding, offered possibilities of all-year-round operation. Settlers

[1]See H. A. Innis, *Problems of Staple Production in Canada* (Toronto, 1933), Chap. II.

[2]Numerous regulations were enacted against the dumping of ballast in the harbours of Newfoundland.

rather than ballast, therefore, were brought to New England. Expansion of settlement contributed to more effective exploitation of the fishery, shipbuilding, and trade and to the decline of control of fishing ships from England. Numerous small New England vessels extended the fishery to the banks and the shores of Nova Scotia, participated in the coastal trade to Newfoundland in spring and summer, and carried products to the West Indies to exchange for sugar and molasses in winter when these products came on the market and there was freedom from hurricanes. Relative absence of unused capacity in New England shipping meant low costs and contributed to rapid economic development which facilitated control over Nova Scotia after its loss to France in the Treaty of Utrecht in 1713. The expansion of New England involved a continued drain of labour from Newfoundland and weakened the position of settlement in that area.

The concern of French fishing ships with the home market and the green fishery led to a late development of the dry fishery in more distant areas not occupied by the English, such as Gaspé. An unbalanced cargo facilitated the addition of trading goods on the outward voyage for development of trade on the St. Lawrence in furs, which with small bulk and high value added little to the cargo of the home voyage. The importance of the Pre-Cambrian formation, and its limitations as to agricultural development, accentuated dependence on the fishing industry in the Maritime regions and on the fur trade in the area drained by the St. Lawrence. Severe competition of fishing ships for the fur trade made monopoly control impossible in the Maritimes and inevitable in the restricted areas of the St. Lawrence. Monopoly control in the fur trade and an unbalanced cargo were accompanied by attempts to reduce outbound cargo from Europe, to restrict settlement, and to increase return cargo by expansion of the fur trade. Similar effects were evident in the trade of the Dutch to New Amsterdam and up the Hudson and by the Iroquois to the Richelieu and to Lake Ontario. Competition between two routes characterized by long ocean voyages and unbalanced cargoes, caused serious losses which culminated in the destruction of the villages of Huron middlemen north of Lake Simcoe. Severe losses in the fur trade, which accompanied monopoly under private enterprise, accentuated restriction of settlement. Intense competition between drainage basins necessitated direct control on the part of the French government in 1663 and active promotion of immigration and settlement and successful war against the Iroquois.

Groseilliers and Radisson attempted to avoid the difficulties of the St. Lawrence by developing trade through Hudson Bay, but they were discouraged by the French who were opposed to the additional costs of maintaining control over two routes.[8] They turned to the English who founded the Hudson's Bay Company. To meet competitive attacks from this alternative route, the French ruthlessly checked that Company's activities prior to 1713. Not only was possible competition checked in the north, but efforts continued to extend the St. Lawrence trade by the construction of military posts at Fort Frontenac, Niagara, and Detroit to prevent competition from the English, successors to the Dutch after 1664 to the south. The success of these efforts was followed by rapid increase in the number of lower grade southern furs brought on the market, a rapid decline in price, attempts to increase prices by valorization schemes, which failed, particularly through declining consumption, which accompanied lowering of the quality of materials used in the manufacture of beaver hats. The results accompanying the activities of the government in strengthening the position of the St. Lawrence by heavy military expenditures were evident in the development of inflation and in the loss of Hudson Bay and Nova Scotia in the Treaty of Utrecht. The persistent effects of unused capacity were evident under private enterprise in restriction of settlement and the necessity of governmental intervention. The consequent increased settlement in turn necessitated expansion of the fur trade to the interior. Inability to control the rate of expansion was particularly serious with a luxury product.

The Hudson's Bay Company, handicapped by limitations of agriculture in Hudson Bay, was similarly compelled to restrict a heavy outbound cargo, and to limit population, with the result that it was in a weak position to resist inroads from the French. The difficulties of combating the smuggling of a light highly valuable commodity such as fur necessitated a highly centralized organization similar to that attempted by the Spanish in the handling of precious metals. Possibilities of smuggling in the St. Lawrence checked efforts at

[8]See G. L. Nute, *Cæsars of the Wilderness* (New York, 1943).

centralization such as matured in the Hudson's Bay Company. The problem of restricted population was eventually solved in part by governmental intervention in the form of military and naval campaigns, the success of which led to the reoccupation of Hudson Bay in the Treaty of Utrecht.

Penetration of the French to the interior and increasing dependence on the fur trade accentuated the weakness of agriculture in the St. Lawrence, with its limitations of soil, climate, and technique, to the extent that New France was not even self-sufficient and was unable to provide support to the fishing regions, particularly of Cape Breton after 1713, or to the French West Indies, or to compete with lumber and fish from New England and agricultural products—especially flour—from New York and Philadelphia. Moreover, the long closed season of the St. Lawrence restricted the possibilities of developing a satisfactory trade to the West Indies. The hurricane season coincided with the open season of the St. Lawrence and the sugar season with the closed season. Inability to link up the St. Lawrence with the fishing industry and the West Indies weakened the French Empire; in contrast with the economic integration of settlement in New England and expansion of the fishing industry and trade to the West Indies and Newfoundland which strengthened the English Empire. Expansion of the fur trade and the fishing industry in New France weakened the French, while integrated development increased the strength of the regions under British control on the Atlantic. After 1713, New England advanced to the fishing regions in the vicinity of Canso and extended trade to Newfoundland and the West Indies. Expanding trade involved exports to, and imports from, the foreign West Indies in spite of legislation such as the Molasses Act of 1733. From the south, New York, with cheap supplies of rum from the West Indies, began to compete more effectively in the interior with French trans-Atlantic, St. Lawrence trade with its dependence on brandy. To the north, the Hudson's Bay Company re-established its position on Hudson Bay but the problem of unbalanced cargo continued; settlement was restricted and exploration and penetration to the interior were limited. Indians were encouraged to bring their furs down to Hudson Bay. Continued competition from the north and the south necessitated continued extension westward of the French fur trade of the St. Lawrence. La Vérendrye and his successors took advantage of the weakness of the Hudson's Bay Company on Hudson Bay by pushing trade to the Saskatchewan and making visits of the Indians to Hudson Bay unnecessary; but increasing costs of transportation weakened the position of the French Empire and contributed to its collapse. Renewed efforts to increase control over the fur trade by expansion westward, and over the fishing industry by fortification of Louisbourg in Cape Breton, were again defeated and followed by the collapse of the French Empire in 1763.

Collapse of the French Empire facilitated expansion of British colonial trade, shown in penetration of Albany traders to the St. Lawrence and to the upper lakes, but the problem of unbalanced cargo in the European Atlantic trade in furs by the St. Lawrence route continued, and with it the necessity for westward expansion. The divergence between the New York and St. Lawrence trade was recognized in regulations permitting extension of trade beyond the posts in 1768, and in the Quebec Act of 1774, which attempted to re-establish territory occupied by the French tributary to Montreal by a boundary line down the Ohio. Penetration to the north-west followed lines worked out by the French. On the Atlantic, expansion of integrated colonial trade increased the tension incidental to increased restriction of West Indies trade through enforcements of the Sugar Act. Pressure in the interior and on the Atlantic contributed to the outbreak of the American Revolution.

After the Revolution, England was scarcely more successful than the French had been in developing an empire based on the St. Lawrence, the Maritimes, and the West Indies. The West Indies lost their influential position in Great Britain, and in spite of paying heavy penalties to build up the Maritimes as a substitute for the American colonies, the latter were unable to provide adequate supplies of foodstuffs for their own needs. The fur trade of the St. Lawrence continued as a drain on agriculture in that area. Fur traders continued to solve their problems by expansion to the Saskatchewan, the Churchill, the Mackenzie, and the rivers draining to the Pacific. Reorganization in the formation of the North West Company, support of West Indies rum, use of vessels on the Great Lakes, and organization of food supply in the interior with reliance on pemmican and the potato, contributed to the achievement. The Hudson's Bay Company, with its persistent problem of unbalanced cargo to Hudson Bay, was again weakened by expansion from the

St. Lawrence and was compelled to make determined efforts to overcome its handicaps and penetrate to the interior, in part by reorganization, and in part by settlement in the Red River district under Lord Selkirk as a means of reducing costs of imported provisions and supplies. The inevitable severe competition between rival organizations—on the one hand from the St. Lawrence with expansion to new territory with unexploited resources as a means of mitigating the increasing cost of transportation, and on the other from Hudson Bay with the necessity of penetration to the interior to meet traders from the St. Lawrence—was followed by outbreaks of hostilities and amalgamation in 1821. Continued expansion from the St. Lawrence and the increasingly difficult problem of an unbalanced cargo, accentuated not only by distance but also by the necessity of travelling upstream with heavy outbound cargo, eventually weakened the North West Company as they had the French. The significance of unbalanced cargoes was evident in the intensity of competition, in the rapid extension westward from the St. Lawrence, in restriction in Hudson Bay, and in the clash which brought amalgamation.

The drain of the fur trade and its opposition to settlement in the St. Lawrence were ended temporarily in the French régime by the active intervention of government, and similarly in the English régime. Restricted settlement on the St. Lawrence, as a result of the characteristics of the fur trade, was overcome not only by active encouragement to migration of the Loyalists, particularly to Upper Canada, by military settlements, and by strong military support in the War of 1812, but also by determined efforts of Great Britain through an extremely high preference to build up the timber trade in order to offset the effects of dependence on European and American supplies during the Napoleonic Wars. The disappearance of the fur trade in the St. Lawrence was followed by exploitation of softwood (white pine) timber. As a bulky commodity with low specific gravity it could be floated down the long continental rivers, and with the manufacture of ships provided its own means of transportation to Great Britain. With a heavy return cargo and empty space on the outbound voyage, its effects were the reverse of the fur trade, and large numbers of settlers were brought out in preference to ballast. Rapid increase of settlement, particularly after 1820, was followed by rapid expansion of agriculture, especially in Upper Canada. Increased production of agricultural products, wheat and flour, in the newly-settled regions of Upper Canada led to demands for construction of canals across the Niagara Peninsula and on the upper St. Lawrence. The difficulties of obtaining financial support for canal construction in newly-settled regions, and increasing demands for cheaper transportation, contributed, together with the depression of the thirties and the pronounced cyclical fluctuations of an economy largely dependent on the timber trade, to the outbreak of the rebellion in 1837, Lord Durham's *Report*, the Act of Union, and creation of a financial structure capable of supporting rapid construction of canals. Concentration on the timber trade, with its unbalanced cargo and the indirect effect on increasing emigration and settlement, was followed by governmental intervention not only in the form of improvements of transportation but also of changes in land policy. Unwholesome conditions of immigration in dilapidated ships suited only to the timber trade, shown in outbreaks of cholera, which spread through the continent, necessitated governmental regulation. The timber trade was encouraged by the development of settlement, as costs of transportation were lowered by securing immigrants for the outbound voyage, but as it expanded in these circumstances, the problems of settlement became more acute. The period of shifting from dependence on the timber trade to dependence on agriculture was essentially a period of difficulty.

After 1821 the fur trade as conducted from Hudson Bay continued to be involved in problems of unbalanced cargo, though they were less acute on account of settlement of Red River, more efficient transportation, and increasing possibilities of regulation. Continued expansion to new territory in the Yukon and Labrador was accompanied by attempts to lower costs, by reducing the heavy incoming upstream cargo. New England traders, restricted by the British Navigation Acts on the Atlantic and free from the restraints of the East India Company on the Pacific, took advantage of the discoveries made by Captain Cook of the art of navigating long distances by reduction of scurvy, and of the resources of furs. On the other hand, Canadian traders, expelled from American territory after the Jay Treaty and the Embargo Act of 1807, pushed into the Pacific coast drainage basin and displaced Astor's establishment on the Columbia in the War of 1812. After amalgamation in 1821, the Western Department by virtue of its distance and its interest in the Pacific, tended to develop along lines independent of the Northern Department. Exhaustion of new territory for the fur trade accentuated economies of operation, particularly in transportation, and contributed to the development of settlement and agriculture, particularly on the Columbia and the Red River. Settlement eventually brought demands for new types of government, shown in the loss of Oregon and in the difficulties leading to the Riel Rebellion and the establishment of the province of Manitoba. The problem of unused capacity in the fur trade, and the necessity of reducing westbound upstream movements of bulky provisions and supplies, resulted in constant expansion westward to the Pacific and the organization of settlement in relation to production of food supplies. In turn agriculture and settlement hastened the decline of the fur trade and provided abutments for the railway bridge. Monopoly in the fur trade receded and new trade routes emerged in which the Hudson's Bay Company deserted the Hudson Bay route and imported goods from the south.

In the Maritimes continuous efforts were made to develop an integrated economy similar to that of New England in a struggle for control over the fishery, trade, and shipping. Concentration of trade in Halifax was followed after the middle of the century, particularly with the advent of steamships, by attempts to overcome the handicaps of the fishing industry, evident in scattered ports, through government construction of short stretches of railway to the Gulf of St. Lawrence and the Bay of Fundy; and in Saint John by construction of a short stretch of railway to the Gulf of St. Lawrence. Competition of railways with shipping brought profound disturbances to an economy based on ships, and shifted interest from external to internal development. Decline of shipping and difficulties of the railways necessitated efforts to extend traffic to the interior by linking the railways to continental systems. An attempt was made to solve the problem of unused railway capacity by Confederation and construction of the Intercolonial Railway.[4]

[4]"It is to be hoped that the folly of expecting any large results from local and isolated railways is already fully demonstrated to both Nova Scotia and New Brunswick, and that it has now become a first consideration with them to direct their attention to the means by which both may be relieved from the consequences of a large debt incurred for works not only unproductive of any directly remunerative results but also unattended by any substantial advantage to our trade or commercial importance. The conviction must have forced itself upon the public mind that we must extricate ourselves from these difficulties

On the St. Lawrence, the inadequacy of canals as a solution to the problems of agriculture in Upper Canada, and the difficulty of securing traffic from the western states in competition with the Erie Canal, improved upper lakes steamboats, and railways, necessitated further governmental intervention in the form of substantial assistance to the Grand Trunk from Sarnia to Montreal and Portland, and later to Rivière du Loup to connect with the Intercolonial to Halifax. Private enterprise with government support was able to build the short line to the American seaboard, but government ownership was essential to link up Maritime railways with the Grand Trunk by the Intercolonial and to supplement water transportation to Montreal during the summer season. As the Act of Union was a financial prerequisite to the St. Lawrence Canals, so Confederation was a financial prerequisite to the Intercolonial. A more balanced cargo, which was available in New York and American ports, pulled Atlantic steamships—for example, the Cunard line—from Canadian ports. In spite of attempts to increase traffic by construction of through lines, the problems of unused capacity became more serious. Construction of a railway to the Pacific offered possibilities of relief.

On the Pacific coast the sudden economic expansion precipitated by the gold rush in the late fifties and early sixties was followed by rapid decline and serious financial difficulties accompanying heavy interest charges on the debt incurred in construction of roads to the

by obtaining connection with the railways of Canada and the United States by one or other of the routes proposed. Much has already been done towards achieving that result" (From a speech by Sir Charles Tupper at Saint John, 1860, quoted in Sir Charles Tupper, *Recollections of Sixty Years in Canada*, Toronto, 1914, pp. 34-5). "There is a little over a hundred miles of railway in the province but owing to some cause which is unintelligible to an outsider and many less important reasons, which are easily understood, this undertaking has burdened the province with a heavy debt and consequently heavy taxation while it has irritated politicians, and been a cause of deferring . . . perhaps for ever . . . many important acts of local legislation. The primary error, undoubtedly, was the making it a government work, instead of leaving it to a company. Heavy sums raised at *six per cent.* on provincial debentures make sad havoc with revenue of the country. And the next great error . . . patent to all . . . is the custom too prevalent in our colonies under the system of representative government, of changing every official, however petty, at every change of government" (F. Duncan, *Our Garrisons in the West*, London, 1864, p. 100). "Provincial isolation and a blundering neglect to make railways which individually are burdens but would become as a grand whole a source of revenue and profit, are among the features at present most apparent in our British American railway system. . . . It is well said, by one of their own journals 'We cannot afford to bear the burden of our present incomplete road'" (*Ibid.*, p. 280).

interior.[5] Construction of a transcontinental railway as a condition on which British Columbia joined Confederation was expected to solve problems of debt in relation to existing transportation facilities in British Columbia and in the St. Lawrence. Substantial governmental support necessitated construction of a road through Canadian territory north of Lake Superior and precluded participation by the Grand Trunk Railway, insistent on building up traffic for its main line to the western states.[6]

Anxiety of the government to solve the problems of public finance, which followed the severe depression of the seventies, by development of traffic for existing transportation facilities enabled Montreal financiers, who had gained materially from the first line from Minneapolis to Winnipeg and from reversal of the flow of traffic from Hudson Bay on the north to the south, to obtain the contract for construction of the Canadian Pacific Railway. Rapid construction of the main line in the prairie regions, adoption of a southern route in spite of recommendations of Sandford Fleming in favour of the northern route, encouragement of immigrants, acquisition of feeders in the industrialized St. Lawrence region, completion of the line to a winter port at Saint John, and extension of ocean services were part of a policy incidental to the overwhelming importance of developing traffic on a transcontinental line. "It was the Oriental traffic that helped to save the Canadian Pacific from the disaster which sunk a hundred and fifty-six American railroads in the depression of 1893-95 and might well have overwhelmed a new railway through Canada depending for its existence on local business."[7] Oriental traffic during the depression was supplemented by economic expansion of British Columbia, particularly in the construction of the Crow's Nest Pass line, in the mines of the Kootenay region, in lumbering, in fishing, and in the gold rush to the Klondike. The tariff designed in the National Policy to support east-west traffic, and the monopoly clause (cancelled 1888), supported the policy of following a southern route across the prairies to check competition from American roads for long-haul traffic.

[5]"Although sentiment in Vancouver Island on the whole was unfavourable to Confederation, the entire mainland including Cariboo, then an important factor, was practically a unit in its favour" (Sir Charles Tupper, *Recollections*, p. 126).

[6]*Ibid.*, p. 140.

[7]J. M. Gibbon, *Steel of Empire* (Toronto, 1935), p. 336.

Determined efforts to maintain control over traffic were accompanied by rapid increase in profits with the turn of the century, and release of contractors after completion of the main line, with its location along the southern route, led to construction of a second main line from Winnipeg north-west to the Yellowhead Pass with government support from the provinces in protest against the burden of monopoly from a transcontinental line supported by a federal government. Control by the Canadian Northern of a line carrying traffic from the prairies to the head of the lakes necessitated extension westward to Vancouver and eastward from the head of the lakes to the St. Lawrence. In Eastern Canada the Grand Trunk was compelled by encroachment from the Canadian Pacific to secure control of local traffic by amalgamation with the Great Western, and to search for means of supplementing through-line traffic. Protection encouraged transcontinental lines and weakened the position of the Grand Trunk main line to the United States. Montreal became the apex of an angle of which one side—the main line of the C.P.R.—extended to British Columbia and the other—the main line of the Grand Trunk—to Sarnia and Chicago. Development of traffic on these lines, deepening of the upper St. Lawrence Canals to 14 feet and of the St. Lawrence Ship Channel to twenty-five feet early in the century, and extension of wireless, enabled Montreal to compete more effectively with New York for grain and for ships. Inability to link up the Intercolonial as a government undertaking with railways under private enterprise which were anxious to take the shortest cut to seaboard, decline of Quebec as contrasted with the rise of Montreal, attempts to tap the clay belt extending westward to Winnipeg in order to provide for possible expansion in northern Quebec and in northern Ontario, and increasing revenue from the tariff led to the construction of the national Transcontinental Railway from Winnipeg to Quebec and its extension to Maritime ports. The more distant Grand Trunk Pacific line, extending from Winnipeg, as the terminus of the National Transcontinental to Prince Rupert, appeared as a possibility of developing through long-haul traffic to the Orient, British Columbia, and Western Canada, and as a further means of checking the effects of monopoly from the Canadian Pacific under the National Policy. Attempts to link the Grand Trunk in the east and the Canadian Northern in the west were destined to defeat through the insistence of private enterprise in the Canadian

Northern on a line to the Great Lakes and industrial areas of the St. Lawrence, and of the federal government in the National Transcontinental on a line opening new territory and recapturing lost ground for the Intercolonial and the Maritimes.

The enormous outlay of capital in canals and transcontinental railways accentuated problems of unused capacity, particularly because of the basic importance of the production and export of wheat from the prairie regions. Construction of elevators and of branch lines on a vast scale in the wheat-producing regions necessitated double tracking of lines to the head of the lakes and additions of lines from Georgian Bay ports to Montreal. Seasonal navigation implied rapid movement of grain and a pronounced peak load of east-bound traffic. Empty cars were distributed over a long period to points throughout the west in preparation for the harvest rush. Seasonal navigation on the lower St. Lawrence facilitated storage of wheat in Buffalo elevators for shipment to New York.

The secular trend of expanding wheat production shown in long-run peak-load problems of transportation, was accompanied by short-run problems of annual fluctuations of crop, and government policy. The tendency of costs incidental to peak-load operation, made more rigid by competitive rates with American lines and the importance of government debt, to fall on regions exposed to world competition in prices of wheat, has involved the struggle for control over elevators, lower rates, the co-operative movement, the Hudson Bay Railway, and shipment via Vancouver and the Panama Canal. Finally, the recent depression and sustained drought led to governmental support of wheat prices and establishment of a wheat board.

The burdens were less conspicuous during the period of rapid expansion from the middle nineties to the beginning of the War on account of increased immigration, branch-and main-line construction, expansion of wheat production, the development of mining in the Cordilleran region, especially the Kootenay and the Klondike. Rapid increase in capital equipment in Western Canada was accompanied by expansion of the industrial areas of the St. Lawrence and of the Maritimes. Provincial government support of hydro-electric power in Ontario to utilize the enormous water powers of Niagara accompanied support by bonuses of the iron and steel industry of the Maritimes and the St. Lawrence for the production of coal, railway cars, rails, and machinery. Similarly rapid increase of population in the west involved provincial government support in the construction of telephone lines and extension of other social services. Decline in rate of expansion in Western Canada brought a sharp decline in the demand for railway cars, rails, and other types of capital equipment, with particularly serious effects for more distant regions such as the Maritimes, and in turn necessitated increased government support in subventions.

The acute difficulties of new transcontinental railways in competition with an established line before traffic had been developed, and the freezing of capital markets with the outbreak of the Great War, led to the appointment of the Drayton-Acworth Commission and formation of the Canadian National Railways to include lines built by private enterprise—namely the Grand Trunk, and its subsidiary, the Grand Trunk Pacific, and the Canadian Northern—and by government—the Intercolonial and the National Transcontinental. These lines were merged, and determined efforts were made to build up long-haul traffic by steamship lines, hotels, and branch lines. The Canadian Pacific, in an attempt to maintain control and to extend traffic, engaged in construction of branch lines, hotels, steamships, and extension of external activities. The upward swing of the business cycle favoured extension of capital equipment by both organizations. The necessity of competing for long-haul traffic in mature economic areas with which private enterprise had been particularly concerned, accentuated the problem of lines built by the government. These lines were essentially developmental and, being undertaken by the government with ample supplies of credit, were built with heavy initial outlays of capital. Consequently, light traffic, as a result of competition from lines built under private enterprise and privately owned and of their essentially developmental character, involved heavy unit costs of operation and maintenance, which were accentuated by heavy sunk costs of construction. Expansion of mining and of the pulp and paper industry, and settlement in northern Ontario and northern Quebec, were of first importance in reducing costs and meeting the deficit of the Canadian National Railway and in offsetting the effects of competition within the Canadian National System with lines to Chicago, and to the north-west, and from the north-west to Quebec and the Maritimes.

The effects of the depression on the Canadian Pacific and the Canadian National have been evident in the passing of dividends and in the extent of Canadian National deficits. The Canadian Pacific has been relatively barred from further participation in expansion and has even been seriously affected by decline in the southern drought areas, but, on the other hand, its entrenched position has served as a powerful bulwark and it has continued to develop external traffic through its steamship lines. The Canadian National has been restricted by competition from the Canadian Pacific and by financial stringency. A more aggressive developmental policy in new territory would ease its difficulties.

The basic importance of transportation in the economic history of Canada has been responsible for the profound effects of unused capacity. The restrictive effect on settlement of an unbalanced cargo from Europe, and of upstream traffic for heavy goods in the fur trade, resulted in governmental intervention on an extensive scale and collapse in the French régime. On the other hand, the expansive effect of an unbalanced cargo in the timber trade, which followed governmental intervention in the form of high preferences and military settlements to overcome the restrictive influences of the fur trade, brought expansion of agriculture and the necessity of further government intervention to solve the problems of improved transportation.

The significance of water transportation in the export of fur and timber involved emphasis on commercial credit. In the fur trade governmental support to military and naval ventures brought problems of government finance and led to inflation. The severity of fluctuations in the timber trade brought disastrous losses to interests concerned. Production and export of wheat necessitated railways and canals and the introduction of long-term credit through corporate and government finance. Fixed interest charges accompanying extensive government support, and insufficient revenue, necessitated further governmental intervention with Confederation, and extension to the Maritimes and the Pacific. Government intervention took the form of ownership and operation of the Intercolonial to the Maritimes and strong support to private enterprise westward to the Pacific. The expansion westward from the St. Lawrence which was typical of the fur trade was also essential to agriculture. The necessities of a transcontinental railway system were evident in the policies of the federal government—for example in tariff and immigration policy—and of the Canadian Pacific Railway; but they implied the development of competing lines to offset the effects of monopoly control, supported by the provinces of the prairie region and the metropolitan centres of Toronto, Quebec, and Halifax, and the emergence of control through the Board of Railway Commissioners, and of statutory rates such as the Crow's Nest Pass Rate Agreement and more recently British Columbia rate adjustment and the Maritime Freight Rates Act. The Hudson Bay Railway was a conspicuous illustration of the continued necessity for, and significance of, governmental intervention in relation to the problems of monopoly in Western Canada. Ostensibly intended to provide relief from the problem of monopoly, it has been regarded as creating additional burdens of debt. Capital equipment essential to the production and export of wheat, in the form of a transcontinental railway, brought acute problems in non-competitive areas, which were temporarily solved, with the assistance of an upward swing of the business cycle and favourable prices of wheat, by further additions of capital equipment in two transcontinental railways. Decline in the rate of expansion, and the depression, emphasized the weight of overhead costs in relation to extensive capital equipment, and the heavy fixed charges involved in government ownership were evident in rigidities of railway rates and interest charges. These factors contributed to a decline in standards of living in the exposed areas and in turn to a reduction in demands for manufactured products from central Canada, to industrial unemployment, to numerous disparities and destructive eddies in the current of economic life—described in the evidence before the Royal Commission on Price Spreads—and to governmental intervention on a vast scale, ranging from the spate of federal legislation of the session 1935 to the cancelling of power contracts by the provincial government of Ontario. Dependence of the Prairie Provinces on wheat, and the tariff, are factors accentuating the burden on Western Canada and are not offset by lower costs through competition for westbound traffic in manufactured products from Eastern Canada. The sharp decline in prices of raw material, especially wheat, and low returns on bulk movements of grain and additional competition from motor transport in the competitive St. Lawrence region compel the railways to search for more remunerative westbound traffic of manufactured products in the face of declining purchasing power in the wheat area. More exposed regions with rigidities of freight rates and interest charges and shrinking income through drought and falling prices, and without an integrated balanced economic structure, have been more seriously affected by political disturbance as evident in the movement for social credit in Alberta. The inadequacy of methods of control, increasing unit costs with shrinkage of volume and plant built for peak-load operations, and limited possibilities of further expansion, have necessitated substantial federal support of the Prairie Provinces in a wide variety of relief measures during the depression, and have brought forth protests from the Maritimes and British Columbia in favour of readjustment of federal-provincial relations.[8]

Problems of unused capacity have had the effect of quickening and accentuating the long-run general trends of economic development and have necessitated governmental intervention as a steadying or remedial factor. In the main, problems have been solved by aggressive developmental measures but limitations have been apparent in the present depression. Governmental intervention as a means of solving problems during a period of expansion creates problems to be solved by new types of government intervention during a depression. Lower tariffs bring relief, particularly to the regions more distant from the St. Lawrence and probably throughout the entire economy, but they do not solve the problems of reducing the violence of the swings incidental to the significance of unused capacity.

The long-run period of depression of the latter part of the last century was accompanied by continued determined efforts to enable the St. Lawrence to compete with New York, and the long-run period of prosperity of a third of a century which followed was marked by the success of those efforts and by further efforts to swing the Canadian economy further to the north to support Quebec and the Maritimes. The failure of those efforts, shown in an enormous debt and heavy deficits, has been accompanied by a retreat. Heavy outlay incidental to government construction and ownership of the railways designed to support the lower St. Lawrence and Maritime regions have accompanied lower rates incidental to water competition and statutory intervention. Narrowing of the range of the economy dependent on the St. Lawrence as a result of the development of a competitive region on the Pacific coast, largely as a consequence of

[8]See "A Note on Problems of Readjustment in Canada" (*Journal of Political Economy*, Dec., 1935) for a discussion of the implications of W. A. Mackintosh, *Economic Problems of the Prairie Provinces* (Toronto, 1935).

the Panama Canal, has complicated the problem. Drastic revision of debts, ranging from the passing dividends on the C.P.R. to agricultural debt adjustment operations, has been inevitable. Transfers to more exposed regions have been gradually developed, but much remains to be done before the implications of unused capacity are understood.

11. THE POLITICAL IMPLICATIONS OF UNUSED CAPACITY

The implications of economic development on the North American continent to the economic history of Europe have been traced in detail and in general and broad generalizations have emerged to describe their character. An attempt has been made to suggest effects of concentration on specific staple products in Canadian economic expansion, particularly in the confused period of shifts to new staples. Unused capacity involved in exploitation of staples had its effect in prolonging the dominance of one staple or in hastening its decline, and contributed powerfully to the disturbance of equilibrium in Canada and in Europe. The heavy outbound cargo from Europe characteristic of the fur trade restricted immigration, and the heavy return cargo characteristic of the timber trade hastened immigration. The role of unused capacity in determining the characteristics of economic development was weakened or strengthened by peculiarities of particular staples.

North America was settled by immigrants crossing from Asia by Bering Strait. The blocking of the polar ice by this narrow gateway left the Pacific Ocean to exercise a moderating influence on the climate of the western part of the continent and to favour the migration of population to Central and South America. Aboriginal culture in North America reflected a marked adaptation to geographical environment worked out over an extended period and consequently had a profound effect on the character of relations with Europe. Migration from Europe was halted by the accessibility of the Atlantic to the Polar Sea and by the inhospitable Greenland ice cap and the Labrador current with the result that the first approach of the Norsemen met defeat. The Pacific had its moderating influence on the vast portion of Northwestern America in Arctic Felix, Alaska and the Mackenzie River, whereas the Atlantic lowered the temperature of the eastern part of North America in Arctic Deserta. In the second effort contact was made from Spain in the sub-tropical areas of Europe with the highly elaborated aboriginal culture in the tropical regions of Central America. Europeans attacked aboriginal culture in areas in which it was most highly developed and brought its abrupt collapse. Reserves of precious metals were looted in Mexico and Peru and the booty taken to Europe.

Concentration on imports of precious metals brought a sharp rise in prices in Spain and the shrivelling of industry and trade. Other countries seized the opportunity to meet the demands of Spain and to secure the advantages of high prices. England with "no treasure but by trade" elaborated mercantile policies designed to attract precious metals. The fishing industry was encouraged in the New World as a means of gaining access to the Spanish market and, after the Armada, England established a foothold on Newfoundland. Early in the seventeenth century she restricted imports of sugar and tobacco from Spain in order that she might produce them in her colonies in the new world and thus secure specie rather than these commodities. Control by Spain of the more densely populated aboriginal territory in the New World compelled English expansion in the Atlantic basin to depend on the migration of English labour in Newfoundland and the northern colonies and the movement of slaves from Africa to the plantation colonies in the south and the West Indies. Trade to India was supported by exports of specie obtained through trade from Spain.

France as a country adjacent to Spain found it unnecessary to establish a foothold in the New World to prepare dried fish for the Spanish market until the latter part of the sixteenth century when the Channel ports became more directly concerned. Finding the English entrenched along the Atlantic coast they developed the industry in the Gulf of St. Lawrence, notably on the Gaspé Peninsula, and thus established a base for the expansion of the fur trade up the St. Lawrence and its tributaries. As Spain was profoundly influenced by her contacts with the aborigines of Central and South America through the supplies of precious metals, France was profoundly influenced by her contacts with the hunting Indians of North America through supplies of furs. France and Spain were directly concerned with the effects of contrast between aboriginal and European cultures whereas England was indirectly concerned. In France and Spain the demands of the upper classes determined the character of relations with the aborigines of North America; in England the supply of English and African labour was significant.

The vast angular-shaped area of Precambrian formation in North America had its implications for drainage systems in the large rivers which flowed along its edge, the St. Lawrence and the Mackenzie, and in the difficult shorter rivers which crossed it in flowing to Hudson Bay. In this area flora and fauna moulded the culture of the hunting Indians while in the later formations to the south soil conditions and climate favoured the agricultural Indians, the Huron Iroquois of the upper St. Lawrence, southern Ontario and northern New York. The Dutch and later the English moved from the Atlantic seaboard south of the St. Lawrence approach and traded with the agricultural Indians by the Hudson River. The French were dependent first on the agricultural villages in the Georgian Bay area but with their annihilation by the Iroquois they were compelled to develop the St. Lawrence areas with their own agricultural base. The English restrained by the agricultural Indians and the Appalachians took full advantage of the possibilities of expansion in trade with the areas bordering on the Atlantic. The enormous handicaps of seasonal migration in the more northernly areas drained by the St. Lawrence hastened the discovery and occupation of the Mississippi across a narrow height of land. La Salle overcame the handicaps of navigation on the Upper St. Lawrence, established posts on the Great Lakes and exploited the fur trade of the head waters of the Mississippi. The flood of lower grade furs from this area was an important cause of the development of inflation.

Attraction of the French to the South led to the establishment of a post at the mouth of the Mississippi early in the eighteenth century and to competition for trade in the interior between New Orleans and Montreal. With the success of a trade unhampered by seasonal navigation the French under La Vérendrye turned from the St. Lawrence to the North West of Lake Superior. In this direction they came into more direct competition with the Hudson's Bay Company. In New France company control broke down particularly after the destruction of the Huron villages and after 1663 the Crown intervened with active measures hastening settlement and trade. Traders such as Radisson and Groseilliers persuaded the English Crown shortly after the Restoration to grant a monopoly to the Hudson's Bay Company in 1670. With little possibility of agricultural development in the vicinity of Hudson Bay posts were established at the mouths of rivers draining into James Bay and Hudson Bay and controlled effectively from London. The problem of smuggling peculiar to commodities of small bulk and high value proved insoluble on the St. Lawrence but it was solved by the highly centralized control from London as apparently it was solved in the shipment of treasure from the new world to Spain.

The interest of France in the fur trade of the St. Lawrence involved dependence on a commodity which fluctuated widely in supply as a result of competition from the Dutch, and later the English from the Hudson River, and the English from Hudson Bay; of wars between Europeans and aborigines; of geographic characteristics evident especially in the size and peculiarities of drainage basins; and of the character of aboriginal cultural traits in relation to the demand for European goods. Fur was a commodity in which not only supply but also demand fluctuated widely. As a luxury product it was exposed to the fluctuations incidental to changes of fashion in the courts of Europe and to the immediate effects of prosperity and depression. The difficulties were shown in the organization of military defence of the St. Lawrence and the consequent centralization of policy in institutions of State and Church, and in the inability to control the price of furs, shown in the collapse of the financial structure after 1700 through inflation. The burdens imposed by the system of defence and centralization led to the emergence of the Hudson's Bay Company in Hudson Bay, and to the failure of the St. Lawrence as a base for provisions for the fishing industry on the Atlantic coast and for sugar plantations of the French West Indies. An integrated Atlantic empire became impossible and the English colonies became a source of provisions for the French in both north temperate, and tropical regions.

Collapse of the French empire in North America brought repercussions which led to collapse of the first British Empire. The extension of the fishing industry from Newfoundland to New England early in the seventeenth century was followed by competition between the west country and the colonists. Adjustments within the British colonial system were hampered by the political influence of the west country and of the sugar planters in the British West Indies. The latter resisted trade between the coastal colonies and the French West Indies and supported the Treaty of Paris, which left Guadaloupe in the French Empire and added Canada to the British Empire, thereby accentuating the disturbance in the balance, between an extended market within the British Empire for molasses and rum in the fur trade, and a narrow supply from the British West Indies.

The disappearance of Louisbourg and the Sugar Act made smuggling more difficult and Imperial restrictions more burdensome. Anglo-American traders reorganized the fur trade of the St. Lawrence after the fall of New France and rebuilt a defence system depending on London instead of Paris. The North West Company solved the problem of the French régime by combining agricultural development in Ontario to support shipping on the Great Lakes for the handling of bulk cargo with the canoe route of the Ottawa for return shipments of furs. It extended trade from the Atlantic to the Pacific.

The second British Empire was profoundly modified by the changes involved in the withdrawal of the American colonies and the collapse of the first empire. Flexibility was substituted for the rigidity which brought collapse of the first empire. The supremacy of parliament was recognized but Lord Mansfield in Campbell vs. Hall (1774) strengthened the position of the Assembly in the colonies, and consequently in Nova Scotia. The Colonial Tax Repeal Act (1778) further strengthened Nova Scotia by providing for control over revenues secured from taxes collected under the colonial system. Nova Scotia was able to press more effectively for revisions of the colonial system to enable her to compete with the United States, particularly as the British West Indies had suffered a decline in influence with the abolition of slavery and the competition of sugar from the East Indies. Moreover, the support of Nova Scotia brought an increase in population which enabled Newfoundland to escape the domination of the West Country. On the St. Lawrence, parliament through the Quebec Act of 1774 denied an assembly to the colony and it was not until 1791 that assemblies were granted to Upper and Lower Canada. The merchants lost control of the fur trade to the northwest after the amalgamation of the North West Company and the Hudson's Bay Company in 1821 but the effects of the loss were offset, and along with New Brunswick the regions gained, as a result of the substantial Imperial preference given to the timber trade. The struggle of Wilkes and others in securing freedom to report the proceedings of parliament opened the door to reform and the destruction of control by vested interests. With the destruction of vested interests representing fish, sugar, timber and ships in the colonial system the way was clear to free trade and responsible government. Whereas New England was hampered by the influence of vested interests operating from the West Country in Newfoundland, and from the West Indies, Nova Scotia was able to take an active part in the defeat of those vested interests.

British North America included the French in the lower St. Lawrence region who had lost their contacts with the mother country except through the Church, population which had migrated from New England to Nova Scotia after 1713, and the Loyalists who migrated from the United States and were settled in pockets from the Atlantic seaboard to the Great Lakes. The region contained groups with the pre-revolutionary background of France steeped in the traditions of the Church in Quebec and with the loyalist traditions of the state particularly in New Brunswick and Ontario which escaped the influence of revolutionary tradition in the United States. British North America was a young country with the oldest pre-revolutionary ideas of Europe. Expulsion of the loyalists from the United States weakened the centralizing tendencies of the colonies and contributed to the trend which culminated in the Civil War, and, reinforced by the British military tradition, strengthened the centralizing tendencies in British North America. The military system with its division of British North America into separate colonies dominated by military power restricted the growth of responsible government. Construction of the Rideau Canal as a military route delayed the construction of other canals.

The subordination of the executive to the assembly which characterized responsible government involved control over revenues which meant control over funds received from lands. Newfoundland with control over land and trade continuously and effectively pressed for exclusion of French, English, Canadian, and American fishermen. Responsible government was interpreted as implying "that the consent of the Community of Newfoundland is regarded by Her Majesty's government as the essential preliminary to any modification of their territorial and maritime rights."[1] From this interpretation the legislature not only waged an effective battle against the French but also resisted efforts on the part of Canada to secure control of her natural resources in proposals for admission to Confederation. Nova Scotia insisted on her rights to the extent of compelling the United States and Great Britain to concede the reciprocity treaty from 1854 to 1866, and of persuading Canada to adopt a per-

[1]Henry Labouchere in a dispatch of March 26, 1857.

missive system, and under Confederation a compulsory system, to exclude American fishermen to the point that the United States conceded the Washington Treaty. With control over natural resources she was able to break the monopoly of the General Mining Association over coal in 1858. Confederation of the colonies left the control over land with the provinces but placed the control over the coastal fisheries under the federal government.

Competition in Western Canada from the French and later the Anglo-American merchants and the North West Company from the St. Lawrence with the Hudson's Bay Company from Hudson Bay assumed an intense form, characteristic of duopoly, and led to monopoly in 1821. The vast area under the control of the Hudson's Bay Company after that date included land owned by virtue of the charter granted in 1670 or that drained by rivers flowing into Hudson Bay, and regions beyond to the Pacific coast under a license for twenty-one years. Under a monopoly, a large surplus population was moved from numerous posts to Red River and to Canada and attracted fresh competition from Americans which weakened the company on the Columbia and on the Pacific coast. The Oregon boundary was finally settled at the 49th parallel in 1846. Vancouver Island was granted to the Hudson's Bay Company in 1849, and on the insistence of the Imperial government, an assembly was elected in 1856. On the mainland the licensing arrangement was brought to an end with the gold rush to the Fraser River and in 1858 a colony was organized. An area which had been systematically organized in defence against settlers from the United States was suddenly over-run by large numbers of people pushing northward in the search for gold. In the following year Vancouver Island was repurchased by the Imperial government. In 1864 a council was set up in British Columbia, but an assembly was refused. The character of the gold rush led Newcastle to write "that the fixed population . . . is not yet large enough to form a sufficient and sound basis of representation, while the migratory element exceeds the fixed and the Indian far outnumbers both together."[2] In 1866 the government of the main-land was united with that of Vancouver Island and the Assembly of the latter disbanded. Problems of finance which arose from the sudden development of a community dependent on placer gold

[2]Cited in A. S. Morton, *A History of the Canadian West to 1870-1* (Toronto, n.d.), p. 785.

hastened the adoption of an arrangement involving the construction of a transcontinental railway and the inclusion of British Columbia in the federal structure. Immediately before the united colony joined Confederation in 1871 an assembly was elected and responsible government was achieved. The natural resources were left in the hands of the province.

The discovery of gold speeded up the construction of a transcontinental railway and in turn had important effects for the prairie region across which it had to be built. The territory under control of the Hudson's Bay Company by virtue of charter was more effectively organized, than that under the licensing arrangement, against encroachment from the St. Lawrence across the Canadian shield but was eventually sold to the Dominion of Canada. The resistance of the Company and the delay in admitting the region to Confederation involved the defeat of efforts to secure responsible government in its full implications. Manitoba became a province but gave up land "for the purposes of the Dominion." The boundaries of Manitoba, Saskatchewan and Alberta were determined along astronomical lines and the provinces of Alberta and Saskatchewan were created in 1905 again without control over land. The "purposes of the Dominion" having been served, and the lands largely alienated for the construction of transcontinental railways, the natural resources were given to the prairie provinces in 1930. Attempts to secure compensation for misuse of the lands by the Dominion have not been completely successful.

With the exception of Nova Scotia, assemblies emerged at a late stage in the second empire and responsible government was slow to mature as a result of slowness in the adoption of parliamentary reform and of the geographic background with its emphasis on waterways and on exports of staples and the creation of vested interests centring about them. The organization of defence in the French régime on the St. Lawrence in opposition to English trade from the south and the north implied a legacy of defence in the English régime, especially after the American revolution. Occupation of New France by conquest and the insistence on defence delayed the introduction of assemblies on the St. Lawrence until 1791 and of responsible government until 1849. The organization of the Hudson's Bay Company for defence against competition from Canada and the United States in Western Canada paralleled the organization for defence on the St. Lawrence. Entrenchment of the Hudson's Bay Company in the fur trade and the sudden changes wrought by the gold rushes on the Pacific Coast contributed to the indefinite delay of responsible government in the prairie provinces.

The bitterness of the struggle for responsible government on the St. Lawrence had repercussions in Western Canada. The provinces which took the place of the colonies in Confederation continued with such important characteristics of responsible government as control of their natural resources. The federal government was concerned primarily with customs for revenue to support transportation improvements in railways and canals, to pay subsidies largely on a population basis and thus to avoid controversies over religion, and to pay interest on debts incurred chiefly in building railways and canals and taken over from the provinces. The exclusion of the federal government from control over natural resources in Eastern Canada and the dominance of the Hudson's Bay Company over a long period checked the growth of assemblies and the achievement of complete responsible government in the prairie region.[3] Land was reserved by the Dominion for the support of railway construction to carry out the agreement with British Columbia.

The use of lands "for purposes of the Dominion" was accompanied by control over competition from the United States in the tariff and in restrictions on the construction of railways to the American boundary. Location of the Canadian Pacific Railway along the southern route left vast areas to the north to be occupied. The recovery following the long depression from the seventies to the nineties was accompanied by important new discoveries of placer beds on the Klondike in the Yukon region. As the Canadian Pacific followed the gold rushes in British Columbia, the Canadian Northern and the Grand Trunk Pacific followed the gold rushes of the Yukon in the territory north of the Canadian Pacific, but exhaustion of land led to dependence on bonds for their construction. The effectiveness with which the Dominion realized its "purposes" was evident in the enormous increase in the production of wheat in the period from 1900 to 1929. The problems which have followed concentration on

[3]See Chester Martin, *"Dominion Lands" policy* (Toronto, 1938); also A. S. Morton, *A History of the Canadian West to 1870-1* (Toronto, n.d.), pp. 914 ff.

wheat have been evident in Western and Eastern Canada in the depression and the war. Deprived of control over natural resources, the attention of the west was concentrated on federal problems such as railway rates, grain marketing, prices, tariffs and debts.

With control over natural resources under the British North America Act and privy council decisions, the province of Ontario began an active policy of development by imposing embargoes on logs and pulpwood cut on crown lands, by supporting public ownership of hydro-electric power and by constructing the Temiskaming and Northern Ontario Railway. Cobalt, Porcupine and Kirkland Lake poured out riches of gold and silver and hydro-electric power sites were developed. The policies were less effective in the pulp and paper industry and it was not until the demand of newspapers in the United States for cheap newsprint brought a reduction of the American tariff and the Province of Quebec and other provinces imposed an embargo after 1910 that the pulp and paper industry migrated with startling rapidity to Quebec, Ontario, and British Columbia and later to New Brunswick, Manitoba and Nova Scotia. The problems of wheat which characterized the policies of the Dominion in fulfilment of its "purposes" in the prairie provinces after 1929 were accompanied by the problems of newsprint which characterized the policies of the provinces with control over their natural resources. Gold mining in Quebec, Ontario and Manitoba offset in part the effects of the depression on wheat and newsprint. Fish, minerals, lumber, pulp and paper, hydro-electric power and the favourable effects of the Panama Canal softened the blow of the depression in British Columbia.

In areas in which responsible government had not been achieved because of control over natural resources by the Dominion Government, the position of provincial administrations reflected the maladjustment of political machinery. It has become obvious that the constitutional arrangements imposed too heavy a burden on the prairie provinces in that numerous makeshifts have been arranged by which the Dominion has attempted to relieve the burden and that the political atmosphere has become disturbed and confused. Manitoba, Alberta and Saskatchewan have shown signs of achieving political maturity. In the area in which responsible government was achieved and control over natural resources was acquired at the expense of exclusion from Confederation, the problem of finance has been scarcely less acute. Newfoundland abandoned responsible government and accepted Commission government. Absence of federal control in Newfoundland has been as disastrous as excessive federal control in the prairie provinces.

The first empire was concerned with the significance of land and the second empire with the significance of trade. Gradually land has assumed increasing importance in the second empire and the Statute of Westminster coincided closely with the return of natural resources to the prairie provinces. The Canadian federal structure has assumed a closer parallel to that of the United States as the feudalization of the second empire approached the feudal character of the first. The dominance of trade in the second empire and concentration on staples imposed heavy burdens on Great Britain until through parliamentary reform she was able to free herself from the control of vested interests in a policy of free trade and in the granting of responsible government to the colonies. The problems of trade in staples evaded by Great Britain became more acute for the colonies. But the colonies resorted to feudalism as the mother country emphasized trade. They began to concentrate on machinery designed to meet internal problems, ranging through Confederation to protection and construction of transcontinental railways. The political machinery was closely adapted to meet the severe economic demands of dependence on staples with their sharp changes in prices and income. Governmental devices stabilized in part and accentuated in part the fluctuations. Support to improvements in transportation was achieved with low interest rates secured by the government, and low costs of transportation provided a tremendous impetus with an increase in prices. The disturbances incidental to dependence on staples, including the essential importance of governmental support, created difficulties within Canada and without. Concentration on large scale production of single staples involved sharp fluctuations in output which bombarded with violent intensity the international economy, to mention specifically the case of wheat. The study of the Canadian economy becomes of crucial significance to an understanding of cyclical and secular disturbances not only within Canada but without. In a sense the economies of frontier countries are storm centres to the modern international economy.

12. IMPERFECT REGIONAL COMPETITION AND POLITICAL INSTITUTIONS ON THE NORTH ATLANTIC SEABOARD

The fishing industry has been conducted on the Atlantic seaboard of North America for centuries through small units of capital equipment—the ship or the small boat. It is essentially dependent on individual initiative and enterprise and was particularly so prior to the introduction of large-scale units of capital in the nineteenth century. Various devices depending chiefly on the size of the unit of equipment were developed to reward the fisherman in proportion to his catch and to stimulate his interest. The dependence on individual initiative was tempered by the necessity of co-operation since it was only rarely that an individual fisherman could command and direct his own capital equipment. The small boat required three to five men, and the ship a crew which was disciplined in relation to its operations. It required, moreover, the support of capital interests whether in providing the ship or the supplies and provisions, but the risks of the industry compelled a wide division of capital interests as a means of insurance. If conducted within narrow geographical limits such as a single port or a number of small ports in a definite region these capital groups had large common interests. The industry was therefore characterized by individual enterprise which was sharply competitive and by types of co-operation ranging from the fishermen of a small boat to the group of merchants in definite regions. The common interests of the group were concerned with finance, markets, and political control over areas of production. The power of each group became concentrated in separate geographic regions in the Atlantic basin, the West Country, Newfoundland, Nova Scotia, and New England, and the effectiveness of the power varied in part with the element of monopoly and imperfect competition. Each community became a centre of aggressiveness and of governmental expansion with the emergence of a centralized merchant group.

The West Country (Cornwall, Devon, Dorset) was a region with a large number of ports which sent out ships to prosecute the fishing industry in Newfoundland. It was able to exercise powerful influence in a mercantilist state and to plead with effect the unity of its prosperity with that of the nation since as a result of its efforts treasure was brought from the Catholic countries of Spain, Portugal, and the Mediterranean, and trained seamen were available for the navy. Attempts made by London interests representing the carrying trade to establish a colony through a joint stock company were defeated through attacks by West country interests in England and in Newfoundland. Their powers were limited, however, to a definite region of the New World and their determined efforts to maintain control of the fishing industry of the Avalon peninsula hastened the migration of settlers to New England on the mainland. West Country ships to Newfoundland took out settlers and their effects to New England as a means of increasing revenue for the voyage. Small units of capital facilitated rapid adjustment in the migration between regions along the Atlantic seaboard. Flexibility of economic organization based on technology accentuated the significance of liquidity preference in the demands of a mercantilist state for specie. Long-term capital interests, defeated in attempts to establish a settlement in Newfoundland, moved to New England.

The growth of settlement, the development of the fishing industry, and increase in shipping led to the emergence of a new centre in New England. It began to compete with the West Country in the markets of Europe but its effects were less direct. Sheltered by the Navigation Acts, shipping flourished and trade expanded from New England to the West Indies and to Europe. Provisions were shipped to the West Indies to be exchanged for sugar, molasses and rum and these with other provisions were shipped to Newfoundland to be exchanged for bills. By insisting that Newfoundland was not a colony the West Country enabled New England interests to argue that it could be used as a warehousing centre under the navigation acts. Their insistence made Newfoundland conspicuously the centre of attention in Parliament after 1688 and emphasized more sharply the view that the mainland colonies were creatures of the Crown and not of Parliament. Demands for liquidity preference in England which fostered the exchange of fish for specie in Spain and Portugal were paralleled and in part thwarted by the demands for liquidity preference in New England which fostered the exchange of provisions and supplies for bills in Newfoundland. The more skilled fishermen migrated from Newfoundland to New England but others remained in Newfoundland through the support of New England in spite of protests of the West Country. The influence of New England in the British parliament was weakened by the increasing interest of its fishing industry in the West Indies where again it came into conflict and was overshadowed by the dominance of the planters of the British West Indies. New England was exposed in parliament to attack on the one hand from the West Country as a competitor in Europe and as a support to settlement in Newfoundland and on the other hand from the British West Indies as a support to settlement in the French West Indies. The influence of New England was evident in the cession of Nova Scotia to Great Britain in 1713 and in the capture of Louisbourg in 1745, and the limits of its influence in the return of Louisbourg to France in 1748. In the Treaty of Paris the influence of the West Indies rather than New England was instrumental in leaving Guadaloupe with France. In this it offered no threat as a competitor within the empire and the fur trade of Canada offered a wider market for British West Indies molasses and rum.

France in contrast with the West Country and New England had no single region dominated by the fishery. It was scattered among a large number of ports on the Channel and in the Bay of Biscay which sent vessels to widely scattered regions in North America including the Banks. The deliberate attempt to offset the handicaps of decentralization in the Old and the New World by the establishment of Placentia, and, after the Treaty of Utrecht in 1713, Louisbourg, was defeated by the absence of an agricultural base. The inability to establish a base was a result of the agricultural limitations of the St. Lawrence region, the handicap of seasonal navigation, the smuggling with the Acadians of the Bay of Fundy, the inability to develop a colony on Prince Edward Island, and the dependence on the English colonies. A centralized fortified area could not survive against the opposition of England and the English colonies. The establishment of Halifax in 1749 and the capture of Louisbourg and Quebec brought to an end the effort of France to dominate the New World.

With the fall of France the antagonism between New England and England was no longer tempered by the existence of a common enemy. New England thrived under the protection of the Navigation Acts and the evasion of legislation designed to favour the West

Indies planters at her expense. The direct influence of the West Indies planters and of the West Country in the corrupt parliaments of Walpole rendered the influence of New England ineffective. Parliament reflected the direct pressure of the West Indies and the West Country but not of New England. As we have seen her ineffectiveness was evident in the Treaty of Paris and in later legislation in which her markets for rum and molasses were widened by the acquisition of Canada but her supplies were narrowed by the influence of the West Indies in leaving Guadaloupe under French control. The rapid and effective activities of New England and the other colonies in resisting a parliament which was under the influence of the West Indies and the West Country was apparent in the short period between the Treaty of Paris and the outbreak of revolution and the Treaty of Versailles.

The sharpness of the break between New England and England facilitated the emergence of new fishing interests from the Channel Islands to Cape Breton and the Gulf of St. Lawrence to take the place of the French and of a new mercantile group centring about Halifax which was quick to press for the advantages of exclusion of New England from the colonial system. Seizing concessions, notably in the Act of 1778, which England had made too late to save the colonies, Nova Scotia pressed for advantageous modifications of the colonial system at the expense of the West Indies. The latter were no longer able to dominate colonial policy in parliament but they succeeded eventually in 1830 in gaining access to the cheaper provisions of the United States whereupon Nova Scotia was compelled to turn (1) to the trade of Newfoundland vacated by New England and (2) to the pursuit of more vigorous tactics in excluding American fishermen from her inshore waters. The growth of autonomy in Nova Scotia was rapid in relation to England and to the United States, compared with New England, and extremely rapid compared with Newfoundland. Expansion of New England was the reverse side of restrictions on Newfoundland by the West Country but the rise of Nova Scotia and difficulties in the West Indies hastened settlement in Newfoundland.

Increased trade from Nova Scotia to Newfoundland favoured the growth of settlement and weakened the position of the West Country. Parliament after the Reform Acts was more pliable and provided a less certain shelter in which the influence of the West Indies and the West Country could be exerted at the expense of Nova Scotia and Newfoundland. The growth of settlement in Newfoundland led to the emergence of representative institutions. But these institutions flowered more quickly as a result of renewed efforts from France in St. Pierre and Miquelon to revive the fisheries by improved techniques and generous bonuses. Newfoundland seized upon control of her natural resources, which came with responsible government, to press steadily toward weakening the French by depriving them of supplies of bait and by excluding them from the French shore in 1904.

Representative institutions in Newfoundland were used not only to oppose France but with parliamentary reform, the decline in influence of vested interests in England, free trade, and responsible government, also the West Country, the Channel Islands, Nova Scotia, and New England. With the abrogation of the Reciprocity Treaty in 1866 Nova Scotia enlisted the support of Canada under Confederation to secure the Washington Treaty. The retreat of New England to the shelter of an expanding internal market under the tariff and the *modus vivendi* arrangement reflected resistance to pressure from Nova Scotia and Canada. Newfoundland resented efforts of Nova Scotia to use her in attempts to secure better arrangements with the United States after the termination of the Washington Treaty in 1885.

The long delay in the growth of representative institutions in Newfoundland incidental to the protracted decline of control from the West Country prior to parliamentary reform in Great Britain was in sharp contrast with the rapid growth of Nova Scotia through the support of a modified colonial system after the American Revolution. Nova Scotia, pressing on New England, sought support in Confederation and New England, pressed from Nova Scotia, sought shelter on the continent. The aggressiveness of Nova Scotia left Newfoundland with no alternative but resistance through accentuation of local autonomy. The burden of industrialism, especially in the construction of railways, carried for Nova Scotia by the Dominion was carried in Newfoundland by herself.

Control by the West Country delayed growth of settlement and in turn of governmental and judicial institutions in Newfoundland.

This control in turn hastened growth of settlement and acquisition of governmental institutions in New England. The accentuated local autonomy of New England contributed to the American Revolution and to the attempt of Nova Scotia to secure advantages under the colonial system. The rapid growth of Nova Scotia led to the support of settlement in Newfoundland and in turn to decline of control from the West Country. The eventual emergence of strong local autonomy in Newfoundland following the struggle between the accentuated autonomies of New England and Nova Scotia in which each turned for support to the Continent led to industrialism, debt, and the loss of responsible government.

Liquidity preference became less effective as a stimulus to trade and competition and political institutions lost the flexibility essential to adjustment. The effectiveness of the demands of the West Country for control over Newfoundland through its dependence on short-term credit and its ability to emphasize the importance of imports of specie from Spain and Portugal, and the increasing demands of New England and the colonies for short-term credit to support an expanding trade, and of an expanding trade for supplies of short-term credit, were factors leading to the break up of the French Empire and in turn of the first British Empire. The importance of short-term credit in the American Revolution and the United States increased the burden of long-term credit essential to the staple trades of Great Britain and supported the trend toward the Reform Acts and the constitutional changes which destroyed protection for interests in timber, shipping, sugar, fur, and other long-term credit trades. Liquidity preference had its implications in the changes in political structure in the West Country, New England, Newfoundland, and England. The power of finance was steadily increased. Destruction of the shelter for staple trades as a result of the trend toward free trade led to a search for new expedients in the development of governments in areas producing staple commodities. The Act of Union and the British North America Act emerged as bases for lowering costs of transportation and to provide support for an accompanying expanding debt structure. The new mercantilism was embedded in constitutional structures.

The significance of liquidity preference in the trend toward free trade in Great Britain was paralleled by the expansion of government finance in Canada. Governmental institutions in Newfoundland, unlike those of Canada, were unable to meet the test of debt expansion under conditions of prosperity and depression nor will they be exposed to the same problems of international adjustment incidental to Canadian success. Political institutions have become less flexible with devices facilitating the handling of credit and the prospects of international adjustment less promising.

13. DECENTRALIZATION AND DEMOCRACY

This paper is concerned with the changes in types of power in the Atlantic basin following the discovery of America. Direct control from Europe under the French, Dutch, Spanish, and British Empires has gradually changed with emergence of independent states in North and South America and of the British Commonwealth of Nations. In Canada European institutions were more strongly entrenched and feudalism continued to exercise a powerful influence, latterly, for example, in the control of natural resources by the provinces. The provinces have become landlords with great disparity of wealth varying with federal policy, technological change, and provincial policy. The changing disparity enhances the complexity of democracy in Canada.

The advantages of the British Empire in its struggle with the French Empire were in part a result of the implications of imperfect competition between drainage basins in the interior as contrasted with more effective competition between the maritime regions of the Atlantic seaboard. In the latter region, imperfect competition was reflected in the slowness with which adjustments were made between the West Country in England, Newfoundland, Nova Scotia and New England. In the interior of the continent competition was less effective in the struggle between traders of various nationalities or of the same nationality as it was carried on between drainage basins. Trunk rivers and tributaries with low heights of land between drainage basins facilitated the tapping of vast regions. The relative effectiveness of competition on the seaboard and in the interior of the continent had implications for the struggle of empire.

In the sixteenth century the French Empire was concerned with the extension of the fishing industry in the New World as a means of strengthening self-sufficiency with access to new supplies of food and to an industry promising naval strength. The English Empire was concerned with the acquisition of specie flowing from the New World of Spain. It concentrated on the dry fishery in Newfoundland and exports to Spain. By the end of the century the French were also influenced by the high prices of Spain only to find that the more accessible sites for the prosecution of the dry fishery were occupied by the English and that it was necessary to penetrate to more distant sites such as the Gaspé region in the Gulf of St. Lawrence.

The interest of France in development of the fishery in relation to her own needs and of England in trade with Spain involved the delay of a century in penetrating the northern part of the continent. In the seventeenth century, France, after comparative failure on the seaboard, established a foothold at Quebec in the protected region of the St. Lawrence. The Hudson River was occupied by the Dutch after Hudson's voyage of 1609, and the Iroquois, driven from the St. Lawrence by the hunting Indians and the French, received support for vigorous counter attacks. Fortifications were extended up the St. Lawrence to Three Rivers, Montreal, and the mouth of the Richelieu, and trade with the agricultural Indians of the Georgian Bay region to the interior by the Ottawa route was protected. In turn the Iroquois were pressed to the interior and proceeded across the east end of Lake Ontario and north to destroy the Huron villages in 1648-9. Concentration on military activity and the restrictions on the fur trade under company control necessitated governmental intervention. The fur trade involved heavy outbound cargo and a light return cargo with the result that settlement was discouraged and that vigorous efforts by the government to encourage immigration were made. The difficulties of the fur trade stimulated the interest of traders such as Radisson and Groseilliers in the alternative outlet by Hudson Bay. The necessity of concentrating on the St. Lawrence precluded the development of the route and Radisson and Groseilliers deserted to the English to assist in the formation of the Hudson's Bay Company in 1670.

The active interest of the French government in the St. Lawrence was accompanied by a determined effort to build up an integrated Atlantic empire. Placentia in Newfoundland was established as a basis of the fishing industry in 1662 and attempts were made to link the St. Lawrence as an agricultural base to the sugar plantations of the West Indies. The effort failed because of the increasing demands of the St. Lawrence. Energy was dissipated in efforts to check competition by the destruction of English posts in Hudson Bay and by the construction of forts along the Great Lakes. Destruction of the Huron villages compelled the French to build up their own trading organization to the interior. Dissipation of resources was evident in the abandonment of Fort Frontenac in 1689 with the capture of posts on James Bay, and its re-establishment in 1694 after their loss in 1693. The uncertainty of returns from furs which followed the success or failure of military and naval activity and the changes in fashion combined, with the increasing debt incidental to expansion in the interior, to produce inflation and the disorganization of economic life in the St. Lawrence. The French West Indies were compelled to rely on the English colonies and on Ireland for supplies and provisions. In the Treaty of Utrecht in 1713 France recognized defeat in retreat from Nova Scotia and Hudson Bay.

Penetration of the St. Lawrence by the French involved restriction of the English to the regions along the Atlantic seaboard. In the seventeenth century, with the exception of the conquest of Quebec from 1629 to 1632, and of Nova Scotia for a short period, England confined her activities to the establishment of colonies along the southern seaboard and in the West Indies. In 1664 New York was captured from the Dutch. Mercantilist policy involved not only the export of dried fish from Newfoundland as a means of securing specie from Spain but also the production of tropical products in the British West Indies as a means of restricting the purchase of those commodities from Spain. The resources of the Atlantic seaboard enabled the colonies to provide provisions and supplies for the British West Indies and even for the French West Indies. The limitations of French integration imposed strains on an inclusive British Empire. Attempts of the West Country to maintain control over Newfoundland and to check settlement facilitated the migration of labour from Newfoundland to New England. On the other hand, the increase in the production of agricultural commodities, lumber, and fish in the English colonies and restrictions on exports to the French West Indies lowered the price of exports to Newfoundland and supported the growth of settlement in spite of West Country hostility. Concentration on the Atlantic seaboard emphasized the importance of naval strength and encouragement of the fishing industry and carrying trade as nurseries for seamen and reserves for ships. The construction of military fortifications was discouraged and the English Empire was never cursed with the problem of dependence on a staple commodity such as fur and the heavy burden of fixed charges incidental to the construction of forts in the interior, and the consequent devastating effects of inflation.

In the sixteenth century the Iroquois had been pushed from the

St. Lawrence and the French built up connections with the Hurons from Georgian Bay by the Ottawa route. In the seventeenth century the Iroquois, pushed to northern New York, established trade relations with the Dutch, and, after 1664, with the English, and through the Hudson-Albany route destroyed the Huron villages. The French were compelled to concentrate on active occupation of the St. Lawrence and to build up a middleman organization to take the place of the Hurons. With French concentration of the St. Lawrence the English occupied Hudson Bay. Unable to maintain control of Hudson Bay and the St. Lawrence in the face of competition from the Hudson River the French withdrew from Hudson Bay in 1713.

With retreat from Hudson Bay, Nova Scotia, and Newfoundland after 1713, France consolidated her position at Louisbourg on Cape Breton and renewed efforts were made to rebuild an empire on a more solid base. But the basic problems of integration were accentuated rather than alleviated. The establishment of a settlement on Cape Breton was handicapped by the limited resources of the area, by the limitations of the St. Lawrence region, and by the difficulty of attracting Acadians from the dyked lands of the Bay of Fundy to the forest lands of Prince Edward Island or of encouraging them to raise grain, rather than livestock, to be smuggled from the Bay of Fundy. The French West Indies were unable to rely on French supplies and provisions and a smuggling trade increased with the English colonies in the West Indies and in Cape Breton. Cheap supplies and provisions from the English colonies were exchanged for rum through both channels. French policy favoured consumption of French brandy in New France, and French West Indies rum was sold to the English.

The St. Lawrence was handicapped by the loss of Hudson Bay, which compelled French traders to extend their trade from Lake Superior to Lake Winnipeg and the Saskatchewan under La Vérendrye and his successors. The long and difficult voyage around the arc of a circle along the edge of the Hudson Bay drainage basin, in competition with the Hudson's Bay Company on Hudson Bay at the centre of the circle, imposed heavy burdens on the colony. Moreover the development of trade from the mouth of the Mississippi meant encroachments on the trade of the St. Lawrence. Fortifications were extended along the Great Lakes to check competition from the English and the Iroquois from Albany and Oswego. In spite of efforts to encourage the iron industry and shipbuilding on the St. Lawrence, France was unable to develop an agricultural and an industrial base to meet the demands of Louisbourg and the West Indies and of Saskatchewan and the Great Lakes. Inflation again broke out and the Seven Years' War brought the collapse of Louisbourg, Quebec, and the French Empire in North America.

Again the inability of the French to develop an integrated Empire had implications for the British Empire. Expansion of production and trade in the English colonies involved an increase in the smuggling trade to the French West Indies. Continued encouragement to the fishing industry and to shipbuilding involved a clash with British West Indies planters anxious to check trade with the French West Indies. The influence of the planters in Great Britain secured the Molasses Act of 1733, which was designed with other legislation to create a monopoly market in Great Britain and to check the trade of surplus tropical products of the French West Indies with the surplus products of the temperate English colonies of the seaboard. The legislation stimulated the smuggling trade through Louisbourg and enhanced the interest in Nova Scotia and Newfoundland. Settlement continued to increase in Newfoundland and the influence of the West Country to decline. With the defeat of France it was expected that the markets of the St. Lawrence would be opened to the products of the British West Indies and that more rigid control would be exercised over the trade between the English colonies and the French West Indies.

Destruction of the French Empire profoundly disturbed the equilibrium of the Atlantic and was followed by the collapse of the British Empire and the loss of the colonies. The Treaty of Versailles recognizing the independence of the United States followed the Treaty of Paris in two decades. Anglo-American traders pushed rapidly into the territory vacated by the French and quickly occupied the region northwest of the Saskatchewan. The English colonies extended the fishing industry to the Gulf of St. Lawrence and participated, in spite of protests from the British West Indies, in smuggling to the French West Indies, which were no longer able to draw even meagre support from the St. Lawrence. Conflicts emerged between the colonies and the British West Indies, between the colonies and Newfoundland, which under West Country influence attempted to check the colonial fishery, and among the colonies themselves, since traders from Albany dependent on the Iroquois middleman organization demanded restriction of trade to the posts, and the St. Lawrence region and traders from Quebec and Montreal, following the organization built up by the French after the destruction of the Huron middlemen, insisted on extending the trade among the Indians. Pallisser's Act in 1775 encouraged the Newfoundland fishery at the expense of the colonies, and the Quebec Act of 1774 enlarged the province of Quebec to extend the control of the St. Lawrence at the expense of Albany. The Hudson's Bay Company in the year of the Quebec Act made its first important move inland in the construction of Cumberland House to check the encroachments of the Anglo-American traders. The complexity of an empire including the West Indies and Newfoundland with strong influential groups in England, the colonies including Nova Scotia in possession of a powerful tradition of Assemblies, a conquered territory in Quebec, and a charter company in Hudson Bay, imposed too severe a strain on the constitutional resources of Great Britain, taxed by the addition of Scotland in 1707 and the corruption of parliament under Walpole and George III. Removal of colonial fears of a major hostile power after the Seven Years' War brought disaster.

The fall of New France and of the French Empire had been a result of the inadequacies of control by France with a continental background, and the dependence on military participation and consequent rigidities. The fall of the British Empire was a result of the inadequacies of control by England with a maritime background and her dependence on naval strength and consequent elasticities.

After the Revolution United Empire Loyalists followed earlier New England immigrants into Nova Scotia, and migrated to the province of Quebec in the Eastern Townships and north of the Great Lakes. The Maritimes were divided into separate colonies, Nova Scotia, New Brunswick, Prince Edward Island, and Cape Breton. Nova Scotia made a deliberate effort to establish a place for itself within the British Empire comparable to that formerly occupied by New England and the American colonies. The influence of the West Indies was weakened particularly with legislation against slavery, as the influence of Nova Scotia became stronger. The latter opposed the re-establishment of trade between the West Indies and the region which had now become the United States, and attempted to develop her own resources, and to build up an *entrepôt* trade from the St. Lawrence and from New England. Protests from the West Indies eventually led to the opening of trade with the United States. As the French had failed to build up an integrated trade between the St. Lawrence, the Maritimes, and the West Indies, so Nova Scotia failed. The difficulties of Nova Scotia in relation to the West Indies were in part a result of the increase in population in Newfoundland. The American Revolution and wars between England and France weakened the control of the West Country and hastened the growth of a resident population. The demands of an increasing population attracted trade from Nova Scotia and weakened her possibilities in relation to West Indies trade. The aggressive influence of Nova Scotia in the Second Empire became more effective in contrast with the West Indies in the First Empire. Efforts to prevent the loss of the American colonies by such measures as the Colonial Tax Repeal Act of 1778 were exploited by Nova Scotia through an Assembly inherited from the old Empire. Whereas Massachusetts was willing to recognize the Crown but refused to recognize the supremacy of the British parliament, Nova Scotia accepted supremacy and secured modifications in imperial legislation enabling her to strengthen her autonomy. The dependence of Nova Scotia on the fishery, shipping, and trade was in contrast with the limited possibilities of the St. Lawrence.

Anglo-American traders driven to the North-West by the extension of immigration to the interior of the United States developed an effective instrument for the command of increasing capital which came with increasing distances. The North West Company emerged with the support of rum from the West Indies restricted in the American market after the Revolution, the development of shipping on the Great Lakes, the organization of food supplies and extension to the Athabasca and the Mackenzie Rivers. Organization of the American fur trade and the Jay Treaty compelled Anglo-American traders to withdraw and to penetrate the North-west as the XY Company. Intensive competition brought amalgamation in 1804. To offset the effects of organization of trade from the St. Lawrence, the Hudson's Bay Company was compelled to re-organize a structure developed in relation to the fur trade on Hudson Bay. The organization of a base for supplies of food and a determination to exact recognition of the ownership of land drained by rivers flowing into Hudson Bay provided the background for the Selkirk settlement. As on the St. Lawrence the French government had been compelled to intervene to prevent retardation of settlement by companies, so on Hudson Bay competition from St. Lawrence traders compelled the Hudson's Bay Company to provide a base for settlement in the Selkirk scheme. The North West Company extended its organization across the continent to the mouth of the Columbia River but was handicapped in the development of Pacific trade. New England, restricted after the Revolution in trade with the British Empire, became active in South America and the Pacific, and built up extensive connections with the Sandwich Islands and the Orient. While the attempt of the North West Company to build up trade on the Pacific failed because of inability of Nova Scotia to build up a trading organization in relation to the St. Lawrence, the West Indies and Newfoundland, but succeeded in developing a transcontinental organization, American traders succeeded in the Pacific regions but failed to develop a transcontinental organization by the Missouri across the plains to the Columbia. The Hunting Indians of the north supported the North West Company but the Plains Indians of the south restricted American organization. Astoria was taken over by the North West Company but arrangements were made to trade with the Orient through Boston firms to avoid the monopoly of the East Indian Company. Limitations of the North West Company on the Pacific contributed to its difficulties in the competitive struggle with the Hudson's Bay Company. In 1821 the two companies were amalgamated and Hudson Bay became the dominant route with the elimination of the St. Lawrence.

As in the French Empire, the St. Lawrence was inadequate as a continental base to support Nova Scotia in relation to the West Indies and Newfoundland, and the fur trade to the interior. In the French Empire brandy was sold in the St. Lawrence at the expense of West Indies rum, and in the British Empire settlement was followed by grain production and concentration on whiskey rather than rum. With supremacy of Hudson Bay settlers on the lower St. Lawrence and in the Great Lakes region turned to the timber trade which emerged through the efforts of Great Britain to build up an alternative supply during the Napoleonic wars. The demands of United Empire Loyalists in the Great Lakes region and of traders in the lower St. Lawrence and the importance of military strength led to the adoption of the Constitutional Act of 1791 and the division of the province of Quebec into Upper and Lower Canada. The resources of Upper and Lower Canada were in the land and of Nova Scotia in the sea. Nova Scotia developed her autonomy in relation to the trade of the Empire whereas Upper and Lower Canada were concerned with the occupation of land by settlers and the exploitation of the forests. The Crown's control over land strengthened the position of the executive, and the Assembly, without the long traditions of Nova Scotia, was less effective in its struggle for responsible government. Military control and settlement in the St. Lawrence, in the British Empire as in the French Empire, strengthened the interest of Europe in finance, while naval control and trade in the Maritimes facilitated the growth of independence. Rebellion broke out in Upper and Lower Canada but Nova Scotia achieved responsible government with peace.

The Reform Act in Great Britain hastened the destruction of shelters which protected the vested interests of staple trades with long term credit, such as sugar, thus contributing to the break-up of the Second Empire. The emergence of free trade compelled realignments in the St. Lawrence essential to the lowering of transportation costs to offset the loss of protection. Canals were built, the provinces of Upper and Lower Canada were united, and credit was provided to strengthen a transport system to compete with the alternative New York route. Canadian tariffs replaced the tariffs of the colonial system. In Nova Scotia, following defeat in checking trade between the United States and the West Indies, determined efforts were made to hamper the American fishery. Success was partially achieved in the opening of American markets in the Reciprocity Treaty. In the St. Lawrence and in Nova Scotia advantages were gained in American trade during the difficult period of compromise between North and South in the United States. With the success of the North in the Civil War, the Reciprocity Treaty came to an end and American tariffs were imposed. New schemes were essential on the St. Lawrence to strengthen its position with the increasing difficulties of the American market and in Nova Scotia to compel a re-opening of the market for fish.

In the territory under the control of the Hudson's Bay Company after 1821, monopoly was strengthened and barricades were built along the Precambrian formation against competition from the south. Signs of strain were evident in the most distant area, in the retreat from the Columbia to Victoria on Vancouver Island after the settlement of the Oregon boundary dispute. In the Red River free trade was conceded by the Hudson's Bay Company to traders from the Mississippi drainage basin to the south in 1849. A major breach in the system came with the discovery of placer gold in the Fraser River in 1857 and the rapid occupation of the Pacific Coast region. The monopoly of the Hudson's Bay Company with that of the East India Company came under attack, and colonial government emerged in British Columbia and Vancouver Island. The entrenchment of the Hudson's Bay Company in the territory drained by rivers flowing into Hudson's Bay held by it under the charter from the Crown yielded only after the joining of the provinces of Ontario, Quebec, Nova Scotia, and New Brunswick in Confederation, and the demand for a solution of their transportation problems by extension of the trunk railway of the St. Lawrence. The policy of imperial defence, which created divisions in British North America after the Treaty of Versailles, successful in the War of 1812, was reversed in the interests of unity and centralization after the Civil War. The policy of division and defence after 1783 left a legacy of control by the provinces over their natural resources in the federal structure which checked the trend toward centralization.

In Newfoundland, revival of the French fishery after the Napoleonic wars was accompanied by determined efforts to hamper it comparable to those of Nova Scotia against the United States. The struggle for responsible government brought control over natural resources and a gradual pressure for exclusion of the French by such measures as were involved in the bait legislation and later in the removal of the French from the French shore, and for exclusion of American, Nova Scotian, Canadian, and English traders and fishermen. The aggressiveness of Canada, supported by Nova Scotia, especially after the abrogation of the Washington Treaty, embittered Newfoundland and made federation impossible.

* * * * *

Throughout the history of northern North America the Maritimes, and especially Nova Scotia, had served as an unsuccessful base of empires. In the French régime, first in Nova Scotia and after 1713 in Cape Breton, attempts to link the St. Lawrence and the French West Indies failed because of the high prices of the St.

Lawrence incidental to the drain of westward expansion in pursuit of the fur trade. In the British régime, Nova Scotia was again unable to take the place of the English colonies in relation to the British West Indies, but she effectively developed a position in the British Empire and assumed an aggressiveness which enabled her to enlist the support of Canada against encroachment from the United States. The price of the enlistment was recognition of Canadian tariffs and acceptance of the high price system of the St. Lawrence. Higgling was evident in the free port policy in the Gaspé region and after Confederation in construction of the Intercolonial Railway and its extension to Sydney, tariffs and subventions on coal and iron, upward revisions of federal subsidies, and the Maritime Freight Rates Act.

Confederation emerged in relation to the problems of the St. Lawrence and the Maritimes and of the Pacific. The resistance of the Hudson's Bay Company, weakened in Red River and on the Pacific, yielded under pressure from the Atlantic and the Pacific. But it was felt in the location of the Canadian Pacific Railway along the southern border, its extension through British Columbia by the Crowsnest Pass line and in its monopolistic measures. The long delay which accompanied the monopoly position of the Hudson's Bay Company was followed by rapid occupation of the prairie regions. Disequilibrium as a result of resistance of the Hudson's Bay Company, characterized by large scale migration from the St. Lawrence and the Maritimes to the United States and by widening of the gauge of the Grand Trunk Railway to link up with the American system at Chicago, was followed by disequilibrium with the sudden opening of the prairies by construction of a transcontinental railway and completion of the St. Lawrence canals to fourteen feet. The long depression was followed by the great boom. The monopoly position of the Canadian Pacific Railway, evident in a favourable capital structure and large dividends, was followed by the pouring in of capital into the region north of the Canadian Pacific Railway, and in the construction of two additional transcontinental railways by the Yellowhead Pass to Vancouver and Prince Rupert. These developments followed support from newly created credit instruments in the prairie provinces and from the interest of the provinces of Ontario and Quebec in the development of natural resources especially after the Privy Council decision of 1898. The Temiskaming and

Northern Ontario Railway, expansion of the mining industry in Cobalt, Porcupine and Kirkland Lake, exploitation of hydro-electric power, particularly in the Ontario Hydro Electric Power Commission, fostered by protection of Nova Scotian coal, and construction of pulp and paper plants through the active intervention first of Ontario and later Quebec and the other provinces, accompanied the extension of transcontinental systems east from Winnipeg.

Rapid occupation of the prairie regions from the late 1890's to about 1930 accompanied the construction of railways and canals to the Atlantic seaboard and after the war the completion of the Panama Canal. As a result of the latter, freight rates were lowered in the areas with high freight rates to the St. Lawrence and the resources of Alberta and British Columbia were developed with striking rapidity. The St. Lawrence was strengthened in its struggle with the Pacific by deepening of the Welland Canal.

The depression coincided with the decline in influence of major technical developments in transportation. Regionalization became more pronounced with competition between the Panama and the St. Lawrence and the development of natural resources, hydro-electric power, pulp and paper and minerals, particularly in the provinces of Ontario and Quebec. Provincialism has paralleled the new industrialism. The increasing demands of the United States with expanding population and declining resources shifted the direction of trade from an east-west to a north-south route particularly in regions other than the Prairie Provinces.

Regionalization has brought complex problems for an economy developed in relation to the St. Lawrence. It has been strengthened by the growth of automotive transport and roads in competition with coal and steam and water and rail. Confederation as an instrument of steam power has been compelled to face the implications of hydro-electric power and petroleum. Confederation has been to an important extent the creation of private enterprise represented by the Canadian Pacific Railway, supported by the federal government in a tariff and railway rate policy, and in the Canadian National Railways. The direct interest of the federal government in the Canadian National Railways cannot be separated from an indirect interest in the Canadian Pacific Railway. The burden of a political structure developed in relation to exploitation of the prairie regions has rested to an important extent on those regions and adjustment involves a struggle between regions which have become concerned with new types of power and the American rather than the European market, and regions which have suffered directly from the difficulties of the European market, and costs of a system of transportation suffering obsolescence from new types of transportation.

Strains on the political structure have been evident on all sides as problems of adjustment have become more acute. Demands on party organization as the basis of government have been almost insuperable. The Senate, in contrast with second chambers in Great Britain and the United States, was created in a period with limited political capacity and little effort has been made to adjust its membership to the increase in talent available. Necessities of party organization have made it a pasture for old party war horses which old age pensions render unnecessary. Regions favoured by the British North America Act with a large number of senators are able to build up powerful party organizations with the promise of tangible rewards.

With limitations of the Senate the strain imposed on the courts has not been lessened. Reform of the civil service has increased the necessity of patronage in judicial appointments. Not only has the foundation of the courts been weakened by patronage but division of authority between the Privy Council and the Supreme Court of Canada has meant lower prestige for the latter. A strong Supreme Court insistent on avoiding an attempt to follow the elections is an essential bulwark to a democracy. We are hearing far too much about peace by power and far too little about equality before the law.

In the House of Commons the exacting demands of party organization have the effect of increasing the power of the Cabinet and of a small group within the Cabinet. Patronage has been increasingly restricted to this group and taken out of the hands of the members. Not only have members of parliament less power but they are selected from a weaker group. Decline in the influence of the press and particularly the amalgamation of newspapers since the last war precludes intense party activity and effective discussion. Editors are compelled to follow a neutral policy without endangering the interests of either party. The radio becomes more effective in the hands of a central party organization but the character of discussion is lowered because of the necessity of appealing to large numbers.[1] Discussion is

[1]Then Tom Corcoran (assistant to the President) offered me a little advice. The day of the printed word, he announced, was over. 'You have no idea what

restricted in the constituencies and in turn in the House of Commons. The increasing dictatorial powers of a small group in the Cabinet and the lowering of the calibre of members of parliament have contributed to the unprecedented breaches in the British tradition of anonymity in the Civil Service. Members of the Civil Service are becoming almost as well known to the public as Ministers. A new Civil Service has emerged with much looser responsibilities to Ministers in charge of Departments. Ministers are able to evade responsibility by using the pronouncements of members of the Civil Service as kites to test public opinion, or by throwing individuals to the wolves when the chase becomes too warm. The power of opposition has been reduced enormously during the war period. Members of the opposition oppose the government in arguments and vote with it. Union government almost prevails in fact if not in name. Opposition consequently becomes effective in separate provinces and provincial parties[2] have emerged on a large scale most obviously in Alberta and Quebec.

The emergence of new parties favours the growth of ideologies and the neglect of practical problems of government. These ideologies range through free enterprise, production for use and not for profit, new democracy, *bloc populaire*, and the like. Bureaucracies give rise to parties with ideologies because they prevent groups from facing immediate problems and leave them with no alternative but party activity. The economics of parties is by no means clearly understood but the supply of parties is associated with the demands of the professions, particularly the legal profession, for advertising, and the demand for parties with the inability of groups to register their views effectively. The complex problems of regionalization in the recent development of Canada render the political structure obsolete and necessitate concentration on the problem of machinery by which interests can become more vocal and their demands be met more efficiently. It is imperative that serious attention should be given to the problem of revising political machinery so that democracy can work out solutions to modern problems. The danger

a good thing it is for your soul to have to address yourself to a big radio audience. You've got to clarify your meaning, make things simple, reduce them to their ultimate essentials if you want to get them over to a big audience, because human beings are a hell of a lot stupider than you would ever think' " (Raymond Moley, *After Seven Years*, New York, 1939, p. 355).

[2]See J. B. Crozier, *History of Intellectual Development on the Lines of Modern Evolution*, Vol III (London, 1901), pp 258-9, on parties in France.

that bureaucracies, including royal commissions, will suggest legislation rather than devices by which the demands of interests can be reflected and discussed previous to the enactment of legislation has been evident.

The dangers of an obsolescent political structure cannot be avoided by patchwork solutions and plans of the bureaucracies. Each region has its conditions of equilibrium in relation to the rest of Canada and to the rest of the world, particularly in relation to Great Britain and the United States. Manipulation of a single instrument such as monetary policy implies a highly elaborate system to determine how far transfers between regions or provinces are necessary. Otherwise full employment will become a racket on the part of the central provinces for getting and keeping what they can. The provinces will require elaborate machinery to protect themselves against exploitation of haphazard federal policies. Provincial finances will reflect the influence of federal activity. The result of neglect of interrelations between the provinces and the Dominion will be evident in increasing division and greater reliance on bureaucracy.

The argument developed in this paper assumes that the end of the second thirty years' war is in sight and that the Pax Britannica will be followed by an effective Pax Americana-Britannica. It assumes that the political scientist[8] can escape from the hocus-pocus of the economist and concentrate on the extremely difficult problems of his own field. He can best make a contribution to economic development by suggested modifications to political machinery.

[8]"A similar revolution of ideas is very rare in the West, and indeed experience shows that innovating legislation is connected not so much with Science as with the scientific air which certain subjects, not capable of exact scientific treatment, from time to time assume. To this class of subjects belonged Bentham's scheme of Law-Reform, and, above all, Political Economy as treated by Ricardo. Both have been extremely fertile sources of legislation during the last fifty years" (Sir Henry Sumner Maine, *Popular Government*, London, 1885, p. 146). "We Englishmen pass on the Continent as masters of the art of government; yet it may be doubted whether, even among us, the science, which corresponds to the art, is not very much in the condition of Political Economy before Adam Smith took it in hand" (*ibid.*, p. 58). "Popular Government and Popular Justice were originally the same thing. The ancient democracies devoted much more time and attention to the exercise of civil and criminal jurisdiction than to the administration of their public affairs; and, as a matter of fact, popular justice has lasted longer, has had a more continuous history, and has received much more observation and cultivation than popular government" (*ibid.*, pp. 89-90). On the problems of government in Great Britain, and, one might add, the more acute problems of government in Canada, see the discussion of the machinery developed in the United States to check the usurpation of the Cabinet (*ibid.*, pp. 196 ff.).

14. TRANSPORTATION AND THE TARIFF

The transportation problem began with the construction of canals and improvements of the St. Lawrence waterways. Railways were built as supplements to the canals to overcome the handicaps of slow transportation and closed seasons of navigation. Transportation was dependent, from the beginning, on government support. The Grand Trunk operated under private enterprise was given strong support by the Government; the canals and the Intercolonial and P.E.I. Railways were constructed by the Government. From the beginning, returns on capital invested were met by earnings on traffic in the case of the railways and to a certain extent in the case of canals by collection of tolls. It was obvious, however, that these means were inadequate, with the result that the tariff was imposed to meet the deficits. The tariff was regarded as a secondary toll or rate on traffic.

Transportation must be considered as a unit, and navigation cannot be isolated from rail transportation nor the Canadian Pacific and private enterprise from the Canadian National and Government ownership. Periodic crises lead to the establishment of Royal Commissions, and the results are in the form of panic literature rather than exhaustive studies of the field as a whole. Nevertheless, the recommendations of Royal Commissions indicate decided trends, especially when considered over a long period.

The overwhelming importance of water transportation in relation to the St. Lawrence contributed to an emphasis on the production and export of staples, as shown in the dominance at various stages of fur and lumber and, with the improvement of transportation by canals and railways, of wheat and agricultural products. Emphasis was on raw materials which were subject to wide fluctuations in returns as a result of prices or yields. Consequently, while on the one hand returns on capital invested by the Government in canals and by the Government and private enterprise in railways were inflexible as far as the Government was concerned, and relatively inflexible (in so far as securities were in the form of bonds rather than stocks) as far as private enterprise was concerned, earnings were subject to wide fluctuations since returns from customs fluctuated with imports, which were directly affected by exports. Returns from freight rates and tolls fluctuated similarly.

During periods of depression government finance was exposed to serious deficits as a result of the importance of staples and of the tariff. Private enterprise in railways was exposed to losses from the same source. On the other hand, the tariff was more flexible than rates, and during a period of depression increases followed the problems of government deficits, and attempts of manufacturers to secure protection from manufactured products dumped by more highly industrialized countries. Increase in the tariff and attempts to stimulate imports of capital by further transportation improvements, coinciding with the prosperity phase of the business cycle, brought a temporary solution to the problem of deficits. Completion of the Intercolonial Railway by the Government in 1876, the national policy of 1878, and the plan to construct the Canadian Pacific Railway were factors overcoming the difficulties of the seventies. The importance of the Government in the construction and deepening of the canals and in the construction of the Intercolonial Railway, and the problems of fixed charges during a period of depression accentuated the importance attached to construction under private enterprise. The tariff tended to impose too heavy a burden on the staple industries. Private enterprise provided for greater flexibility without the danger of fixed charges and deficits during the depression stage. The determined attempts to enlist the interests of private capitalists for construction of the Canadian Railway, and the generous support in land, money and railways made possible avoidance of inflexible drains on the Government and provided a flexible financial structure for private enterprise.

Inflexibility of the tariff downwards contributed to the difficulties during the period of prosperity which began with the discovery of gold in the Klondike in 1896, the opening of the Kootenay by the Crowsnest Pass Railway and the lowering of railway rates on settlers' effects and grain which accompanied the same development, completion of the St. Lawrence waterways to fourteen-foot draught, the opening of the West and its accompanying increase in immigration of labour and importation of capital. Expansion made possible a marked increase in dividends to Canadian Pacific shareholders, and a marked increase in surplus from the tariff which provided support for government construction of the Transcontinental Railway from

Moncton to Winnipeg, and for construction of the Canadian Northern and the Grand Trunk Pacific under private enterprise with governmental assistance. With the war, the elasticity of private enterprise was not in evidence and the Canadian Northern, the Grand Trunk Pacific and the Grand Trunk came into the hands of the Government. Attempts to locate a scapegoat for the present railroad problem have led to charges that the Laurier administration was responsible in not forcing an amalgamation of the Canadian Northern and the Grand Trunk Pacific and that the Borden administration should have refused assistance to the Canadian Northern Railway at the onset of the war. It is important to emphasize that expansion of credit in the period from 1900 to 1914 facilitated expansion of railroads with government assistance, and under private enterprise, by the Canadian Pacific Railway. In the war and the post-war period further expansion of credit, which followed the enormous speculative boom of the United States, led to marked expansion on the part of the Canadian Pacific and Canadian National Railways. Again attempts to locate a scapegoat were in evidence.

The problem of government finance became acute with the depression, partly because natural resources have not shown adequate resilience. Expansion of credit crystallized with government ownership into heavy fixed charges. Moreover, the loss of traffic was responsible for operating deficits which accumulated with fixed charges. Private enterprise representing the alternative of elasticity was forced to give evidence of inelasticity by passing dividends. Government finance, in so far as it was related to lands and railroads, was dependent on earnings and on continued application of the tariff. Elimination of the elasticity feature, as shown in the disappearance of C.P.R. dividends, accentuated the burden of government finance. Formation of an arbitration board centred directly on the problem of solving the inelastic factors, and rendered more urgent an analysis of the position of the tariff and of government finance generally. The efficacy of the tariff from the standpoint of waterways and railways varied in part with imports, and in turn with exports and accordingly with earnings dependent on railway rates and traffic. Deficits on the railways and on canals were directly linked to returns from the tariff. The more complicated phases of the problem arise from the marked expansion incidental to rapid exploitation of virgin natural resources, accentuated by the prosperity phases of the business cycle. Whereas the tariff, by remaining at a high level, or by an increase, may lead to a substantial increase in revenue without affecting relatively the position of the burden, if this is followed by an increased expenditure on the part of the Government, and by new flotations of capital, the fixed charges increase rapidly. This results in increasing surpluses being devoted to an increasing extent to the payment of interest charges on capital when they should be devoted to an increasing extent to capital. As a result, during periods of depression, fixed charges on capital invested during the boom period become a serious burden. The burden may be borne without serious difficulty, provided the chief exports continue in a strong competitive position in relation to other exporting areas. On the other hand, failing exploitation of virgin natural resources may seriously accentuate the burden. The tariff tends to become inadequate as a result and it may, by virtue of protective features, add to the burden. The impasse which developed under these conditions, and which was evident in the depression, can be met in part by further improvements in transportation such as the St. Lawrence waterway, which will lower costs of transportation and strengthen the position of Canada as a wheat producer. The difficulties are obvious but not insuperable. It is a temporary solution and serves to emphasize the importance of making the tariff a more flexible and scientific instrument. During a period of prosperity the tariff should be raised to act as a brake and to provide for surpluses not only to meet the short-run railway operating deficits of Canadian transportation, but also the interest and depreciation of capital. If railroad rates are lowered at the beginning of a period of prosperity tariff rates should be raised accordingly. A scientific application of the tariff offers at least a partial solution to the dilemma which arises from fluctuations in a country dependent on staples, especially wheat, and in turn on government ownership and fixed charges. Lowering the tariff during the period of a depression and raising the tariff during a period of prosperity might do much to alleviate the problems of the staple-producing areas.

The disappearance of elasticity in railroad finance which follows the passing of dividends on common stock in the Canadian Pacific Railway and emergence of an arbitral board involve consideration of fresh standards for rate adjustment. It is no longer feasible to regard seven per cent. dividends on common stock of the Canadian Pacific Railway as a measuring rod for railway rates and it may no longer be feasible to regard the financially healthy state of the Canadian Pacific Railway as a guide. This arrangement implied that rates providing satisfactory returns for the Canadian Pacific did not necessarily provide satisfactory returns for the Government Railways. Earnings from these rates were necessarily supplemented by support from the Government to make up deficits either in terms of deficits on operation or of interest on capital. Assuming that an arbitral board mantains an even balance between the two railroads and avoids encroachment of the Canadian Pacific on the Canadian National or of the Canadian National on the Canadian Pacific, rates must be adjusted in relation to the total capital structure of the railways rather than to the capital structure of the line dominated by private enterprise. It becomes possible and essential that the burden of railroad finance be adjusted more closely to the relative ability of supporting areas. Assuming relative stability in the production of raw materials as a result of exhaustion of natural resources the tariff must assume to an increasing extent the position of a toll, as Galt originally planned, and should approximate the deficit on transportation finance. Consequently the tariff and railway rates but particularly the former must be linked in more direct fashion to the problem of returns on investment, whether in terms of government ownership or private enterprise. The tariff may serve to operate as a new base, in the place of dividends on Canadian Pacific stock, by which deficits on the Canadian National and on canals should approximate returns from the tariff and railway rates should provide in addition earnings on the Canadian National adequate to provide returns on Canadian Pacific securities.

Aside from the problem of meeting deficits on transportation, the public debt of Canada (provincial, municipal and Federal) is of serious proportions. The transportation problem accentuated the difficulties and forced consideration of fiscal and monetary policy. Fiscal difficulties and inelasticity of structure have steadily driven toward a realignment of monetary policy. Commercial credit in a young country subject to wide fluctuations has been subject to systematic protection by banking policy and banking legislation.

Governmental credit and corporate credit have suffered as a result of their relatively weaker position in the credit structure. Continued expansion of government credit in terms of continued deficits and increasing rigidity have become imperative factors in the appointment of a Royal Commission on banking and in the recommendation and establishment of new machinery designed to eliminate strains and so introduce unity, strength and flexibility.

15. REFLECTIONS ON RUSSIA

In *The Russian Peasant and Other Studies* (London, 1945), Sir John Maynard has written in a preface: "It is inevitable that one who writes about Russia in the very crisis of the struggle now convulsing the world should have his mind focused upon the ultimate relations of the Western powers with the vast federation of peoples who form the bridge between Europe and Asia. . . . Neither group must try to force its own ideas, political, economic or social, upon the other. . . . On the other hand there must be agreement upon foreign policy . . . agreement . . . upon the necessity of agreement." Two worlds which do not understand each other are suddenly faced with the necessity of working out compromises. In the words of E. J. Dillon, Russia as a community without "the cement of hypocrisy" and accustomed to direct relations is compelled to develop a spirit of compromise to deal with nations which have been masters of it.

It would be presumptuous of the present writer to attempt to throw light on the problem. The effects of a first experience in a plane, the speed of travel by air, lack of knowledge of the Russian language and the first contact with the Asiatic continent and with a new power celebrating its coming out party must leave any observer in a state of confusion. But an experienced student has said that one must spend ten days or ten years in Russia. To be trained in a subject which has its roots in the West and which has suffered from the characteristic disease of specialization and to realize suddenly that a vast powerful organization built around the efforts of 180 million people has arisen with little interest in this specialization is to find oneself compelled to search for possible contacts in the broader approach of its history.

Writings on Russia reflect the bitterness of civil war, only less bitter than religious war, whether written by those sympathetic to Trotsky or by those sympathetic to Stalin. Few individuals are interested in dispassionate discussion.

Lack of knowledge about Russia is not only a result of the intensely partisan character of writings, but also of the deliberate policy of defence which has largely characterized Russian history. Strategy in countries emphasizing naval power in the West has always stressed the principle of attack. Suddenly one realizes that in a vast continental area, defence is the key to ultimate success. The strategy of defence springs forward to a position which it has not occupied since the castles of the medieval period before the invention of gunpowder. The success of defence in secrecy, destruction or supervision of contacts with the outside world, a distinct railway gauge, a difficult language for Europeans which with Marxian indoctrination was impenetrable to propaganda, concentration on a small single party, control over the press and radio, have been evident in the underestimation of Russian strength by the Germans and by the Allies. Confusion in the Western world was in part a result of the interest in ideologies and the neglect of factors of military strength. Journalists affected by the age-old tendency of the printing industry to push to the left found themselves suddenly confronted by a powerful centralized force which was essentially right. The right which thought of Russia as left was even more confused than the left which found she was right.

The social scientist from Canada will be particularly impressed with the difficulties. The Canadian has no revolutionary tradition —the influence of the Church in Quebec is that of pre-revolutionary France, the influence of the state in Ontario and in English-speaking provinces is that of the Loyalist—the counter-revolutionary of the American revolution. This is an island of counter-revolution in a world of revolutionary traditions. In the long series of revolutions beginning with Cromwell and continuing through the American revolution, the French revolution and the Russian revolution, we occupy a unique position. Russia as the latest product of revolutionary technique is the most difficult for us to understand. The revolutionaries in Russia had made an intensive study of revolutions. The political revolution in Russia as in other countries with a revolutionary tradition has meant the spread and improvement of revolutionary techniques as well as industrial techniques from the West. Canadians have perhaps a point of approach in that they understand the industrial revolution.

The major task of the new régime was the building up of an army. Its success scarcely needs comment. Industry and agriculture were drastically reorganized to supply men and material. The revolution, the counter revolution, the purges, the Stalin-Hitler pact, were concentrated on the army and defence on capital equipment and producer's goods. In developing the resources of the Ural mountains or of other parts of Russia, building up industrial areas in Siberia, opening up routes to the Arctic from the East and the West, establishing air bases across Siberia to Alaska, the major concern was preparation for war against ultimate aggression from the West. Five-year plans, devices for speeding up production and large scale importations of capital equipment and technical skill were enthusiastically supported to the same end.

A war economy concerned with the production of capital equipment implies concentration on self-sufficiency and a relative neglect of consumer goods and a high standard of living. The emphasis on consumer's goods and the use of advertising as a device for persistently educating the consumer to a higher standard of living which characterizes the English-speaking countries of the Western World is necessarily absent. Emphasis on producer's goods involves little need for advertising. Whereas an economy which emphasizes consumer's goods is characterized by communication industries largely dependent on advertising and by constant efforts to reach the largest number of readers or listeners, an economy emphasizing producer's goods is characterized by communication industries largely dependent on government support. As a result of this contrast a common public opinion in Russia and the West is difficult to achieve. In a consumer's goods economy news is an important device for the sale of advertising, but informed news is neglected. Inability to appraise the military strength of France and Russia was a result. The countries of the free press are characterized by underground movements. Information will be shared provided it is off the record and not for publication. It would be unfair to use Canada as an illustration since even platform discussion must avoid numerous topics. The numerous parties in English-speaking Canada suggest that even the same language does not prevent deliberately building up differences which render a common approach impossible. In Russia with a limited press, conversation occupies a more important place. In the countries of the West and in Russia it has become much easier for governments to proceed without regard to public opinion. Mr. Baldwin stated that he would not have won an election if he had provided all the necessary information. The differences in language and alphabet make an approach through a well-informed public opinion in both countries extremely difficult. Consequently a heavy task is imposed on the respective embassies and on diplomatic conferences. Rapid advances in methods of communication has meant a shift of the control of governments from the highly skilled diplomat to the relatively unskilled and inexperienced. The governing classes have been exposed on a large scale to technological unemployment. While David Hume remarked that all governments are influenced by public opinion the influence varies with circumstances. A decline in the effectiveness of public opinion means a resort to reliance on displays of force. The tendency to rely on force is accentuated by the necessity of discussion in the simplest possible terms of the relative advantages of systems. System is a fighting word and the emotional excitement surrounding it obscures even a realization of the necessity of intelligence. There is no system in Russia or in the West and governments are compelled to meet problems as they arise.

The disappearance of the nations of the counter-revolution, Germany and Japan, has both simplified and made more difficult the problem of agreement. Germany opposed the revolution and expelled Marx only to find his influence hastening the revolution in Russia. Intellectual vigour has disappeared in the defeated countries and independent thought has been burned out. An indoctrinated nation can be quickly indoctrinated with new ideologies once independence has disappeared. Co-operation between Russia and the Anglo-Saxon world becomes the major problem of the West. In the language of the economist the problems of duopoly are perhaps simpler than those of oligopoly but the simplicity has created problems of its own.

If we are to take seriously the suggestion of Sir Halford MacKinder that control of the heartland of Asia implies control of the world, the major problem of Russia for the West is in her ability to adapt a traditional defensive policy. Her imperialism differs fundamentally from the imperialism of the Anglo-Saxon world as a continental military economy differs from a maritime naval economy. The size of Russia in itself is a tribute to the effectiveness of the imperialism of the old régime and of the new. With diverse languages, religions, races, and regions she has developed an effective technique of government. The imperialism of continental Asia must be regarded as complementary to the imperialism of the Anglo-Saxon world.

The traditions of Anglo-Saxons differ from continental Europe as continental Europe differs from Russia. Anglo-Saxons and continental Europe have been profoundly influenced by the great contributions of the Roman Empire in law and religion. Communities that have been schooled in the traditions of Roman law and the Roman Church differ sharply from communities influenced by the traditions of Russia as they have been developed in the Byzantine Empire. The Orthodox Church emerged from the Greek rather than the Roman tradition. As a distinguished Russian scientist explained to me, Russians prefer the Gospel of St. John. The revolution destroyed the position of the Orthodox Church in Russia as earlier revolutions weakened the position of the Roman Church in the West. Law is perhaps more disciplinary than religion and the task of developing complex codes more difficult in Russia than in countries more directly influenced by the Roman law or by common law. Law assumes force and raises the question as to the place of the army and public opinion.

The problem of Russia will continue to centre around the farmer. "Every civilized community in Europe has found it necessary in one way or other to regulate the relations of landlord and tenant, and to save the latter from the capricious and ruinous rapacity of the former. In France it was effected at the Revolution, and with terrible suddenness in the autumn of 1789. In Germany, Stein and Hardenberg saw that a change was imperative after the humiliation of Jena. In Holland it was a later reform, as it was in Scandinavia. In Denmark which forty years ago was as miserable and as turbulent as Ireland, it was the benevolent work of Bishop Monrad, the enlightened minister who had to bear the brunt of the scandalously unjust Schleswig-Holstein War. In Russia, it was the work of the late emperor. I do not say that in every case, the reform was done in the best way, but I am assured that the reform had to be done."[1] The Crimean War cut off the markets of Europe for wheat, raised the price of wheat in North America and accentuated difficulties in Russia which led to the emancipation of the serf in 1861. The cumulative effect of lower costs of transportation of wheat from North America culminating in the opening of Western Canada after 1900 is the background to the events including the assassination of the Czar which led to the Russian revolution. Trotsky reminds us that a revolution

[1]Rogers, James Edwin Thorold, *The Economic Interpretation of History* (New York and London), p. 175.

cannot succeed without control of the army. The old régime had been shaken by the demands of large scale organization characteristic of the army in the war with Japan, and collapsed in the face of the strains of the last war. The peasant was the army and demanded recognition of the age old traditions of the village or the commune. Political revolution facilitated the spread of the industrial revolution as a solution to the labour problem of Russian agriculture. The seasonal problem, even more acute than that of Western Canada, places a heavy load on administration if the worst effects of drought and famine are to be avoided. Increasing population accentuates the necessity of concentration on industrial growth, the installation of capital equipment on an enormous scale and a raising of the standard of living. The Red Army may serve as a temporary solution of the problem by absorbing surplus labour and raising the standard of living but it cannot be regarded as a permanent and satisfactory alternative.

The ability to approach a new major problem on the part of Russia and the West will be the test of civilization. The late Justice Holmes once stated that the first sign of being civilized is the questioning of one's principles. The decision to celebrate the 220th anniversary of the Academy of Sciences is an indication of a broad statesmanlike approach to a world problem of understanding, and recognition of the possibilities of using science as a common approach—almost the only universal common basis left. Nationalism inevitably creates inefficiency and bigotry even in science and the enormous literature in the various fields in different languages becomes a major handicap. In the social sciences, it is significant that English economic history has gained enormously from the contributions of Russian students. Both groups have much to learn from each other and probably no countries have more to learn through exchange of information than Canada and Russia.

Political economy as developed in the Western world will be compelled to broaden its range and to discuss the implications of competition between languages, religions and cultural phenomena largely neglected by it. Russia has been a storm centre of history largely because of the instability of climate and its effects on migrations. Dependence on agriculture gives a more stable base for society but implies exposure to the effects of geography. Continental militarism and naval armament involve strains which few economies have survived. Concentration on a conscripted army has meant bureaucracy and inefficiency. In the Anglo-Saxon world the addition of a conscripted standing army to naval strength involves similar burdens. Avoidance of a standing army strengthens democratic tendencies and makes for the flexibility and efficiency of industry. Flexibility of military strength accompanies flexibility in the use of manpower and capital equipment. The West has gained from pliability of public opinion since up to the present it has invariably shown the absolutely essential power to throw up the particular individual necessary for a crisis. But succession involves acute difficulties in the West and not less acute difficulties in Russia. A common world view has become indispensable.

The significance of Greek civilization to East and West provides an approach to modern problems. Both groups in the word of Jaeger are Hellenocentric. Again following Jaeger "the world-wide historical importance of the Greeks as educators was derived from their new awareness of the position of the individual in the community. And in fact there could be no sharper contrast than that between the modern man's keen sense of his own individuality and the self-abnegation of the pre-Hellenistic Orient, made manifest in the sombre majesty of Egypt's pyramids and the royal tombs and monuments of the East. As against the Oriental exaltation of one God-king far above all natural proportions (which expresses a metaphysical view of life totally foreign to us) and the Oriental suppression of the great mass of the people (which is a corollary of that quasi-religious exaltation of the monarch), the beginning of Greek history appears to be the beginning of a new conception of the value of the individual."[2] "Other nations made gods, kings, spirits; the Greeks alone made men."

Russia has shared in the heritage of the Mediterranean civilization but she has been dominated by the Greek or the Eastern rather than the Latin or the Western branch. The Roman Empire continued in the East until the fall of Constantinople in 1453. Byzantine civilization conserved the literature of Greece and with the fall of Constantinople turned it over to the West with consequences evident in the Renaissance. In the West with the invasion of the barbarians and the fall of the political power of Rome the Church developed

[2]See Werner Jaeger, *Paideia: The Ideals of Greek Culture* (Oxford, 1939), XIX.

its monarchical system under the influence of Roman law. In the East political power remained in the hands of monarchies and spiritual power based on Greek philosophical thought was in the hands of the councils. In other words political power was monarchical and spiritual power democratic in the East and political power was democratic and spiritual power monarchical in the West. The monarchical organization of the spiritual power in the West has served as a check to the growth of totalitarianism but the democratic organization of the spiritual power in the East has left it exposed to the tyranny of the state. But the character of absolute power in the West, about which Acton spoke, in the spiritual world, contributed to the splintering of religious organizations in Protestantism and to the strengthening of power in the temporal world in the modern state. The power of the democratic type of spiritual organization in spite of the encroachment of the temporal power in the East has been evident in the tenacity with which Eastern peoples have held to the Greek Orthodox Church in the face of centuries of persecution.

In the West monarchical organization of the spiritual power insisted on celibacy of the clergy and on the Latin vulgate. Indeed opposition[3] to the translation of the scriptures from Latin to the vernacular was in part a result of the attempt to check the influence of scriptures translated into the vernacular—Slavic and Bulgarian—in the Eastern church. The break between the East and West became more and more pronounced.

The influence of Plato through Augustine has dominated the later religious and political history of Western Europe. Augustine elaborated the position of the individual and the necessity of the integration of personality. He attacked classicism as guilty of secular pride, the original sin. The doctrine of original sin and in turn of grace became a weapon of devastating power against attempts to build up the divine right of emperors and it proved no less devastating against the ecclesiasticism of the spiritual power. Wycliffe returned to it when he saw the papacy in Babylonian captivity at Avignon and from him the Reformation spread through Huss, Luther and Calvin. Protestantism had its roots in Platonism and St. Augustine.[4] The

[3]Margaret Deanesly, *The Lollard Bible and other medieval Biblical versions* (Cambridge, 1920), p. 23.

[4]See C. N. Cochrane, *Christianity and Classical Culture* (Oxford, 1940).

implications of the Reformation were evident in the unhappy alliance of Church and State in Lutheranism, the basis of democratic development in Calvinism,[5] and the problem of countries which remained Catholic. While revolutions accompanied constitutional change in Protestant countries they never assumed the violence which characterized Catholic countries notably in France. The sharpness of the doctrine of original sin was not adequate to secure constitutional change in Roman Catholic countries and resort was had in France to the deism, and atheism, of the eighteenth century. Greek philosophy provided the powerful dynamic which broke down political hierarchies and protected western civilization against the inefficiencies of absolutism and bureaucracy either through revolution or constitutional change. Resistance was strong in Roman Catholic countries but stronger in Lutheran Germany. The revolutionary tradition which swept the nations of the western world failed in Germany. The philosophic weapons of individualism were met by the rise of Prussia and of the bureaucratic movement. Marx developed new weapons in the class struggle and the dictatorship of the proletariat but again without appreciable influence.

In the East the Byzantine tradition, weakened after the fall of Constantinople, emerged in Russia. The Greek Orthodox Church with its reliance on councils was exposed to the domination of the monarchy and became part of the elaborate structure of absolutism. Here the weapons of Marx were sharpened and improved in the hands of Lenin and others, atheism was given a more conspicuous position, and the structure collapsed. The political and ecclesiastical hierarchy of Russia, a vast area with a large illiterate population, without the disciplinary effects of a public opinion based on printing and the price system and the traditions of Roman law, was unable to withstand the effects of the new weapons. In turn the fall of Germany followed. Byzantine civilization had nursed Greek culture and turned it over to the West with the fall of Constantinople. After the impact had been made on the West it returned to the East to bring about the destruction of the inheritors of the Byzantine tradition. At long last Greek philosophy had worked its will on the west. The transfer of Greek philosophy to the West had brought the Renaissance and the modern world and it remains to ask whether the return

[5]See Ernst Troeltsch, *The Social Teaching of the Christian Churches* (London, 1931).

movement of Greek philosophy to the East will bring a second renaissance. The pendulum swung from the absolutism of Russia to the democracies of the West and from the authoritarianism of the West to the revolution in Russia.

A revolutionary tradition such as has prevailed in the history of the West involves not only the development of the technique of constitutional change but also the loss of valuable elements in the community. A revolution burns off the intellectual resources of communities and imposes enormous strains on the reserves of a people. It is not without significance that Germany became the home of scholars in the nineteenth century. The demands of political compromise in countries with a revolutionary tradition made for continuous exhaustion. The extension of the mathematical[6] device as a means of checking discussion, and bringing it to an end by an appeal to a majority vote, offers little or no relief.

Our first duty is to conserve and strengthen our heavily depleted intellectual and spiritual resources. The time has at last arrived when the Platonic problem of the state in contrast with the problem of the individual must be solved or rather the problem which Plato left unsolved must be met. Attempts to solve it in the Platonic fashion in the nineteenth and twentieth centuries have been all but fatal to western civilization. We have been told often enough that the industrial revolution has at last solved the problem of scarcity but full employment, in a world of famine, full employment without butter, is upon us.

Machine industry has never shown any particular regard for the individual—in fact it has catered to many of our worst vices and has produced luxuries which have proved all too expensive. One of the first points at which it began its inroads on the West was in the field of knowledge. The printing industry made available the vast treasures of Greece and hastened the Renaissance, but very quickly pushed on to less happy results and divided the modern west along the lines of the vernacular languages. Latin very quickly ceased to serve as a language of unity in Europe and it became more and more difficult to maintain a common intellectual life. More and more effectively each nation developed its own narrow outlook and the possibilities of breaking through the ever rising and ever broaden-

[6]See E. D. Martin, *The behaviour of crowds, a psychological study* (New York, 1920).

ing walls disappeared. The few remaining channels of intercommunication were poisoned and division reached its inevitable end.

That the problem is acute will be shown in a study of the views about other nations within the bounds of any nation. Only the stories of major disasters other than war can be expected to cross language borders without serious damage. Stories of war are perhaps the least trustworthy of all as we have reason to know. The spearhead of the newspaper is the headline and to be effective must be constantly changed. A continuous carefully worked out position taking into account the innumerable ramifications of any action is impossible through dependence on headlines and is difficult even in the editorials. The editorial, like most sober institutions including the university, is influenced by the news. The Anglo-Saxon Press was restricted during the war in its comments on the Allies or on foreign countries and was deliberately propagandist in its attempts to emphasize allied strength or to corrupt enemy strength. Even before the war information in the English press leading to the abdication of Edward VIII was suppressed. Dependence on the headline and limitations of the press inevitably made for superficial information and an unstable public opinion which can be dominated by political leaders in control of parliament or the radio. And we are a long way from Plato's ideal of government by those who dislike to govern.

Russia as the latest country to come under the revolution adopted an intensive propaganda as a device to check a possible counter-revolution. Its effectiveness was shown in the survival of two civil wars and of the last war. This implied not only propaganda in the press but in the development of new shrines such as Lenin's tomb, in the use of such names as Stalin (steel) by leaders, and in literature, the stage and the ballet. They have developed a censorship exercised through control over admissions of foreign correspondents in Russia which does not mean admission of radical papers but rather of conservative papers, and control over material sent out by foreign correspondents. The effectiveness of propaganda in Russia explains its ineffectiveness abroad. This does not refer to the efforts of the Communist party in various countries which on the whole have been almost a complete failure but to the unfortunate impression which knowledge of the existence of censorship creates. News from Russia is distrusted and foreign correspondents who return from Russia are distrusted whether they report violently in favour of Russia or violently against. The problem becomes acute with the high state of sales resistance which has been built up in countries served by newspapers paid for by advertisers. Russia has never been systematically exposed to the tradition of continuity and instability of the price system. In Russia, dominance of the press by the government and limited retail development which accompanies limited advertising implies unity and effective domestic propaganda, whereas in Anglo-Saxon countries extensive retail development and extensive advertising implies unwillingness to believe anything which does not get into the headlines, and not even that, including Russian news. It is difficult to estimate the effectiveness of propaganda. The completely free discussion of the irrepressible Russians suggests that propaganda has been as completely successful in Russia as it has in Anglo-Saxon countries. Russia may have an advantage in the greater possibility of being unpredictable[7] but unpredictability is not an asset in the long run. But underneath is a feeling of confidence even if expressed in such negative fashion as that by a friend of the late Samuel Harper. "The trouble is you never can be sure that these Russians will let you down."[8]

The necessity of cutting away the underbrush and of enabling us to see each other has become imperative. Whether the United Nations Organization will serve as a common clearing house for disputes and whether discussion will be effective in influencing public opinion remains an important problem but we must not underestimate the long and experienced training of leaders in democratic countries in dominating the news, nor the effectiveness with which political leaders in Russia dominate news. Internal problems in both regions will be reflected in hostile attacks on the foreign policy of the other regions. Smouldering coals of prejudice will be carefully damped down to be blown into a raging fire of hatred when domestic political difficulties become acute. No statesman can afford to forfeit "the rights of hostility—at all times half the fortune of a politician" (Sir Henry Taylor). Unfortunately the history of Canada has been largely involved in stirring up animosity toward other countries, in order to strengthen unity, to mention only the acute controversies

[7]See Arthur Koestler, *The Yogi and the Commissar* (London, 1945), p. 202.

[8]*The Russia I believe in, The Memoirs of Samuel N. Harper, 1902-1941* (Chicago, 1945), p. 265.

with the United States after the abrogation of the Washington treaty in order to bind the interests of the Maritimes to those of the rest of Canada. It is the task of Canadians to make determined efforts to understand the Anglo-Saxon world at least and not to become a menace because of our inability to solve our own problems. We no longer have even the excuse of loyalty for pursuing any other course. Otherwise we justify and gain the suspicion of all concerned. Naval power has shifted from Great Britain to the Anglo-Saxon world, and Canada will no longer serve as a sort of weather vane indicating war in Great Britain and involving the United States and the Anglo-Saxon world.

"All higher civilization springs from the differentiation of social classes," but the problem of recruiting new sources of power and energy is peculiar neither to Russia nor to Anglo-Saxon countries. Certainly the latter can hardly claim to have solved the problem of always keeping open the ladders from the bottom to the top. Fortunately in both areas the revolutionary tradition admits of a more rapid shift in personnel though not as rapid as many would suggest. Whether the United Nations Organization will make for greater or less flexibility remains to be seen. It will be clear that the future involves great difficulties if we are able to be well informed about each other's problems. The number of channels are few and muddy.

Cultural achievement may serve as a device to evade censorship and to provide weapons for the human spirit. Even with repression it produces aberrations in specialization. Encyclopædias preceded the French revolution and novels the Russian revolution. But even here the destructive influences of revolutions prevent major developments.

As there are two wants connatural to man, so are there two main directions of human activity, pervading in modern times the whole civilized world; and constituting and sustaining that nationality which yet it is their tendency, and, more or less, their effect, to transcend and to moderate—trade and literature. These were they, which, after the dismemberment of the old Roman world, gradually reduced the conquerors and the conquered at once into several nations and a common Christendom. . . .

But without trade and literature, mutually commingled, there can be no nation; without commerce and science, no bond of nations. As the one hath for its object the wants of the body, real or artificial, the desires for which are for the greater part, nay, as far as the origination of trade and commerce is concerned, altogether excited from without; so the other has for its origin, as well as for its object, the wants of the mind, the gratification of which is a natural and necessary condition of its growth and sanity." (Coleridge.)

The universities must attack the problem of understanding. Science has become intensely concerned with military secrets. For the subject of the social sciences one may quote from a letter of Turgot. "He who does not forget that there are political states separated from one another and diversely constituted, will never treat well of any question of political economy."[9]

[9]To Mlle. Lespinasse, January 26, 1770. *Letters,* II, 800, cited in W. Stark, *The history of economics in its relations to social development* (London, 1945), p. 69.

INDEX

www.ingramcontent.com/pod-product-compliance
Lightning Source LLC
LaVergne TN
LVHW090800070826
844660LV00022B/1037

9781487522926